Introduction to Computing Using Python

Using Python

Second Edition

Introduction to Computing Using Python

An Application Development Focus

Second Edition

Ljubomir Perkovic
DePaul University

VICE PRESIDENT AND DIRECTOR	Laurie Rosatone
SENIOR DIRECTOR	Don Fowley
SENIOR ACQUISITIONS EDITOR	Bryan Gambrel
PROJECT SPECIALIST	Marcus Van Harpen
EDITORIAL ASSISTANT	Jessy Moor
EXECUTIVE MARKETING MANAGER	Dan Sayre
SENIOR CONTENT MANAGER	Elle Wagner
SENIOR PRODUCTION EDITOR	John Curley
PROOFREADER	Betty Pessagno
COMPOSITOR	B. Praveen Kumar for SPi Global
COVER PHOTO	©simon2579/iStockphoto

This book was set in TEX Gyre Termes 10 and TEX Gyre Heros 10 by Ljubomir Perković and printed and bound by Quad Graphics/Versailles. The cover was printed by Quad Graphics/Versailles.

This book is printed on acid-free paper. ∞

Founded in 1807, John Wiley & Sons, Inc. has been a valued source of knowledge and understanding for more than 200 years, helping people around the world meet their needs and fulfill their aspirations. Our company is built on a foundation of principles that include responsibility to the communities we serve and where we live and work. In 2008, we launched a Corporate Citizenship Initiative, a global effort to address the environmental, social, economic, and ethical challenges we face in our business. Among the issues we are addressing are carbon impact, paper specifications and procurement, ethical conduct within our business and among our vendors, and community and charitable support. For more information, please visit our website: www.wiley.com/go/citizenship.

Evaluation copies are provided to qualified academics and professionals for review purposes only, for use in their courses during the next academic year. These copies are licensed and may not be sold or transferred to a third party. Upon completion of the review period, please return the evaluation copy to Wiley. Return instructions and a free of charge return mailing label are available at www.wiley.com/go/returnlabel. If you have chosen to adopt this textbook for use in your course, please accept this book as your complimentary desk copy. Outside of the United States, please contact your local sales representative.

Library of Congress Cataloging-in-Publication Data

Perkovic, Ljubomir.
  Introduction to computing using Python : an application development focus / Ljubomir Perkovic, DePaul University. – Second edition.
     pages cm
  Includes index.
  ISBN 978-1-118-89094-3 (pbk.)
1. Python (Computer program language) 2. Object-oriented programming (Computer science) 3. Computer programming. I. Title.
QA76.73.P98P47 2015
005.1'17–dc23   2015008087

ISBN: 978-1-118-89094-3

Printed in the United States of America

10 9 8 7 6 5 4 3

To my father, Milan Perković (1937–1970),

who did not get the chance to complete his book.

Contents

Preface   xvii

Online Textbook Supplements xviii
For Students: How to Read This Book xviii
Overview of the Book xix
What Is New in This Edition? xxii
For Instructors: How to Use This Book xxiii

1

Introduction to Computer Science   1

1.1 Computer Science 2
     What Do Computing Professionals Do? 2
     Models, Algorithms, and Programs. 3
     Tools of the Trade 3
     What Is Computer Science? 4
1.2 Computer Systems 4
     Computer Hardware 4
     Operating Systems 5
     Networks and Network Protocols 6
     Programming Languages 7
     Software Libraries 7
1.3 Python Programming Language 8
     Short History of Python 8
     Setting Up the Python Development Environment 8
1.4 Computational Thinking 9
     A Sample Problem 9
     Abstraction and Modeling 10
     Algorithm 10
     Data Types 11
     Assignments and Execution Control Structures 12
Chapter Summary 13

2

Python Data Types   15

2.1 Expressions, Variables, and Assignments 16
    Algebraic Expressions and Functions 16
    Boolean Expressions and Operators 18
    Variables and Assignments 20
    Variable Names 22
2.2 Strings 23
    String Operators 23
    Indexing Operator 25
2.3 Lists and Tuples 27
    List Operators 27
    Lists Are Mutable, Strings Are Not 29
    Tuples, or "Immutable Lists" 29
    List and Tuple Methods 31
2.4 Objects and Classes 33
    Object Type 33
    Valid Values for Number Types 35
    Operators for Number Types 36
    Creating Objects 37
    Implicit Type Conversions 38
    Explicit Type Conversions 39
    Class Methods and Object-Oriented Programming 40
2.5 Python Standard Library 41
    Module `math` 41
    Module `fractions` 42
E-Book Case Study: Turtle Graphics 43
Chapter Summary 43
Solutions to Practice Problems 44
Exercises 45

3

Imperative Programming   51

3.1 Python Programs 52
    Our First Python Program 52
    Python Modules 54
    Built-In Function `print()` 54
    Interactive Input with `input()` 55
    Function `eval()` 56

3.2 Execution Control Structures 57

One-Way Decisions 57
Two-Way Decisions 60
Iteration Structures 62
Nesting Control Flow Structures 65
Function `range()` 66

3.3 User-Defined Functions 67

Our First Function 67
Function Input Arguments 68
`print()` versus `return` 70
Function Definitions Are "Assignment" Statements 71
Comments 72
Docstrings 72

3.4 Python Variables and Assignments 74

Mutable and Immutable Types 75
Assignments and Mutability 76
Swapping 77

3.5 Parameter Passing 78

Immutable Parameter Passing 79
Mutable Parameter Passing 80

E-Book Case Study: Automating Turtle Graphics 81
Chapter Summary 81
Solutions to Practice Problems 82
Exercises 85
Problems 86

4

Text Data, Files, and Exceptions   91

4.1 Strings, Revisited 92

String Representations 92
The Indexing Operator, Revisited 94
String Methods 95

4.2 Formatted Output 98

Function `print()` 98
String Method `format()` 100
Lining Up Data in Columns 102
Getting and Formatting the Date and Time 105

4.3 Files 107

File System 107
Opening and Closing a File 109
Patterns for Reading a Text File 112
Writing to a Text File 115

4.4 Errors and Exceptions 116
    Syntax Errors 116
    Built-In Exceptions 117
E-Book Case Study: Image Files 119
Chapter Summary 119
Solutions to Practice Problems 120
Exercises 121
Problems 124

5

Execution Control Structures 127

5.1 Decision Control and the if Statement 128
    Three-Way (and More!) Decisions 128
    Ordering of Conditions 130
5.2 for Loop and Iteration Patterns 131
    Loop Pattern: Iteration Loop 131
    Loop Pattern: Counter Loop 132
    Loop Pattern: Accumulator Loop 134
    Accumulating Different Types 135
    Loop Patterns: Nested Loop 137
5.3 More on Lists: Two-Dimensional Lists 139
    Two-Dimensional Lists 140
    Two-Dimensional Lists and the Nested Loop Pattern 141
5.4 while Loop 143
    while Loop Usage 143
5.5 More Loop Patterns 145
    Iteration Patterns: Sequence Loop 145
    Loop Pattern: Infinite Loop 147
    Loop Pattern: Loop and a Half 147
5.6 Additional Iteration Control Statements 149
    break Statement 149
    continue Statement 150
    pass Statement 151
E-Book Case Study: Image Processing 151
Chapter Summary 151
Solutions to Practice Problems 152
Exercises 155
Problems 157

6

Containers and Randomness 165

6.1 Dictionaries 166
    User-Defined Indexes as Motivation for Dictionaries 166
    Dictionary Class Properties 167
    Dictionary Operators 169
    Dictionary Methods 170
    A Dictionary as a Substitute for the Multiway `if` Statement . . . 173
    Dictionary as a Collection of Counters 173
    `tuple` Objects Can Be Dictionary Keys 176
6.2 Sets 177
    Using the `set` Constructor to Remove Duplicates 178
    `set` Operators 179
    `set` Methods 180
6.3 Character Encodings and Strings 181
    Character Encodings 181
    ASCII 182
    Unicode 183
    UTF-8 Encoding for Unicode Characters 185
6.4 Module `random` 186
    Choosing a Random Integer 187
    Choosing a Random "Real" 188
    Shuffling, Choosing, and Sampling at Random 189
E-Book Case Study: Games of Chance 190
Chapter Summary 190
Solutions to Practice Problems 190
Exercises 194
Problems 195

7

Namespaces 203

7.1 Encapsulation in Functions 204
    Code Reuse 204
    Modularity (or Procedural Decomposition) 205
    Encapsulation (or Information Hiding) 205
    Local Variables 205
    Namespaces Associated with Function Calls 206
    Namespaces and the Program Stack 207

7.2 Global versus Local Namespaces 211
      Global Variables 211
      Variables with Local Scope 212
      Variables with Global Scope 212
      Changing Global Variables Inside a Function 214
7.3 Exceptional Control Flow 215
      Exceptions and Exceptional Control Flow 215
      Catching and Handling Exceptions 216
      The Default Exception Handler 218
      Catching Exceptions of a Given Type 218
      Multiple Exception Handlers 219
      Controlling the Exceptional Control Flow 220
7.4 Modules as Namespaces 223
      Module Attributes 223
      What Happens When Importing a Module 224
      Module Search Path 224
      Top-Level Module 226
      Different Ways to Import Module Attributes 228
7.5 Classes as Namespaces 230
      A Class Is a Namespace 230
      Class Methods Are Functions Defined in the Class Namespace . . 231
E-Book Case Study: Debugging with a debugger 231
Chapter Summary 232
Solutions to Practice Problems 232
Exercises 233
Problems 236

8

Object-Oriented Programming

239

8.1 Defining a New Python Class 240
      Methods of Class Point 240
      A Class and Its Namespace 241
      Every Object Has an Associated Namespace 242
      Implementation of Class Point 242
      Instance Variables 243
      Instances Inherit Class Attributes 244
      Class Definition, More Generally 245
      Documenting a Class 246
      Class Animal 247
8.2 Examples of User-Defined Classes 248
      Overloaded Constructor Operator 248
      Default Constructor 249
      Playing Card Class 250

8.3 Designing New Container Classes. 251

Designing a Class Representing a Deck of Playing Cards 251
Implementing the Deck (of Cards) Class 252
Container Class Queue 254
Implementing a Queue Class 255

8.4 Overloaded Operators 256

Operators Are Class Methods 257
Making the Class Point User Friendly 258
Contract between the Constructor and the repr() Operator . . . 260
Making the Queue Class User Friendly 262

8.5 Inheritance 264

Inheriting Attributes of a Class 264
Class Definition, in General 267
Overriding Superclass Methods 267
Extending Superclass Methods 270
Implementing a Queue Class by Inheriting from list 271

8.6 User-Defined Exceptions 272

Raising an Exception 273
User-Defined Exception Classes 274
Improving the Encapsulation of Class Queue 274

E-Book Case Study: Indexing and Iterators 275
Chapter Summary 275
Solutions to Practice Problems 276
Exercises 279
Problems 281

9

Graphical User Interfaces

291

9.1 Basics of tkinter GUI Development 292

Widget Tk: The GUI Window. 292
Widget Label for Displaying Text 292
Displaying Images 294
Packing Widgets 295
Arranging Widgets in a Grid 297

9.2 Event-Based tkinter Widgets 299

Button Widget and Event Handlers 299
Events, Event Handlers, and mainloop() 301
The Entry Widget 302
Text Widget and Binding Events 305
Event Patterns and the tkinter Class Event 306

9.3 Designing GUIs 308

Widget Canvas 308
Widget Frame as an Organizing Widget 311

9.4 OOP for GUIs 313
     GUI OOP Basics. 313
     Shared Widgets Are Assigned to Instance Variables 315
     Shared Data Are Assigned to Instance Variables 317
E-Book Case Study: Developing a Calculator 318
Chapter Summary 319
Solutions to Practice Problems 319
Exercises 323
Problems 324

10

Recursion   329

10.1 Introduction to Recursion 330
     Functions that Call Themselves 330
     Stopping Condition 331
     Properties of Recursive Functions 332
     Recursive Thinking 332
     Recursive Function Calls and the Program Stack 334
10.2 Examples of Recursion 336
     Recursive Number Sequence Pattern 336
     Fractals 338
     Virus Scanner 342
     Linear recursion 345
10.3 Run Time Analysis 347
     The Exponent Function 347
     Counting Operations 349
     Fibonacci Sequence 349
     Experimental Analysis of Run Time 351
10.4 Searching 354
     Linear Search 354
     Binary Search 354
     Linear versus Binary Search 356
     Uniqueness Testing 357
     Selecting the kth Largest (Smallest) Item 358
     Computing the Most Frequently Occurring Item 359
E-Book Case Study: Tower of Hanoi 359
Chapter Summary 360
Solutions to Practice Problems 360
Exercises 362
Problems 363

11

The Web and Search

371

11.1 The World Wide Web 372
    Web Servers and Web Clients 372
    "Plumbing" of the WWW 373
    Naming Scheme: Uniform Resource Locator 373
    Protocol: HyperText Transfer Protocol 374
    HyperText Markup Language 375
    HTML Elements 376
    Tree Structure of an HTML Document 377
    Anchor HTML Element and Absolute Links 377
    Relative Links 378

11.2 Python WWW API 379
    Module `urllib.request` 379
    Module `html.parser` 381
    Overriding the `HTMLParser` Handlers 383
    Module `urllib.parse` 384
    Parser That Collects HTTP Hyperlinks 385

11.3 String Pattern Matching 387
    Regular Expressions 387
    Python Standard Library Module `re` 390

E-Book Case Study: Web Crawler 391
Chapter Summary 392
Solutions to Practice Problems 392
Exercises 394
Problems 395

12

Databases and Data Processing

399

12.1 Databases and SQL 400
    Database Tables 400
    Structured Query Language 402
    Statement SELECT 402
    Clause WHERE 404
    Built-In SQL Functions 406
    Clause GROUP BY 406
    Making SQL Queries Involving Multiple Tables 407
    Statement CREATE TABLE 409
    Statements INSERT and UPDATE 409

12.2 Database Programming in Python 410
      Database Engines and SQLite 410
      Creating a Database with sqlite3 411
      Committing to Database Changes and Closing the Database . . . 412
      Querying a Database Using sqlite3. 413
12.3 Functional Language Approach 415
      List Comprehension 415
      MapReduce Problem-Solving Framework 417
      MapReduce, in the Abstract 420
      Inverted Index 421
12.4 Parallel Computing 423
      Parallel Computing 423
      Class Pool of Module multiprocessing 424
      Parallel Speedup 427
      MapReduce, in Parallel 428
      Parallel versus Sequential MapReduce 429
E-Book Case Study: Data Interchange 431
Chapter Summary 432
Solutions to Practice Problems 432
Exercises 435
Problems 436

Index   440

Preface

This textbook is an introduction to programming, computer application development, and the science of computing. It is meant to be used in a college-level introductory programming course. More than just an introduction to programming, the book is a broad introduction to computer science concepts and to the tools used for modern computer application development.

The computer programming language used in the book is Python, a language that has a gentler learning curve than most. Python comes with powerful software libraries that make complex tasks—such as developing a graphics application or finding all the links in a web page—a breeze. In this textbook, we leverage the ease of learning Python and the ease of using its libraries to do more computer science *and* to add a focus on modern application development. The result is a textbook that is a broad introduction to the field of computing and modern application development.

The textbook's pedagogical approach is to introduce computing concepts and Python programming in a breadth-first manner. Rather than covering computing concepts and Python structures one after another, the book's approach is more akin to learning a natural language, starting from a small general-purpose vocabulary and then gradually extending it. The presentation is in general problem oriented, and computing concepts, Python structures, algorithmic techniques, and other tools are introduced when needed, using a "right tool at the right moment" model.

The book uses the imperative-first and procedural-first paradigm but does not shy away from discussing objects early. User-defined classes and object-oriented programming are covered later, when they can be motivated and students are ready. The last three chapters of the textbook and the associated case studies use the context of web crawling, search engines, and data mining to introduce a broad array of topics. These include foundational concepts such as recursion, regular expressions, depth-first search, data compression, and Google's MapReduce framework, as well as practical tools such as GUI widgets, HTML parsers, SQL, JSON, I/O streams, and multicore programming.

This textbook can be used in a course that introduces computer science and programming to computer science majors. Its broad coverage of foundational computer science topics as well as current technologies will give the student a broad understanding of the field *and* a confidence to develop "real" modern applications that interact with the web and/or a database. The textbook's broad coverage also makes it ideal for students who need to master programming and key computing concepts but will not take more than one or two computing courses.

The Book's Technical Features

The textbook has a number of features that engage students and encourage them to get their hands dirty. For one, the book makes heavy use of *examples that use the Python interactive shell*. Students can easily reproduce these one-liners on their own. After doing so, students will likely continue experimenting further using the immediate feedback of the interactive shell.

Throughout the textbook, there are inline *practice problems* whose purpose is to reinforce concepts just covered. The solutions to these problems appear at the end of the corresponding chapter or case study, allowing students to check their solution or take a peek in case they are stuck.

The textbook uses Caution boxes to warn students of potential pitfalls. It also uses Detour boxes to briefly explore interesting but tangential topics. The large number of boxes, practice problems, figures, and tables create visual breaks in the text, making reading the volume more approachable for students.

Finally, the textbook contains a *large number of end-of-chapter problems*, many of which are unlike problems typically found in an introductory textbook.

The *E-Book Edition* of the textbook includes additional material consisting of 11 case studies. Each case study is associated with a chapter (2 through 12) and showcases the concepts and tools covered in the chapter in context. The case studies include additional problems, including practice problems with solutions.

Online Textbook Supplements

These textbook supplements are available on the textbook web site:

- PowerPoint slides for each chapter
- Learning objectives for each section
- Code examples appearing in the book
- Exercise and problem solutions (for instructors only)
- Exam problems (for instructors only)

For Students: How to Read This Book

This book is meant to help you master programming and develop computational thinking skills. Programming and computational thinking are hands-on activities that require a computer with a Python integrated development environment as well as a pen and paper for "back-of-the-envelope" calculations. Ideally, you should have those tools next to you as you read this book.

The book makes heavy use of small examples that use Python's interactive shell. Try running those examples in your shell. Feel free to experiment further. It's very unlikely the computer will burst into flames if you make a mistake!

You should also attempt to solve all the practice problems as they appear in the text. Problem solutions appear at the end of the corresponding chapter. If you get stuck, it's OK to peek at the solution; after doing so, try solving the problem without peeking.

The text uses Caution boxes to warn you of potential pitfalls. These are very important and should not be skipped. The Detour boxes, however, discuss topics that are only tangentially related to the main discussion. You may skip those if you like. Or you may go further and explore the topics in more depth if you get intrigued.

At some point while reading this text, you may get inspired to develop your own app, whether a card game or an app that keeps track of a set of stock market indexes in real time. If so, just go ahead and try it! You will learn a lot.

Overview of the Book

This textbook consists of 12 chapters that introduce computing concepts and Python programming in a breadth-first manner. The E-Book Edition also includes case studies that showcase concepts and tools covered in the chapters in context.

Tour of Python and Computer Science

Chapter 1 introduces the *basic computing concepts and terminology*. Starting with a discussion of what computer science is and what developers do, the concepts of modeling, algorithm development, and programming are defined. The chapter describes the computer scientist's and application developer's toolkit, from logic to systems, with an emphasis on programming languages, the Python development environment, and computational thinking.

Chapter 2 covers *core built-in Python data types*: the integer, Boolean, floating-point, string, list, and tuple types. To illustrate the features of the different types, the Python interactive shell is used. Rather than being comprehensive, the presentation focuses on the purpose of each type and the differences and similarities between the types. This approach motivates a more abstract discussion of objects and classes that is ultimately needed for mastering the proper usage of data types. The E-Book case study takes advantage of this discussion to introduce Turtle graphics classes that enable students to do simple, fun graphics interactively.

Chapter 3 introduces *imperative and procedural programming, including basic execution control structures*. This chapter presents programs as a sequence of Python statements stored in a file. To control how the statements are executed, basic conditional and iterative control structures are introduced: the one-way and two-way if statements as well as the simplest for loop patterns of iterating through an explicit sequence or a range of numbers. The chapter introduces functions as a way to neatly package a small application; it also builds on the material on objects and classes covered in Chapter 2 to describe how Python does assignments and parameter passing. The E-Book case study uses the visual context of Turtle graphics to motivate automation through programs and abstraction through functions.

The first three chapters provide a *shallow* but *broad* introduction to Python programming and computers science. Core Python data types and basic execution control structures are introduced so students can write simple but complete programs early. Functions are introduced early as well to help students conceptualize what a program is doing, that is, what inputs it takes and what output it produces. In other words, abstraction and encapsulation of functions is used to help students better understand programs.

Focus on Algorithmic Thinking

Chapter 4 covers *text and file processing in more depth*. It continues the coverage of strings from Chapter 2 with a discussion of string value representations, string operators and methods, and formatted output. File input/output (I/O) is introduced as well and, in particular, the different patterns for reading text files. Finally, the context of file I/O is used to motivate a discussion of exceptions and the different types of exceptions in Python. The E-Book case study discusses how image files (typically stored as binary files rather than text files) are read and written and how images can be processed using Python.

Chapter 5 covers *execution control structures and loop patterns in depth*. Basic conditional and iteration structures were introduced in Chapter 3 and then used in Chapter 4 (e.g., in the context of reading files). Chapter 5 starts with a discussion of multiway conditional statements. The bulk of the chapter is spent on describing the different loop patterns: the various ways `for` loops and `while` loops are used. Multidimensional lists are introduced as well, in the context of the nested loop pattern. More than just covering Python loop structures, this core chapter describes the different ways that problems can be broken down. Thus, the chapter fundamentally is about *problem solving and algorithms*. The E-Book case study looks underneath the hood of image processing and describes how classic image processing algorithms can be implemented.

Chapter 6 completes the textbook's coverage of *Python's built-in container data types and their usage*. The dictionary, set, and tuple data types are motivated and introduced. This chapter also completes the coverage of strings with a discussion of character encodings and Unicode. Finally, the concept of randomness is introduced in the context of selecting and permuting items in containers. The E-Book case study makes use of concepts introduced in this chapter to show how a blackjack application can be developed.

Chapters 4 through 6 represent the second layer in the breadth-first approach this textbook takes. One of the main challenges students face in an introductory programming course is mastering conditional and iteration structures and, more generally, the computational problem-solving and algorithm development skills. The critical Chapter 5, on patterns of applying execution control structures, appears *after* students have been using *basic* conditional statements and iteration patterns for several weeks and have gotten somewhat comfortable with the Python language. Having gained some comfort with the language and basic iteration, students can focus on the algorithmic issues rather than less fundamental issues, such as properly reading input or formatting output.

Managing Program Complexity

Chapter 7 shifts gears and focuses on the software development process itself and the problem of managing larger, more complex programs. It introduces *namespaces as the foundation for managing program complexity*. The chapter builds on the coverage of functions and parameter passing in Chapter 3 to motivate the software engineering goals of code reuse, modularity, and encapsulation. Functions, modules, and classes are tools that can be used to achieve these goals, fundamentally because they define separate namespaces. The chapter describes how namespaces are managed during normal control flow and during exceptional control flow, when exceptions are handled by exception handlers. The E-Book case study builds on this chapter's content to show how to use a debugger to find bugs in a program or, more generally, to analyze the execution of the program.

Chapter 8 covers the *development of new classes in Python and the object-oriented programming (OOP) paradigm*. The chapter builds on Chapter 7's uncovering of how Python classes are implemented through namespaces to explain how new classes are developed. The chapter introduces the OOP concepts of operator overloading—central to Python's design philosophy—and inheritance—a powerful OOP property that will be used in Chapters 9 and 11. Through abstraction and encapsulation, classes achieve the desirable software engineering goals of modularity and code reuse. The context of abstraction and encapsulation is then used to motivate user-defined exception classes. The E-Book case study goes one step further and illustrates the implementation of iterative behavior in user-defined container classes.

Chapter 9 introduces *graphical user interfaces (GUIs) and showcases the power of the OOP approach for developing GUIs.* It uses the Tk widget toolkit, which is part of the Python Standard Library. The coverage of interactive widgets provides the opportunity to discuss the event-driven programming paradigm. In addition to introducing GUI development, the chapter also showcases the power of OOP to achieve modular and reusable programs. The E-Book case study illustrates this in the context of implementing a basic calculator GUI.

The broad goal of Chapters 7 though 9 is to introduce students to the issues of program complexity and code organization. They describe how namespaces are used to achieve functional abstraction and data abstraction and, ultimately, encapsulated, modular, and reusable code. Chapter 8 provides a comprehensive discussion of user-defined classes and OOP. The full benefit of OOP, however, is best seen in context, which is what Chapter 9 is about. Additional contexts and examples of OOP are shown in later chapters and specifically in Sections 11.2, 12.3, and 12.4 as well as in the Chapter 10 case study. Chapters 7 though 9 provide a foundation for the students' future education in data structures and software engineering methodologies.

Crawling through Foundations and Applications

Chapters 10 through 12, the last three chapters of the textbook, cover a variety of advanced topics, from fundamental computer science concepts like recursion, regular expressions, data compression, and depth-first search, to practical and contemporary tools like HTML parsers, JSON, SQL, and multicore programming. The theme used to motivate and connect these topics is the development of web crawlers, search engines, and data mining apps. The theme, however, is loose, and each individual topic is presented independently to allow instructors to develop alternate contexts and themes for this material as they see fit.

Chapter 10 introduces foundational computer science topics: *recursion, search, and the run-time analysis of algorithms.* The chapter starts with a discussion of how to think recursively. This skill is then put to use on a wide variety of problems from drawing fractals to virus scanning. This last example is used to illustrate depth-first search. The benefits and pitfalls of recursion lead to a discussion of algorithm run-time analysis, which is then used in the context of analyzing the performance of various list search algorithms. This chapter puts the spotlight on the theoretical aspects of computing and forms a basis for future coursework in data structures and algorithms. The E-Book case study considers the Tower of Hanoi problem and shows how to develop a visual application that illustrates the recursive solution.

Chapter 11 introduces the *World Wide Web as a central computing platform and as a huge source of data* for innovative computer application development. HTML, the language of the web, is briefly discussed before tools to access resources on the web and parse web pages are covered. To grab the desired content from web pages and other text content, regular expressions are introduced. A benefit of touching HTML parsing and regular expressions in an introductory course is that students will be familiar with their uses in context before rigorously covering them in a formal languages course. The E-Book case study makes use of the different topics covered in this chapter to show how a basic *web crawler* can be developed.

Chapter 12 covers *databases and the processing of large data sets.* The database language SQL is briefly described as well as a Python's database application programming interface in the context of storing data grabbed from a web page. Given the ubiquity of databases in today's computer applications, it is important for students to get an early exposure to them and their use (if for no other reason than to be familiar with them before their first internship). The coverage of databases and SQL is introductory only and should be considered merely a basis for a later database course. This chapter also considers how to leverage the multiple cores available on computers to process big data sets more quickly. Google's MapReduce problem-solving framework is described and used as a context for introducing list comprehensions and the functional programming paradigm. This chapter forms a foundation for further study of databases, programming languages, and data mining. The E-Book case study uses this last context to discuss *data interchange* or how to format and save data so that it is accessible, easily and efficiently, to any program that needs it.

What Is New in This Edition?

The big change between the first and second editions of the textbook is a structural one. A clear separation now exists between the foundational material covered in a chapter and the case study illustrating the concepts covered in the chapter. The case studies have been moved out of the chapters and are now grouped together in the E-Book Edition of the textbook. There are two benefits from this structural change. First, the coverage of the textbook chapters is now more focused on foundational material. The streamlined content, together with a switch to a Black&White format, allows the new Print Edition of the textbook to be priced less than the previous one. The second benefit of moving the case studies to the E-Book Edition is that the move gives more space for the case studies to be enriched. Four new case studies appear in the new edition, and there is now a case study associated with every chapter of the textbook (except the "non-technical" introductory chapter).

In addition to this structural change, new material has been added, some material has been moved, errata have been corrected, and the presentation has been improved. We outline these changes next.

In Chapter 2, we have added coverage of the tuple type (covered in Chapter 6 in the first edition). This move is justified because the tuple type is a key built-in type in Python that is used by many Standard Library modules and Python applications. For example, tuple objects are used by the image processing modules discussed in the case studies associated with Chapters 4 and 5. Because the tuple type is very similar to the list type, this additional content adds very little to the time needed to cover Chapter 2.

In Chapter 3, the presentation of functions has been improved. In particular, there are more examples and practice problems to help illustrate the passing of different numbers and types of function parameters. The Chapter 4 case study has been replaced with a new one on processing image files. The new case study gives students an exciting opportunity to see the textbook material in the context of visual media. Also, the material on processing and formating date and time strings has been moved to Section 4.2. The important Chapter 5 has, in the second edition, an associated case study on implementing image processing algorithms. This material again uses the attractive context of visual media to illustrate fundamental concepts such as nested loops.

Chapter 6 no longer includes coverage of the tuple type (moved to Chapter 2). Chapter 7 has, in the second edition, an associated case study on debugging and the use of a debugger. It effectively uses the concepts covered in the chapter to provide students with a new tool that will help them with debugging. Chapters 8 and 9 have changed only slightly. Chapter 10 has a deeper and more explicit coverage of linear recursion and its relationship to iteration. Chapter 11 has few changes. Finally, Chapter 12 has, in the second edition, an associated case study on data interchange which will help students gain practical experience working with data sets.

Finally, about 60 practice and end-of-chapter problems have been added to the book.

For Instructors: How to Use This Book

The material in this textbook was developed for a two quarter course sequence introducing computer science and programming to computer science majors. The book therefore has more than enough material for a typical 15-week course (and probably just the right amount of material for a class of well-prepared and highly motivated students).

The first six chapters of the textbook provide a comprehensive coverage of imperative/procedural programming in Python. They are meant to be covered in order, but it is possible to cover Chapter 5 before Chapter 4. Furthermore, the topics in Chapter 6 may be skipped and then introduced as needed.

Chapters 7 through 9 are meant to be covered in order to effectively showcase OOP. It is important to cover Chapter 7 before Chapter 8 because it demystifies Python's approach to class implementation and allows the more efficient coverage of OOP topics such as operator overloading and inheritance. It is also beneficial, though not necessary, to cover Chapter 9 after Chapter 8 because it provides a context in which OOP is shown to provide great benefits.

Chapters 9 through 12 are all optional, depend only on Chapters 1 through 6—with the few exceptions noted—and contain topics that can, in general, be skipped or reordered at the discretion of the course instructor. Exceptions are Section 9.4, which illustrates the OOP approach to GUI development, as well as Sections 11.2, 12.3, and 12.4, all of which make use of user-defined classes. All these should follow Chapter 8.

Instructors using this book in a course that leaves OOP to a later course can cover Chapters 1 through 7 and then choose topics from the non-OOP sections of Chapters 9 through 12. Instructors wishing to cover OOP should use Chapters 1 through 9 and then choose topics from Chapters 10 through 12.

Acknowledgments

The material for the first edition of this textbook was developed over three years in the context of teaching the CSC 241/242 course sequence (Introduction to Computer Science I and II) at DePaul University. In those three years, six separate cohorts of computer science freshmen moved through the course sequence. I used the different cohorts to try different pedagogical approaches, reorder and reorganize the material, and experiment with topics usually not taught in a course introducing programming. The continuous reorganization and experimentation made the course material less fluid and more challenging than necessary, especially for the early cohorts. Amazingly, students maintained their enthusiasm through the low points in the course, which in turn helped me maintain mine. I thank them all wholeheartedly for that.

I would like to acknowledge the faculty and administration of DePaul's School of Computing for creating a truly unique academic environment that encourages experimentation and innovation in education. Some of them also had a direct role in the creation and shaping of this textbook. Associate Dean Lucia Dettori scheduled my classes so I had time to write. Curt White, an experienced textbook author, encouraged me to start writing and put in a good word for me with publishing house John Wiley & Sons. Massimo DiPierro, the creator of the web2py web framework and a far greater Python authority than I will ever be, created the first outline of the content of the CSC241/242 course sequence, which was the initial seed for the book. Iyad Kanj taught the first iteration of CSC241 and selflessly allowed me to mine the material he developed. Amber Settle is the first person other than me to use this textbook in her course; thankfully, she had great success, though that is at least as much due to her excellence as a teacher. Craig Miller has thought more deeply about fundamental computer science concepts and how to explain them than anyone I know; I have gained some of his insights through many interesting discussions, and the textbook has benefited from them. Finally, Marcus Schaefer improved the textbook by doing a thorough technical review of more than half of the book.

My course lecture notes would have remained just that if Nicole Dingley, a Wiley book rep, had not suggested that I make them into a textbook. Nicole put me in contact with Wiley editor Beth Golub, who made the gutsy decision to trust a foreigner with a strange name and no experience writing textbooks to write a textbook. Wiley senior designer Madelyn Lesure, along with my friend and neighbor Mike Riordan, helped me achieve the simple and clean design of the text. Finally, Wiley senior editorial assistant Samantha Mandel worked tirelessly on getting my draft chapters reviewed and into production. Samantha has been a model of professionalism and good grace throughout the process, and she has offered endless good ideas for making the book better.

The final version of the book is similar to the original draft in surface only. The vast improvement over the initial draft is due to the dozens of reviewers, many of them anonymous. The kindness of strangers has made this a better book and has given me a new appreciation for the reviewing process. The reviewers have been kind enough not only to find problems but also offer solutions. For their careful and systematic feedback, I am grateful. Some of the reviewers, including David Mutchler (Rose-Hulman Institute of Technology), who offered his name and email for further correspondence, went beyond the call of duty and helped excavate the potential that lay buried in my early drafts. Jonathan Lundell also provided a technical review of the last chapters in the book. Because of time constraints, I was not able to incorporate all the valuable suggestions I received from them, and the responsibility for any any omissions in the textbook are entirely my own.

I would like to thank, in particular, the following faculty who made use of the first edition in their courses and gave me invaluable feedback: Ankur Agrawal (Manhattan College), Albert Chan (Fayetteville State University), Gabriel Ferrer (Hendrix College), David G. Kay (University of California, Irvine), Gerard Ryan (New Jersey Institute of Technology), Sridhar Seshadri (University of Texas at Arlington), Richard Weiss (Evergreen State College), and Michal Young (University of Oregon). I have tried my best to incorporate their suggestions in this second edition.

Finally, I would like to thank my spouse, Lisa, and daughters, Marlena and Eleanor, for the patience they had with me. Writing a book takes a huge amount of time, and this time can only come from "family time" or sleep since other professional obligations have set hours. The time I spent writing this book resulted in my being unavailable for family time or my being crabby from lack of sleep, a real double whammy. Luckily, I had the foresight to adopt a dog when I started working on this project. A dog named Muffin inevitably brings more joy than any missing from me... So, thanks to Muffin.

About the Author

Ljubomir Perkovic is an associate professor at the School of Computing of DePaul University in Chicago. He received a Bachelor's degree in mathematics and computer science from

Hunter College of the City University of New York in 1990. He obtained his Ph.D. in algorithms, combinatorics, and optimization from the School of Computer Science at Carnegie Mellon University in 1998.

Professor Perkovic started teaching the introductory programming sequence for majors at DePaul in the mid-2000s. His goal was to share with beginning programmers the excitement that developers feel when working on a cool new app. He incorporated into the course concepts and technologies used in modern application development. The material he developed for the course forms the basis of this book.

His research interests include computational geometry, distributed computing, graph theory and algorithms, and computational thinking. He has received a Fulbright Research Scholar award for his research in computational geometry and a National Science Foundation grant for a project to expand computational thinking across the general education curriculum.

Introduction to Computer Science

1.1 Computer Science   2

1.2 Computer Systems   4

1.3 Python Programming Language   8

1.4 Computational Thinking   9

Chapter Summary   13

IN THIS INTRODUCTORY CHAPTER, we provide the context for the book and introduce the key concepts and terminology that we will be using throughout. The starting point for our discussion are several questions. What is computer science? What do computer scientists and computer application developers do? And what tools do they use?

Computers, or more generally computer systems, form one set of tools. We discuss the different components of a computer system including the hardware, the operating system, the network and the Internet, and the programming language used to write programs. We specifically provide some background on the Python programming language, the language used in this book.

The other set of tools are the reasoning skills, grounded in logic and mathematics, required to develop a computer application. We introduce the idea of computational thinking and illustrate how it is used in the process of developing a small web search application.

The foundational concepts and terminology introduced in this chapter are independent of the Python programming language. They are relevant to any type of application development regardless of the hardware or software platform or programming language used.

1.1 Computer Science

This textbook is an introduction to programming. It is also an introduction to Python, the programming language. But most of all, it is an introduction to computing and how to look at the world from a computer science perspective. To understand this perspective and define what computer science is, let's start by looking at what computing professionals do.

What Do Computing Professionals Do?

One answer is to say: they write programs. It is true that many computing professionals do write programs. But saying that they write programs is like saying that screenwriters (i.e., writers of screenplays for movies or television series) write text. From our experience watching movies, we know better: screenwriters invent a world and plots in it to create stories that answer the movie watcher's need to understand the nature of the human condition. Well, maybe not all screenwriters.

So let's try again to define what computing professionals do. Many actually do *not* write programs. Even among those who do, what they are really doing is developing computer applications that address a need in some activity we humans do. Such computing professionals are often called *computer application developers* or simply *developers*. Some developers even work on applications, like computer games, that are not that different from the imaginary worlds, intricate plots, and stories that screenwriters create.

Not all developers develop computer games. Some create financial tools for investment bankers, and others create visualization tools for doctors (see Table 1.1 for other examples.)

What about the computing professionals who are *not* developers? What do they do? Some talk to clients and elicit requirements for computer applications that clients need.

Table 1.1 The range of computers science. Listed are examples of human activities and, for each activity, a software product built by computer application developers that supports performing the activity.

Activity	Computer Application
Defense	Image processing software for target detection and tracking
Driving	GPS-based navigation software with traffic views on smartphones and dedicated navigation hardware
Education	Simulation software for performing dangerous or expensive biology laboratory experiments virtually
Farming	Satellite-based farm management software that keeps track of soil properties and computes crop forecasts
Films	3D computer graphics software for creating computer-generated imagery for movies
Media	On-demand, real-time video streaming of television shows, movies, and video clips
Medicine	Patient record management software to facilitate sharing between specialists
Physics	Computational grid systems for crunching data obtained from particle accelerators
Political activism	Social network technologies that enable real-time communication and information sharing
Shopping	Recommender system that suggests products that may be of interest to a shopper
Space exploration	Mars exploration rovers that analyze the soil to find evidence of water

Others are managers who oversee an application development team. Some computing professionals support their clients with newly installed software and others keep the software up to date. Many computing professionals administer networks, web servers, or database servers. Artistic computing professionals design the interfaces that clients use to interact with an application. Some, such as the author of this textbook, like to teach computing, and others offer information technology (IT) consulting services. Finally, more than a few computing professionals have become entrepreneurs and started new software businesses, many of which have become household names.

Regardless of the ultimate role they play in the world of computing, all computing professionals understand the basic principles of computing, how computer applications are developed, and how they work. Therefore, the training of a computing professional always starts with the mastery of a programming language and the software development process. In order to describe this process in general terms, we need to use slightly more abstract terminology.

Models, Algorithms, and Programs

To create a computer application that addresses a need in some area of human activity, developers invent a *model* that represents the "real-world" environment in which the activity occurs. The model is an abstract (imaginary) representation of the environment and is described using the language of logic and mathematics. The model can represent the objects in a computer game, stock market indexes, an organ in the human body, or the seats on an airplane.

Developers also invent *algorithms* that operate in the model and that create, transform, and/or present information. An algorithm is a sequence of instructions, not unlike a cooking recipe. Each instruction manipulates information in a very specific and well-defined way, and the execution of the algorithm instructions achieves a desired goal. For example, an algorithm could compute collisions between objects in a computer game or the available economy seats on an airplane.

The full benefit of developing an algorithm is achieved with the *automation* of the execution of the algorithm. After inventing a model and an algorithm, developers implement the algorithm as a *computer program* that can be executed on a *computer system*. While an algorithm and a program are both descriptions of step-by-step instructions of how to achieve a result, an algorithm is described using a language that we understand but that cannot be executed by a computer system, and a program is described using a language that we understand *and* that can be executed on a computer system.

At the end of this chapter, in Section 1.4, we will take up a sample task and go through the steps of developing a model and an algorithm implementing the task.

Tools of the Trade

We already hinted at a few of the tools that developers use when working on computer applications. At a fundamental level, developers use logic and mathematics to develop models and algorithms. Over the past half century or so, computer scientists have developed a vast body of knowledge—grounded in logic and mathematics—on the theoretical foundations of information and computation. Developers apply this knowledge in their work. Much of the training in computer science consists of mastering this knowledge, and this textbook is the first step in that training.

The other set of tools developers use are computers, of course, or more generally computer systems. They include the hardware, the network, the operating systems, and also the programming languages and programming language tools. We describe all these systems in more detail in Section 1.2. While the theoretical foundations often transcend changes in technology, computer system tools are constantly evolving. Faster hardware, improved operating systems, and new programming languages are being created almost daily to handle the applications of tomorrow.

What Is Computer Science?

We have described what application developers do and also the tools that they use. What then is computer science? How does it relate to computer application development?

While most computing professionals develop applications for users outside the field of computing, some are studying and creating the theoretical and systems tools that developers use. The field of computer science encompasses this type of work. Computer science can be defined as the study of the theoretical foundations of information and computation and their practical implementation on computer systems.

While application development is certainly a core driver of the field of computer science, its scope is broader. The computational techniques developed by computer scientists are used to study questions on the nature of information, computation, and intelligence. They are also used in other disciplines to understand the natural and artificial phenomena around us, such as phase transitions in physics or social networks in sociology. In fact, some computer scientists are now working on some of the most challenging problems in science, mathematics, economics, and other fields.

We should emphasize that the boundary between application development and computer science (and, similarly, between application developers and computer scientists) is usually not clearly delineated. Much of the theoretical foundations of computer science have come out of application development, and theoretical computer science investigations have often led to innovative applications of computing. Thus many computing professionals wear two hats: the developer's and the computer scientist's.

1.2 Computer Systems

A computer system is a combination of hardware and software that work together to execute application programs. The hardware consists of physical components—that is, components that you can touch, such as a memory chip, a keyboard, a networking cable, or a smartphone. The software includes all the nonphysical components of the computer, including the operating system, the network protocols, the programming language tools, and the associated application programming interface (API).

Computer Hardware

The computer *hardware* refers to the physical components of a computer system. It may refer to a desktop computer and include the monitor, the keyboard, the mouse, and other external devices of a computer desktop and, most important, the physical "box" itself with all its internal components.

The core hardware component inside the box is the *central processing unit* (CPU) . The CPU is where the computation occurs. The CPU performs computation by fetching program instructions and data and executing the instructions on the data. Another key internal component is *main memory*, often referred to as *random access memory* (RAM). That is where program instructions and data are stored when the program executes. The CPU fetches instructions and data from main memory and stores the results in main memory.

The set of wirings that carry instructions and data between the CPU and main memory is commonly called a *bus*. The bus also connects the CPU and main memory to other internal components such as the hard drive and the various *adapters* to which external devices (such as the monitor, the mouse, or the network cables) are connected.

The *hard drive* is the third core component inside the box. The hard drive is where files are stored. Main memory loses all data when the computer is shut down; the hard drive, however, is able to store a file whether the computer is powered on or off. The hard drive also has a much, much higher capacity than main memory.

The term *computer system* may refer to a single computer (desktop, laptop, smartphone, or pad). It may also refer to a collection of computers connected to a network (and thus to each other). In this case, the hardware also includes any network wiring and specialized network hardware such as *routers*.

It is important to understand that most developers do not work with computer hardware directly. It would be extremely difficult to write programs if the programmer had to write instructions directly to the hardware components. It would also be very dangerous because a programming mistake could incapacitate the hardware. For this reason, there exists an *interface* between application programs written by a developer and the hardware.

Operating Systems

An application program does not directly access the keyboard, the computer hard drive, the network (and the Internet), or the display. Instead it requests the *operating system* (OS) to do so on its behalf. The operating system is the software component of a computer system that lies between the hardware and the application programs written by the developer. The operating system has two complementary functions:

1. The OS protects the hardware from misuse by the program or the programmer and
2. The OS provides application programs with an interface through which programs can request services from hardware devices.

In essence, the OS manages access to the hardware by the application programs executing on the machine.

DETOUR

Origins of Today's Operating Systems

The mainstream operating systems on the market today are Microsoft Windows and UNIX and its variants, including Linux and Apple OS X.

The UNIX operating system was developed in the late 1960s and early 1970s by Ken Thompson at AT&T Bell Labs. By 1973, UNIX was reimplemented by Thompson and Dennis Ritchie using C, a programming language just created by Ritchie. As it was free for anyone to use, C became quite popular, and programmers *ported* C and UNIX to various computing platforms. Today, there are several versions of UNIX, including Apple's Mac OS X.

The origin of Microsoft's Windows operating systems is tied to the advent of personal computers. Microsoft was founded in the late 1970s by Paul Allen and Bill Gates. When IBM developed the IBM Personal Computer (IBM PC) in 1981, Microsoft provided the operating system called MS DOS (Microsoft Disk Operating System). Since then Microsoft has added a graphical interface to the operating system and renamed it Windows. The latest version is Windows 7.

Linux is a UNIX-like operating sytem developed in the early 1990s by Linus Torvalds. His motivation was to build a UNIX-like operating system for personal computers since, at the time, UNIX was restricted to high-powered workstations and mainframe computers. After the initial development, Linux became a community-based, *open source* software development project. That means that any developer is welcome to join in and help in the further development of the Linux OS. Linux is one of the best examples of successful open-source software development projects.

Networks and Network Protocols

Many of the computer applications we use daily require the computer to be connected to the Internet. Without an Internet connection, you cannot send an email, browse the web, listen to Internet radio, or update your software. In order to be connected to the Internet, though, you must first connect to a network that is part of the Internet.

A computer network is a system of computers that can communicate with each other. There are several different network communication technologies in use today, some of which are wireless (e.g., Wi-Fi) and others that use network cables (e.g., Ethernet).

An *internetwork* is the connection of several networks. The *Internet* is an example of an internetwork. The Internet carries a vast amount of data and is the platform upon which the World Wide Web (WWW) and email are built.

DETOUR

Beginning of the Internet

On October 29, 1969, a computer at the University of California at Los Angeles (UCLA) made a network connection with a computer at the Stanford Research Institute (SRI) at Stanford University. The ARPANET, the precursor to today's Internet, was born.

The development of the technologies that made this network connection possible started in the early 1960s. By that time, computers were becoming more widespread and the need to connect computers to share data became apparent. The Advanced Research Projects Agency (ARPA), an arm of the U.S. Department of Defense, decided to tackle the issue and funded network research at several American universities. Many of the networking technologies and networking concepts in use today were developed during the 1960s and then put to use on October 29, 1969.

The 1970s saw the development of the TCP/IP network protocol suite that is still in use today. The protocol specifies, among other things, how data travels from one computer on the Internet to another. The Internet grew rapidly during the 1970s and 1980s but was not widely used by the general public until the early 1990s, when the World Wide Web was developed.

Programming Languages

What distinguishes computers from other machines is that computers can be programmed. What this means is that instructions can be stored in a file on the hard drive, and then loaded into main memory and executed on demand. Because machines cannot process ambiguity the way we (humans) can, the instructions must be precise. Computers do exactly what they are told and cannot understand what the programmer "intended" to write.

The instructions that are actually executed are *machine language* instructions. They are represented using binary notation (i.e., a sequence of 0s and 1s). Because machine language instructions are extremely hard to work with, computer scientists have developed programming languages and language translators that enable developers to write instructions in a human readable language and then translate them into machine language. Such language translators are referred to as *assemblers*, *compilers*, or *interpreters*, depending on the programming language.

There are many programming languages out there. Some of them are specialized languages meant for particular applications such as 3D modeling or databases. Other languages are *general-purpose* and include C, C++, C#, Java, and Python.

While it is possible to write programs using a basic text editor, developers use *Integrated Development Environments* (IDEs) that provide a wide array of services that support software development. They include an editor to write and edit code, a language translator, automated tools for creating binary executables, and a *debugger*.

DETOUR

Computer Bugs

When a program behaves in a way that was not intended, such as crashing, freezing the computer, or simply producing erroneous output, we say that the program has a *bug* (i.e., an error). The process of removing the error and correcting the program is called *debugging*. A *debugger* is a tool that helps the developer find the instructions that cause the error.

The term "bug" to denote an error in a system predates computers and computer science. Thomas Edison, for example, used the term to describe faults and errors in the engineering of machines all the way back in the 1870s. Interestingly, there have also been cases of *actual* bugs causing computer failures. One example, as reported by computing pioneer Grace Hopper in 1947, is the moth that caused the Mark II computer at Harvard, one of the earliest computers, to fail.

Software Libraries

A general-purpose programming language such as Python consists of a small set of general-purpose instructions. This core set does not include instructions to download web pages, draw images, play music, find patterns in text documents, or access a database. The reason why is essentially because a "sparser" language is more manageable for the developer.

Of course, there are application programs that need to access web pages or databases. Instructions for doing so are defined in *software libraries* that are separate from the core language, and they must be explicitly *imported* into a program in order to be used. The description of how to use the instructions defined in a library is often referred to as the *application programming interface* (API).

1.3 Python Programming Language

In this textbook, we introduce the Python programming language and use it to illustrate core computer science concepts, learn programming, and learn application development in general. In this section, we give some background on Python and how to set up a Python IDE on your computer.

Short History of Python

The Python programming language was developed in the late 1980s by Dutch programmer Guido van Rossum while working at CWI (the Centrum voor Wiskunde en Informatica in Amsterdam, Netherlands). The language was not named after the large snake species but rather after the BBC comedy series *Monty Python's Flying Circus*. Guido van Rossum happens to be a fan. Just like the Linux OS, Python eventually became an open source software development project. However, Guido van Rossum still has a central role in deciding how the language is going to evolve. To cement that role, he has been given the title of "Benevolent Dictator for Life" by the Python community.

Python is a general-purpose language that was specifically designed to make programs very readable. Python also has a rich library making it possible to build sophisticated applications using relatively simple-looking code. For these reasons, Python has become a popular application development language *and* also the preferred "first" programming language.

CAUTION

> ### Python 2 versus Python 3
>
> There are currently two major versions of Python in use. Python 2 was originally made available in 2000; its latest release is 2.7. Python 3 is a new version of Python that fixes some less-than-ideal design decisions made in the early development of the Python language. Unfortunately, Python 3 is not backward compatible with Python 2. This means that a program written using Python 2 usually will not execute properly with a Python 3 interpreter.
>
> In this textbook, we have chosen to use Python 3 because of its more consistent design. To learn more about the difference between the two releases, see:
>
> ```
> http://wiki.python.org/moin/Python2orPython3
> ```

Setting Up the Python Development Environment

If you do not have Python development tools installed on your computer already, you will need to download a Python IDE. The official list of Python IDEs is at

```
http://wiki.python.org/moin/IntegratedDevelopmentEnvironments
```

We illustrate the IDE installation using the standard Python development kit that includes the IDLE IDE. You may download the kit (for free) from:

```
http://python.org/download/
```

Listed there are installers for all mainstream operating systems. Choose the appropriate one for your system and complete the installation.

To get started with Python, you need to open a Python *interactive shell* window. The IDLE interactive shell included with the Python IDE is shown in Figure 1.1.

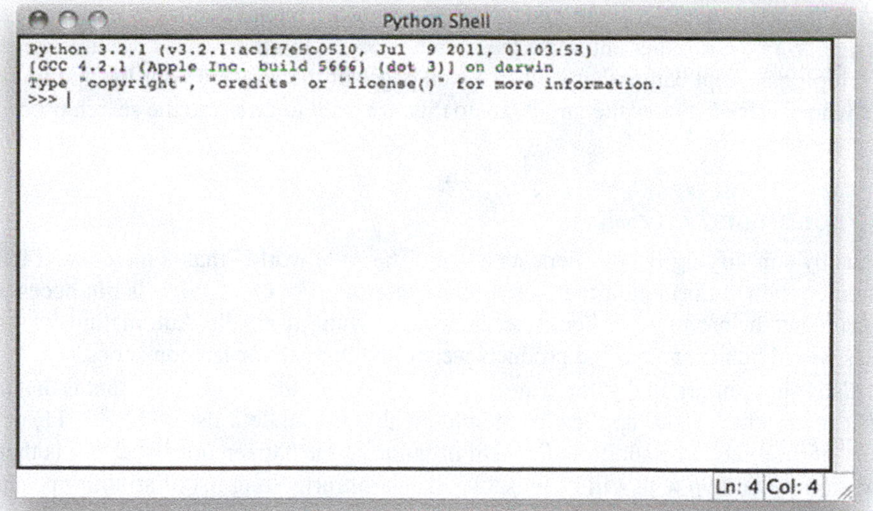

Figure 1.1 The IDLE IDE.
The IDLE Integrated
Development Environment
is included in the standard
implementation of Python.
Shown is the IDLE
interactive shell. At the >>>
prompt, you can type single
Python instructions. The
instruction is executed by
the Python interpreter when
the Enter/Return key is
pressed.

The interactive shell expects the user to type a Python instruction. When the user types the instruction `print('Hello world')` and then presses the Enter/Return key on the keyboard, a greeting is printed:

```
Python 3.2.1 (v3.2.1:ac1f7e5c0510, Jul  9 2011, 01:03:53)
[GCC 4.2.1 (Apple Inc. build 5666) (dot 3)] on darwin
Type "copyright", "credits" or "license()" for more information.
>>> print('Hello world')
Hello world
```

The interactive shell is used to execute single Python instructions like `print('Hello world')`. A program typically consists of multiple instructions that must be stored in a file before being executed.

1.4 Computational Thinking

In order to illustrate the software development process and introduce the software development terminology, we consider the problem of automating a web search task. To model the relevant aspects of the task and describe the task as an algorithm, we must *understand* the task from a "computational" perspective. *Computational thinking* is a term used to describe the intellectual approach through which natural or artificial processes or tasks are understood and described as computational processes. This skill is probably the most important one you will develop in your training as a computer scientist.

A Sample Problem

We are interested in purchasing about a dozen prize-winning novels from our favorite online shopping web site. The thing is, we do not want to pay full price for the books. We would rather wait and buy the books on sale. More precisely, we have a target price for each book and will buy a book only when its sale price is below the target. So, every couple of days, we visit the product web page of every book on our list and, for each book, check whether the price has been reduced to below our target.

As computer scientists, we should not be satisfied with manually visiting web page after web page. We would rather automate the search process. In other words, we are interested in developing an application that visits the web pages of the books on our list and finds the books whose price is below the target. To do this, we need to describe the search process in computational terms.

Abstraction and Modeling

We start by simplifying the problem statement. The "real world" that is the context for the problem contains information that is not really relevant. For example, it is not necessarily important that the products are books, let alone prize-winning novels. Automating the search process would be the same if the products were climbing gear or fashion shoes.

It also is not important that there are 12 products on our list. More important is that there is *a list* (of products); our application should be able to handle a list of 12, 13, 11, or any number of products. The additional benefit of ignoring the "dozen novels" detail is that the application we end up with will be reusable on an arbitrarily long list of arbitrary products.

What are the relevant aspects of the problem? One is that each product has an associated web page that lists its price. Another is that we have a target price for each product. Finally, the web itself is a relevant aspect as well. We can summarize the relevant information as consisting of:

a. the web

b. a list that contains addresses of product web pages

c. a list that contains target prices

Let's call the first list `Addresses` and the second `Targets`.

We need to be a bit more precise with the descriptions of our lists because it is not clear how addresses in list `Addresses` correspond to target prices in list `Targets`. We clarify this by numbering the products 0, 1, 2, 3, . . . (computer scientists start counting from 0) and then ordering the addresses and targets so the web page address and target price of a product are in the same position in their respective list, as shown in Figure 1.2.

Figure 1.2 Lists of web page addresses and target prices. The web page address and target price for product 0 are first in their respective lists. For product 1, they are both second, for product 2, they are third, etc.

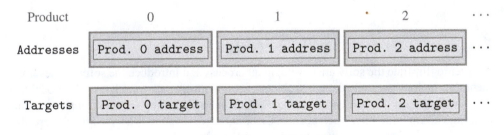

The process of distilling the relevant aspects of a problem is called *abstraction*. It is a necessary step, so the problem is described precisely, using the language of logic and mathematics. The result of abstraction is a *model* that represents all the relevant aspects of the problem.

Algorithm

The search application we want to develop should "visit" product web pages "one after another" and, for each product, "check" whether the price has been reduced to below the target price. While this description of how the application should work may be clear to us, it is not quite precise enough. For example, what do we mean by "visit," "one after another," and "check"?

When we "visit" a web page, we are really downloading it and displaying it in our browser (or reading it). When we say that we are going to visit pages "one after another," we need to be clear that each page will be visited exactly once; we also should be explicit about the order in which the pages will be visited. Finally, in order to "check" whether the price has been reduced enough, we need to first find the price in the web page.

To facilitate the eventual implementation of the search process as a computer program, we need to describe the search using more precise step-by-step instructions or, in other words, an algorithm. The algorithm should consist of an unambiguous description of the steps that, when executed on a specified input, produce the desired output.

We start the development of the algorithm by clearly specifying the *input* data (i.e., the information we start with) and the *output* data (i.e., the information we desire to obtain):

Input: An ordered list of web page addresses called `Addresses` and an ordered list of target prices called `Targets` of the same size

Output: (Printed on the screen.) Web page addresses for products whose price is less than the target price

Now we can describe the algorithm:

```
1   Let N be the number of products in list Addresses.
2
3   For every product I = 0, 1, ..., N-1, execute these statements:
4
5       Let ADDR be the address in list Addresses for product I
6
7       Download the web page whose address is ADDR and
8           let PAGE be the content of this web page
9
10      Find in PAGE the current price of product I and
11          let CURR be this value
12
13      Let TARG be the product I target price from list Targets
14
15      If CURR < TARG:
16          Print ADDR
```

This description of the algorithm is not real code that can be executed on a computer. It is simply a precise description of what we need to do to acomplish a task and is often refered to as *pseudocode*. An algorithm can also be described using actual executable code. In the rest of this book, we will describe our algorithms using Python programs.

Data Types

The description of the search algorithm includes references to various data:

    a. N, the number of products

    b. ADDR, the address of a web page

    c. PAGE, the content of a web page

    d. CURR and TARG, the current and target prices

    e. The lists Addresses and Targets

The names N, I, ADDR, PAGE, CURR, and TARG are called *variables*, just as in algebra. The names Addresses and Targets are also variables. The purpose of variables is to store values so that they can be retrieved later. For example, the value of ADDR, set in line 5 of the algorithm, is retrieved to be printed in line 16.

Let's take a closer look at the *type of values* these data can have. The number of products N will be a nonnegative integer value. The current price CURR and the target price TARG will be positive numbers likely using decimal point notation; we describe them as positive non-integer numbers. What about the "value" of the web page address ADDR and the "value" of the web page content? Both are best described as sequences of characters (we ignore non-text content). Finally, we have the two lists. The list of addresses Addresses is an ordered sequence of addresses (which are character sequences), whereas the list of target prices Targets is an ordered sequence of prices (which are numbers).

The *data type* refers to the range of values data can have (e.g., integer, non-integer number, sequence of characters, or list of other values) *and also* to the operations that can be performed on the data. In the algorithm, we perform the following operations, among others, on the data:

a. We compare numbers CURR and TARG

b. We find the address of product I in list Addresses

c. We search the web page content for a price

d. We create a sequence 0, 1, 2, ..., N-1 from integer N

In case **a.**, we make the assumption that number types can be compared. In case **b.**, we assume that we can retrieve product I from list Addresses. In case **c.**, we assume that we can search a sequence of characters and look for something that looks like a price. In case **d.**, we assume that we can create a sequence from 0 up to and not including an integer.

The point we are making is this: An algorithm consists of instructions that manipulate data and how the data is allowed to be manipulated depends on the data type. Consider case **d.**, for example. While this operation makes sense for integer data type N, it does not make sense at all for, say, the web page address data ADDR. So the integer data type supports the operation of creating a sequence, whereas the "character sequence" data type does not.

So, in order to be able to think "computationally," we really need to know what types of data we can use and what operations can be performed on that data. Because we will think "computationally" in the context of Python programming, we will need to know the data types and the operations that Python supports. Our first order of business is thus to learn Python's core data types and, in particular, the different operations that these data types support. This will be the topic of Chapter 2.

Assignments and Execution Control Structures

In addition to *different types of data*, the product search algorithm we developed uses *different kinds of instructions*. Several instructions in the algorithm assign a value to a variable:

a. In line 1, we assign a value to variable N.

b. In line 5, we assign a value to variable ADDR.

c. In line 8, we assign a value to variable PAGE.

d. In line 11, we assign a value to variable CURR.

e. In line 13, we assign a value to variable TARG.

While the values assigned to the variables are of different types, the same kind of instruction is used to do the assignment. This kind of instruction is called an *assignment statement*.

A different kind of instruction is used in line 15. This instruction compares the current price CURR with the target price TARG; if the value of CURR is less than the value of TARG— and only then—the statement in line 16 is executed (and the value of ADDR is printed). The If instruction in line 15 is a kind of instruction referred to as a *conditional control structure*.

Line 3 illustrates yet another kind of instruction. This instruction will repeatedly execute the statements in lines 5 to 16, once for every value of I. So, the statements 5 to 16 will be executed for I equal to 0, and then again for I equal to 1, and then again for I equal to 2, and so on. After the statements 5 to 16 have been executed for I equal to N-1, the execution of the instruction in line 3 is complete. This instruction is referred to as an *iteration control structure*. The word *iteration* means "the action of repeating a process." The process that is repeated in our algorithm is the execution of statements in lines 5 to 16.

Conditional and iteration control structures are together referred to as *execution control structures*. Execution control structures are used to control the *flow of execution* of the statements in a program. In other words, they determine the order in which the statements are executed, under what conditions, and how many times. Together with assignment statements, execution control structures are the fundamental building blocks for describing computational solutions to problems and developing algorithms. We introduce Python's execution control structures in Chapter 3, after having reviewed Python's core data types in Chapter 2.

Chapter Summary

This chapter introduces the field of computer science, the work computer scientists and developers do, and the tools that computer scientists and developers use.

Computer science studies, on one hand, the theoretical foundations of information and computation and, on the other, the hands-on techniques to implement applications on computer systems. Computer application developers use the concepts and techniques of computer science in the context of application development. They formulate abstract representations that model a particular real or imaginary environment, create algorithms that manipulate data in the model, and then implement the algorithm as a program that can be executed on a computer system.

The computer science tools include the abstract tools of math and logic and the concrete computer system tools. Computer system tools include the hardware and the software. In particular, they include the programming language and the programming language tools through which the developer ultimately controls the different system components.

The abstract tools that computer scientists use are the computational thinking skills, based on logic and mathematics, that are necessary to describe problems, tasks, and processes through the lens of abstraction and computation. In order to be able to do this, we need to master a language of abstraction and computation. The best way to do this, of course, is to master a programming language. In effect, the programming language is the glue that connects the system and the abstract tools of a developer. That is why mastery of a programming language is the core skill of a computer scientist.

Python Data Types

2.1 Expressions, Variables, and Assignments 16

2.2 Strings 23

2.3 Lists and Tuples 27

2.4 Objects and Classes 33

2.5 Python Standard Library 41

E-Book Case Study: Turtle Graphics 43

Chapter Summary 43

Solutions to Practice Problems 44

Exercises 45

IN THIS CHAPTER, we introduce a very small subset of Python. While small, it is broad enough to start doing interesting things right away. In the next chapters we fill in the details. We begin by using Python as a calculator that evaluates algebraic expressions. We then introduce variables as a way to "remember" results of such evaluations. Finally we show how Python works with values other than numbers: values to represent logical values true and false, text values, and lists of values.

Having seen the core types of data supported by Python, we take a step back and define precisely the concept of a data type and that of an object that stores a value of a given type. With data stored in objects, we can ignore how the data is represented and stored in the computer and work only with the abstract but familiar properties that the object's type makes explicit. This idea of abstracting important properties is a central one in computer science to which we come back several times.

In addition to the core, built-in data types, Python comes with a large library of additional types organized into modules. We use two math modules to illustrate usage of the Python Standard Library.

2.1 Expressions, Variables, and Assignments

Let's start with something familiar. We use the Python IDE interactive shell as a calculator to evaluate Python expressions, starting with simple algebraic expressions. Our goal is to illustrate how Python is intuitive and usually behaves the way you would expect.

Algebraic Expressions and Functions

At the interactive shell prompt >>> , we type an algebraic expression, such as 3 + 7, and hit the ⎡Enter⎤ key on the keyboard to view the result of evaluating the expression:

```
>>> 3 + 7
10
```

Let's try expressions that use different algebraic operators:

```
>>> 3 * 2
6
>>> 5 / 2
2.5
>>> 4 / 2
2.0
```

In the first two expressions, integers are added or multiplied and the result is an integer, which is what you expect. In the third expression, an integer is divided by another and the result is shown in decimal point notation. This is because when an integer is divided by another, the result is not necessarily an integer. The rule in Python is to return a number with a decimal point and a fractional part, even when the result is an integer. This is illustrated in the last expression, where integer 4 is divided by 2 and the result shown is 2.0 rather than 2.

Values without the decimal point are said to be of type *integer* or simply `int`. Values with decimal points and fractional parts are said to be of type *floating point* or simply `float`. Let us continue evaluating expressions using values of both types:

```
>>> 2 * 3 + 1
7
>>> (3 + 1) * 3
12
>>> 4.321 / 3 + 10
11.440333333333333
>>> 4.321 / (3 + 10)
0.3323846153846154
```

Multiple operators are used in these expressions, which raises the question: In what order should the operations be evaluated? The standard algebra *precedence rules* apply in Python: Multiplication and division take precedence over addition and subtraction and, just as in algebra, parentheses are used when we want to explicitly specify the order in which operations should take place. If all else fails, expressions are evaluated from using the *left-to-right evaluation* rule. This last rule is used in the next expression, where the addition is executed *after* the subtraction:

```
>>> 3 - 2 + 1
2
```

All the expressions we have evaluated so far are plain algebraic *expressions* involving number values (of type `int` or type `float`), algebraic operators (such as +, -, /, and *), and parentheses. When you hit the ⟨Enter⟩ key, the Python interpreter will read the expression and evaluate it in a way that you expect. Here is one more, slightly unusual, example of an algebraic expression:

```
>>> 3
3
```

Python evaluates expression 3 to . . . 3.

The two types of number values, `int` and `float`, have somewhat different properties. For example, when two `int` values are added, subtracted, or multiplied, the result is an `int` value. If at least one `float` value appears in the expression, however, the result is always a `float` value. Note that a `float` value is also obtained when two integer values (e.g., 4 and 2) are divided.

Several other algebraic operators are commonly used. To compute 2^4, you need to use the *exponentiation* operator **:

```
>>> 2**3
8
>>> 2**4
16
```

So x^y is computed using the Python expression `x**y`.

In order to obtain the integer quotient and the remainder when two integer values are divided, operators // and % are used. The // operator in expression `a//b` returns the integer quotient obtained when integer a is divided by integer b. The % operator in expression `a%b` computes the remainder obtained when integer a is divided by integer b. For example:

```
>>> 14 // 3
4
>>> 14 % 3
2
```

In the first expression, 14 // 3 evaluates to 4 because 3 goes into 14 four times. In the second expression, 14 % 3 evaluates to 2 because 2 is the remainder when 14 is divided by 3.

Python also supports mathematical functions of the kind you have used in an algebra class. Recall that, in algebra, the notation

```
f(x) = x + 1
```

is used to define function `f()` that takes an input, denoted by x, and returns a value, which is `x + 1` in this case. In order to use this function on input value 3, for example, you would use the notation `f(3)`, which evaluates to 4.

Python functions are similar. For example, the Python function `abs()` can be used to compute the absolute value of a number value:

```
>>> abs(-4)
4
>>> abs(4)
4
>>> abs(-3.2)
3.2
```

Some other functions that Python makes available are `min()` and `max()`, which return the minimum or maximum, respectively, of the input values:

```
>>> min(6, -2)
-2
>>> max(6, -2)
6
>>> min(2, -4, 6, -2)
-4
>>> max(12, 26.5, 3.5)
26.5
```

Practice Problem 2.1

Write Python algebraic expressions corresponding to the following statements:

(a) The sum of the first five positive integers

(b) The average age of Sara (age 23), Mark (age 19), and Fatima (age 31)

(c) The number of times 73 goes into 403

(d) The remainder when 403 is divided by 73

(e) 2 to the 10th power

(f) The absolute value of the difference between Sara's height (54 inches) and Mark's height (57 inches)

(g) The lowest price among the following prices: $34.99, $29.95, and $31.50

Boolean Expressions and Operators

Algebraic expressions evaluate to a number, whether of type `int` or `float` or one of the other number types that Python supports. In an algebra class, expressions other than algebraic expressions are also common. For example, the expression $2 < 3$ does not evaluate to a number; it evaluates to either `True` or `False` (`True` in this case). Python can also evaluate such expressions, which are called *Boolean expressions*. Boolean expressions are expressions that evaluate to one of two *Boolean values*: `True` or `False`. These values are said to be of Boolean type, a type just like `int` and `float` and denoted `bool` in Python.

Comparison operators (such as $<$ or $>$) are commonly used operators in Boolean expressions. For example:

```
>>> 2 < 3
True
>>> 3 < 2
False
>>> 5 - 1 > 2 + 1
True
```

The last expression illustrates that algebraic expressions on either side of a comparison operators are evaluated before the comparison is made. As we will see later in this chapter, algebraic operators take precedence over comparison operators. For example, in `5 - 1 > 2 + 1`, the operators - and + are evaluated first, and then the comparison is made between the resulting values.

In order to check equality between values, the comparison operator == is used. Note that the operator has two = symbols, not one. For example:

```
>>> 3 == 3
True
>>> 3 + 5 == 4 + 4
True
>>> 3 == 5 - 3
False
```

There are a few other logical comparison operators:

```
>>> 3 <= 4
True
>>> 3 >= 4
False
>>> 3 != 4
True
```

The Boolean expression 3 <= 4 uses the <= operator to test whether the expression on the left (3) is *less than or equal to* the expression of the right (4). The Boolean expression evaluates to True, of course. The >= operator is used to test whether the operand on the left is greater than or equal to the operand on the right. The expression 3 != 4 uses the != (not equal) operator to test whether the expressions on the left and right evaluate to different values.

Translate the following statements into Python Boolean expressions and evaluate them:

  (a) The sum of 2 and 2 is less than 4.

  (b) The value of 7 // 3 is equal to 1 + 1.

  (c) The sum of 3 squared and 4 squared is equal to 25.

  (d) The sum of 2, 4, and 6 is greater than 12.

  (e) 1387 is divisible by 19.

  (f) 31 is even. (Hint: what does the remainder when you divide by 2 tell you?)

  (g) The lowest price among \$34.99, \$29.95, and \$31.50 is less than \$30.00.

Practice Problem 2.2

Just as algebraic expression can be combined into larger algebraic expression, Boolean expressions can be combined together using Boolean operators and , or , and not to form larger Boolean expressions. The and operator applied to two Boolean expressions will evaluate to True if both expressions evaluate to True; if either expression evaluates to False, then it will evaluate to False:

```
>>> 2 < 3 and 4 > 5
False
>>> 2 < 3 and True
True
```

Both expressions illustrate that comparison operators are evaluated before Boolean operators. This is because comparison operators take precedence over Boolean operators, as we will see later in this chapter.

The or operator applied to two Boolean expressions evaluates to `False` only when both expressions are false. If either one is true or if both are true, then it evaluates to `True`.

```
>>> 3 < 4 or 4 < 3
True
>>> 3 < 2 or 2 < 1
False
```

The `not` operator is a *unary* Boolean operator, which means that it is applied to a *single* Boolean expression (as opposed to the *binary* Boolean operators `and` and `or`). It evaluates to `False` if the expression is true or to `True` if the expression is false.

```
>>> not (3 < 4)
False
```

DETOUR

George Boole and Boolean Algebra

George Boole (1815–1864) developed Boolean algebra, the foundation upon which the digital logic of computer hardware and the formal specification of programming languages are built.

Boolean algebra is the algebra of values true and false. Boolean algebra includes operators `and`, `or`, and `not`, which can be used to create Boolean expressions, expressions that evaluate to true or false. The *truth tables* below define how these operators evaluate.

p	q	p and q
true	true	true
true	false	false
false	true	false
false	false	false

p	q	p or q
true	true	true
true	false	true
false	true	true
false	false	false

p	not p
true	false
false	true

Variables and Assignments

Let us continue with our algebra theme for a bit more. As we already know from algebra, it is useful to assign names to values, and we call those names *variables*. For example, value 3 may be assigned to variable x in an algebra problem as follows: $x = 3$. The variable x can be thought of as a name that enables us to retrieve value 3 later on. In order to retrieve it, we just need to evaluate x in an expression.

The same can be done in Python. A value can be assigned to a variable:

```
>>> x = 4
```

The statement `x = 4` is called an *assignment statement*. The general format of an assignment statement is:

```
<variable> = <expression>
```

An expression we refer to as `<expression>` lies on the right-hand side of the = operator; it can be an algebraic, Boolean, or other kind of expression. On the left-hand side is a variable referred to as `<variable>`. The assignment statement assigns to `<variable>` the value that `<expression>` evaluates to. In the last example, x is assigned value 4.

Once a value has been assigned to a variable, the variable can be used in a Python expression:

```
>>> x
4
```

When Python evaluates an expression containing a variable, it will evaluate the variable to its assigned value and then perform the operations in the expression:

```
>>> 4 * x
16
```

An expression involving variables may appear on the right side of an assignment statement:

```
>>> counter = 4 * x
```

In statement counter = 4 * x, x is first evaluated to 4, then the expression 4 * 4 is evaluated to 16, and then 16 gets assigned to variable counter:

```
>>> counter
16
```

So far, we have defined two variable names: x with value 4 and counter with value 16. What about, say, the value of variable z that has not been assigned yet? Let's see:

```
>>> z
Traceback (most recent call last):
  File "<pyshell#1>", line 1, in <module>
    z
NameError: name 'z' is not defined
```

Not sure what we expected . . . but here we got our first (and, unfortunately, not the last) error message. It turns out that if a variable—z in this case—has not been assigned a value, it just does not exist. When Python tries to evaluate an unassigned name, an error will occur and a message (such as name 'z' is not defined) is printed out. We will learn more about errors (also called *exceptions*) in Chapter 4.

Write Python statements that correspond to the actions below and execute them:
  (a) Assign integer value 3 to variable a.
  (b) Assign 4 to variable b.
  (c) Assign to variable c the value of expression a * a + b * b.

Practice Problem 2.3

You may remember from algebra that the value of a variable can change. The same is true with Python variables. For example, suppose that the value of variable x is initially 4:

```
>>> x
4
```

Now let's assign value 7 to variable x:

```
>>> x = 7
>>> x
7
```

So the assignment statement x = 7 changed the value of x from 4 to 7.

CAUTION

Assignment and Equality Operators

Be careful to distinguish the assignment statement = and the equality operator ==. This is an assignment statement that assigns 7 to variable x:

```
>>> x = 7
```

The following, however, is a Boolean expression that compares the value of variable x with number 7 and returns `True` if they are equal:

```
>>> x == 7
True
```

The expression evaluates to `True` because variable x has value 7.

Variable Names

The characters making up a variable name can be lowercase and uppercase letters from the alphabet (a through z and A through Z), the underscore character (_), and, except for the first character, digits 0 through 9:

- `myList` and `_list` are OK, but `5list` is not.
- `list6` and `l_2` are OK, but `list-3` is not.
- `mylist` and `myList` are different variable names.

Even when a variable name is "legal" (i.e., follows the rules), it might not be a "good" name. Here are some generally accepted conventions for designing good names:

- A name should be meaningful: Name `price` is better than name `p`.
- For a multiple-word name, use either the underscore as the delimiter (e.g., `temp_var` and `interest_rate`) or *camelCase* capitalization (e.g., `tempVar`, `TempVar`, `interestRate` or `InterestRate`); pick one style and use it consistently throughout your program.
- Shorter meaningful names are better than longer ones.

In this textbook, all variable names start with a lowercase character.

DETOUR

Variable Names in Python 3 and Beyond

The restriction on the characters used for variable names is true only for Python versions before 3.0. Those versions of Python use the ASCII character encoding (which includes characters in the English alphabet only and is described in more detail in Chapter 6) as the default character set.

Starting with Python 3.0, the Unicode character encoding (also discussed in Chapter 6) is the default character encoding. With this change, many more characters (e.g., Cyrillic, Chinese, or Arabic characters) can be used in variable names. The change reflects the important social and economic role that globalization has in today's world.

> At this moment, most programming languages still require names of variables and other objects to use the ASCII character encoding. For this reason, while this textbook follows the Python 3.0 and later standards, we restrict ourselves to the ASCII character encoding when devising variable names.

The names below are used as reserved keywords of the Python language. You cannot use them other than as Python commands.

False	break	else	if	not	while
None	class	except	import	or	with
True	continue	finally	in	pass	yield
and	def	for	is	raise	
as	del	from	lambda	return	
assert	elif	global	nonlocal	try	

2.2 Strings

In addition to number and Boolean types, Python supports a large number of other, more complex, types. The Python string type, denoted `str`, is used to represent and manipulate text data or, in other words, a sequence of characters, including blanks, punctuation, and various symbols. A string value is represented as a sequence of characters that is enclosed within quotes:

```
>>> 'Hello, World!'
'Hello, World!'
>>> s = 'hello'
>>> s
'hello'
```

The first expression, `'Hello, world!'`, is an expression that contains just one string value and it evaluates to itself, just as expression 3 evaluates to 3. The statement `s = 'hello'` assigns string value `'hello'` to variable s. Note that s evaluates to its string value when used in an expression.

String Operators

Python provides operators to process text (i.e., string values). Like numbers, strings can be compared using comparison operators: ==, !=, <, >, and so on. Operator ==, for example, returns `True` if the strings on either side of the operator have the same value:

```
>>> s == 'hello'
True
>>> t = 'world'
>>> s != t
True
>>> s == t
False
```

While == and != test whether or not two strings are equal, the comparison operators < and > compare strings using the dictionary order:

```
>>> s < t
True
>>> s > t
False
```

(For now, we appeal to intuition when referring to *dictionary order*; we define it precisely in Section 6.3.)

The + operator, when applied to two strings, evaluates to a new string that is the *concatenation* (i.e., the joining) of the two strings:

```
>>> s + t
'helloworld'
>>> s + ' ' + t
'hello world'
```

In the second example, the names s and t are evaluated to the string values 'hello' and 'world', respectively, which are then concatenated with the single blank space string ' '. If we can *add* two strings, can we, perhaps, *multiply* them?

```
>>> 'hello ' * 'world'

Traceback (most recent call last):
  File "<pyshell#146>", line 1, in <module>
    'hello ' * 'world'
TypeError: cannot multiply sequence by non-int of type 'str'
```

Well . . . it doesn't look like we can. If you take a moment and think about it, it is not really clear what multiplying two strings would mean anyway. Adding them (i.e., concatenating them) makes more sense. Overall, the design of the Python programming language and the meaning of the standard operators (+, *, /, etc.) for various types of values (integer, floating point, Boolean, string, etc.) is intuitive. So, intuitively, what do you think should happen when a string gets multiplied by an integer? Let's try it:

```
>>> 3 * 'A'
'AAA'
>>> 'hello ' * 2
'hello hello '
>>> 30 * '-'
'------------------------------'
```

Multiplying a string s by an integer k gives us a string obtained by concatenating k copies of string s. Note how we easily obtained a line (useful for presenting your simple text output, say) by multiplying string '-' 30 times.

With the in operator, we can check whether a character appears in a string:

```
>>> s = 'hello'
>>> 'h' in s
True
>>> 'g' in s
False
```

Usage	Explanation
x in s	True if string x is a substring of string s, and false otherwise
x not in s	False if string x is a substring of string s, and true otherwise
s + t	Concatenation of string s and string t
s * n, n * s	Concatenation of n copies of s
s[i]	Character of string s at index i
len(s)	Length of string s

Table 2.1 String operators.
Only a few commonly used string operators are shown; many more are available. To obtain the full list in your interactive shell, use the `help()` documentation function:
```
>>> help(str)
```

The in operator also can be used to check whether a string appears in another:
```
>>> 'll' in s
True
```

Since 'll' appears in string s, we say that 'll' is a *substring* of s.

The length of a string can be computed using the len() function:
```
>>> len(s)
5
```

In Table 2.1, we summarize the usage and explanation for commonly used string operators.

Practice Problem 2.4

Start by executing the assignment statements:
```
>>> s1 = 'ant'
>>> s2 = 'bat'
>>> s3 = 'cod'
```

Write Python expressions using s1, s2, and s3 and operators + and * that evaluate to:

(a) 'ant bat cod'

(b) 'ant ant ant ant ant ant ant ant ant ant '

(c) 'ant bat bat cod cod cod'

(d) 'ant bat ant bat ant bat ant bat ant bat ant bat ant bat '

(e) 'batbatcod batbatcod batbatcod batbatcod batbatcod '

Indexing Operator

The individual characters of a string can be accessed using the *indexing operator* []. We define the concept of an *index* first. The index of a character in a string is the character's offset (i.e., position in the string) with respect to the first character. The first character has index 0, the second has index 1 (because it is one away from the first character), the third character has index 2, and so on. The indexing operator [] takes a nonnegative index i and returns a string consisting of the single character at index i (see Figure 2.1):
```
>>> s[0]
'h'
>>> s[1]
'e'
>>> s[4]
'o'
```

Figure 2.1 The string index and index operator. Index 0 refers to the first character, while index i refers to the character that is i positions to the right of the first character. Expression s[0], using the indexing operator [], evaluates to string 'h'; s[1] evaluates to 'e'; s[4] evaluates to 'o'.

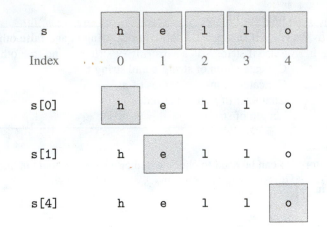

Practice Problem 2.5

Start by executing the assignment:

    s = '0123456789'

Now write expressions using string s and the indexing operator that evaluate to:

(a) '0'

(b) '1'

(c) '6'

(d) '8'

(e) '9'

Negative indexes may be used to access the characters from the back (right side) of the string. For example, the last character and second to last can be retrieved using negative indexes −1 and −2, respectively (see also Figure 2.2):

```
>>> s[-1]
'o'
>>> s[-2]
'l'
```

Figure 2.2 Index operator using negative indexes. The index −1 refers to the last character; so s[-1] evaluates to string 'o'. s[-2] evaluates to 'l'.

Negative Index	−5	−4	−3	−2	−1
s	h	e	l	l	o
Index	0	1	2	3	4
s[-1]	h	e	l	l	o
s[-2]	h	e	l	l	o

We have only scratched the surface of the text-processing capabilities of Python. We will come back to strings and text processing several times in this textbook. For now, we continue our tour of Python's data types.

2.3 Lists and Tuples

In many situations we organize data into a list: a shopping list, a list of courses, a list of contacts on your cell phone, a list of songs in your audio player, and so on. In Python, lists are usually stored in a type of object called a *list*. A list is a sequence of objects. The objects can be of any type: numbers, strings, even other lists. For example, here is how we would assign to the variable `pets` the list of strings representing several pets:

```
>>> pets = ['goldfish', 'cat', 'dog']
```

The variable `pets` evaluates to the list:

```
>>> pets
['goldfish', 'cat', 'dog']
```

In Python, a list is represented as a comma-separated sequence of objects enclosed within square brackets. An empty list is represented as `[]`. Lists can contain items of different types. For example, the list named `things` in

```
>>> things = ['one', 2, [3, 4]]
```

has three items: the first is string `'one'`, the second is integer 2, and the third item is list `[3, 4]`.

List Operators

Most of the string operators we have seen in the previous section can be used on lists in similar ways. For example, the items in the list may be accessed individually using the indexing operator, just as individual characters can be accessed in a string:

```
>>> pets[0]
'goldfish'
>>> pets[2]
'dog'
```

Figure 2.3 illustrates the list `pets` along with the indexing of the list items. Negative indexes can be used too:

```
>>> pets[-1]
'dog'
```

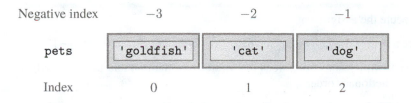

Figure 2.3 A list of string objects. List pets is a sequence of objects. The first object, at index 0, is string `'goldfish'`. Positive and negative indexes can be used, just like for strings.

Table 2.2 List operators and functions. Only some of the commonly used list operators are shown here. To obtain the full list in your interactive shell, use the `help()` documentation function:

```
>>> help(list)
```

Usage	Explanation
`x in lst`	True if object x is in list `lst`, false otherwise
`x not in lst`	False if object x is in list `lst`, true otherwise
`lstA + lstB`	Concatenation of lists `lstA` and `lstB`
`lst * n, n * lst`	Concatenation of n copies of list `lst`
`lst[i]`	Item at index i of list `lst`
`len(lst)`	Length of list `lst`
`min(lst)`	Smallest item in list `lst`
`max(lst)`	Largest item in list `lst`
`sum(lst)`	Sum of items in list `lst`

The length of a list (i.e., the number of items in it) is computed using function `len()`:

```
>>> len(pets)
3
```

Like strings, lists can be "added," meaning that they can be *concatenated*. They can also be "multiplied" by an integer k, which means that k copies of the list are concatenated:

```
>>> pets + pets
['goldfish', 'cat', 'dog', 'goldfish', 'cat', 'dog']
>>> pets * 2
['goldfish', 'cat', 'dog', 'goldfish', 'cat', 'dog']
```

If you want to check whether string `'rabbit'` is in the list, you can use the in operator in a Boolean expression that evaluates to True if string `'rabbit'` appears in list `pets`:

```
>>> 'rabbit' in pets
False
>>> 'dog' in pets
True
```

In Table 2.2 we summarize the usage of some of the string operators. We include in the table functions `min()`, `max()`, and `sum()`, which can take a list as input and return the smallest item, the largest item, or the sum of the items, respectively, in the list:

```
>>> lst = [23.99, 19.99, 34.50, 120.99]
>>> min(lst)
19.99
>>> max(lst)
120.99
>>> sum(lst)
199.46999999999997
```

Practice Problem 2.6

First execute the assignment

```
words = ['bat', 'ball', 'barn', 'basket', 'badminton']
```

Now write two Python expressions that evaluate to the first and last, respectively, word in `words`, in dictionary order.

Lists Are Mutable, Strings Are Not

An important property of lists is that they are *mutable*. What that means is that the content of a list can be changed. For example, suppose that we want to be more specific about the type of cat in list `pets`. We would like `pets[1]` to evaluate to `'cymric cat'` instead of just plain `'cat'`. To do this, we assign `'cymric cat'` to `pets[1]`:

```
>>> pets[1] = 'cymric cat'
>>> pets
['goldfish', 'cymric cat', 'dog']
```

So, the list no longer contains the string `'cat'` at index 1; instead, it contains the string `'cymric cat'`.

While lists are mutable, strings are not. What that means is that we cannot change the individual characters of a string value. For example, suppose that we misspelled the type of cat:

```
>>> myCat = 'cymric bat'
```

We would like to correct the mistake by changing the character at index 7 from a `'b'` to a `'c'`. Let's try:

```
>>> myCat[7] = 'c'
Traceback (most recent call last):
  File "<pyshell#35>", line 1, in <module>
    myCat[7] = 'c'
TypeError: 'str' object does not support item assignment
```

The error message essentially says that individual characters (items) of a string cannot be changed (assigned to). We say that strings are *immutable*. Does that mean that we are stuck with a misspelled value for myCat? No, not at all. We can simply reassign a brand *new value* to variable myCat:

```
>>> myCat = 'cymric cat'
>>> myCat
'cymric cat'
```

We will discuss assignments to strings and lists—and other immutable and mutable types—further in Section 3.4.

Tuples, or "Immutable Lists"

In addition to lists, Python also supports *tuples* which, in many ways, behave like lists except that tuples are immutable. A tuple object contains a sequence of values separated by commas and enclosed in parentheses (`( )`) instead of brackets (`[ ]`):

```
>>> days = ('Mo', 'Tu', 'We')
>>> days
('Mo', 'Tu', 'We')
```

The parentheses are optional in simple expressions like this assignment:

```
>>> days = 'Mo', 'Tu', 'We', 'Th'
>>> days
('Mo', 'Tu', 'We', 'Th')
```

All operators shown in Table 2.2 can be used on tuples as well as lists. For example:

```
>>> 'Fr' in days
False
>>> week = days + ('Fr', 'Sa', 'Su')
>>> week
('Mo', 'Tu', 'We', 'Th', 'Fr', 'Sa', 'Su')
>>> len(week)
7
>>> 2*week
('Mo', 'Tu', 'We', 'Th', 'Fr', 'Sa', 'Su', 'Mo', 'Tu', 'We', 'Th',
 'Fr', 'Sa', 'Su')
```

In particular, the indexing operator can be used to access tuple items using the item's offset as the index, just like in lists:

```
>>> days[2]
'We'
```

However, any attempt to change a tuple results in an error:

```
>>> days[4] = 'th'
Traceback (most recent call last):
  File "<pyshell#261>", line 1, in <module>
    days[4] = 'th'
TypeError: 'tuple' object does not support item assignment
```

So, as in lists, items in tuples are ordered and can be accessed using an index (offset). Unlike lists, tuples are immutable: once a tuple is created, it cannot be changed. To learn more about operators that can be used on tuples, read the online documentation or simply use the documentation function `help()`. We'll have to wait a bit to understand when one should use a tuple instead of a list to store a sequence of data. We will see examples illustrating that in Sections 3.4, 3.5, and 6.1.

CAUTION

One-Item Tuple

Suppose we need to create a one-item tuple, such as:

```
>>> days = ('Mo')
```

Let's evaluate the value and type of the object days:

```
>>> days
'Mo'
>>> type(days)
<class 'str'>
```

What we got is no `tuple` at all! It's just string `'Mo'`. The parentheses were essentially ignored. Let's do another example to clarify what's going on:

```
>>> t = (3)
>>> t
3
>>> type(3)
```

```
<class 'int'>
```

It's clear that the parentheses are treated as parentheses should be in an arithmetic expression. In fact, the same was true when we evaluated (`'Mo'`); while surrounding strings with parentheses may seem odd, the Python string operators * and + do sometimes require us to use them to indicate the order in which string operations should be evaluated, as the next example shows:

```
>>> ('Mo'+'Tu')*3
'MoTuMoTuMoTu'
>>> 'Mo'+('Tu'*3)
'MoTuTuTu'
```

How do we create a one element tuple? What differentiates the parentheses in a general `tuple` from parentheses in an expression is that enclosed in the `tuple` parentheses will be comma-separated items. So, the commas make the difference, and all we need to do is add a comma after the first, and only, item to get a one-item tuple object:

```
>>> days = ('Mo',)
```

Let's check that we got a `tuple` object:

```
>>> days
('Mo',)
>>> type(days)
<class 'tuple'>
```

List and Tuple Methods

We have seen functions that operate on lists such as, for example, the `min()` function:

```
>>> numbers = [6, 9, 4, 22]
>>> min(numbers)
4
```

In expression `min(numbers)`, we say that function `min()` is *called* with one input argument, the list `numbers`.

There are also functions that are called *on* lists. For example, to add `'guinea pig'` to list `pets`, we would call function `append()` on list `pets` as follows:

```
>>> pets.append('guinea pig')
>>> pets
['goldfish', 'cymric cat', 'dog', 'guinea pig']
```

Let's do this again and add another `'dog'` to list `pets`:

```
>>> pets.append('dog')
>>> pets
['goldfish', 'cymric cat', 'dog', 'guinea pig', 'dog']
```

Note the special way the function `append()` is called:

Table 2.3 Some list methods. Functions `append()`, `insert()`, `pop()`, `remove()`, `reverse()`, and `sort()` modify the list `lst`. To obtain the full listing of list methods in your interactive shell, use the `help()` documentation function:
`>>> help(list)`

Usage	Explanation
`lst.append(item)`	Adds item to the end of list `lst`
`lst.count(item)`	Returns the number of occurrences of `item` in list `lst`
`lst.index(item)`	Returns the index of the first occurrence of `item` in list `lst`
`lst.insert(index, item)`	Inserts `item` into list just before index `index`
`lst.pop()`	Removes last item in the list
`lst.remove(item)`	Removes first occurrence of `item` in the list
`lst.reverse()`	Reverses the order of items in the list
`lst.sort()`	Sorts the list

```
pets.append('guinea pig')
```

This should be interpreted as follows: function `append()` is called on list `pets` with input `'guinea pig'`. The effect of executing the statement `pets.append('guinea pig')` is that the input argument `'guinea pig'` is added at the end of list `pets`.

The function `append()` is a `list` function. What this means is that function `append()` cannot be called on its own; it always has to be called on some list `lst`, using the notation `lst.append()`. We will refer to such functions as *methods*.

Another example of a list method is the `count()` method. When called on a list with an input argument, it returns the number of times the input argument appears in the list:

```
>>> pets.count('dog')
2
```

Again, we say that method `count()` is called on list `pets` (with input argument `'dog'`).

To remove the first occurrence of `'dog'`, we can use the `list` method `remove()`:

```
>>> pets.remove('dog')
>>> pets
['goldfish', 'cymric cat', 'guinea pig', 'dog']
```

The `list` method `reverse()` reverses the order of the objects:

```
>>> pets.reverse()
>>> pets
['dog', 'guinea pig', 'cymric cat', 'goldfish']
```

Some commonly used list methods are shown in Table 2.3. You can view a listing of *all* list methods in the interactive shell using the `help()` documentation function:

```
>>> help(list)
Help on class list in module builtins:
...
```

The `sort()` method sorts the items in the list in increasing order, using the ordering that "naturally" applies to the objects in the list. Since list `pets` contains string objects, the order will be lexicographical (i.e., dictionary order):

```
>>> pets.sort()
>>> pets
['cymric cat', 'dog', 'goldfish', 'guinea pig']
```

A list of numbers would be sorted using the usual increasing number order:

```
>>> lst = [4, 2, 8, 5]
>>> lst.sort()
>>> lst
[2, 4, 5, 8]
```

What would happen if we tried to sort a list containing numbers and strings? Since strings and integers cannot be compared, the list cannot be sorted and an error would occur. Check it.

Given the list of student homework grades

```
>>> grades = [9, 7, 7, 10, 3, 9, 6, 6, 2]
```

write:

(a) An expression that evaluates to the number of 7 grades

(b) A statement that changes the last grade to 4

(c) An expression that evaluates to the maximum grade

(d) A statement that sorts the list `grades`

(e) An expression that evaluates to the average grade

Practice Problem 2.7

Before moving on, let's discuss the methods that can be used on tuples. We have said that tuples behave like lists except that they are immutable. Looking at Table 2.3, you will note that all but two list methods modify the list they are called on. The two methods are `count()` and `index()` and they happen to be the only two tuple methods.

2.4 Objects and Classes

We have so far seen how to use several types of values that Python supports: `int`, `float`, `bool`, `str`, `list`, and `tuple`. Our presentation has been informal to emphasize the often-intuitive approach Python uses to manipulate values. Intuition takes us only so far, though. At this point, we step back for a moment to understand more formally what we mean by a *type*, and by *operators* and *methods* supported by the type.

In Python, every value, whether a simple integer value (such as 3) or a more complex value (such as the string `'Hello, World!'` or the list `['hello', 4, 5]`) is stored in memory as an *object*. It is useful to think of an object as a container for the value that sits inside your computer's memory.

The container idea captures the motivation behind objects. The actual representation and processing of, say, integer values on a computer system is quite complicated. Doing arithmetic with integer values, however, is quite straightforward. Objects are containers for values, integer or other, that hide the complexity of integer storage and processing and provide the programmer with only the information she needs: the value of the object and what kind of operations can be applied to it.

Object Type

Every object has associated with it a *type* and a *value*. We illustrate this in Figure 2.4 with four objects: an integer object with value 3, a floating point object with value 3.0, a string object with value `'Hello World'`, and a list object with value `[1, 1, 2, 3, 5, 8]`.

Figure 2.4 Four objects.
Illustrated are four objects of
different types. Each object
has a type and a value.

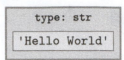
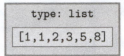

An *object's type* indicates what kind of values the object can hold and what kind of operations can be performed on the object. The types we have seen so far include the integer (`int`), floating point (`float`), Boolean (`bool`), string (`str`), and list (`list`) types. The Python `type()` function can be used to determine an object's type:

```
>>> type(3)
<class 'int'>
>>> type(3.0)
<class 'float'>
>>> type('Hello World')
<class 'str'>
>>> type([1, 1, 2, 3, 5, 8])
<class 'list'>
```

When used on a variable, the `type()` function will return the type of the object the variable refers to:

```
>>> a = 3
>>> type(a)
<class 'int'>
```

CAUTION

Variables Do Not Have a Type

It is important to note that a variable does not have a type. A variable is just a name. Only the object it refers to has a type. So, when we see

```
>>> type(a)
<class 'int'>
```

it really means that the object that variable a *currently* refers to is of type integer.

We emphasize *currently* because the type of object that a refers to may change. For example, if we assign 3.0 to a:

```
a = 3.0
```

then a will refer to a `float` value:

```
>>> type(a)
<class 'float'>
```

The Python programming language is said to be *object-oriented* because values are always stored in objects. In programming languages other than Python, values of certain types are not stored in abstract entities such as objects but explicitly in memory. The term *class* is used to refer to types whose values are stored in objects. Because every value in Python is stored in an object, every Python type is a class. In this book, we will use *class* and *type* interchangeably.

Earlier in this chapter, we introduced several Python number types informally. To illustrate the concept of the *object's type*, we now discuss their behaviors more precisely.

Valid Values for Number Types

Every object has a *value* that must be legal for the object's type. For example, an integer object can have value 3 but not 3.0 or 'three'. The integer values can be arbitrarily large. For example, we can create an integer object whose value is 2^{1024}:

```
>>> x = 2**1024
>>> x
179769313486231590772930519078902473361797697894230657273430080
...
71633505106845862982399472459384797163048353563296242241372166
```

Actually, there is a limit to how large the value stored in an integer object can be: The value is limited by the available computer memory. This is simply because it is not possible to store an integer value that has more digits than can be stored in the computer memory.

The Python floating point (float) type is used to represent real numbers as fractions with finite decimal representations:

```
>>> pi = 3.141592653589793
>>> 2.0**30
1073741824.0
```

While integer values can have an arbitrarily large number of digits (limited only by the size of the computer memory), the number of bits used to represent float values is limited, typically to 64 bits on today's laptop and desktop computers. This implies several things. First, this means that very, very large numbers cannot be represented:

```
>>> 2.0**1024
Traceback (most recent call last):
  File "<pyshell#92>", line 1, in <module>
    2.0**1024
OverflowError: (34, 'Result too large')
```

An error occurs when we attempt to define a float value that requires more bits than is available to represent float values. (Note that this can occur only with floating point values; the integer value 2**1024 is OK, as we have already seen.) Also, smaller fractional values will only be approximated rather than represented exactly:

```
>>> 2.0**100
1.2676506002282294e+30
```

What does this notation mean? This notation is called *scientific notation*, and it represents the value $1.2676506002282294 \cdot 10^{30}$. Compare this with the full precision of the corresponding integer value:

```
>>> 2**100
1267650600228229401496703205376
```

Small fractional values will also be approximated:

```
>>> 2.0**-100
7.888609052210118e-31
```

and very small values are approximated by 0:

```
>>> 2.0**-1075
0.0
```

Operators for Number Types

Python provides operators and built-in mathematical functions like `abs()` and `min()` to construct algebraic expressions. Table 2.4 lists the arithmetic expression operators available in Python.

Table 2.4 Number-type operators. Listed are the operators that can be used on number objects (e.g., `bool`, `int`, `float`). If one of the operands is a `float`, the result is always a `float` value; otherwise, the result is an `int` value, except for the division (/) operator, which always gives a `float` value.

Operation	Description	Type (if x and y are integers)
x + y	Sum	Integer
x - y	Difference	Integer
x * y	Product	Integer
x / y	Division	Float
x // y	Integer division	Integer
x % y	Remainder of x // y	Integer
-x	Negative x	Integer
abs(x)	Absolute value of x	Integer
x**y	x to the power y	Integer

For every operation other than division (/), the following holds: If both operands x and y (or just x for unary operations - and `abs()`) are integers, the result is an integer. If one of the operands is a `float` value, the result is a `float` value. For division (/), the result is a `float` value, regardless of the operands.

Comparison operators are used to compare values. There are six comparison operations in Python, as shown in Table 2.5. Note that in Python, comparisons can be chained arbitrarily:

```
>>> 3 <= 3 < 4
True
```

When an expression contains more than one operator, evaluating the expression requires that an order is specified. For example, does the expression 2 * 3 + 1 evaluate to 7 or 8?

```
>>> 2 * 3 + 1
7
```

The *order* in which operators are evaluated is defined either *explicitly* using parentheses or *implicitly* using either the *operator precedence* rules or the *left-to-right evaluation* rule if the operators have the same precedence. The operator precedence rules in Python follow

Table 2.5 Comparison operators. Two numbers of the same or different type can be compared with the comparison operators.

Operation	Description
<	Less than
<=	Less than or equal
>	Greater than
>=	Greater than or equal
==	Equal
!=	Not equal

Operator	Description
`[expressions...]`	List definition
`x[]`, `x[index:index]`	Indexing operator
`**`	Exponentiation
`+x, -x`	Positive, negative signs
`*, /, //, %`	Product, division, integer division, remainder
`+, -`	Addition, subtraction
`in, not in, <, <=, >, >=,` `<>, !=, ==`	Comparisons, including membership and identity tests
`not x`	Boolean NOT
`and`	Boolean AND
`or`	Boolean OR

Table 2.6 Operator precedence. The operators are listed in order of precedence from highest on top to lowest at the bottom; operators in the same row have the same precedence. Higher-precedence operations are performed first, and equal precedence operations are performed in left-to-right order.

the usual algebra rules and are illustrated in Table 2.6. Note that relying on the left-to-right rule is prone to human error, and good developers prefer to use parentheses instead. For example, rather than relying on the left-to-right rule to evaluate expression:

```
>>> 2 - 3 + 1
0
```

a good developer would use parentheses to clearly indicate her intent:

```
>>> (2 - 3) + 1
0
```

In what order are the operators in the following expressions evaluated?

(a) `2 + 3 == 4 or a >= 5`

(b) `lst[1] * -3 < -10 == 0`

(c) `(lst[1] * -3 < -10) in [0, True]`

(d) `2 * 3**2`

(e) `4 / 2 in [1, 2, 3]`

Practice Problem 2.8

Creating Objects

To create an integer object with value 3 (and assign it to variable x), we can use this statement:

```
>>> x = 3
```

Note that the type of the integer object that is created is not explicitly specified. Python also supports a way to create objects that makes the object type explicit:

```
>>> x = int(3)
>>> x
3
```

The function `int()` is called a *constructor*; it is used to *explicitly* instantiate an integer object. The value of the object is determined by the function argument: The object created with `int(3)` has value 3. If no argument is given, a default value is given to the object.

```
>>> x = int()
>>> x
0
```

So the default value for integers is 0.

The constructor functions for the floating point, list, and string types are `float()`, `list()`, and `str()`, respectively. We illustrate their usage with no argument to determine the default values for those types. For float objects, the default value is 0.0:

```
>>> y = float()
>>> y
0.0
```

The default values for strings and lists are, respectively, `' '` (the empty string) and `[]` (the empty list):

```
>>> s = str()
>>> s
' '
>>> lst = list()
>>> lst
[]
```

Implicit Type Conversions

If an algebraic or logical expression involves operands of different types, Python will convert each operand to the type that *contains* the others. For example, `True` is converted to 1 before integer addition is executed to give an integer result:

```
>>> True + 5
6
```

The reason for this seemingly strange behavior is that the Boolean type is really just a "subtype" of the integer type, as illustrated in Figure 2.5. Boolean values `True` and `False` typically behave like values 1 and 0, respectively, in almost all contexts.

Figure 2.5 Number types conversions. In an arithmetic expression with operands of different types, values are converted to the type that contains the others, where containment is as shown. Conversion from integer to float may result in an overflow.

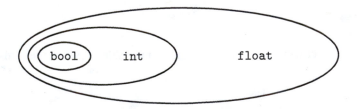

Because integers can be written using decimal-point notation (3 is 3.0) but not vice versa (2.65 cannot be represented as an integer), the `int` type is contained in the float type, as shown in Figure 2.5. Consider, for example, the expression `3 + 0.35` in which an `int` value and a `float` value are added. The `float` type contains the `int` type so 3 is converted to 3.0 before floating point addition of two float values is done:

```
>>> 3 + 0.35
3.35
```

Conversion from int to float

Recall that the range of values that int objects can have is much larger than the range of float objects. While the int type is contained in the float type, this doesn't imply that int values can *always* be converted to a float value. For example, the expression 2**10000+3 evaluates without difficulties to an int value, but its conversion to float results in an overflow:

```
>>> 2**10000+3.0
Traceback (most recent call last):
  File "<pyshell#139>", line 1, in <module>
    2**10000+3.0
OverflowError: Python int too large to convert to C double
```

Explicit Type Conversions

Type conversions can also be done explicitly using the constructor functions we just introduced. For example, the int() constructor creates an integer from a float input argument; it does so by removing the fractional part of the argument:

```
>>> int(3.4)
3
>>> int(-3.6)
-3
```

The float() constructor applied to an integer will change the representation to a floating point one, unless an overflow occurs.

```
>>> float(3)
3.0
```

The conversion from string to a number type will work only if it makes sense (i.e., the string is a valid representation of a value of the type); otherwise it results in an error:

```
>>> int('3.4')
Traceback (most recent call last):
  File "<pyshell#123>", line 1, in <module>
    int('3.4')
ValueError: invalid literal for int() with base 10: '3.4'
>>> float('3.4')
3.4
```

The string constructor str(), when applied to a number, returns the string representation of the number:

```
>>> str(2.72)
'2.72'
```

Practice Problem
2.9

What is the type of the object that these expressions evaluate to?

(a) `False + False`

(b) `2 * 3**2.0`

(c) `4 // 2 + 4 % 2`

(d) `2 + 3 == 4 or 5 >= 5`

Class Methods and Object-Oriented Programming

One way to think of a type (i.e., class) is to see it as the set of all operators and methods that can be applied to objects of the class. The `list` class, for example, can be defined by the operators and methods of the `list` class, some of which were shown in Figures 2.2 and 2.3. We have used, for example, `list` methods `append()`, `count()`, and `remove()` as follows:

```
>>> pets = ['goldfish', 'cat', 'dog']
>>> pets.append('guinea pig')
>>> pets.append('dog')
>>> pets
['goldfish', 'cat', 'dog', 'guinea pig', 'dog']
>>> pets.count('dog')
2
>>> pets.remove('dog')
>>> pets
['goldfish', 'cat', 'guinea pig', 'dog']
>>> pets.reverse()
>>> pets
['dog', 'guinea pig', 'cat', 'goldfish']
```

To see all the methods supported by the class `list`, use the `help()` documentation tool:

```
>>> help(list)
```

We now formally explain the notation used in the previous method calls. In every case, we have a `list` object, `pets`, followed by a dot (`.`), followed by the method (function) call. The meaning of, say,

```
pets.append('guinea pig')
```

is: *The* `list` *method* `append()` *is* *called on* the `list` object `pets` with string input `'guinea pig'`. In general, the notation

```
o.m(x,y)
```

means that method `m` is called on object `o` with inputs `x` and `y`. The method `m` should be a method of the class object `o` belongs to.

Every operation done in Python is a method invocation of this format. You may wonder because expression `x + y` does not seem to fit this format, but as we will see in Chapter 8, it does. This approach to manipulating data, where the data is stored in objects and methods are invoked on objects, is called *object-oriented programming* (OOP). OOP is a powerful approach to code organization and development. We will learn a lot more about it in Chapter 8.

2.5 Python Standard Library

The core Python programming language comes with functions such as `max()` and `sum()` and classes such as `int`, `str`, and `list`. While those are by no means all the built-in Python functions and classes, the core Python language is deliberately small for efficiency and ease-of-use purposes. In addition to the core functions and classes, Python has many, many more functions and classes defined in the Python Standard Library. The Python Standard Library consists of thousands of functions and classes organized into components called `modules`.

Each module contains a set of functions and/or classes related to a particular application domain. More than 200 built-in modules together form the Python Standard Library. Each module in the Standard Library contains functions and classes to support application programming in a certain domain. The Standard Library includes modules to support, among others:

- Network programming
- Web application programming
- Graphical user interface (GUI) development
- Database programming
- Mathematical functions
- Pseudorandom number generators

We will eventually use all of these modules. Right now we will see how to use the `math` and `fraction` modules.

Module `math`

The core Python language supports only basic mathematical operators; we have learned about them earlier in this chapter. For other mathematical functions such as the square root function or the trigonometric functions, the math module is required. The math module is a library of mathematical constants and functions. To use a math module function, the module must first be explicitly imported:

```
>>> import math
```

The `import` statement makes available all the math functions defined in module `math`. (We leave the more detailed explanation of how the `import` statement works for the next chapter and also Chapter 6.)

The square root function `sqrt()` is defined in module `math`, but we cannot use it like this:

```
>>> sqrt(3)
Traceback (most recent call last):
  File "<pyshell#28>", line 1, in <module>
    sqrt(3)
NameError: name 'sqrt' is not defined
```

Clearly, the Python interpreter doesn't know about `sqrt`, the name of the square root function. We must tell the interpreter explicitly where (i.e., which module) to look for it:

```
>>> math.sqrt(3)
1.7320508075688772
```

Table 2.7 Module `math`.
Listed are some functions
and constants in the
module. *After* importing the
module, you can obtain the
full list in your interactive
shell using the `help()`
function:

```
>>> help(math)
```

Function	Explanation
`sqrt(x)`	$\sqrt{x}$
`ceil(x)`	$\lceil x \rceil$ (i.e., the smallest integer $\geq x$)
`floor(x)`	$\lfloor x \rfloor$ (i.e., the largest integer $\leq x$)
`cos(x)`	$\cos(x)$
`sin(x)`	$\sin(x)$
`log(x, base)`	$\log_{base}(x)$
`pi`	3.141592653589793
`e`	2.718281828459045

Table 2.7 lists some of the commonly used functions defined in the math module. Also shown are two mathematical constants defined in the module. The value of variable `math.pi` is an approximation for the mathematical constant π, and the value of `math.e` is an approximation for the Euler constant e.

**Practice Problem
2.10**

Write Python expressions corresponding to the following:

(a) The length of the hypotenuse in a right triangle whose other two sides have lengths `a` and `b`

(b) The value of the expression that evaluates whether the length of the above hypotenuse is 5

(c) The area of a disk of radius `a`

(d) The value of the Boolean expression that checks whether a point with coordinates `x` and `y` is inside a circle with center (a, b) and radius `r`

Module `fractions`

The `fractions` module makes available a new type of number: the `Fraction` type. The `Fraction` type is used to represent fractions and do rational arithmetic, such as:

$$\frac{1}{2} + \frac{3}{4} = \frac{\cdot 5}{4}$$

To use the `fractions` module, we first need to import it:

```
>>> import fractions
```

To create a `Fraction` object, we use the `Fraction()` constructor with two arguments: a numerator and a denominator. Here is how we can define $\frac{3}{4}$ and $\frac{1}{2}$:

```
>>> a = fractions.Fraction(3, 4)
>>> b = fractions.Fraction(1, 2)
```

Note how we must specify where the class `Fractions` is defined: in the `fractions` module. When we evaluate expression `a`, we get

```
>>> a
Fraction(3, 4)
```

Note that `a` does *not* evaluate to 0.75.

As with other numbers, `Fraction` objects can be added, and the result is a `Fraction` object:

```
>>> c = a + b
>>> c
Fraction(5, 4)
```

What is the difference between the `float` type and the `fractions.Fraction` type? We mentioned earlier that `float` values are stored in the computer using a limited number of bits, typically 64 of them. That means that the range of values that `float` objects can store is limited. For example, 0.5^{1075} cannot be represented as a `float` value and thus evaluates to 0:

```
>>> 0.5**1075
0.0
```

The range of values representable with `fractions.Fraction` objects is much, much larger and limited only by the available memory, just as for the `int` type. So we can easily compute $\frac{1}{2}^{1075}$:

```
>>> fractions.Fraction(1, 2)**1075
Fraction(1, 4048045066146212367049906934378346140991132995282842367
1380271605486067913599069378392076740287424899037415572863362382277
9617474771586953734026799881477019843034848553132722728933815484186
4326824795353569454901371240149668493853972362067112983191126816201
1302471753910466682923046100506437265501729201252661541548218698956
8)
```

Why not always use the `fractions.Fraction` type? Because expressions involving `float` values evaluate much, much faster than expressions involving `fractions.Fraction` values.

E-Book Case Study: Turtle Graphics

In our first case study, we use a graphics tool to (visually) illustrate the concepts covered in this chapter: objects, classes and class methods, object-oriented programming, and modules. The tool, Turtle graphics, allows a user to draw lines and shapes in a way that is similar to using a pen on paper.

Chapter Summary

This chapter is an overview of Python concepts and its core built-in data types.

We introduce the interactive shell as a way to evaluate expressions. We start first with algebraic expressions that evaluate to a number and then Boolean expressions that evaluate to values `True` or `False`. We also introduce variables and the assignment statement, which is used to give a variable name to a value.

This chapter introduces the core Python built-in types: `int`, `float`, `bool`, `str`, `list`, and `tuple`. We go over the built-in number operators and explain the difference between the number types `int`, `float`, and `bool`. We introduce the string (`str`) operators (we leave string methods for Chapter 4); we cover, in particular, the important indexing operator. For the `list` and `tuple` types, we introduce both their operators and methods.

After defining several built-in classes, we step back and define the concept of an object and of a class. We then use those concepts to define class constructors and type conversion.

Python's Standard Library includes many modules that contain functions and types beyond the built-in ones. We introduce the useful math module that gives us access to many classic math functions.

Solutions to Practice Problems

2.1 The expressions are:

  (a) `1 + 2 + 3 + 4 + 5`

  (b) `(23 + 19 + 31) / 3)`

  (c) `403 // 73`

  (d) `403 % 73`

  (e) `2**10`

  (f) `abs(54 - 57)`

  (g) `min(34.99, 29.95, 31.50)`

2.2 The Boolean expressions are:

  (a) `2 + 2 < 4` which evaluates to `False`

  (b) `7 // 3 == 1 + 1` which evaluates to `True`

  (c) `3**2 + 4**2 == 25` which evaluates to `True`

  (d) `2 + 4 + 6 > 12` which evaluates to `False`

  (e) `1387 % 19 == 0` which evaluates to `True`

  (f) `31 % 2 == 0` which evaluates to `False`

  (g) `min(34.99, 29.95, 31.50) < 30.00` evaluates to `True`

2.3 The sequence of statements in the interactive shell is:

```
>>> a = 3
>>> b = 4
>>> c = a * a + b * b
```

2.4 The expressions are:

  (a) `s1 + ''+ s2 + ''+ s3`

  (b) `10 * (s1 + '')`

  (c) `s1 + '' + 2 * (s2 + '') + 2 * (s3 + '') + s3`

  (d) `7 * (s1 + ''+ s2 + '')`

  (e) `3 * (2 * s2 + s3 + '')`

2.5 The expressions are:
(a) `s[0]`, (b) `s[1]`, (c) `s[6]`, (d) `s[8]`, and (e) `s[9]`.

2.6 The expressions are `min(words)` and `max(words)`.

2.7 The method calls are:

  (a) `grades.count(7)`

  (b) `grades[-1] = 4`

  (c) `max(grades)`

  (d) `grades.sort()`

  (e) `sum(grades) / len(grades)`

2.8 The order is indicated using parentheses:

  (a) `((2 + 3) == 4) or (a >= 5)`

  (b) `(((lst[1]) * (-3)) < (-10)) == 0`

  (c) `(((lst[1]) * (-3)) < (-10)) in [0, True]`

  (d) `2 * (3**2)`

  (e) `(4 / 2) in [1, 2, 3]`

2.9 Check these solutions for yourself by evaluating all the expressions in the interactive shell.

  (a) While the two operands are Boolean, the + operator is an `int` operator, not a `bool` operator. The result (0) is an `int` value.

  (b) A `float` value.

  (c) An `int` value.

  (d) The expressions on both sides of the `or` operator evaluate to `bool` values, so the result is a `bool` value.

2.10 The expressions are:

  (a) `math.sqrt(a**2 + b**2)`

  (b) `math.sqrt(a**2 + b**2) == 5`

  (c) `math.pi * a**2`

  (d) `(x - a)**2 + (y - b)**2 < r**2`

Exercises

2.11 Write Python expressions corresponding to these statements:

  (a) The sum of negative integers -7 through -1

  (b) The average age of a group of kids at a summer camp given than 17 are 9 years old, 24 are 10 years old, 21 are 11 years old, and 27 are 12 years old

  (c) 2 to the power -20

  (d) The number of times 61 goes into 4356

  (e) The remainder when 4365 is divided by 61

2.12 Start by evaluating, in the interactive shell, the assignment:

```
>>> s1 = '-'
>>> s2 = '+'
```

Now write string expressions involving `s1` and `s2` and string operators `+` and `*` that evaluate to:

  (a) `'-+'`

  (b) `'-+-'`

  (c) `'+--'`

  (d) `'+--+--'`

   (e) `'+--+--+--+--+--+--+--+--+'`

   (f) `'+-+++--+-+++--+-+++--+-+++--+-+++--'`

Try to make your string expressions as succinct as you can.

2.13 Start by running, in the shell, the following assignment statement:

```
>>> s = 'abcdefghijklmnopqrstuvwxyz'
```

Now write expressions using string s and the indexing operator that evaluate to `'a'`, `'c'`, `'z'`, `'y'`, and `'q'`.

2.14 Start by executing

```
s = 'goodbye'
```

Then write a Boolean expression that checks whether:

   (a) The first character of string s is `'g'`

   (b) The seventh character of s is `'g'`

   (c) The first two characters of s are `'g'` and `'a'`

   (d) The next to last character of s is `'x'`

   (e) The middle character of s is `'d'`

   (f) The first and last characters of string s are equal

   (g) The last four characters of string s match the string `'tion'`

Note: These seven statements should evaluate to True, False, False, False, True, False, and False, respectively.

2.15 Write Python expressions corresponding to these statements:

   (a) The number of characters in the word "anachronistically" is 1 more than the number of characters in the word "counterintuitive."

   (b) The word "misinterpretation" appears earlier in the dictionary than the word "misrepresentation."

   (c) The letter "e" does not appear in the word "floccinaucinihilipilification."

   (d) The number of characters in the word "counterrevolution" is equal to the sum of the number of characters in words "counter" and "resolution."

2.16 Write the corresponding Python assignment statements:

   (a) Assign 6 to variable a and 7 to variable b.

   (b) Assign to variable c the average of variables a and b.

   (c) Assign to variable inventory the list containing strings `'paper'`, `'staples'`, and `'pencils'`.

   (d) Assign to variables first, middle and last the strings `'John'`, `'Fitzgerald'`, and `'Kennedy'`.

   (e) Assign to variable fullname the concatenation of string variables first, middle, and last. Make sure you incorporate blank spaces appropriately.

2.17 Using variables defined in Exercise 2.16, write Boolean expressions corresponding to the following logical statements and evaluate the expressions:

   (a) The sum of 17 and −9 is less than 10.

   (b) The length of list inventory is more than five times the length of string fullname.

   (c) c is no more than 24.

(d) 6.75 is between the values of integers `a` and `b`.

(e) The length of string `middle` is larger than the length of string `first` and smaller than the length string `last`.

(f) Either the list `inventory` is empty or it has more than 10 objects in it.

2.18 Write Python statements corresponding to the following:

(a) Assign to variable `flowers` a list containing strings `'rose'`, `'bougainvillea'`, `'yucca'`, `'marigold'`, `'daylilly'`, and `'lilly of the valley'`.

(b) Write a Boolean expression that evaluates to True if string `'potato'` is in list `flowers`, and evaluate the expression.

(c) Assign to list `thorny` the sublist consisting of the first three objects in list `flowers`.

(d) Assign to list `poisonous` the sublist consisting of just the last object of list `flowers`.

(e) Assign to list `dangerous` the concatenation of lists `thorny` and `poisonous`.

2.19 Start by assigning to variable `answers` a list containing an arbitrary sequence of strings `'Y'` and `'N'`. For example:

```
answers = ['Y', 'N', 'N', 'Y', 'N', 'Y', 'Y', 'Y', 'N', 'N', 'N']
```

Write Python statements corresponding to the following:

(a) Assign to variable `numYes` the number of occurrences of `'Y'` in list `answers`.

(b) Assign to variable `numNo` the number of occurrences of `'N'` in list `answers`.

(c) Assign to variable `percentYes` the percentage of strings in `answers` that are `'Y'`.

(d) Sort the list `answers`.

(e) Assign to variable `f` the index of the first occurrence of `'Y'` in sorted list `answers`.

2.20 Write an expression involving a three-letter string `s` that evaluates to a string whose characters are the characters of `s` in reverse order. If `s` is `'top'`, the expression should evaluate to `'pot'`.

2.21 Write an expression involving strings `s` and `t` containing the last name and the first name, respectively, of a person that evaluates to the person's initials. If the two strings contained the first and last name of this book's author, the expression would evaluate to `'LP'`.

2.22 The range of a list of numbers is the largest difference between any two numbers in the list. Write a Python expression that computes the range of a list of numbers `lst`. If the list `lst` is, say, `[3, 7, -2, 12]`, the expression should evaluate to 14 (the difference between 12 and −2).

2.23 Start by assigning to variables `monthsL` and `monthsT` a list and a tuple, respectively, both containing strings `'Jan'`, `'Feb'`, `'Mar'`, and `'May'`, in that order. Then attempt the following with both containers:

(a) Insert string `'Apr'` between `'Mar'` and `'May'`.

(b) Append string `'Jun'`.

(c) Pop the container.

(d) Remove the second item in the container.

(e) Reverse the order of items in the container.

(f) Sort the container.

Note: when attempting these on tuple `monthsT` you should expect errors.

2.24 Start by assigning to variable grades a list containing an arbitrary sequence of grades (strings) 'A', 'B', 'C', 'D', and 'F'. For example:

```
grades = ['B','B','F','C','B','A','A','D','C','D','A','A','B']
```

Write a sequence of Python statements that ultimately produce a list count that contains the numbers of occurrences of each grade in list grades in alphabetic order. For the given example, the list count should be [4, 4, 2, 2, 1].

2.25 Repeat Problem 2.24 with the following modification: variable grades is defined to be of type tuple rather than of type list:

```
grades = ('B','B','F','C','B','A','A','D','C','D','A','A','B')
```

Variable count should still refer to a list.

2.26 A dartboard of radius 10 and the wall it is hanging on are represented using the two-dimensional coordinate system, with the board's center at coordinate $(0, 0)$. Variables x and y store the x- and y-coordinate of a dart hit. Write an expression using variables x and y that evaluates to True if the dart hits (is within) the dartboard, and evaluate the expression for these dart coordinates:

(a) $(0, 0)$

(b) $(10, 10)$

(c) $(6, -6)$

(d) $(-7, 8)$

2.27 A ladder put up right against a wall will fall over unless put up at a certain angle less than 90 degrees. Given variables length and angle storing the length of the ladder and the angle that it forms with the ground as it leans against the wall, write a Python expression involving length and angle that computes the height reached by the ladder. Evaluate the expression for these values of length and angle:

(a) 16 feet and 75 degrees

(b) 20 feet and 0 degrees

(c) 24 feet and 45 degrees

(d) 24 feet and 80 degrees

Note: You will need to use the trig formula:

$$\text{height} = \text{length} * \sin(\text{angle})$$

The math module sin() function takes its input in radians. You will thus need to convert the angle given in degrees to the angle given in radians using:

$$\text{radians} = \frac{\pi * \text{degrees}}{180}$$

2.28 Write the relevant Python expression or statement, involving a list of numbers lst and using list operators and methods for these specifications:

(a) An expression that evaluates to the index of the middle element of lst

(b) An expression that evaluates to the middle element of lst

(c) A statement that sorts the list lst in descending order

(d) A statement that removes the first number of list lst and puts it at the end

Note: If a list has even length, then the middle element is defined to be the rightmost of the two elements in the middle of the list.

2.29 Add one or more pairs of parentheses to each expression so that it evaluates to True.
   (a) $0 == 1 == 2$
   (b) $2 + 3 == 4 + 5 == 7$
   (c) $1 < -1 == 3 > 4$
For each expression, explain in what order the operators were evaluated.

2.30 Using an example of your own, explicitly convert some string to a list. Describe, in your own words, the behavior of the list constructor on a string input.

2.31 In this chapter we have covered some, but not all, methods of class list. Using the following interactive session as an aid, explain in your own words what the list methods extend(), copy(), and clear() do.

```
>>> lst = [2, 3, 4]
>>> lst.extend([5, 6])
>>> lst
[2, 3, 4, 5, 6]
>>> lst2 = lst.copy()
>>> lst2
[2, 3, 4, 5, 6]
>>> lst.clear()
>>> lst
[]
>>> lst2
[2, 3, 4, 5, 6]
```

Imperative Programming

3.1 Python Programs   52

3.2 Execution Control Structures   57

3.3 User-Defined Functions   67

3.4 Python Variables and Assignments   74

3.5 Parameter Passing   78

E-Book Case Study: Automating Turtle Graphics   81

Chapter Summary   81

Solutions to Practice Problems   82

Exercises   85

Problems   86

IN THIS CHAPTER, we discuss how to develop Python programs. A Python program is a sequence of Python statements that are executed in order. To achieve different program behavior depending on a condition, we introduce a few decision and iteration control flow structures that control whether and how many times particular statements are executed.

As we develop more code, we will note that, often, the same group of Python statements is used repeatedly and implements a task that can be described abstractly. Python gives developers the ability to wrap code into functions so that the code can be executed with just one function call. One benefit of functions is code reuse. Another is that they simplify the developer's job by (1) hiding the code implementing the function from the developer and (2) making explicit the abstract task achieved by the code. This chapter introduces how Python functions are defined and how parameters are passed when functions are called.

The concepts covered in this chapter are fundamental programming language concepts, not just Python concepts. This chapter also introduces the process of breaking down problems into steps that can be described computationally using Python statements.

3.1 Python Programs

In Chapter 2, we used the interactive shell to evaluate Python expressions and execute single Python statements. A Python *program* that implements a computer application is a sequence of multiple Python statements. This sequence of Python statements is stored in one or more files created by the developer using an editor.

Our First Python Program

In order to write your first program, you will need to use the editor that is included in the Python IDE you are using. How the editor is opened depends on the IDE. For example, if you are using the IDLE Python IDE, click on the `File` tab in the IDLE window and then on the `New Window` button. This will open up a new window, which you will use to type your first Python program.

Module: hello.py

```
1  line1 = 'Hello Python developer...'
2  line2 = 'Welcome to the world of Python!'
3  print(line1)
4  print(line2)
```

This program consists of four statements, one in each line. Lines 1 and 2 have assignment statements and lines 3 and 4 are calls to the `print()` function. Once you have typed the program, you will want to execute it. You can do so using your Pyton IDE; again, the steps you need to take to run your program will depend on the type of IDE you are using. For example, if you are using the IDLE IDE, just hit key `F5` on your keyboard (or, using your mouse, click on the `Run` tab of the IDLE shell window menu and then on the `Run Module` button). You will be asked to save the program in a file. The file name must have the suffix `'.py'`. After you have saved the file (as `hello.py`, say, in a folder of your choice), the program is executed, and this is printed in the interactive shell:

```
>>> ========================= RESTART =========================
>>>
Hello Python developer...
Welcome to the world of Python!
```

The Python interpreter has executed all the statements in the program in order, from line 1 to line 4. Figure 3.1 shows the *flowchart* of this program. A flowchart is a diagram that illustrates the flow of execution of a program. In this first example, the flowchart shows that the four statements are executed in order from top to bottom.

CAUTION

Restarting the Shell

When we executed `hello.py`, the Python interpreter printed this line before the actual program output:

```
>>> ========================= RESTART =========================
...
```

This line indicates that the Python shell got restarted. Restarting the shell has the effect of erasing all the variables that have been defined in the shell so far. This is necessary because the program must execute in a blank-slate, default shell environment.

The interactive shell can also be restarted directly. In IDLE, you would do so by clicking on the Shell tag in the IDLE window and then on the Restart Shell button. In the next example, we restart the shell after variable x has been assigned 3 and expression x has evaluated to 3:

```
>>> x = 3
>>> x
3
>>> ======================= RESTART ===========================
>>> x
Traceback (most recent call last):
  File "<pyshell#4>", line 1, in <module>
    x
NameError: name 'x' is not defined
>>>
```

In the restarted shell, note that x is no longer defined.

An application program is typically run from outside a software development environments such as IDLE, so it is important to know how to execute Python programs at the command line. An easy way to run your program is to run this command at the prompt of a command line window:

```
> python hello.py
Hello Python developer...
Welcome to the world of Python!
```

(Make sure you run the program from within the folder containing the Python program.)

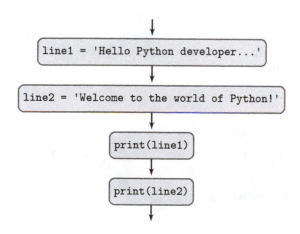

Figure 3.1 First program flowchart. Each statement of the program is inside its own box; the program execution flow is shown using arrows connecting the boxes.

DETOUR

Python Modules

The file `hello.py` we have created and saved is an example of a *user-defined* Python module. In Chapter 2, we have used the term *module* to describe the built-in Standard Library components `math`, `fractions`, and `turtle`. Those are *built-in* Python modules. What is common between `hello.py` and the built-in modules we have seen?

A module is simply a file containing Python code. Every file containing Python code and whose file name ends in `.py` is a Python module. The file `hello.py` we created is a module, and so are files `math.py`, `fractions.py` and `turtle.py` hidden in some folder on your computer and implementing the corresponding Standard Library components.

The code in a module is, of course, meant to be executed. For example, when we ran `hello.py` by hitting ⃞F5⃞, the code in the module got executed, from beginning to end. When we execute an `import` statement on a module such as `math` or `turtle`, it is equivalent to hitting ⃞F5⃞ (well, not quite, but we will handle that in Chapter 7). When we execute

```
>>> import math
```

the code in the file `math.py` gets executed. That Python code just happens to define a bunch of math functions.

Built-In Function `print()`

Our first program has two lines of code in which the function `print()` is used. This function prints, within the interactive shell, whatever argument is given to it. For example, if given a number, it prints the number:

```
>>> print(0)
0
```

Similarly, if given a list, it prints it:

```
>>> print([0, 0, 0])
[0, 0, 0]
```

A string argument is printed without the quotes:

```
>>> print('zero')
zero
```

If the input argument contains an expression, the expression is evaluated and the result is printed:

```
>>> x = 0
>>> print(x)
0
```

Note that, in our first program, each `print()` statement "printed" its argument on a separate line.

Interactive Input with `input()`

Often an executing program needs to interact with the user. The `input()` function is used for that purpose. It is always used on the right side of an assignment statement, as in:

```
>>> x = input('Enter your first name: ')
```

When Python executes this `input()` function, it will first print its input argument (string `'Enter your first name: '`) in the shell:

```
Enter your first name:
```

and then it will interrupt the execution and wait for the user to type something at the key-board. The printed string `'Enter your first name: '` is essentially a prompt. When the user types something and hits the Enter/Return key on her keyboard, the execution will resume and whatever the user has typed will be assigned to variable `name`:

```
>>> name = input('Enter your first name: ')
Enter your first name: Ljubomir
>>> name
'Ljubomir'
```

Note that Python treats as a string whatever the user types (e.g., Ljubomir in the example).

The `input()` function is meant to be used in a program. We illustrate this with a more personalized version of the `hello.py` greeting program. The next program asks the user to enter his first and last name and then prints a personalized greeting on the screen.

Module: input.py

```
1  first = input('Enter your first name: ')
2  last = input('Enter your last name: ')
3  line1 = 'Hello '+ first + ' ' + last + '...'
4  print(line1)
5  print('Welcome to the world of Python!')
```

When we run this program, the statement in line 1 is executed first; it prints the message `'Enter your first name: '` and interrupts the execution of the program until the user types something using the keyboard and presses the Enter/Return key. Whatever the user typed is assigned to variable `first`. Line 2 is similar. In line 3, string concatenation is used to create the greeting string printed in line 4. Here is a sample execution of the program:

```
>>>
Enter your first name: Ljubomir
Enter your last name: Perkovic
Hello Ljubomir Perkovic...
Welcome to the world of Python!
```

CAUTION

Function `eval()`

If you expect the user to enter a value that is *not* a string, you need to explicitly ask Python to evaluate what the user types *as a Python expression* using the `eval()` function.

The function `eval()` takes a string as input and evaluates the string as if it were a Python expression. Here are some examples:

```
>>> eval('3')
3
>>> eval('3 + 4')
7
>>> eval('len([3, 5, 7, 9])')
4
```

The function `eval()` can be used together with the function `input()` when we expect the user to type an expression (a number, a list, etc.) when requested. All we need to do is wrap the `eval()` function around the `input()` function: The effect is that whatever the user types will be evaluated as an expression. For example, here is how we would ensure that a number entered by the user is treated as a number:

```
>>> x = eval(input('Enter x: '))
Enter x: 5
```

We check that x is indeed a number and not a string:

```
>>> x == 5
True
>>> x == '5'
False
```

Implement a program that requests the current temperature in degrees Fahrenheit from the user and prints the temperature in degrees Celsius using the formula

$$\texttt{celsius} = \frac{5}{9}(\texttt{fahrenheit} - 32)$$

Your program should execute as follows:

**Practice Problem
3.1**

```
>>>
Enter the temperature in degrees Fahrenheit: 50
The temperature in degrees Celsius is 10.0
```

3.2 Execution Control Structures

A Python program is a sequence of statements that are executed in succession. In the short programs we have seen so far, the same sequence of statements is executed, in order starting from the statement in line 1 and regardless of the values input by the user, if any. That is not what we usually experience when using an application on a computer. Computer applications usually do different things depending on the values input. For example, the game you just finished playing may stop or continue running, depending on whether you click on the Exit or the Play Again button. We now introduce Python statements that can control which statements are executed and which statements should be executed repeatedly.

One-Way Decisions

Suppose we want to develop a program that asks the user to enter the current temperature and then prints an appropriate message *only if* it is more than 86 degrees. This program would behave as shown if the user enters 87:

```
>>>
Enter the current temperature: 87
It is hot!
Be sure to drink liquids.
```

The program would behave as shown if the user enters 67:

```
>>>
Enter the current temperature: 67
```

In other words, if the temperature is 86 or less, no message is printed. If the temperature is more than 86, then the message

```
It is hot!
Be sure to drink liquids.
```

is printed.

To achieve the described behavior (i.e., the conditional execution of a code fragment) there has to be a way to control *whether* to execute a fragment of code based on a condition. If the condition is true, then the code fragment is executed; otherwise it is not.

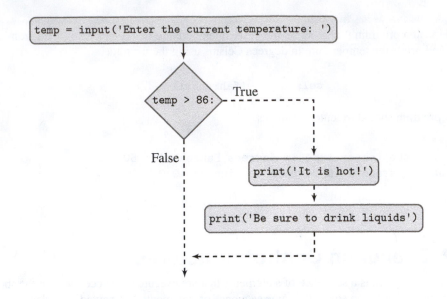

The if statement is used to implement conditional execution. Here is how we would use the if statement to implement the desired program:

Module: oneWay.py

```
1   temp = eval(input('Enter the current temperature: '))
2
3   if temp > 86:
4       print('It is hot!')
5       print('Be sure to drink liquids.')
```

(Note the use of a blank line to make the program more readable.) The if statement encompasses line 3 through 5 in the program. In line 3, the if keyword is followed by the condition temp > 86. If the condition evaluates to True, the indented statements below line 3 are executed. If the condition temp > 86 evaluates to False, those indented statements are *not* executed. Figure 3.2 illustrates (using dashed lines) the two possible execution flows for the program.

Now suppose that we need to add a feature to our program: We would like the program to print 'Goodbye!' before terminating, whether or not the temperature input by the user is high. The program would need to behave as follows:

```
>>>
Enter the current temperature: 87
It is hot!
Be sure to drink liquids.
Goodbye.
```

or as follows

```
>>>
Enter the current temperature: 67
Goodbye.
```

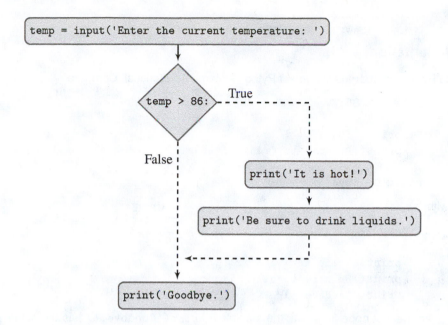

Figure 3.3 Flowchart for program oneWay2. Regardless of whether the if statement condition is true or false, the statement print('Goodbye.') is executed *after* the if statement.

A print('Goodbye') needs to be executed after the if statement. This means that the print('Goodbye') statement must be placed in the program (1) below the indented if block of code and (2) with the same indentation as the first line of the if statement:

Module: oneWay2.py

```
1  temp = eval(input('Enter the current temperature: '))
2
3  if temp > 86:
4      print('It is hot!')
5      print('Be sure to drink liquids.')
6
7  print('Goodbye.')
```

After line 3 of this program is executed, either the indented block of code in lines 4 and 5 is executed, or it is not. Either way, the execution resumes with the statement in line 7. The flowchart corresponding to program oneWay2.py is shown in Figure 3.3.

In general, the format of an if statement is:

```
if <condition>:
    <indented code block>
<non-indented statement>
```

The first line of an if statement consists of the if keyword, followed by Boolean expression <condition> (i.e., an expression that evaluates to True or False), followed by a colon, which indicates the end of the condition. Below the first line and indented with respect to the if keyword will be the block of code that is executed if condition evaluates to True.

If <condition> evaluates to False, the indented block of code is skipped. In either case, regardless of whether the indented code has been executed, the execution continues with the Python statement <non-indented statement> directly below, and with the same indentation as, the first line of the if statement.

CAUTION

Indentation

In Python, proper indentation of Python statements is critical. Compare

```python
if temp > 86:

    print('Its hot!')
    print('Be sure to drink liquids.')

print('Goodbye.')
```

with

```python
if temp > 86:

    print('It is hot!')
    print('Be sure to drink liquids.')
    print('Goodbye.')
```

In the first code fragment, the statement `print('Goodbye.')` has the same indentation as the first line of the `if` statement. It is therefore a statement that is executed *after* the `if` statement, regardless of whether the `if` statement condition is true or false.

In the second code fragment, the statement `print('Goodbye.')` is indented with respect to the first line of the `if` statement. It is therefore part of the block that is executed only if the `if` statement condition is true.

Practice Problem 3.2

Translate these conditional statements into Python `if` statements:

(a) If age is greater 62, print `'You can get your pension benefits'`.

(b) If name is in list `['Musial', 'Aaraon', 'Williams', 'Gehrig', 'Ruth']`, print `'One of the top 5 baseball players, ever!'`.

(c) If `hits` is greater than 10 and `shield` is 0, print `'You are dead...'`.

(d) If at least one of the Boolean variables `north`, `south`, `east`, and `west` is True, print `'I can escape.'`.

Two-Way Decisions

In a one-way decision `if` statement, an action is performed only if a condition is true. Then, whether the condition is true or false, execution resumes with the statement following the `if` statement. In other words, no special action is performed if the condition is false.

Sometimes, however, that is not what we want. We may need to perform one action when the condition is true and another if the condition is false. Continuing with the temperature example, suppose we would like to print an alternative message if the value of `temp` is not greater than 86. We can achieve this behavior with a new version of the `if` statement, one that uses the `else` clause. We use program `twoWay.py` to illustrate this.

```
1   temp = eval(input('Enter the current temperature: '))
2
3   if temp > 86:
4
5       print('It is hot!')
6       print('Be sure to drink liquids.')
7
8   else:
9
10      print('It is not hot.')
11      print('Bring a jacket.')
12
13  print('Goodbye.')
```

Module: twoWay.py

When line 3 of the program is executed, there are two cases. If the value of `temp` is greater than 86, the indented block

```
print('It is hot!')
print('Be sure to drink liquids.')
```

is executed. If `temp` is not greater than 86, the indented block below `else` is executed instead:

```
print('It is not hot.')
print('Bring a jacket.')
```

In both cases, execution resumes with the statement following, and indented the same as, the `if/else` statement (i.e., the statement in line 13). The flowchart illustrating the two possible execution flows is shown in Figure 3.4.

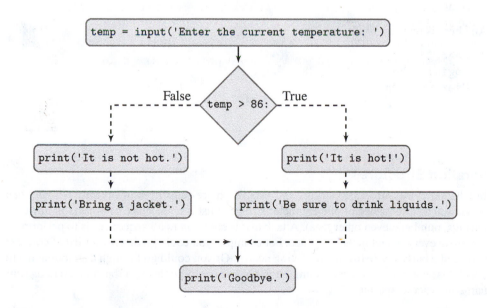

Figure 3.4 Flowchart for program `twoWay`. If the condition `temp > 86` is true, the body of the `if` statement gets executed; if false, the body of the `else` clause gets executed. In both cases, execution resumes with the statements after the `if/else` pair of statements.

The more general version of the if statement has the following format:

```
if <condition>:
    <indented code block 1>
else:
    <indented code block 2>
<non-indented statement>
```

The indented code section `<indented code block 1>` is executed if `<condition>` evaluates to True; if `<condition>` evaluates to False, the indented code section `<indented code block 2>` is executed instead. After executing one or the other code block, execution resumes with the statement `<non-indented statement>`.

Practice Problem 3.3

Translate these into Python `if`/`else` statements:

(a) If `year` is divisible by 4, print 'Could be a leap year.'; otherwise print 'Definitely not a leap year.'

(b) If list `ticket` is equal to list `lottery`, print 'You won!'; else print 'Better luck next time...'

Practice Problem 3.4

Implement a program that starts by asking the user to enter a login id (i.e., a string). The program then checks whether the id entered by the user is in the list `['joe', 'sue', 'hani', 'sophie']` of valid users. Depending on the outcome, an appropriate message should be printed. Regardless of the outcome, your function should print `'Done.'` before terminating. Here is an example of a successful login:

```
>>>
Login: joe
You are in!
Done.
```

And here is one that is not:

```
>>>
Login: john
User unknown.
Done.
```

Iteration Structures

In Chapter 2 we introduced strings and lists. Both are sequences of objects. A string can be viewed as a sequence of one-character strings; a list is a sequence of objects of any type (strings, numbers, even other lists). A task that is common to all sequences is to perform an action on every object in the sequence. For example, you could go down your list of contacts and send a party invite to contacts living nearby. Or you could go through a shopping list to check that you purchased everything on it. Or you could go through the characters of your name in order to spell it.

Let's use this last example. Suppose we would like to implement a short program that spells the string entered by the user:

```
>>>
Enter a word: Lena
The word spelled out:
L
e
n
a
```

The program first requests the user to enter a string. Then, after printing the line `'The word spelled out:'`, the characters of the string entered by the user are printed one per line. We can start the implementation of this program as follows:

```
name = input('Enter a word: ')
print('The word spelled out:')
...
```

In order to complete this program, we need a method that will allow us to execute a `print()` statement *for every character* of the string `name`. The Python `for` loop statement can be used to do exactly this. This program implements the behavior we want:

Module: spelling.py

```
1  name = input('Enter a word: ')
2  print('The word spelled out: ')
3
4  for char in name:
5      print(char)
```

The `for` loop statement encompasses lines 4 and 5 of the program. In line 4, `char` is a variable name. The `for` loop statement will repeatedly assign characters of string `name` to variable `char`. If `name` is string `'Lena'`, `char` will first have value `'L'`, then `'e'`, then `'n'`, and finally `'a'`. For each value of `char`, the indented print statement `print(char)` is executed. Figure 3.5 illustrates the workings of this loop.

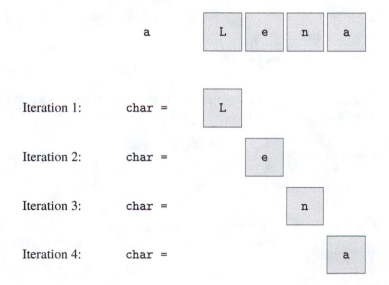

Figure 3.5 Iteration through a string. The variable `char` is assigned `'L'` in iteration 1, `'e'` in iteration 2, `'n'` in iteration 3, and `'a'` in iteration 4; in every iteration, the current value of `char` is printed. So when `char` is `'L'`, `'L'` gets printed; when `char` is `'e'`, `'e'` gets printed, and so on.

The `for` loop can also be used to iterate over the items of a list. In the next example, we use, in the interactive shell, a `for` loop to iterate over string objects representing my pets:

```
>>> animals = ['fish', 'cat', 'dog']
>>> for animal in animals:
        print(animal)

fish
cat
dog
```

The `for` loop executes the indented section `print(animal)` three times, once for each value of `animal`; the value of `animal` is first `'fish'`, then `'cat'`, and finally `'dog'`, as illustrated in Figure 3.6.

Figure 3.6
Iteration through a list.
The value of variable `animal` is set to `'fish'` in iteration 1, then to `'cat'` in iteration 2, and finally to `'dog'`. In each iteration, the value of `animal` is printed.

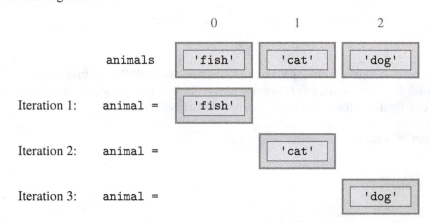

CAUTION

The `for` Loop Variable

The variable char in

```
for char in name:
    print(char)
```

and the variable animal in

```
for animal in animals:
    print(animal)
```

are just variable names, chosen to make the program more meaningful. We could have just as easily written the loops with, say, variable name x:

```
for x in name:
    print(x)
```

```
for x in animals:
    print(x)
```

Note: If we change the name of the `for` loop variable, we also need to change any occurrence of it in the body of the `for` loop.

In general, the `for` loop statement has this format:

```
for <variable> in <sequence>:
    <indented code block >
<non-indented code block>
```

The `for` loop will successively assign objects from `<sequence>` to `<variable>`, in order as they appear from left to right. The `<indented code block>`, typically called the *body* of the `for` loop, is executed once for every value of `<variable>`. We say that the `for` loop *iterates* through the objects in the sequence. After `<indented code block>` has been executed for the last time, execution resumes with the statements after the `for` loop; they will be below, and use the same indentation as, the first line of the `for` loop statement.

Nesting Control Flow Structures

Let's use the `for` loop to write a program that combines a `for` loop and an `if` statement. We would like to write an application that starts by asking the user to enter a phrase. After the user has done so, the program will print all the vowels in the phrase, and no other letter. The program should behave like this:

```
>>>
Enter a phrase: test case
e
a
e
```

This program will consist of several components. We need an `input()` statement to read in the phrase, a `for` loop to iterate over the characters of the input string, and, in every iteration of the `for` loop, an `if` statement to check whether the current character is a vowel. If so, it gets printed. Next is the complete program.

Module: for.py

```
1  phrase = input('Enter a phrase: ')
2
3  for c in phrase:
4      if c in 'aeoiuAEIOU':
5          print(c)
```

Note that we combined a `for` loop and an `if` statement and that indentation is used to specify the body of each. The `if` statement body is just `print(c)` while the `for` loop statement body is:

```
if c in 'aeiouAEIOU':
    print(c)
```

Implement a program that requests from the user a list of words (i.e., strings) and then prints on the screen, one per line, all four-letter strings in the list.

Practice Problem 3.5

```
>>>
Enter word list: ['stop', 'desktop', 'top', 'post']
stop
post
```

Function `range()`

We just saw how the `for` loop is used to iterate over the items of a list or the characters of a string. It is often necessary to iterate over a sequence of numbers in a given range, even if the list of numbers is not explicitly given. For example, we may be searching for a divisor of a number. Or we could be iterating over the indexes 0, 1, 2, ... of a sequence object. The built-in function `range()` can be used together with the `for` loop to iterate over a sequence of numbers in a given range. Here is how we can iterate over the integers 0, 1, 2, 3, 4:

```
>>> for i in range(5):
        print(i)

0
1
2
3
4
```

Function `range(n)` is typically used to iterate over the integer sequence $0, 1, 2, \ldots, n-1$. In the last example, variable `i` is set to 0 in the first iteration; in the following iterations, `i` gets assigned values 1, 2, 3, and finally 4 (as $n = 5$). As in previous `for` loop examples, the indented code section of the `for` loop is executed in every iteration, for every value of `i`.

Practice Problem 3.6

Write the for loop that will print these sequences of numbers, one per line, in the interactive shell.

(a) Integers from 0 to 9 (i.e., 0, 1, 2, 3, 4, 5, 6, 7, 8, 9)

(b) Integers from 0 to 1 (i.e., 0, 1)

The `range()` function can also be used to iterate over more complex sequences of numbers. If we would like the sequence to start at a nonzero number `start` and end *before* number end, we make the function call `range(start,end)`. For example, this `for` loop iterates over the sequence 2, 3, 4:

```
>>> for i in range(2, 5):
        print(i)

2
3
4
```

In order to generate sequences that use a step size other than 1, a third argument can be used. The function call `range(start, end, step)` can be used to iterate over the sequence of integers starting at `start`, using a step size of `step` and ending before `end`. For example, the next loop will iterate over the sequence 1, 4, 7, 10, 13:

```
>>> for i in range(1, 14, 3):
        print(i)
```

The sequence printed by the `for` loop starts at 1, uses a step size of 3, and ends before 14. Therefore it will print 1, 4, 7, 10, and 13.

Write the `for` loop that will print the following sequences of numbers, one per line.

Practice Problem
3.7

  (a) Integers from 3 up to and including 12

  (b) Integers from 0 up to but not including 9, but with a step of 2 instead of the default of 1 (i.e., 0, 2, 4, 6, 8)

  (c) Integers from 0 up to but not including 24 with a step of 3

  (d) Integers from 3 up to but not including 12 with a step of 5

3.3 User-Defined Functions

We have already seen and used several built-in Python functions. The function `len()`, for example, takes a sequence (a string or a list, say) and returns the number of items in the sequence:

```
>>> len('goldfish')
8
>>> len(['goldfish', 'cat', 'dog'])
3
```

Function `max()` can take two numbers as input and returns the maximum of the two:

```
>>> max(4, 7)
7
```

Function `sum()` can take a list of numbers as input and returns the sum of the numbers:

```
>>> sum([4, 5, 6, 7])
22
```

Some functions can even be called without arguments:

```
>>> print()
```

In general, a function takes 0 or more input arguments and returns a result. One of the useful things about functions is that they can be called, using a single-line statement, to complete a task that really requires multiple Python statements. Even better, usually the developer using the function does not need to know what those statements are. Because developers do not need to worry about how functions work, functions simplify the development of programs. For this reason, Python and other programming languages make it possible for developers to define their own functions.

Our First Function

We illustrate how functions are defined in Python by developing a Python function named `f` that takes a number x as input and computes and returns the value $x^2 + 1$. We expect this function to behave like this:

```
>>> f(9)
82
>>> 3 * f(3) + 4
34
```

Function f() can be defined in a Python module as:

```
1  def f(x):
2      res = x**2 + 1
3      return res
```

In order to use function f() (to compute, say, f(3) or f(9)), we first have to execute this function definition statement by running the module containing it (e.g., by pressing F5). After the function definition statement has been executed, function f() can be used.

You can also define function f() directly in the interactive shell in this way:

```
>>> def f(x):
        res = x**2 + 1
        return res
```

After you have defined function f(), you can use it just like any other built-in function.

The Python function definition statement has this general format:

```
def <function name> (<0 or more variables>):
    <indented function body>
```

A function definition statement starts with the def keyword. Following it is the name of the function; in our example, the name is f. Following the name and in parentheses are the variable names that stand in for the input arguments, if any. In function f(), the x in

```
def f(x):
```

has the same role as x in the math function $f(x)$: to serve as the name for the input value.

The first line of the function definition ends with a colon. Below and *indented* is the body of the function, a set of Python statements that implement the function. They are executed whenever the function is called. If a function is to return a value, then the return statement is used to specify the value to be returned. In our case, the value of variable res is returned. The execution of a function ends when the return statement is executed or when the last statement in the function body is executed.

Practice Problem 3.8

Define, directly in the interactive shell, function perimeter() that takes, as input, the radius of a circle (a nonnegative number) and returns the perimeter of the circle. A sample usage is:

```
>>> perimeter(1)
6.283185307179586
>>> perimeter (2)
12.566370614359172
```

Remember that you will need the value of π (defined in module math) to compute the perimeter.

Function Input Arguments

The function f() is defined to take a single input argument, and variable x is the variable name that refers to the input argument. To define a function with more than one argument, we need to have a distinct variable name for every input argument.

For example, if we want to define a function called `squareSum()` that takes two numbers x and y as input and returns the sum of their squares $x^2 + y^2$, we need to define function `squareSum()` so there is a variable name for input argument x, say x, and another variable name for input argument y, say y:

```
1   def squareSum(x, y):
2       return x**2 + y**2
```

Module: ch3.py

(Note that we chose to implement function `squareSum()` using a single `return` statement, unlike the implementation of `f()` which uses an additional assignment statement.)

Implement function `average()` that takes two numbers as input and returns the average of the numbers. You should write your implementation in a module you will name `average.py`. A sample usage is:

```
>>> average(1,3)
2.0
>>> average(2, 3.5)
2.75
```

Practice Problem 3.9

The functions we have defined so far all take one or more numbers as input arguments. Functions can take other types of input arguments, of course, including strings and lists.

Implement function `noVowel()` that takes a string s as input and returns `True` if no character in s is a vowel, and `False` otherwise (i.e., some character in s is a vowel).

```
>>> noVowel('crypt')
True
>>> noVowel('cwm')
True
>>> noVowel('car')
False
```

Practice Problem 3.10

Implement function `allEven()` that takes a list of integers and returns `True` if all integers in the list are even, and False otherwise.

```
>>> allEven([8, 0, -2, 4, -6, 10])
True
>>> allEven([8, 0, -1, 4, -6, 10])
False
```

Practice Problem 3.11

Not all functions need to return a value, as we will see in the next example.

print() **versus** return

As another example of a user-defined function, we develop a personalized hello() function. It takes as input a name (a string) and *prints* a greeting:

```
>>> hello('Sue')
Hello, Sue!
```

We implement this function in the same module as function f():

Module: ch3.py

```
1  def hello(name):
2      print('Hello, '+ name + '!')
```

When function hello() is called, it will print the concatenation of string 'Hello, ', the input string, and string '!'.

Note that function hello() *prints* output on the screen; it does not *return* anything. What is the difference between a function calling print() or returning a value?

CAUTION

Statement return **versus Function** print()

A common mistake is to use the print() function instead of the return statement inside a function. Suppose we had defined our first function f() in this way:

```
def f(x):
    print(x**2 + 1)
```

It would seem that such an implementation of function f() works fine:

```
>>> f(2)
5
```

However, when used in an expression, function f() will not work as expected:

```
>>> 3 * f(2) + 1
5
Traceback (most recent call last):
  File '<pyshell#103>', line 1, in <module>
    3 * f(2) + 1
TypeError: unsupported operand type(s) for *:
            'int' and 'NoneType'
```

When evaluating f(2) in the expression 3 * f(2) + 1, the Python interpreter evaluates (i.e., executes) f(2), which *prints* the value 5. You can actually see this 5 in the line before the "Traceback" error line.

So f() *prints* the computed value, but it does not *return* it. This means that f(2) *returns nothing* and thus evaluates to *nothing* in an expression. Actually, Python has a name for the "nothing" type: It is the 'NoneType' referred to in the error message shown. The error itself is caused by the attempt to multiply an integer value with "nothing."

That said, it is perfectly OK to call print() inside a function, as long as the intent is to print rather than return a value.

Write function `negatives()` that takes a list as input and *prints*, one per line, the *negative* values in the list. The function should not return anything.

Practice Problem
3.12

```
>>> negatives([4, 0, -1, -3, 6, -9])
-1
-3
-9
```

Function Definitions Are "Assignment" Statements

To illustrate that function definitions are really ordinary Python statements, similar in fact to assignment statements, we use this short program:

```
1  s = input('Enter square or cube: ')
2  if s == 'square':
3      def f(x):
4          return x*x
5  else:
6      def f(x):
7          return x*x*x
```

Module: dynamic.py

In it, function `f()` is defined within a Python program, just as an assignment statement can be in a program. The actual definition of `f()` depends on the input entered by the user at execution time. By typing `cube` at the prompt, function `f()` is defined to be the cubic function:

```
>>>
Enter square or cube: cube
>>> f(3)
27
```

If, however, the user types `square`, then `f()` would be the quadratic function.

First Define the Function, Then Use It

Python does not allow calling a function before it is defined, just as a variable cannot be used in an expression before it is assigned.

Knowing this, try to figure out why running this module would result in an error:

```
print(f(3))

def f(x):
    return x**2 + 1
```

Answer: When a module is executed, the Python statements are executed top to bottom. The `print(f(3))` statement will fail because the name `f` is not defined yet.

CAUTION

Will we get an error when running this module?

```
def g(x):
    return f(x)

def f(x):
    return x**2 + 1
```

Answer: No, because functions `f()` and `g()` are not *executed* when the module is run, they are just defined. After they are defined, they can both be executed without problems.

Comments

Python programs should be well documented for two reasons:

1. The user of the program should understand what the program does.
2. The developer who develops and/or maintains the code should understand how the program works.

Documentation for the program developer and the future maintainer is important because undocumented code is harder to maintain, even by the programmer who wrote the code. Such documentation is done mainly using comments written by the function developer right next the program.

A comment is anything that follows the # symbol in a line. Here is how we add comments to explain the implementation of function `f()`:

Module: ch3.py

```
1  def f(x):
2      res = x**2 + 1  # compute x**2 + 1 and store value in res
3      return res      # return value of res
```

The comment—anything that follows # in the line—is ignored by Python.

While comments are necessary, it is also important not to overcomment. Comments should not make it difficult to read the program. Ideally, your programs should use meaningful variable names and simple, well-designed code so the program is, or is almost, self-explanatory. Comments should be used to identify the main components of the program and explain the trickier parts.

Docstrings

Functions should also be documented for the function users. The built-in functions we have seen so far all have documentation that can be viewed using function `help()`. For example:

```
>>> help(len)
Help on built-in function len in module builtins:

len(...)
    len(object) -> integer

    Return the number of items of a sequence or mapping.
```

Section 3.3 User-Defined Functions 73

If we use help on our first function f(), surprisingly we get some documentation as well.

```
>>> help(f)
Help on function f in module __main__:

f(x)
```

In order to get something more useful, however, the function developer needs to add a special comment to the function definition, one that will be picked up by the help() tool. This comment, called a *docstring*, is a string that should describe what the function does and must be placed directly below the first line of a function definition. Here is how we would add docstring 'returns x**2 + 1' to our function f():

```
1  def f(x):
2      'returns x**2 + 1'
3      res = x**2 + 1   # compute x**2 + 1 and store value in res
4      return res       # return value of res
```

Module: ch3.py

Let's also add a docstring to our function hello():

```
1  def hello(name):
2      'a personalized hello function'
3      print('Hello,' + name + ' !')
```

Module: ch3.py

With the docstrings in place, the help() function will use them as part of the function documentation. For example, the docstring 'returns x**2 + 1' is displayed when viewing the documentation for function f():

```
>>> help(f)
Help on function f in module __main__:

f(x)
    returns x**2 + 1
```

Similarly, the docstring is displayed when viewing the documentation for hello():

```
>>> help(hello)
Help on function hello in module __main__:

hello(name)
    a personalized hello function
```

Add appropriate docstrings to functions average() and negatives() from Practice Problems 3.9 and 3.12. Check your work using the help() documentation tool. You should get, for example:

```
>>> help(average)
Help on function average in module __main__:

average(x, y)
    returns average of x and y
```

Practice Problem 3.13

3.4 Python Variables and Assignments

Functions are either called from within the interactive shell or by another program, which we will refer to as the calling program. In order to be able to design functions, we need to understand how values created in the calling program—or the interactive shell—are passed as input arguments to the function. To do this, however, we first need to understand exactly what happens in an assignment statement.

Let's consider this question in the context of the assignment a = 3. First, let's note that before executing this assignment, the identifier a does not exists:

```
>>> a
Traceback (most recent call last):
  File "<pyshell#15>", line 1, in <module>
    a
NameError: name 'a' is not defined
```

When the assignment

```
>>> a = 3
```

is executed, the integer object 3 and its name a are created. Python will store the name in a table maintained by Python. This is illustrated in Figure 3.7.

Figure 3.7 Assignments to new variables. The int object (with value) 3 is assigned to variable a, the float object 3.0 is assigned to b, the str object 'hello' is assigned to c, and the list object [2, 3, 5, 8, 11] is assigned to d.

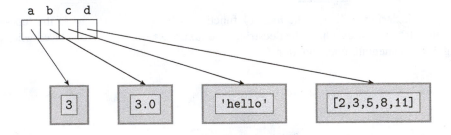

The variable a now refers to the integer object with value 3:

```
>>> a
3
```

Figure 3.7 shows that additional variables are in the table: variable b referring to float object 3.0, variable c referring to str object 'hello', and variable d referring to list object [2, 3, 5, 8, 11]. In other words, it illustrates that these assignments have also been made:

```
>>> b = 3.0
>>> c = 'hello'
>>> d = [2, 3, 5, 8, 11]
```

In general, a Python assignment statement has this syntax:

```
<variable> = <expression>
```

The <expression> to the right of the = assignment operator is evaluated, and the resulting value is stored in an object of the appropriate type; then the object is assigned to <variable>, which is said to *refer* to the object or to be *bound* to the object.

Mutable and Immutable Types

Subsequent assignments to **a**, such as

```
>>> a = 6
```

will reuse the existing name **a**. The result of this assignment is that variable **a** will refer to another object, integer object 6. The `int` object 3 no longer is referred to by a variable, as shown in Figure 3.8.

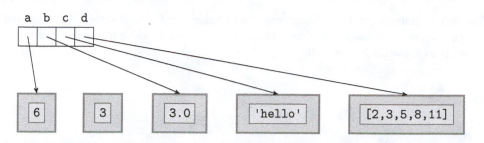

Figure 3.8 Assigning an immutable object to an existing variable. The `int` object 6 is assigned to existing variable a; the `int` object 3 is no longer assigned to a variable and can no longer be accessed.

The important thing to note is that the assignment a = 6 did not change the value of the integer object 3. Instead, a new integer object 6 is created, and variable a now refers to it. In fact, there is no way to change the value of the object containing value 3. This illustrates an important feature of Python: Python `int` objects cannot be changed. Integer objects are not the only objects that cannot be modified. Types whose objects cannot be modified are called *immutable*. All Python number types (`bool`, `int`, `float`, and `complex`) are immutable.

We saw in Chapter 2 that a list object *can* change. For example:

```
>>> d = [2, 3, 5, 8, 11]
>>> d[3] = 7
>>> d
[2, 3, 5, 7, 11]
```

The list d is modified in the second statement: the entry at index 3 is changed to 7, as shown in Figure 3.9. Types whose objects can be modified are called *mutable* types. The list type

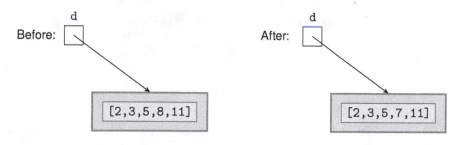

Figure 3.9 Lists are mutable. The assignment d[3] = 7 replaces the object at index 3 of d with new `int` object 7.

is mutable. The number types are immutable. What about the string type?

```
>>> c = 'hello'
>>> c[1] = 'i'
Traceback (most recent call last):
  File "<pyshell#23>", line 1, in <module>
    c[1] = 'i'
TypeError: 'str' object does not support item assignment
```

We cannot modify a character of string object. The string type is *immutable*.

Assignments and Mutability

We often have the situation when multiple variables refer to the same object. (This is, in particular, the case when a value is passed as an input to a function.) We need to understand what happens when one of the variables is assigned another object. For example, suppose we do:

```
>>> a = 3
>>> b = a
```

The first assignment creates an integer object with value 3 and gives it name a. In the second assignment, the expression a evaluates to the integer object 3, which then receives another name, b, as shown in Figure 3.10:

Figure 3.10 Multiple references to the same object. The assignment b = a evaluates the expression to the right of the = sign to object 3 and assigns that object to variable b.

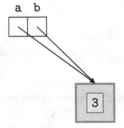

Variables a and b both refer to the same integer object 3. Now, what happens when we assign something else to a?

```
>>> a = 6
```

The assignment a = 6 does not change the value of the object from 3 to 6 because the int type is immutable. Variable a should now refer to a new object with value 6. What about b?

```
>>> a
6
>>> b
3
```

Variable b still refers to the object with value 3, as shown in Figure 3.11:

Figure 3.11 Multiple assignments and mutability. If a and b refer to the same object 3 and then object 6 is assigned to a, b will still refer to object 3.

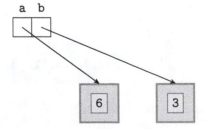

The point is this: If two variables refer to the same immutable object, that modifying one variable will not affect the other.

Now let's consider what happens with lists. We start by assigning a list to a and then assigning a to b.

```
>>> a = [3, 4, 5]
>>> b = a
```

We expect a and b to refer to the same list. That is indeed the case, as shown in Figure 3.12:

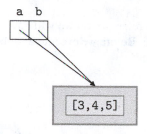

Figure 3.12 Multiple assignments on a mutable object. Both a and b refer to the same list; the assignment b[1] = 8 and the assignment a[-1] = 16 will change the same list, so any change to the list referred by b will change the list referred to by a and vice versa.

Now let's see what happens when we assign a new object to b[1]:

```
>>> b[1] = 8
>>> b
[3, 8, 5]
>>> a
[3, 8, 5]
```

As we saw in Chapter 2, lists can be modified. The list b is modified by the assignment b[1] = 8. But because variable a is bound to the same list, a will be changed as well. Similarly, changes to list a will modify list b: assignment a[-1] = 16 will make new object 16 be the last object in lists a and b.

Draw a diagram representing the state of names and objects after this execution:

```
>>> a = [5, 6, 7]
>>> b = a
>>> a = 3
```

Practice Problem 3.14

Swapping

We now consider a fundamental assignment problem. Let a and b refer to two distinct integer values:

```
>>> a = 6
>>> b = 3
```

Suppose we need to swap the values of a and b. In other words, after the swap, a will refer to 3 and b will refer to 6, as shown in Figure 3.13.

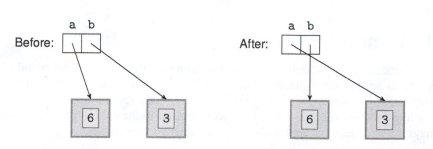

Figure 3.13 Swapping values. Variables a and b swap the objects they refer to; Python supports the multiple assignment statement, which makes swapping easy.

If we start by assigning the value of b to a:

```
a = b
```

then variable a will refer to the same object that variable b refers to. So we will have both a and b refer to 3, and we would have "lost" integer object 6. Before we execute a = b, we must save a reference to 6 and then assign that to b at the end:

```
>>> temp = a    # temp refers to 6
>>> a = b       # a refers to 3
>>> b = temp    # b refers to 6
```

In Python, there is a much simpler way to achieve the swap. Python supports the multiple assignment statement:

```
>>> a = 6
>>> b = 3
>>> a, b = b, a
>>> a
3
>>> b
6
```

In the multiple assignment statement a, b = b, a, the two expressions on the right of = are evaluated to two objects and then each is assigned to the corresponding variable.

Before we move on from our discussion of Python assignments, we note another cool Python feature. A value can be assigned to several variables simultaneously:

```
>>> i = j = k = 0
```

The three variables i, j, and k are all set to 0.

Practice Problem 3.15

Suppose a nonempty list team has been assigned. Write a Python statement or statements that swap the first and last value of the list. So, if the original list is:

```
>>> team = ['Ava', 'Eleanor', 'Clare', 'Sarah']
```

then the resulting list should be:

```
>>> team
['Sarah', 'Eleanor', 'Clare', 'Ava']
```

3.5 Parameter Passing

With a better understanding of how assignments happen in Python, we can understand how input arguments are passed in function calls. Functions are either called from within the interactive shell or by another program. We refer to either as the *calling program*. The input arguments in a function call are *names* of objects created in the calling program. These names may refer to objects that are mutable or immutable. We consider each case separately.

Immutable Parameter Passing

We use the function g() to discuss the effect of passing a reference to an immutable object in a function call.

Module: ch3.py

```
1  def g(x):
2      x = 5
```

Let's start by assigning integer 3 to variable name a:

```
>>> a = 3
```

In this assignment statement, integer object 3 is created and given name a, as shown in Figure 3.14:

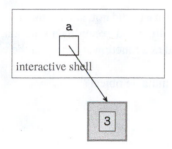

Figure 3.14 An assignment in the main program. Integer object 3 is assigned name a in the main program, the interactive shell.

This figure illustrates that name a has been defined in the context of the interactive shell. It refers to an integer object whose value is 3. Now let's call function g() with name a as the input argument:

```
>>> g(a)
```

When this function call is made, the argument a is evaluated first. It evaluates to integer object 3. Now, recall that function g() was defined as:

```
def g(x):
    x = 5
```

The name x in def g(x): is now set to refer to the input integer object 3. In effect, it is as if we have executed the assignment x = a:

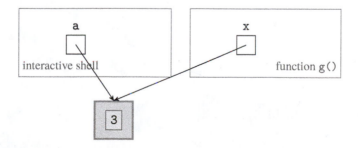

Figure 3.15 Parameter passing. The function call g(a) passes the reference a as the input argument. Variable x, defined at the beginning of the execution of g(), will be assigned this reference. Both a and x will refer to the same object.

Thus, at the start of the execution of g(a), two variables refer to the single object 3: variable a defined in the interactive shell and variable x defined in function g() (see Figure 3.15).

During the execution of g(a), variable x is assigned 5. Since integer objects are immutable, x no longer refers to 3 but to new integer object 5, as shown in Figure 3.16. Variable a, however, still refers to object 3.

Figure 3.16 Immutable parameter passing. When x = 5 is executed, x will refer to a new integer object with value 5. The integer object with value 3 is unchanged. The name a in the main program, the interactive shell, still refers to it.

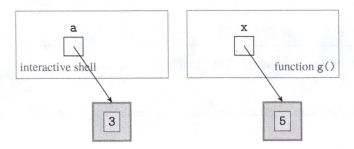

The point of this example is this. The function g() did not, and cannot, modify the value of a in the interactive shell. In general, when calling and executing a function, the function will not modify the value of any variable passed as a function argument if the variable refers to an immutable object.

What if, however, we pass a reference to a mutable object?

Mutable Parameter Passing

We use the next function to see what happens when the name of a mutable object is passed as the argument of a function call.

Module: ch3.py

```
1  def h(lst):
2      lst[0] = 5
```

Consider what happens when we execute:

```
>>> myList = [3, 6, 9, 12]
>>> h(myList)
```

In the assignment statement, a list object is created and assigned name myList. Then the function call h(myList) is made. When function h() starts executing, the list referred to by myList will be assigned to variable name lst defined in the function definition of h(). So we have the situation illustrated in Figure 3.17.

Figure 3.17 Mutable parameter passing. The function call h() passes the reference to a list as an argument. So name myList in the interactive shell and name lst in h() now refer to the same list.

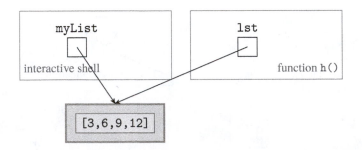

While executing function h(), lst[0] is assigned 5 and so lst[0] will refer to new object 5. Since lists are mutable, the list object referred to by lst changes. Because variable myList in the interactive shell refers to the same list object, it means that the list object referred to by myList changes as well. We illustrate this in Figure 3.18.

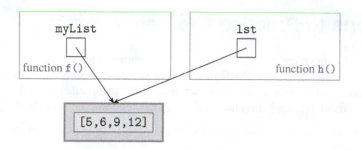

This example illustrates that when a mutable object, like list object `[3,6,9,12]`, is passed as an argument in a function call, it *may* be modified by the function.

Implement function `swapFL()` that takes a list as input and swaps the first and last elements of the list. You may assume the list will be nonempty. The function should not return anything.

Practice Problem 3.16

```
>>> ingredients = ['flour', 'sugar', 'butter', 'apples']
>>> swapFL(ingredients)
>>> ingredients
['apples', 'sugar', 'butter', 'flour']
```

E-Book Case Study: Automating Turtle Graphics

It is very common for the same fragment of code to be used repeatedly in different parts of a program. In this case study, we show the benefit of wrapping such a fragment of code into a function and replacing with a function call every instance of the code fragment in the program. The case study effectively illustrates the basic software engineering concepts of (functional) encapsulation and abstraction.

Chapter Summary

Chapter 3 introduces tools for writing Python programs and basic program development concepts. We start by writing very simple interactive programs that use built-in functions `print()`, `input()`, and `eval()`. Then, to create programs that execute differently depending on the input entered by the user, we introduce the `if` statement. We describe its one-way and two-way decision formats.

We introduce next the `for` loop statement, in its simplest form: as a way to iterate over the items of a list or the characters of a string. We also introduce the `range()` function, which enables iteration over a sequence of integers in a given range.

A focus of this chapter is how to define new functions in Python. The syntax of a function definition statement is introduced. We pay special attention to parameter passing (i.e., how parameters are passed when calling a function). To understand parameter passing, we take a closer look at how assignments work. Finally, we introduce the ways to document a function, through comments and a docstring.

Solutions to Practice Problems

3.1 An input() statement is used to request a temperature. The value entered by the user is treated as a string. One way to convert the string value to a number is with the eval() function, which evaluates the string as an expression. An arithmetic expression is used for the conversion from degrees Fahrenheit to degrees Celsius, and the result is then printed.

```
fahr = eval(input('Enter the temperature in degrees Fahrenheit: '))
cels = (fahr - 32) * 5 / 9
print('The temperature in degrees Celsius is', cels)
```

3.2 The if statement in the interactive shell is shown without the result of the execution:

```
>>> if age > 62:
        print('You can get your pension benefits!')
>>> if name in ['Musial','Aaron','Williams','Gehrig','Ruth']:
        print('One of the top 5 baseball players, ever!')
>>> if hits > 10 and shield == 0:
        print('You\'re dead ...')
>>> if north or south or east or west:
        print('I can escape.')
```

3.3 The if statement in the interactive shell is shown without the result of the execution:

```
>>> if year % 4 == 0:
        print('Could be a leap year.')
    else:
        print('Definitely not a leap year.')
>>> if ticket == lottery:
        print('You won!')
    else:
        print('Better luck next time...')
```

3.4 List users is defined first. The id is then requested using function input(). The condition id in users is used in an if statement to determine the appropriate message:

```
users = ['joe', 'sue', 'hani', 'sophie']
id = input('Login: ')
if id in users:
    print('You are in!')
else:
    print('User unknown.')
print('Done.')
```

Figure 3.19 presents the flowchart describing the different execution flows of this program.

3.5 We use a for loop to iterate through the words in the list. For each word, we check whether it has length 4; if so, we print it.

```
wordList = eval(input('Enter word list: '))
for word in wordList:
  if len(word) == 4:
    print(word)
```

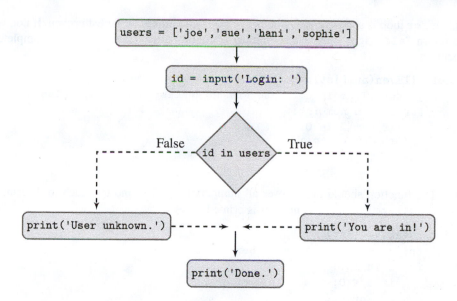

**Figure 3.19 Program
flowchart.** The solid arrows
show the execution flow that
always occurs. The dashed
arrows show the possible
execution flows that occur
depending on a condition.

3.6 The `for` loops are:

```
>>> for i in range(10):
        print(i)
>>> for i in range(2):
        print(i)
```

3.7 We omit the complete `for` loop:
(a) `range(3, 13)`, (b) `range(0, 10, 2)`, (c) `range(0, 24, 3)`, and (d) `range(3, 12, 5)`.

3.8 The perimeter of a circle of radius r is $2\pi r$. The math function needs to be imported so that the value `math.pi` can be obtained:

```
import math
def perimeter(radius):
    return 2 * math.pi * radius
```

3.9 The function `average()` takes two inputs. We use variable names x and y to refer to the input arguments. The average of x and y is `(x+y)/2`:

```
def average(x, y):
    return (x + y) / 2
```

3.10 We need to use a `for` loop to check whether or not each character of the input string is a vowel. If yes, we can return `False` immediately. We can return `True` only after all the characters have been checked, that is, when the `for` loop has completed execution.

```
def noVowel(s):
    'return True if string s contains no vowel, False otherwise'
    for c in s:
        if c in 'aeiouAEIOU':
            return False
    return True
```

3.11 A `for` loop is used to check whether or not each number in the list is even. If not, we can return `False` right away. We can return `True` only after the `for` loop has completed execution.

```
def allEven(numList):
    'return True is all integers in numList are even, False otherwise'
    for num in numList:
        if num%2 != 0:
            return False
    return True
```

3.12 The function should iterate over all numbers in the list and test each to determine whether it is negative; if so, the number is printed.

```
def negatives(lst):
    'prints the negative numbers in list lst'
    for i in lst:
        if i < 0:
            print(i)
```

3.13 The docstrings are shown in the solutions of the respective Practice Problems.

3.14 When variable a is assigned 3, a is bound to the new object 3. Variable b is still bound to the list object.

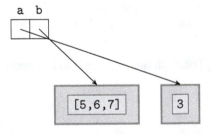

3.15 The multiple assignment statement is the easiest way to achieve the swap:

```
>>> team[0], team[-1] = team[-1], team[0]
```

Another way would be to use a temporary variable `temp`:

```
>>> temp = team[0]
>>> team[0] = team[-1]
>>> team[-1] = temp
```

3.16 This function just wraps the swapping code we developed in the previous practice problem.

```
def swapFL(lst):
    lst[0], lst[-1] = lst[-1], lst[0]
```

Exercises

3.17 Use the `eval()` function to evaluate these strings as Python expressions:

(a) `'2 * 3 + 1'`

(b) `'hello'`

(c) `"'hello' + ' ' + 'world!'"`

(d) `"'ASCII'.count('I')"`

(e) `'x = 5'`

Which evaluations result in an error? Explain why.

3.18 Assume a, b, and c have been defined in the interactive shell as shown:

```
>>> a, b, c = 3, 4, 5
```

Within the interactive shell, write `if` statements that print `'OK'` if:

(a) a is less than b.

(b) c is less than b.

(c) The sum of a and b is equal to c.

(d) The sum of the squares a and b is equal to c squared.

3.19 Repeat the previous problem with the additional requirement that `'NOT OK'` is printed if the condition is false.

3.20 Write a `for` loop that iterates over a list of strings `lst` and prints the first three characters of every word. If `lst` is the list `['January', 'February', 'March']` then the following should be printed:

```
Jan
Feb
Mar
```

3.21 Write a for loop that iterates over a list of numbers `lst` and prints the even numbers in the list. For example, if `lst` is `[2, 3, 4, 5, 6, 7, 8, 9]`, then the numbers 2, 4, 6, and 8 should be printed.

3.22 Write a `for` loop that iterates over a list of numbers `lst` and prints the numbers in the list whose square is divisible by 8. For example, if `lst` is `[2, 3, 4, 5, 6, 7, 8, 9]`, then the numbers 4 and 8 should be printed.

3.23 Write for loops that use the function `range()` and print the following sequences:

(a) 0 1

(b) 0

(c) 3 4 5 6

(d) 1

(e) 0 3

(f) 5 9 13 17 21

Problems

Note: In the programs that use interactive input of nonstring values, you will need to use the function `eval()` to force Python to treat the user's input as a Python expression (rather than just a string).

3.24 Implement a program that requests a list of words from the user and then prints each word in the list that is not `'secret'`.

```
>>>
Enter list of words: ['cia','secret','mi6','isi','secret']
cia
mi6
isi
```

3.25 Implement a program that requests a list of student names from the user and prints those names that start with letters A through M.

```
>>>
Enter list: ['Ellie', 'Steve', 'Sam', 'Owen', 'Gavin']
Ellie
Gavin
```

3.26 Implement a program that requests a nonempty list from the user and prints on the screen a message giving the first and last element of the list.

```
>>>
Enter a list: [3, 5, 7, 9]
The first list element is 3
The last list element is 9
```

3.27 Implement a program that requests a positive integer n from the user and prints the first four multiples of n.

```
>>>
Enter n: 5
0
5
10
15
```

3.28 Implement a program that requests an integer n from the user and prints on the screen the squares of all numbers from 0 up to, but not including, n.

```
>>>
Enter n: 3
0
1
4
```

3.29 Implement a program that requests a positive integer n and prints on the screen all the positive divisors of n. *Note:* 0 is not a divisor of any integer, and n divides itself.

```
>>>
Enter n: 49
1
7
49
```

3.30 Implement a program that requests four numbers (integer or floating-point) from the user. Your program should compute the average of the first three numbers and compare the average to the fourth number. If they are equal, your program should print `'Equal'` on the screen.

```
>>>
Enter first number: 4.5
Enter second number: 3
Enter third number: 3
Enter last number: 3.5
Equal
```

3.31 Implement a program that requests the user to enter the x and y coordinates (each between -10 and 10) of a dart and computes whether the dart has hit the dartboard, a circle with center $(0, 0)$ and radius 8. If so, string `It is in!` should be printed on the screen.

```
>>>
Enter x: 2.5
Enter y: 4
It is in!
```

3.32 Write a program that requests a positive four-digit integer from the user and prints its digits. You are not allowed to use the string data type operations to do this task. Your program should simply read the input as an integer and process it as an integer, using standard arithmetic operations (+, *, -, /, %, etc).

```
>>>
Enter n: 1234
1
2
3
4
```

3.33 Implement function `reverse_string()` that takes as input a three-letter string and returns the string with its characters reversed.

```
>>> reverse_string('abc')
'cba'
>>> reverse_string('dna')
'and'
```

3.34 Implement function `pay()` that takes as input two arguments: an hourly wage and the number of hours an employee worked in the last week. Your function should compute and return the employee's pay. Any hours worked beyond 40 is overtime and should be paid at 1.5 times the regular hourly wage.

```
>>> pay(10, 35)
350
>>> pay(10, 45)
475.0
```

3.35 The probability of getting n heads in a row when tossing a fair coin n times is 2^{-n}. Implement function `prob()` that takes a nonnegative integer n as input and returns the probability of n heads in a row when tossing a fair coin n times.

```
>>> prob(1)
0.5
>>> prob(2)
0.25
```

3.36 Implement function `reverse_int()` that takes a three-digit integer as input and returns the integer obtained by reversing its digits. For example, if the input is 123, your function should return 321. You are not allowed to use the string data type operations to do this task. Your program should simply read the input as an integer and process it as an integer using operators such as `//` and `%`. You may assume that the input integer does not end with the 0 digit.

```
>>> reverse_int(123)
321
>>> reverse_int(908)
809
```

3.37 Implement function `points()` that takes as input four numbers x_1, y_1, x_2, y_2 that are the coordinates of two points (x_1, y_1) and (x_2, y_2) in the plane. Your function should compute:

- The slope of the line going through the points, unless the line is vertical
- The distance between the two points

Your function should *print* the computed slope and distance in the following format. If the line is vertical, the value of the slope should be string `'infinity'`. *Note:* Make sure you convert the slope and distance values to a string before printing them.

```
>>> points(0, 0, 1, 1)
The slope is 1.0 and the distance is 1.41421356237
>>> points(0, 0, 0, 1)
The slope is infinity and the distance is 1.0
```

3.38 Implement function `abbreviation()` that takes a day of the week as input and returns its two-letter abbreviation.

```
>>> abbreviation('Tuesday')
'Tu'
```

3.39 The computer game function `collision()` checks whether two circular objects collide; it returns `True` if they do and `False` otherwise. Each circular object will be given by its radius and the (x, y) coordinates of its center. Thus the function will take six numbers as input: the coordinates x_1 and y_1 of the center and the radius r_1 of the first circle, and the coordinates x_2 and y_2 of the center and the radius r_2 of the second circle.

```
>>> collision(0, 0, 3, 0, 5, 3)
True
>>> collision(0, 0, 1.4, 2, 2, 1.4)
False
```

3.40 Implement function `partition()` that splits a list of soccer players into two groups. More precisely, it takes a list of first names (strings) as input and prints the names of those soccer players whose first name starts with a letter between and including A and M.

```
>>> partition(['Eleanor', 'Evelyn', 'Sammy', 'Owen', 'Gavin'])
Eleanor
Evelyn
Gavin
```

3.41 Write function `lastF()` that takes as input two strings of the form `'FirstName'` and `'LastName'`, respectively, and returns a string of the form `'LastName, F.'`. (Only the initial should be output for the first name.)

```
>>> lastF('Albert', 'Camus')
'Camus, A.'
```

3.42 Implement function `avg()` that takes as input a list that contains lists of numbers. Each number list represents the grades a particular student received for a course. For example, here is an input list for a class of four students:

```
[[95, 92, 86, 87], [66, 54], [89, 72, 100], [33, 0, 0]]
```

The function avg should *print*, one per line, every student's average grade. You may assume that every list of grades is nonempty, but you may *not* assume that every student has the same number of grades.

```
>>> avg([[95, 92, 86, 87], [66, 54], [89, 72, 100], [33, 0, 0]])
90.0
60.0
87.0
11.0
```

3.43 The computer game function `hit()` takes five numbers as input: the x and y coordinates of the center and the radius of a circle C, and the x and y coordinates of a point P. The function should return `True` if point P is inside or on circle C and `False` otherwise.

```
>>> hit(0, 0, 3, 3, 0)
True
>>> hit(0, 0, 3, 4, 0)
False
```

3.44 Write a function `distance()` that takes as input a number: the time elapsed (in seconds) between the flash and the sound of thunder. Your function should return the distance to the lightning strike in kilometers. The speed of sound is approximately 340.29 meters per second; there are 1000 meters in one kilometer.

```
>>> distance(3)
1.0208700000000002
```

Text Data, Files, and Exceptions

4.1 Strings, Revisited 92

4.2 Formatted Output 98

4.3 Files 107

4.4 Errors and Exceptions 116

E-Book Case Study: Image Files 119

Chapter Summary 119

Solutions to Practice Problems 120

Exercises 121

Problems 124

IN THIS CHAPTER, we focus on the Python tools and problem-solving patterns for processing text and files.

We take a running start by continuing the discussion of the string class we began in Chapter 2. We discuss, in particular, the extensive set of string methods that give Python powerful text-processing capabilities. We then go over the text-processing tools Python provides to control the format of output text. We focus, in particular, on tools for interpreting and creating strings that contain date and time data.

After having mastered text processing, we cover files and file input/output (I/O) (i.e., how to read from and write to files from within a Python program). Much of today's computing involves the processing of text content stored in files. We define several patterns for reading files that prepare the file content for processing.

Working with data coming interactively from the user or from a file introduces a source of errors for our program that we cannot really control. We go over the common errors that can occur and introduce the concept of an exception and the default exceptional control flow.

4.1 Strings, Revisited

In Chapter 2 we introduced the string class `str`. Our goal then was to show that Python supported values other than numbers. We showed how string operators make it possible to write string expressions and process strings in a way that is as familiar as writing algebraic expressions. We also used strings to introduce the indexing operator `[]`.

In this section we cover strings and what can be done with them in more depth. We show, in particular, a more general version of the indexing operator and many of the commonly used string methods that make Python a strong text-processing tool.

String Representations

We already know that a string value is represented as a sequence of characters that is enclosed within quotes, whether single or double quotes:

```
>>> "Hello, World!"
'Hello, World!'
>>> 'hello'
'hello'
```

CAUTION

Forgetting Quote Delimiters

A common mistake when writing a string value is to forget the quotes. If the quotes are omitted, the text will be treated as a name (e.g., a variable name), not a string value. Since, typically, there will be no value assigned to the variable, an error will result. Here is an example:

```
>>> hello
Traceback (most recent call last):
  File "<pyshell#35>", line 1, in <module>
    hello
NameError: name 'hello' is not defined
```

The error message reported that name `hello` is not defined. In other words, the expression `hello` was treated as a variable, and the error was the result of trying to evaluate it.

If quotes delimit a string value, how do we construct strings that contain quotes? If the text contains a single quote, we can use double quote delimiters, and vice versa:

```
>>> excuse = 'I am "sick"'
>>> fact = "I'm sick"
```

If the text contains both type of quotes, then the *escape sequence* \' or \" is used to indicate that a quote is not the string delimiter but is part of the string value. So, if we want to create the string value

```
I'm "sick".
```

we would write:

```
>>> excuse = 'I\'m "sick"'
```

Let's check whether this worked:

```
>>> excuse
'I\'m "sick"'
```

Well, this doesn't seem to work. We would like to see: `I'm "sick"`. Instead we still see the escape sequence `\'`. To have Python print the string nicely, with the escape sequence `\'` properly interpreted as an apostrophe, we need to use the `print()` function. The `print()` function takes as input an expression and prints it on the screen; in the case of a string expression, the `print()` function will interpret any escape sequence in the string and omit the string delimiters:

```
>>> print(excuse)
I'm "sick"
```

In general, an escape sequence in a string is a sequence of characters starting with a \ that defines a special character and that is interpreted by function `print()`.

String values defined with the single- or double-quote delimiters must be defined in a single line. If the string is to represent multiline text, we have two choices. One is to use *triple quotes*, as we do in this poem by Emily Dickinson:

```
>>> poem = '''
To make a prairie it takes a clover and one bee, -
One clover, and a bee,
And revery.
The revery alone will do
If bees are few.
'''
```

Let's see what the variable poem evaluates to:

```
>>> poem
'\nTo make a prairie it takes a clover and one bee, -\nOne clover
, and a bee,\nAnd revery.\nThe revery alone will do\nIf bees are
few.\n'
```

We have here another example of a string containing an escape sequence. The escape sequence \n stands in for a *new line character*. When it appears in a string argument of the `print()` function, the new line escape sequence \n starts a new line:

```
>>> print(poem)

To make a prairie it takes a clover and one bee, -
One clover, and a bee,
And revery.
The revery alone will do
If bees are few.
```

Another way to create a multiline string is to encode the new line characters explicitly:

```
>>> poem = '\nTo make a prairie it takes a clover and one bee, -\n
One clover, and a bee,\nAnd revery.\nThe revery alone
will do\nIf bees are few.\n'
```

The Indexing Operator, Revisited

In Chapter 2, we introduced the indexing operator []:

```
>>> s = 'hello'
>>> s[0]
'h'
```

The indexing operator takes an index i and returns the single-character string consisting of the character at index i.

The indexing operator can also be used to obtain a *slice* of a string. For example:

```
>>> s[0:2]
'he'
```

The expression s[0:2] evaluates to the slice of string s *starting* at index 0 and ending *before* index 2. In general, s[i:j] is the substring of string s that starts at index i and ends at index j-1. Here are more examples, also illustrated in Figure 4.1:

```
>>> s[3:4]
'l'
>>> s[-3:-1]
'll'
```

The last example shows how to get a slice using negative indexes: The substring obtained starts at index −3 and ends *before* index −1 (i.e., at index −2). If the slice we want starts at the first character of a string, we *can* drop the first index:

```
>>> s[:2]
'he'
```

In order to obtain a slice that ends at the last character of a string, we must drop the second index:

```
>>> s[-3:]
'llo'
```

Figure 4.1 Slicing. s[0:2] evaluates to the slice of string s starting at index 0 and ending before index 2. Expression s[:2] evaluates to the same slice. Expression s[3:4] is equivalent to s[3]. Expression s[-3:-1] is the slice of string s that starts at index −3 and ends before index −1.

Reverse Index	-5	-4	-3	-2	-1
s	h	e	l	l	o
Index	0	1	2	3	4
s[0:2]	h	e	l	l	o
s[3:4]	h	e	l	l	o
s[-3:-1]	h	e	l	l	o

Start by executing the assignment:

```
s = '0123456789'
```

Now write expressions using string s and the indexing operator that evaluate to:

(a) '234'

(b) '78'

(c) '1234567'

(d) '0123'

(e) '789'

CAUTION

Slicing Lists

The indexing operator is one of many operators that are shared between the string and the list classes. The indexing operator can also be used to obtain a slice of a list. For example, if pets is defined as

```
>>> pets = ['goldfish', 'cat', 'dog']
```

we can get slices of pets with the indexing operator:

```
>>> pets[:2]
['goldfish', 'cat']
>>> pets[-3:-1]
['goldfish', 'cat']
>>> pets[1:]
['cat', 'dog']
```

A slice of a list is a *list*. In other words, when the indexing operator is applied to a list with two arguments, it will return a list. Note that this is unlike the case when the indexing operator is applied to a list with only one argument, say an index i; in that case, the *item* of the list at index i is returned.

String Methods

The string class supports a large number of methods. These methods provide the developer with a text-processing toolkit that simplifies the development of text-processing applications. Here we cover some of the more commonly used methods.

We start with the string method `find()`. When it is invoked on string s with one string input argument `target`, it checks whether `target` is a substring of s. If so, it returns the index (of the first character) of the first occurrence of string `target`; otherwise, it returns -1. For example, here is how method `find()` is invoked on string `message` using target string `'top secret'`:

```
>>> message = '''This message is top secret and should not
be divulged to anyone without top secret clearance'''
>>> message.find('top secret')
16
```

Index 16 is output by method `find()` since string `'top secret'` appears in string `message` starting at index 16.

The method `count()`, when called by string `s` with string input argument `target`, returns the number of times `target` appears as a substring of `s`. For example:

```
>>> message.count('top secret')
2
```

The value 2 is returned because string `'top secret'` appears twice in `message`.

The function `replace()`, when invoked on string `s`, takes two string inputs, `old` and `new`, and outputs a copy of string `s` with every occurrence of substring `old` replaced by string `new`. For example:

```
>>> message.replace('top', 'no')
'This message is no secret and should not\n
be divulged to anyone without no secret clearance'
```

Has this changed the string `message`? Let's check:

```
>>> print(message)
This message is top secret and should not
be divulged to anyone without top secret clearance
```

So string `message` was *not* changed by the `replace()` method. Instead, a copy of `message`, with appropriate substring replacements, got returned. This string cannot be used later on because we have not assigned it a variable name. Typically, the `replace()` method would be used in an assignment statement like this:

```
>>> public = message.replace('top', 'no')
>>> print(public)
This message is no secret and should not
be divulged to anyone without no secret clearance
```

Recall that strings are immutable (i.e., they cannot be modified). This is why string method `replace()` returns a (modified) copy of the string invoking the method rather than changing the string. In the next example, we showcase a few other methods that return a modified copy of the string:

```
>>> message = 'top secret'
>>> message.capitalize()
'Top secret'
>>> message.upper()
'TOP SECRET'
```

Method `capitalize()`, when called by string `s`, makes the first character of `s` uppercase; method `upper()` makes *all* the characters uppercase.

The very useful string method `split()` can be called on a string in order to obtain a list of words in the string:

```
>>> 'this is the text'.split()
['this', 'is', 'the', 'text']
```

In this statement, the method `split()` uses the blank spaces in the string `'this is the text'` to create word substrings that are put into a list and returned. The method `split()` can also be called with a delimiter string as input: The delimiter string is used in place of the blank space to break up the string. For example, to break up the string

```
>>> x = '2;3;5;7;11;13'
```

into a list of number, you would use ';' as the delimiter:

```
>>> x.split(';')
['2', '3', '5', '7', '11', '13']
```

Finally, another useful string method is `translate()`. It is used to replace certain characters in a string with others based on a mapping of characters to characters. Such a mapping is constructed using a special type of string method that is called not by a string object but by the string class `str` itself:

```
>>> table = str.maketrans('abcdef', 'uvwxyz')
```

The variable `table` refers to a "mapping" of characters a,b,c,d,e,f to characters u,v,w,x,y,z, respectively. We discuss this mapping more thoroughly in Chapter 6. For our purposes here, it is enough to understand its use as an argument to the method `translate()`:

```
>>> 'fad'.translate(table)
'zux'
>>> 'desktop'.translate(table)
'xysktop'
```

The string returned by `translate()` is obtained by replacing characters according to the mapping described by `table`. In the last example, d and e are replaced by x and y, but the other characters remain the same because mapping `table` does not include them.

A partial list of string methods is shown in Table 4.1. Many more are available, and to view them all, use the `help()` tool:

```
>>> help(str)
...
```

Usage	Returned Value
s.capitalize()	A copy of string s with the first character capitalized if it is a letter in the alphabet
s.count(target)	The number of occurrences of substring target in string s
s.find(target)	The index of the first occurrence of substring target in string s
s.lower()	A copy of string s converted to lowercase
s.replace(old, new)	A copy of string s in which every occurrence of substring old, when string s is scanned from left to right, is replaced by substring new
s.translate(table)	A copy of string s in which characters have been replaced using the mapping described by table
s.split(sep)	A list of substrings of strings s, obtained using delimiter string sep; the default delimiter is the blank space
s.strip()	A copy of string s with leading and trailing blank spaces removed
s.upper()	A copy of string s converted to uppercase

Table 4.1 **String methods.** Only some of the commonly used string methods are shown. Since strings are immutable, none of these methods mutates string s. Methods count() and find() return an integer, method split() returns a list, and the remaining methods return a (usually) modified copy of string s.

Assuming that variable `forecast` has been assigned string

```
'It will be a sunny day today'
```

write Python statements corresponding to these assignments:

(a) To variable `count`, the number of occurrences of string `'day'` in string `forecast`.

(b) To variable `weather`, the index where substring `'sunny'` starts.

(c) To variable `change`, a copy of `forecast` in which every occurrence of substring `'sunny'` is replaced by `'cloudy'`.

4.2 Formatted Output

The results of running a program are typically shown on the screen or written to a file. Either way, the results should be presented in a way that is visually effective. The Python output formatting tools help achieve that. In this section we learn how to format output using features of the `print()` function and the string `format()` method. We also look at how strings containing a date and time are interpreted and created.

Function `print()`

The `print()` function is used to print values onto the screen. Its input is an object and it prints a *string representation* of the object's value. (We explain where this string representation comes from in Chapter 8.)

```
>>> n = 5
>>> print(n)
5
```

Function `print()` can take an arbitrary number of input objects, not necessarily of the same type. The values of the objects will be printed in the same line, and blank spaces (i.e., characters `' '`) will be inserted between them:

```
>>> r = 5/3
>>> print(n, r)
5 1.66666666667
>>> name = 'Ida'
>>> print(n, r, name)
5 1.66666666667 Ida
```

The blank space inserted between the values is just the default separator. If we want to insert semicolons between values instead of blank spaces, we can do that too. The `print()` function takes an optional separation argument sep, in addition to the objects to be printed:

```
>>> print(n, r, name, sep=';')
5;1.66666666667;Ida
```

The argument `sep=';'` specifies that semicolons should be inserted to separate the printed values of `n`, `r`, and `name`.

In general, when the argument `sep=<some string>` is added to the arguments of the `print()` function, the string `<some string>` will be inserted between the values. Here are

some common uses of the separator. If we want to print each value separated by the string
', ' (comma and blank space) we would write:

```
>>> print(n, r, name, sep=', ')
5, 1.66666666667, Ida
```

If we want to print the values in separate lines, the separator should be the new line character,
'\n':

```
>>> print(n, r, name, sep='\n')
5
1.66666666667
Ida
```

Write a statement that prints the values of variables `last`, `first`, and `middle` in one line, separated by a horizontal tab character. (The Python escape sequence for the horizontal tab character is \t.) If the variables are assigned like this:

Practice Problem 4.3

```
>>> last = 'Smith'
>>> first = 'John'
>>> middle = 'Paul'
```

the output should be:

```
Smith   John    Paul
```

The `print()` function supports another formatting argument, end, in addition to sep. Normally, each successive `print()` function call will print in a separate line:

```
>>> for name in ['Joe', 'Sam', 'Tim', 'Ann']:
        print(name)

Joe
Sam
Tim
Ann
```

The reason for this behavior is that, by default, the `print()` statement appends a new line character (\n) to the arguments to be printed. Suppose that the output we really want is:

```
Joe! Sam! Tim! Ann!
```

(We just saw our good friends, and we are in an exclamatory kind of mood.) When the argument end=<some string> is added to the arguments to be printed, the string <some string> is printed after all the arguments have been printed. If the argument end=<some string> is missing, then the default string '\n', the new line character, is printed instead; this causes the current line to end. So, to get the screen output in the format we want, we need to add the argument end = '! ' to our `print()` function call:

```
>>> for name in ['Joe', 'Sam', 'Tim', 'Ann']:
        print(name, end='! ')

Joe! Sam! Tim! Ann!
```

| Practice Problem 4.4 | Write function `even()` that takes a positive integer n as input and *prints* on the screen all numbers between, and including, 2 and n divisible by 2 or by 3, using this output format: |

```
>>> even(17)
2, 3, 4, 6, 8, 9, 10, 12, 14, 15, 16,
```

String Method `format()`

The `sep` argument can be added to the arguments of a `print()` function call to insert the same string between the values printed. Inserting the same separator string is not always what we want. Consider the problem of printing the day and time in the way we expect to see time, given these variables:

```
>>> weekday = 'Wednesday'
>>> month = 'March'
>>> day = 10
>>> year = 2010
>>> hour = 11
>>> minute = 45
>>> second = 33
```

What we want is to call the `print()` function with the preceding variables as input arguments and obtain something like:

```
Wednesday, March 10, 2010 at 11:45:33
```

It is clear that we cannot use a separator argument to obtain such an output. One way to achieve this output would be to use string concatenation to construct a string in the right format:

```
>>> print(weekday+', '+month+' '+str(day)+', '+str(year)
    +' at '+str(hour)+':'+str(minute)+':'str(second))
SyntaxError: invalid syntax (<pyshell#36>, line 1)
```

Ooops, I made a mistake. I forgot a + before `str(second)`. That fixes it (check it!) but we should not be satisfied. The reason why I messed up is that the approach I used is very tedious and error prone. There is an easier, and far more flexible, way to format the output. The string (`str`) class provides a powerful class method, `format()`, for this purpose.

The `format()` string method is invoked on a string that represents the format of the output. The arguments of the `format()` function are the objects to be printed. To explain the use of the `format()` function, we start with a small version of our date and time example, in which we only want to print the time:

```
>>> '{0}:{1}:{2}'.format(hour, minute, second)
'11:45:33'
```

The objects to be printed (`hour`, `minute`, and `second`) are arguments of the `format()` method. The string invoking the `format()` function—that is, the string `'{0}:{1}:{2}'`—is the format string: It describes the output format. All the characters outside the curly braces—that is, the two colons (`':'`)—are going to be printed as is. The curly braces `{0}`, `{1}`, and `{2}` are *placeholders* where the objects will be printed. The numbers 0, 1, and 2 explicitly indicate that the placeholders are for the first, second, and third arguments of the `format()` function call, respectively. See Figure 4.2 for an illustration.

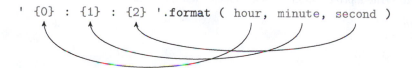

Figure 4.2 Output formatting. The arguments of the `format()` function are printed at the positions indicated by the curly brace placeholders.

Figure 4.3 shows what happens when we move the indexes 0, 1, and 2 in the previous example:

```
>>> '{2}:{0}:{1}'.format(hour, minute, second)
'33:11:45'
```

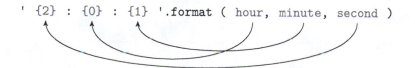

Figure 4.3 Explicit placeholder mapping.

The default, when no explicit number is given inside the curly braces, is to assign the first placeholder (from left to right) to the first argument of the `format()` function, the second placeholder to the second argument, and so on, as shown in Figure 4.4:

```
>>> '{}:{}:{}'.format(hour, minute, second)
'11:45:33'
```

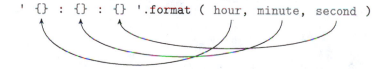

Figure 4.4 Default placeholder mapping.

Let's go back to our original goal of printing the date *and* time. The format string we need is `'{}, {} {}, {} at {}:{}:{}'` assuming that the `format()` function is called on variables `weekday`, `month`, `day`, `year`, `hours`, `minutes`, `seconds` in that order.

We check this (see also Figure 4.5 for the illustration of the mapping of variables to placeholders):

```
>>> print('{}, {} {}, {} at {}:{}:{}'.format(weekday, month,
            day, year, hour, minute, second))
Wednesday, March 10, 2010 at 11:45:33
```

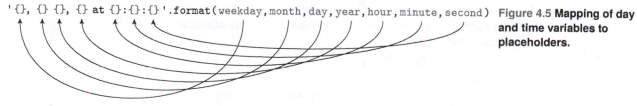

Figure 4.5 Mapping of day and time variables to placeholders.

Practice Problem 4.5

Assume variables `first`, `last`, `street`, `number`, `city`, `state`, `zipcode` have already been assigned. Write a print statement that creates a mailing label:

```
John Doe
123 Main Street
AnyCity, AS 09876
```

assuming that:

```
>>> first = 'John'
>>> last = 'Doe'
>>> street = 'Main Street'
>>> number = 123
>>> city = 'AnyCity'
>>> state = 'AS'
>>> zipcode = '09876'
```

Lining Up Data in Columns

We now consider the problem of presenting data "nicely" lined up in columns. To motivate the problem, just think about how the From, Subject and Date fields in your email client are organized, or how the train or airline departure and arrival information is shown on screens. As we start dealing with larger amount of data, we too sometimes will need to present results in column format.

To illustrate the issues, let's consider the problem of properly lining up values of functions i^2, i^3 and 2^i for $i = 1, 2, 3, \ldots$ Lining up the values properly is useful because it illustrates the very different growth rates of these functions:

```
i     i**2    i**3    2**i
1       1       1       2
2       4       8       4
3       9      27       8
4      16      64      16
5      25     125      32
6      36     216      64
7      49     343     128
8      64     512     256
9      81     729     512
10    100    1000    1024
11    121    1331    2048
12    144    1728    4096
```

Now, how can we obtain this output? In our first attempt, we add a `sep` argument to the `print()` function to insert an appropriate number of spaces between the values printed in each row:

```
>>> print('i    i**2    i**3    2**i')
>>> for i in range(1,13):
        print(i, i**2, i**3, 2**i, sep='      ')
```

The output we get is:

```
i     i**2    i**3    2**i
1       1       1       2
2       4       8       4
3       9      27       8
4      16      64      16
5      25     125      32
6      36     216      64
7      49     343     128
8      64     512     256
9      81     729     512
10      100    1000    1024
11      121    1331    2048
12      144    1728    4096
```

While the first few rows look OK, we can see that the entries in the same column are not properly lined up. The problem is that a fixed-size separator pushes entries farther to the right as the number of digits in the entry increases. A fixed-size separator is not the right tool for the job. The proper way to represent a column of numbers is to have all the unit digits line up. What we need is a way to fix the width of each column of numbers and print the values *right-justified* within these fixed-width columns. We can do that with format strings.

Inside the curly braces of a format string, we can specify how the value mapped to the curly brace placeholder should be presented; we can specify its *field width*, *alignment*, *decimal precision*, *type*, and so on.

We can specify the *(minimum) field width* with a decimal integer defining the number of character positions reserved for the value. If not specified or if the specified field width is insufficient, then the field width will be determined by the number of digits/characters in the displayed value. Here is an example:

```
>>> '{0:3},{1:5}'.format(12, 354)
'  12,   354'
```

In this example, we are printing integer values 12 and 354. The format string has a placeholder for 12 with '0:3' inside the braces. The 0 refers to the first argument of the `format()` function (12), as we've seen before. Everything after the ':' specifies the formatting of the value. In this case, 3 indicates that the width of the placeholder should be 3. Since 12 is a two-digit number, an extra blank space is added in front. The placeholder for 354 contains '1:5', so an extra two blank spaces are added in front.

When the field width is larger than the number of digits, the default is to right-justify—that is, push the number value to the right. Strings are left-justified. In the next example, a field of width 10 characters is reserved for each argument `first` and `last`. Note that extra blanks are added after the string value:

```
>>> first = 'Bill'
>>> last = 'Gates'
>>> '{:10}{:10}'.format(first, last)
'Bill      Gates     '
```

The *precision* is a decimal number that specifies how many digits should be displayed before and after the decimal point of a floating-point value. It follows the field width and a period separates them. In the next example, the field width is 8 but only four digits of the

Table 4.2 **Integer presentation types.** They allow an integer value to be output in different formats.

Type	Explanation
b	Outputs the number in binary
c	Outputs the Unicode character corresponding to the integer value
d	Outputs the number in decimal notation (default)
o	Outputs the number in base 8
x	Outputs the number in base 16, using lowercase letters for the digits above 9
X	Outputs the number in base 16, using uppercase letters for the digits above 9

floating-point value are displayed:

```
>>> '{:8.4}'.format(1000 / 3)
'   333.3'
```

Compare this with the unformatted output:

```
>>> 1000 / 3
333.3333333333333
```

The *type* determines how the value should be presented. The available integer presentation types are listed in Table 4.2. We illustrate the different integer type options on integer value 10:

```
>>> n = 10
>>> '{:b}'.format(n)
'1010'
>>> '{:c}'.format(n)
'\n'
>>> '{:d}'.format(n)
'10'
>>> '{:x}'.format(n)
'a'
```

Two of the presentation-type options for floating-point values are f and e. The type option f displays the value as a fixed-point number (i.e., with a decimal point and fractional part).

```
>>> '{:6.2f}'.format(5 / 3)
'  1.67'
```

In this example, the format specification ':6.2f' reserves a minimum width of 6 with exactly two digits past the decimal point for a floating-point value represented as a fixed-point number. The type option e represents the value in scientific notation in which the exponent is shown after the character e:

```
>>> '{:e}'.format(5 / 3)
'1.666667e+00'
```

This represents $1.666667 \cdot 10^0$.

Now let's go back to our original problem of presenting the values of functions i^2, i^3, and 2^i for $i = 1, 2, 3, \ldots$ up to at most 12. We specify a minimum width of 3 for the values i and 6 for the values of i^2, i^3, and 2^i to obtain the output in the desired format.

```
1  def growthrates(n):
2      'prints values of below 3 functions for i = 1, ..., n'
3      print(' i   i**2   i**3   2**i')
4      formatStr = '{0:2d} {1:6d} {2:6d} {3:6d}'
5      for i in range(2, n+1):
6          print(formatStr.format(i, i**2, i**3, 2**i))
```

Module: ch4.py

Implement function `roster()` that takes a list containing student information and prints out a roster, as shown below. The student information, consisting of the student's last name, first name, class, and average course grade, will be stored in that order in a list. Therefore, the input list is a list of lists. Make sure the roster printed out has 10 slots for every string value and 8 for the grade, including 2 slots for the decimal part.

Practice Problem 4.6

```
>>> students = []
>>> students.append(['DeMoines', 'Jim', 'Sophomore', 3.45])
>>> students.append(['Pierre', 'Sophie', 'Sophomore', 4.0])
>>> students.append(['Columbus', 'Maria', 'Senior', 2.5])
>>> students.append(['Phoenix', 'River', 'Junior', 2.45])
>>> students.append(['Olympis', 'Edgar', 'Junior', 3.99])
>>> roster(students)
Last       First      Class      Average Grade
DeMoines   Jim        Sophomore      3.45
Pierre     Sophie     Sophomore      4.00
Columbus   Maria      Senior         2.50
Phoenix    River      Junior         2.45
Olympia    Edgar      Junior         3.99
```

Getting and Formatting the Date and Time

Programs often need to interpret or produce strings that contain a date and time. In addition, they may also need to obtain the current time. The current date and time are obtained by "asking" the underlying operating system. In Python, the `time` module provides an API to the operating system time utilities as well as tools to format date and time values. To see how to use it, we start by importing the `time` module:

```
>>> import time
```

Several functions in the `time` module return some version of the current time. The `time()` function returns the time in seconds since *the epoch*:

```
>>> time.time()
1268762993.335
```

You can check the epoch for your computer system using another function that returns the time in a format very different from `time()`:

```
>>> time.gmtime(0)
time.struct_time(tm_year=1970, tm_mon=1, tm_mday=1, tm_hour=
0, tm_min=0, tm_sec=0, tm_wday=3, tm_yday=1, tm_isdst=0)
```

DETOUR

Epoch, Time, and UTC Time

Computers keep track of time by keeping track of the number of seconds since a certain point in time, *the epoch*. On UNIX- and Linux-based computers (including Mac OS X), the epoch starts at 00:00:00 of January 1, 1970, Greenwich time.

In order to keep track of the correct number of seconds since the epoch, computers need to know how long a second takes. Every computer has in its central processing unit (CPU) a quartz clock for this purpose (and also to control the length of the "clock cycle"). The problem with quartz clocks is that they are not "perfect" and will deviate from "real time" after a while. This is a problem with today's networked computers because many Internet applications require the computers to agree on time (at least within a small error).

Today's networked computers keep synchronizing their quartz clocks with time servers across the Internet whose job is to serve the "official time" called the Coordinated Universal Time, or UTC time. UTC is the average time of about a dozen atomic clocks and is supposed to track the mean solar time (based on Earth's rotation around the sun) at the Royal Observatory in Greenwich, England.

With time servers across the Internet serving this internationally agreed standard time, computers can agree on what time it is (within a small error).

The type, `time.struct_time`, of the object returned by function `gmtime()` is a tuple-like type. Although the type is unfamiliar to us, it is not difficult to see that the epoch (i.e., the time and date 0 seconds since the epoch) is 00:00:00 on January 1, 1970 UTC. It is UTC time because the function `gmtime()`, if given integer input `s`, returns the UTC time `s` seconds since the start of the epoch. If no argument is given to the function `gmtime()`, it will return the *current* UTC time. The related function `localtime()` returns the *local time zone* current time instead:

```
>>> time.localtime()
time.struct_time(tm_year=2010, tm_mon=3, tm_mday=16, tm_hour=
13, tm_min=50, tm_sec=46, tm_wday=1, tm_yday=75, tm_isdst=1)
```

The output format is not very readable (and is not designed to be). Module `time` provides a formatting function `strftime()` that outputs time in the desired format. This function takes a *format string* and the time returned by `gmtime()` or `localtime()` and outputs the time in a format described by the format string. Here is an example, illustrated in Figure 4.6:

```
>>> time.strftime('%A %b/%d/%y %I:%M %p', time.localtime())
'Tuesday Mar/16/10 02:06 PM'
```

Figure 4.6 Mapping directives. The directives %A, %b, %d, %y, %I, %M, and %p map to date and time values in the output string according to the map described in Table 4.3.

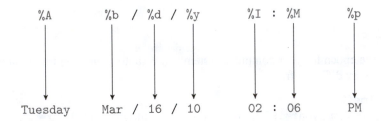

In this example, `strftime()` prints the time returned by `time.localtime()` in the format specified by the format string `'%A %b/%d/%y %I:%M %p'`. The format string includes *directives* %A, %b, %d, %y, %I, %M, and %p that specify what date and time values to output at the directive's location, using the mapping shown in Table 4.3. All the other characters (/, :, and the blank spaces) of the format string are copied to the output as is.

Directive	Output
%a	Abbreviated weekday name
%A	Full weekday name
%b	Abbreviated month name
%B	Full month name
%d	The day of the month as a decimal number between 01 and 31
%H	The hours as a number between 00 and 23
%I	The hours as a number between 01 and 12
%M	The minutes as a number between 00 and 59
%p	AM or PM
%S	Seconds as a number between 00 and 61
%y	Year without century as a number between 00 and 99
%Y	Year as a decimal number
%Z	Time zone name

Table 4.3 Time format string directives. Only some of the commonly used directives for formatting date and time values are shown.

Start by setting `t` to be the local time $1,500,000,000$ seconds from the start of January 1, 1970 UTC:

```
>>> import time
>>> t = time.localtime(1500000000)
```

Construct the next strings by using the string time format function `strftime()`:

(a) `'Thursday, July 13 2017'`

(b) `'09:40 PM Central Daylight Time on 07/13/2017'`

(c) `'I will meet you on Thu July 13 at 09:40 PM.'`

Practice Problem 4.7

4.3 Files

A file is a sequence of bytes stored on a secondary memory device, such as a disk drive. A file could be a text document or spreadsheet, an HTML file, or a Python module. Such files are referred to as text files. Text files contain a sequence of characters that are encoded using some encoding (ASCII, utf-8, etc.). A file also can be an executable application (like python.exe), an image, or an audio file. These files are referred to as *binary files* because they are just a sequence of bytes and there is no encoding.

All files are managed by the file system, which we introduce next.

File System

The file system is the component of a computer system that organizes files and provides ways to create, access, and modify files. While files may be physically stored on various

Figure 4.7 Mac OS X file system organization. The file system consists of text files (e.g., example.txt and chin.txt) and binary files (e.g., date) and folders (the blue rectangles) organized into a tree hierarchy; the root of tree is a folder named /. The figure shows only a fragment of a file system that usually consists of thousands of folders and many more files.

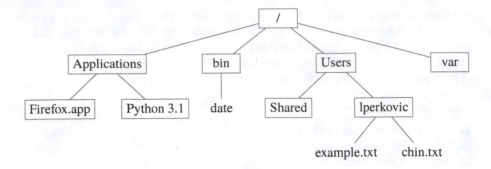

secondary (hardware) memory devices, the file system provides a uniform view of the files that hides the differences between how files are stored on the different hardware devices. The effect is that reading or writing files is the same, whether the file is on a hard drive, flash memory stick, or DVD-RW.

Files are grouped together into *directories* or *folders*. A folder may contain other folders in addition to (regular) files. The file system organizes files and folders into a tree structure. The MAC OS X file system organization is illustrated in Figure 4.7. It is a convention in computer science to draw hierarchical tree structures upside down with the root of the tree on top.

The folder on top of the hierarchy is called the *root directory*. In UNIX, Mac OS X, and Linux file systems, the root folder is named /; in the MS Windows OS, every hardware device will have its own root directory (e.g., C:\). Every folder and file in a file system has a name. However, a name is not sufficient to locate a file efficiently. Every file can be specified using a *pathname* that is useful for locating the file efficiently. The file pathname can be specified in two ways.

The *absolute pathname* of a file consists of the sequence of folders, starting from the root directory, that must be traversed to get to the file. The absolute pathname is represented as a string in which the sequence of folders is separated by forward (/) or backward (\) slashes, depending on the operating system.

For example, the absolute pathname of folder `Python 3.1` is

```
/Applications/Python 3.1
```

while the absolute pathname of file `example.txt` is

```
/Users/lperkovic/example.txt
```

This is the case on UNIX, Mac OS X, and Linux boxes. On a Windows machine, the slashes are backward and the "first slash," the name of the root folder, is instead C:\.

Every command or program executed by the computer system has associated with it a *current working directory*. When using the command shell, the current working directory is typically listed at the shell prompt. When executing a Python module, the current working directory is typically the folder containing the module. After running a Python module from within the interactive shell (e.g., by pressing F5 in the IDLE interactive shell), the folder containing the module becomes the current working directory for the interactive shell commands that follow.

The *relative pathname* of a file is the sequence of directories that must be traversed, starting from the current working directory, to get to the file. If the current working directory is `Users`, the relative pathname of file `example.txt` in Figure 4.7 is

```
lperkovic/example.txt
```

If the current working directory is `lperkovic`, the relative pathname of executable file `date` is

```
../../bin/date
```

The double-period notation (`..`) is used to refer to the *parent folder*, which is the folder containing the current working directory.

Opening and Closing a File

Processing a file consists of these three steps:

1. Opening a file for reading or writing

2. Reading from the file and/or writing to the file

3. Closing the file

The built-in function `open()` is used to open a file, whether the file is a text file or a binary file. In order to read file `example.txt`, we must first open it:

```
infile = open('example.txt', 'r')
```

The function `open()` takes three string arguments: a file name and, optionally, a mode and an encoding; we will not discuss the encoding argument until Chapter 6. The file name is really the pathname (absolute or relative) of the file to be opened. In the last example, the file relative pathname is `example.txt`. Python will look for a file named `example.txt` in the current working directory (recall that this will be the folder containing the module that was last imported); if no such file exists, an exception occurs. For example:

```
>>> infile = open('sample.txt')
Traceback (most recent call last):
  File "<pyshell#339>", line 1, in <module>
    infile = open('sample.txt')
IOError: [Errno 2] No such file or directory: 'sample.txt'
```

The file name could also be the absolute path of the file such as, for example

```
/Users/lperkovic/example.txt
```

on a UNIX box or

```
C:/Users/lperkovic/example.txt
```

on a Windows machine.

CAUTION

Backslashes or Forward Slashes in File System Paths?

In UNIX, Linux, and Mac OS X systems, the forward slash / is used as the delimiter in a path. In Microsoft Window systems, the backslash \ is used:

```
C:\Users\lperkovic\example.txt
```

That said, Python will accept the forward slash / in paths on a Windows system. This is a nice feature because the backslash \ inside a string is interpreted as the start of an escape sequence.

The *mode* is a string that specifies how we will interact with the opened file. In function call open('example.txt', 'r'), the mode 'r' indicates that the opened file will be read from; it also specifies that the file will be read from as a text file.

In general, the mode string may contain one of r, w, a, or r+ to indicate whether the file should be opened for reading, writing, appending, or reading *and* writing, respectively. If missing, the default is r. In addition, t or b could also appear in the mode string: t indicates that the file is a text file, while b indicates it is a binary file. If neither is present, the file will be opened as a text file. So open('example.txt', 'r') is equivalent to open('example.txt', 'rt'), which is equivalent to open('example.txt'). This is all summarized in Table 4.4.

Table 4.4 File mode. The file mode is a string that describes how the file will be used: read from, written to, or both, byte by byte or using a text encoding.

Mode	Description
r	Reading mode (default)
w	Writing mode; if the file already exists, its content is wiped out
a	Append mode; writes are appended to the end of the file
r+	Reading and writing mode (beyond the scope of this book)
t	Text mode (default)
b	Binary mode

The difference between opening a file as a text or binary file is that binary files are treated as a sequence of bytes and are not decoded when read or encoded when written to. Text files, however, are treated as encoded files using some encoding.

The open() function returns an object of an *Input* or *Output Stream* type that supports methods to read and/or write characters. We refer to this object as a *file object*. Different modes will give us file objects of different file types. Depending on the mode, the file type will support all or some of the methods described in Table 4.5.

The separate read methods are used to read the content of the file in different ways. We show the difference between the three on file example.txt whose content is:

File: example.txt

```
1   The 3 lines in this file end with the new line character.
2
3   There is a blank line above this line.
```

We start by opening the file for reading as a text input stream:

```
>>> infile = open('example.txt')
```

Table 4.5 File methods. File objects such as those returned by the open() function support these methods.

Method Usage	Explanation
infile.read(n)	Read n characters from the file infile or until the end of the file is reached, and return characters read as a string
infile.read()	Read characters from file infile until the end of the file and return characters read as a string
infile.readline()	Read file infile until (and including) the new line character or until end of file, whichever is first, and return characters read as a string
infile.readlines()	Read file infile until the end of the file and return the characters read as a list lines
outfile.write(s)	Write string s to file outfile
file.close()	Close the file

With every opened file, the file system will associate a *cursor* that points to a character in the file. When the file is first opened, the cursor typically points to the beginning of the file (i.e., the first character of the file), as shown in Figure 4.8. When reading the file, the characters that are read are the characters that start at the cursor; if we are writing to the file, then anything we write will be written starting at the cursor position.

We now use the `read()` function to read just one character. The `read()` function will return the first character in the file as a (one-character) string.

```
>>> infile.read(1)
'T'
```

After the character `'T'` is read, the cursor will move and point to the next character, which is `'h'` (i.e., the first unread character); see Figure 4.8. Let's use the `read()` function again, but now to read five characters at a time. What is returned is a string of the five characters following the character `'T'` we initially read:

```
>>> infile.read(5)
'he 3 '
```

The function `readline()` will read characters from the file up to the end of the line (i.e., the new line character `\n`) or until the end of the file, whichever happens first. Note that in our case the last character of the string returned by `readline()` is the new line character:

```
>>> infile.readline()
'lines in this file end with the new line character.\n'
```

The cursor now points to the beginning of the second line, as shown in Figure 4.8. Finally, we use the `read()` function without arguments to read the remainder of the file:

```
>>> infile.read()
'\nThere is a blank line above this line.\n'
```

The cursor now points at the "End-Of-File" (EOF) character, which indicates the end of the file.

Initially:	The 3 lines in this file end with the new line character. There is a blank line above this line.
After `read(1)`:	The 3 lines in this file end with the new line character. There is a blank line above this line.
After `read(5)`:	The 3 lines in this file end with the new line character. There is a blank line above this line.
After `readline()`:	The 3 lines in this file end with the new line character. There is a blank line above this line.
After `read()`:	The 3 lines in this file end with the new line character. There is a blank line above this line.

Figure 4.8 Reading file `example.txt`. When a file is read, the cursor will move as the characters are read and always point to the first unread character. After `read(1)`, the character `'T'` is read and the cursor will move to point at `'h'`. After `read(5)`, the string `'he 3 '` is read and the cursor will move to point at `'l'`. After `readline()`, the rest of the first line is read and the cursor moves to point at the beginning of the second line which happens to be empty (except for the new line character.)

To close the opened file that `infile` refers to, you just do:

```
infile.close()
```

Closing a file releases the file system resources that keep track of information about the opened file (i.e., the cursor position information).

CAUTION

Line Endings

If a file is read from or written to as a binary file, the file is just a sequence of bytes and there are no lines. An encoding must exist to have a code for a new line (i.e., a new line character). In Python, the new line character is represented by the escape sequence \n. However text file formats are platform dependent, and different operating systems use a different byte sequence to encode a new line:

- MS Windows uses the \r\n 2-character sequence.
- Linux/UNIX and Mac OS X use the \n character.
- Mac OS up to version 9 uses the \r character.

Python translates platform-dependent line-ends into \n when reading and translates \n back to platform-dependent line-ends when writing. By doing this, Python becomes platform independent.

Patterns for Reading a Text File

Depending on what you need to do with a file, there are several ways to access the file content and prepare it for processing. We describe several patterns to open a file for reading and read the content of the file. We will use the file `example.txt` again to illustrate the patterns:

```
1   The 3 lines in this file end with the new line character.
2
3   There is a blank line above this line.
```

One way to access the text file content is to read the content of the file into a string object. This pattern is useful when the file is not too large and string operations will be used to process the file content. For example, this pattern can be used to search the file content or to replace every occurrence of a substring with another.

We illustrate this pattern by implementing function `numChars()`, which takes the name of a file as input and returns the number of characters in the file. We use the `read()` function to read the file content into a string:

Module: ch4.py

```
1   def numChars(filename):
2       'returns the number of characters in file filename'
3       infile = open(filename, 'r')
4       content = infile.read()
5       infile.close()
6
7       return len(content)
```

When we run this function on our example file, we obtain:

```
>>> numChars('example.txt')
98
```

Practice Problem
4.8

Write function `stringCount()` that takes two string inputs—a file name and a target string—and returns the number of occurrences of the target string in the file.

```
>>> stringCount('example.txt', 'line')
4
```

The file reading pattern we discuss next is useful when we need to process the words of a file. To access the words of a file, we can read the file content into a string and use the string `split()` function, in its default form, to split the content into a list of words. (So, our definition of a word in this example is just a contiguous sequence of nonblank characters.) We illustrate this pattern on the next function, which returns the number of words in a file. It also prints the list of words, so we can see the list of words.

Module: ch4.py

```
1  def numWords(filename):
2      'returns the number of words in file filename'
3      infile = open(filename, 'r')
4      content = infile.read()      # read the file into a string
5      infile.close()
6
7      wordList = content.split()   # split file into list of words
8      print(wordList)              # print list of words too
9      return len(wordList)
```

Shown is the output when the function is run on our example file:

```
>>> numWords('example.txt')
['The', '3', 'lines', 'in', 'this', 'file', 'end', 'with',
 'the', 'new', 'line', 'character.', 'There', 'is', 'a',
 'blank', 'line', 'above', 'this', 'line.']
20
```

In function `numWords()`, the words in the list may include punctuation symbols, such as the period in `'line.'`. It would be nice if we removed punctuation symbols before splitting the content into words. Doing so is the aim of the next problem.

Practice Problem
4.9

Write function `words()` that takes one input argument—a file name—and returns the list of actual words (without punctuation symbols `!,.:;?`) in the file.

```
>>> words('example.txt')
['The', '3', 'lines', 'in', 'this', 'file', 'end', 'with',
 'the', 'new', 'line', 'character', 'There', 'is', 'a',
 'blank', 'line', 'above', 'this', 'line']
```

Sometimes a text file needs to be processed *line by line*. This is done, for example, when searching a web server log file for records containing a suspicious IP address. A log file is a file in which every line is a record of some transaction (e.g., the processing of a web page request by a web server). In this third pattern, the `readlines()` function is used to obtain the content of the file as a list of lines. We illustrate the pattern on a simple function that counts the number of lines in a file by returning the length of this list. It also will print the list of lines so we can see what the list looks like.

Module: ch4.py

```
1  def numLines(filename):
2      'returns the number of lines in file filename'
3      infile = open(filename, 'r')   # open the file and read it
4      lineList = infile.readlines()  # into a list of lines
5      infile.close()
6
7      print(lineList)                # print list of lines
8      return len(lineList)
```

Let's test the function on our example file. Note that the new line character \n is included in each line:

```
>>> numLines('example.txt')
['The 3 lines in this file end with the new line character.\n',
 '\n', 'There is a blank line above this line.\n']
3
```

All file processing patterns we have seen so far read the whole file content into a string or a list of strings (lines). This approach is OK if the file is not too large. If the file is large, a better approach would be to process the file line by line; that way we avoid having the whole file in main memory. Python supports iteration over lines of a file object. We use this approach to print each line of the example file:

```
>>> infile = open('example.txt')
>>> for line in infile:
        print(line,end='')

The 3 lines in this file end with the new line character.

There is a blank line above this line.
```

In every iteration of the `for` loop, the variable `line` will refer to the next line of the file. In the first iteration, variable `line` refers to the line `'The three lines in ...'`; in the second, it refers to `'\n'`; and in the final iteration, it refers to `'There is a blank ...'`. Thus, at any point in time, only one line of the file needs to be kept in memory.

Practice Problem 4.10

Implement function `myGrep()` that takes as input two strings, a file name and a target string, and prints every line of the file that contains the target string as a substring.

```
>>> myGrep('example.txt', 'line')
The 3 lines in this file end with the new line character.
There is a blank line above this line.
```

Writing to a Text File

In order to write to a text file, the file must be opened for writing:

```
>>> outfile = open('test.txt', 'w')
```

If there is no file `test.txt` in the current working directory, the `open()` function will create it. If a file `text.txt` exists, its content will be erased. In both cases, the cursor will point to the beginning of the (empty) file. (If we wanted to add more content to the (existing) file, we would use the mode `'a'` instead of `'w'`.)

Once a file is opened for writing, function `write()` is used to write strings to it. It will write the string starting at the cursor position. Let's start with a one-character string:

```
>>> outfile.write('T')
1
```

The value returned is the number of characters written to the file. The cursor now points to the position after T, and the next write will be done starting at that point.

```
>>> outfile.write('his is the first line.')
22
```

In this write, 22 characters are written to the first line of the file, right after T. The cursor will now point to the position after the period.

```
>>> outfile.write(' Still the first line...\n')
25
```

Everything written up until the new line character is written in the same line. With the `'\n'` character written, what follows will go into the second line:

```
>>> outfile.write('Now we are in the second line.\n')
31
```

The `\n` escape sequence indicates that we are done with the second line and will write the third line next. To write something other than a string, it needs to be converted to a string first:

```
>>> outfile.write('Non string value like '+str(5)+' must be
                   converted first.\n')
49
```

Here is where the string `format()` function is helpful. To illustrate the benefit of using string formatting, we print an exact copy of the previous line using string formatting:

```
>>> outfile.write('Non string value like {} must be converted
                   first.\n'.format(5))
49
```

Just as for reading, we must close the file after we are done writing:

```
>>> outfile.close()
```

The file `test.txt` will be saved in the current working directory and will have this content:

```
1   This is the first line. Still the first line...
2   Now we are in the second line.
3   Non string value like 5 must be converted first.
4   Non string value like 5 must be converted first.
```

CAUTION

Flushing the Output

When a file is opened for writing, a buffer is created in memory. All writes to the file are really writes to this buffer; nothing is written onto the disk, at least not just yet.

The reason for not writing to disk is that writing to secondary memory such as a disk takes a long time, and a program making many writes would be very slow if each write had to be done onto the secondary memory. What this means though is that no file is created in the file system until the file and the writes are *flushed*. The `close()` function will flush writes from the buffer to the file on disk before closing, so it is critical not to forget to close the file. You can also flush the writes without closing the file using the `flush()` function:

```
>>> outfile.flush()
```

4.4 Errors and Exceptions

We usually try to write programs that do not produce errors, but the unfortunate truth is that even programs written by the most experienced developers sometimes crash. And even if a program is perfect, it could still produce errors because the data coming from outside the program (interactively from the user or from a file) is malformed and causes errors in the program. This is a big problem with server programs, such as web, mail, and gaming servers: We definitely do not want an error caused by a bad user request to crash the server. Next we study some of the types of errors that can occur before and during program execution.

Syntax Errors

Two basic types of errors can occur when running a Python program. Syntax errors are errors that are due to the incorrect format of a Python statement. These errors occur while the statement or program is being translated to machine language and before it is being executed. A component of Python's interpreter called a *parser* discovers these errors. For example, expression:

```
>>> (3+4]
SyntaxError: invalid syntax
```

is an invalid expression that the parser cannot process. Here are some more examples:

```
>>> if x == 5
SyntaxError: invalid syntax
>>> print 'hello'
SyntaxError: invalid syntax
>>> lst = [4;5;6]
SyntaxError: invalid syntax
>>> for i in range(10):
print(i)
SyntaxError: expected an indented block
```

In each of these statements, the error is due to an incorrect syntax (format) of a Python statement. So these errors occur before Python has even a chance of executing the statement on the given arguments, if any.

Explain what causes the syntax error in each statement just listed. Then write a correct version of each Python statement.

Practice Problem 4.11

Built-In Exceptions

We now focus on errors that occur during the execution of the statement or program. They do not occur because of a malformed Python statement or program but rather because the program execution gets into an erroneous state. Here are some examples. Note that in each case, the syntax (i.e., the format of the Python statement) is correct.

An error caused by a division by 0:

```
>>> 4 / 0
Traceback (most recent call last):
  File "<pyshell#52>", line 1, in <module>
    4 / 0
ZeroDivisionError: division by zero
```

An error caused by an invalid list index:

```
>>> lst = [14, 15, 16]
>>> lst[3]
Traceback (most recent call last):
  File "<pyshell#84>", line 1, in <module>
    lst[3]
IndexError: list index out of range
```

An error caused by an unassigned variable name:

```
>>> x + 5
Traceback (most recent call last):
  File "<pyshell#53>", line 1, in <module>
    x + 5
NameError: name 'x' is not defined
```

An error caused by incorrect operand types:

```
>>> '2' * '3'
Traceback (most recent call last):
  File "<pyshell#54>", line 1, in <module>
    '2' * '3'
TypeError: cant multiply sequence by non-int of type 'str'
```

An error caused by an illegal value:

```
>>> int('4.5')
Traceback (most recent call last):
  File "<pyshell#80>", line 1, in <module>
    int('4.5')
ValueError: invalid literal for int() with base 10: '4.5'
```

In each case, an error occurs because the statement execution got into an invalid state. Dividing by 0 is invalid and so is using a list index that is outside of the range of valid indexes for the given list. When this happens, we say that the Python interpreter *raises an exception*. What this means is that an object gets created, and this object contains all the information relevant to the error. For example, it will contain the error message that indicates what happened and the program (module) line number at which the error occurred. (In the preceding examples, the line number is always 1 because there is only one statement in an interactive shell statement "program.") When an error occurs, the default is for the statement or program to crash and for error information to be printed.

The object created when an error occurs is called an *exception*. Every exception has a type (a type as in int or list) that is related to the type of error. In the last examples, we saw these exception types: ZeroDivisionError, IndexError, NameError, TypeError, and ValueError. Table 4.6 describes these and a few other common errors.

Let's see a few more examples of exceptions. An OverflowError object is raised when a floating-point expression evaluates to a floating-point value outside the range of values representable using the floating-point type. In Chapter 3, we saw this example:

```
>>> 2.0**10000
Traceback (most recent call last):
  File "<pyshell#92>", line 1, in <module>
    2.0**10000
OverflowError: (34, 'Result too large')
```

Interestingly, overflow exceptions are not raised when evaluating integer expressions:

```
>>> 2**10000
199506311688075838488374216268358508382349683188619245485200894985
... # many more lines of numbers
04558034168269497871413160632106863915116817743304792596709376
```

(You may recall that values of type int are, essentially, unbounded.)

The KeyboardInterrupt exception is somewhat different from other exceptions because it is interactively and explicitly raised by the program user. By hitting ⌈Ctrl⌉-⌈C⌉ during the execution of a program, the user can interrupt a running program. This will cause the

Table 4.6 Common exception types. When an error occurs during program execution, an exception object is created. The type of this object depends on the type of error that occured. Only a few of the built-in exception types are listed.

Exception	Explanation
KeyboardInterrupt	Raised when user hits Ctrl-C, the interrupt key
OverflowError	Raised when a floating-point expression evaluates to a value that is too large
ZeroDivisionError	Raised when attempting to divide by 0
IOError	Raised when an I/O operation fails for an I/O-related reason
IndexError	Raised when a sequence index is outside the range of valid indexes
NameError	Raised when attempting to evaluate an unassigned identifier (name)
TypeError	Raised when an operation or function is applied to an object of the wrong type
ValueError	Raised when an operation or function has an argument of the right type but incorrect value

program to get into an erroneous, interrupted, state. The exception raised by the Python interpreter is of type `KeyboardInterrupt`. Users typically hit Ctrl - C to interrupt a program (when, for example, it runs too long):

```
>>> for i in range(2**100):
        pass
```

The Python statement `pass` does nothing (for real)! It is used wherever code is required to appear (as in the body of a `for` loop) but no action is to be done. By hitting Ctrl - C , we stop the program and get a `KeyboardInterrupt` error message:

```
>>> for i in range(2**100):
        pass

KeyboardInterrupt
```

An `IOError` exception is raised when an input/output operation fails. For example, we could be trying to open a file for reading but a file with the given name does not exist:

```
>>> infile = open('exaple.txt')
Traceback (most recent call last):
  File "<pyshell#55>", line 1, in <module>
    infile = open('exaple.txt')
IOError: [Errno 2] No such file or directory: 'exaple.txt'
```

An `IOError` exception is also raised when a user attempts to open a file she is not permitted to access.

E-Book Case Study: Image Files

Our focus in this chapter has been on text processing and on reading and writing text files using Python. In this case study, we see how image files (typically stored as binary files rather than text files) are read and written and how images can be processed using Python. We also take this opportunity to show how one installs Python modules that are not in the Python Standard Library but are listed in the Python Package Index (PyPi), the official third-party software repository for Python.

Chapter Summary

In this chapter we introduce Python text-processing and file-processing tools.

We revisit the string `str` class that was introduced in Chapter 2 and describe the different ways string values can be defined, using single, double, or triple quotes. We describe how to use escape sequences to define special characters in strings. Finally, we introduce the methods supported by the class `str`, as only string operators were covered in Chapter 2.

A string method we focus on is method `format()`, which is used to control the format of the string when printed using the `print()` function. We explain the syntax of format strings that describe the output format. After having mastered string output formatting, you will be able to focus on more complex aspects of your programs rather than on achieving the desired output format. We also introduce the valuable Standard Library module `time` that provides functions to obtain the time and also formatting functions that output time in a desired format.

This chapter also introduces file-processing tools. We first explain the concepts of a file and of a file system. We introduce methods to open and close a file and methods `read()`, to read a file, and `write()`, to write a string to a file. Depending on how a file will be processed, there are different patterns for reading a file, and we describe them.

Programming errors were discussed informally in previous chapters. Because of the higher likelihood of errors when working with files, we formally discuss what errors are and define exceptions. We list the different types of exceptions students are likely to encounter.

Solutions to Practice Problems

4.1 The expressions are:
(a) `s[2:5]`, (b) `s[7:9]`, (c) `s[1:8]`, (d) `s[:4]`, and (e) `s[7:]` (or `s[-3:]`).

4.2 The method calls are:

(a) `count = forecast.count('day')`

(b) `weather = forecast.find('sunny')`

(c) `change = forecast.replace('sunny', 'cloudy')`

4.3 The tab character is used as the separator.

```
>>> print(last, first, middle, sep='\t')
```

4.4 The function `range()` is used to iterate over integers from 2 to n; each such integer is tested and, if divisible by 2 or 3, printed with a `end = ', '` argument.

```
def even(n)
    for i in range(2, n+1):
        if i%2 == 0 or i%3 == 0:
            print(i, end=', ')
```

4.5 We only need to place a comma and two new line characters appropriately:

```
>>> fstring = '{} {}\n{} {}\n{}, {} {}'
>>> print(fstring.format(first,last,number,street,city,state,zipcode))
```

4.6 The solution uses the floating-point presentation type `f`:

```
def roster(students):
    'prints average grade for a roster of students'
    print('Last      First      Class      Average Grade')
    for student in students:
        print('{:10}{:10}{:10}{:8.2f}'.format(student[0],
            student[1], student[2], student[3]))
```

4.7 The format strings are obtained as shown:

(a) `time.strftime('%A, %B %d %Y', t)`

(b) `time.strftime('%I:%M %p %Z Central Daylight Time on %m/%d/%Y',t)`

(c) `time.strftime('I will meet you on %a %B %d at %I:%M %p.', t)`

4.8 Making the file content into a string allows the use of string functions to count the number of occurrences of substring target.

```
def stringCount(filename, target):
    'returns the number of occurrences of target in file filename'
    infile = open(filename)
    content = infile.read()
    infile.close()
    return content.count(target)
```

4.9 To remove punctuation from a text, one can use the string `translate()` method to replace every punctuation character with the empty string `''`:

```
def words(filename):
    'returns the list of words in file filename'
    infile = open(filename, 'r')
    content = infile.read()
    infile.close()
    table = str.maketrans('!,.:;?', 6*' ')
    content=content.translate(table)
    content=content.lower()
    return content.split()
```

4.10 Iterating over the lines of the file does the job:

```
def myGrep(filename, target):
    'prints every line of file filename containing string target'
    infile = open(filename)
    for line in infile:
        if target in line:
            print(line, end='')
```

4.11 The causes of the syntax errors and the correct versions are as follows:

(a) The left parenthesis and the right bracket do not match. The intended expression is probably either (3+4) (evaluating to integer 7) or [3+4] (evaluating to a list containing integer 7).

(b) The column is missing; the correct expression is `if x == 5:`.

(c) `print()` is a function and thus must be called with parentheses and with arguments, if any, inside them; the correct expression is `print('hello')`.

(d) The objects in a list are separated by commas: `lst=[4,5,6]` is correct.

(e) The statement(s) in the body of a for loop must be indented.

```
>>> for i in range(3):
        print(i)
```

Exercises

4.12 Start by running, in the interactive shell, this assignment statement:

```
>>> s = 'abcdefghijklmnopqrstuvwxyz'
```

Now write expressions using string s and the indexing operator that evaluate to `'bcd'`, `'abc'`, `'defghijklmnopqrstuvwx'`, `'wxy'`, and `'wxyz'`.

4.13 Let string s be defined as:

```
s = 'abcdefghijklmnopqrstuvwxyz'
```

Write Python Boolean expressions that correspond to these propositions:

(a) The slice consisting of the second and third character of s is `'bc'`.

(b) The slice consisting of the first 14 characters of s is `'abcdefghijklmn'`.

(c) The slice of s excluding the first 14 characters is `'opqrstuvwxyz'`.

(d) The slice of s excluding the first and last characters is `'bcdefghijklmnopqrstuvw'`.

4.14 Translate each part into a Python statement:

(a) Assign to variable `log` the next string, which happens to be a fragment of a log of a request for a text file from a web server:

```
128.0.0.1 - - [12/Feb/2011:10:31:08 -0600] "GET /docs/test.txt HTTP/1.0"
```

(b) Assign to variable `address` the substring of `log` that ends before the first blank space in log, using the string method `split()` and the indexing operator.

(c) Assign to variable `date` the splice of string `log` containing the date (12/Feb ... -6000), using the indexing operator on string `log`.

4.15 For each of the below string values of s, write the expression involving s and the string methods `split()` that evaluates to list:

```
['10', '20', '30', '40', '50', '60']
```

(a) s = `'10 20 30 40 50 60'`

(b) s = `'10,20,30,40,50,60'`

(c) s = `'10&20&30&40&50&60'`

(d) s = `'10 - 20 - 30 - 40 - 50 - 60'`

4.16 Implement a program that requests three words (strings) from the user. Your program should print Boolean value `True` if the words were entered in dictionary order; otherwise nothing is printed.

```
>>>
Enter first word: bass
Enter second word: salmon
Enter third word: whitefish
True
```

4.17 Translate each part into a Python statement using appropriate string methods:

(a) Assign to variable `message` the string `'The secret of this message is that it is secret.'`

(b) Assign to variable `length` the length of string `message`, using operator `len()`.

(c) Assign to variable `count` the number of times the substring `'secret'` appears in string `message`, using string method `count()`.

(d) Assign to variable `censored` a copy of string `message` with every occurrence of substring `'secret'` replaced by `'xxxxxx'`, using string method `replace()`.

4.18 Suppose variable s has been assigned in this way:

```
s = '''It was the best of times, it was the worst of times; it
was the age of wisdom, it was the age of foolishness; it was the
epoch of belief, it was the epoch of incredulity; it was ...'''
```

(The beginning of *A Tale of Two Cities* by Charles Dickens.) Then do the following, in order:

(a) Write a sequence of statements that produce a copy of s, named newS, in which characters ., ,, ;, and \n have been replaced by blank spaces.

(b) Remove leading and trailing blank spaces in newS (and name the new string newS).

(c) Make all the characters in newS lowercase (and name the new string newS).

(d) Compute the number of occurrences in newS of string 'it was'.

(e) Change every occurrence of was to is (and name the new string newS).

(f) Split newS into a list of words and name the list listS.

4.19 Write Python statements that print the next formatted outputs using the already assigned variables first, middle, and last:

```
>>> first = 'Marlena'
>>> last = 'Sigel'
>>> middle = 'Mae'
```

(a) Sigel, Marlena Mae
(b) Sigel, Marlena M.
(c) Marlena M. Sigel
(d) M. M. Sigel
(e) Sigel, M.

4.20 Given string values for the sender, recipient, and subject of an email, write a string format expression that uses variables sender, recipient, and subject and that prints as shown here:

```
>>> sender = 'tim@abc.com'
>>> recipient = 'tom@xyz.org'
>>> subject = 'Hello!'
>>> print(???)                 # fill in
From: tim@abc.com
To: tom@xyz.org
Subject: Hello!
```

4.21 Write Python statements that print the values of π and the Euler constant e in the shown formats:

(a) pi = 3.1, e = 2.7
(b) pi = 3.14, e = 2.72
(c) pi = 3.141593e+00, e = 2.718282e+00
(d) pi = 3.14159, e = 2.71828

Problems

4.22 Write a function `month()` that takes a number between 1 and 12 as input and returns the three-character abbreviation of the corresponding month. Do this without using an `if` statement, just string operations. *Hint:* Use a string to store the abbreviations in order.

```
>>> month(1)
'Jan'
>>> month(11)
'Nov'
```

4.23 Write a function `average()` that takes no input but requests that the user enter a sentence. Your function should return the average length of a word in the sentence.

```
>>> average()
Enter a sentence: A sample sentence
5.0
```

4.24 Implement function `cheer()` that takes as input a team name (as a string) and prints a cheer as shown:

```
>>> cheer('Huskies')
How do you spell winner?
I know, I know!
H U S K I E S !
And that's how you spell winner!
Go Huskies!
```

4.25 Write function `vowelCount()` that takes a string as input and counts and prints the number of occurrences of vowels in the string.

```
>>> vowelCount('Le Tour de France')
a, e, i, o, and u appear, respectively, 1, 3, 0, 1, 1 times.
```

4.26 The cryptography function `crypto()` takes as input a string (i.e., the name of a file in the current directory). The function should print the file on the screen with this modification: Every occurrence of string `'secret'` in the file should be replaced with string `'xxxxxx'`.

File: crypto.txt

```
>>> crypto('crypto.txt')
I will tell you my xxxxxx. But first, I have to explain
why it is a xxxxxx.

And that is all I will tell you about my xxxxxx.
```

4.27 Write a function `fcopy()` that takes as input two file names (as strings) and copies the content of the first file into the second.

File: example.txt

```
>>> fcopy('example.txt','output.txt')
>>> open('output.txt').read()
'The 3 lines in this file end with the new line character.\n\n
 There is a blank line above this line.\n'
```

4.28 Implement function `links()` that takes as input the name of an HTML file (as a string) and returns the number of hyperlinks in that file. To do this you will assume that each hyperlink appears in an anchor tag. You also need to know that every anchor tag ends with the substring `</a>`.

Test your code on HTML file `twolinks.html` or any HTML file downloaded from the web into the folder where your program is.

```
>>> links('twolinks.html')
2
```

File: twolinks.html

4.29 Write a function `stats()` that takes one input argument: the name of a text file. The function should print, on the screen, the number of lines, words, and characters in the file; your function should open the file only once.

```
>>> stats('example.txt')
line count: 3
word count: 20
character count: 98
```

File: example.txt

4.30 Implement function `distribution()` that takes as input the name of a file (as a string). This one-line file will contain letter grades separated by blanks. Your function should print the distribution of grades, as shown.

```
>>> distribution('grades.txt')
6 students got A
2 students got A-
3 students got B+
2 students got B
2 students got B-
4 students got C
1 student  got C-
2 students got F
```

File: grades.txt

4.31 Implement function `duplicate()` that takes as input the name (a string) of a file in the current directory and returns `True` if the file contains duplicate words and `False` otherwise.

```
>>> duplicate('Duplicates.txt')
True
>>> duplicate('noDuplicates.txt')
False
```

File: Duplicates.txt

File: noDuplicates.txt

4.32 The function `censor()` takes the name of a file (a string) as input. The function should open the file, read it, and then write it into file `censored.txt` with this modification: Every occurrence of a four-letter word in the file should be replaced with string `'xxxx'`.

```
>>> censor('example.txt')
```

File: example.txt

Note that this function produces no output, but it does create file `censored.txt` in the current folder.

Execution Control Structures

5.1 Decision Control and the `if` Statement   128

5.2 `for` Loop and Iteration Patterns   131

5.3 More on Lists: Two-Dimensional Lists   139

5.4 `while` Loop   143

5.5 More Loop Patterns   145

5.6 Additional Iteration Control Statements   149

E-Book Case Study: Image Processing   151

Chapter Summary   151

Solutions to Practice Problems   152

Exercises   155

Problems   157

THIS CHAPTER COVERS, in more depth, the Python statements and techniques that provide control over what code blocks will be executed when and how often.

We start the discussion with the Python decision control structure, the `if` statement. The `if` statement was introduced in Chapter 3 in its one-way and two-way formats. We introduce here the general format: a multiway decision control structure that allows an arbitrary number of conditions and associated alternative code blocks to be defined.

We provide next an in-depth coverage of the Python iteration control structures and techniques. Two Python statements provide the ability to execute a block of code repeatedly: the `for` loop and the `while` loop. Both are used in many different ways. The bulk of this chapter is spent on the different iteration patterns, and when and how to use them.

Understanding different iteration patterns is really about understanding different approaches to breaking up problems and solving them iteratively. This chapter is thus fundamentally about problem solving.

5.1 Decision Control and the `if` Statement

The `if` statement is the fundamental decision control structure that enables alternative code blocks to be executed based on some conditions. In Chapter 3 we introduced the Python `if` statement. We first saw it in its simplest form, the one-way decision format:

```
if <condition>:
    <indented code block>
<non-indented statement>
```

The statements in `<indented code block>` are executed only if `<condition>` is `True`; if `<condition>` is `False`, no alternative code block is executed. Either way, execution resumes with the statement `<non-indented statement>` that is below and with the same indentation as the `if` statement.

The two-way decision format of the `if` statement is used when two alternative code blocks have to be executed depending on a condition:

```
if <condition>:
    <indented code block 1>
else:
    <indented code block 2>
<non-indented statement>
```

If condition is true, `<indented code block 1>` is executed; otherwise, `<indented code block 2>` is executed. Note that the conditions under which the two code blocks get executed are mutually exclusive. In either case, execution again resumes with the statement `<non-indented statement>`.

Three-Way (and More!) Decisions

The most general format of the Python `if` statement is the multiway (three or more) decision control structure:

```
if <condition1>:
    <indented code block 1>
elif <condition2>:
    <indented code block 2>
elif <condition3>:
    <indented code block 3>
else:                    # there could be more elif statements
    <indented code block last>
<non-indented statement>
```

This statement is executed in this way:

- If `<condition1>` is true, then `<indented code block 1>` is executed.
- If `<condition1>` is false but `<condition2>` is true, then `<indented code block 2>` is executed.
- If `<condition1>` and `<condition2>` are false but `<condition3>` is true, then `<indented code block 3>` is executed.
- If no condition is true, then `<indented code block last>` is executed.

In all cases, the execution will resume with the statement `<non-indented statement>`.

The `elif` keyword stands for "else if". An `elif` statement is followed by a condition just like the `if` statement. An arbitrary number of `elif` statements can follow one `if` statement, and an `else` statement may follow them all (but is optional). Associated with every `if` and `elif` statement, and also with the optional `else` statement, is an indented code block. Python will execute the code block of the *first condition* that evaluates to `True`; no other code block is executed. If no condition evaluates to `True` and an `else` statement exists, the code block of the `else` statement is executed.

In function `temperature()` shown next, we expand the temperature example from Chapter 3 to illustrate the three-way `if` statement:

Module: ch5.py

```
1  def temperature(t):
2      'prints message based on temperature value t'
3      if t > 86:
4          print('It is hot!')
5      elif t > 32:
6          print('It is cool.')
7      else:                        # t <= 32
8          print('It is freezing!')
```

For a given value of `t`, the indented code block of the first condition that is true is executed; if neither the first nor second condition is true, then the indented code corresponding to the `else` statement is executed:

```
>>> temperature(87)
It is hot!
>>> temperature(86)
It is cool.
>>> temperature(32)
It is freezing!
```

The flowchart of the possible executions of this function is shown in Figure 5.1.

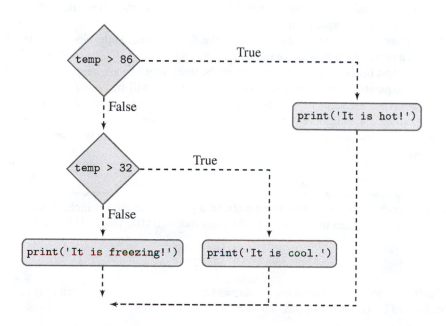

Figure 5.1 Flowchart of function `temperature()`. First checked is the condition `t > 86`. If true, then the statement `print('It is hot!')` is executed. If false, then the condition `t > 32` is checked. If true, then the statement `print('It is cool!')` is executed. If false, then the statement `print('It is freezing!')` is executed.

Ordering of Conditions

There is an issue with multiway decision structures that does not exist with one- or two-way `if` statements. The order in which the conditions appear in a multiway `if` statement is important. To see this, try to figure out what is wrong with the order of the conditions in the next implementation of the function `temperature()`.

```python
def temperature(t):
    if t > 32:
        print('It is cool.')
    elif t > 86:
        print('It is hot!')
    else:
        print('It is freezing!')
```

The problem with this implementation is that `'It is cool'` will be printed for *all* values of t greater than 32. So, if t is 104, what is printed is `'It is cool.'`. In fact, `'It is hot!'` will never get printed, no matter how high the value of t is. The issue is that conditions `t > 32` and `t > 86` are not *mutually exclusive*, as conditions corresponding to code blocks in a two-way decision structure are.

One way to fix the wrong implementation is to make the conditions mutually exclusive explicitly:

```python
def temperature(t):
    if 32 < t <= 86:         # add t <= 86 condition
        print('It is cool.')
    elif t > 86:
        print('It is hot!')
    else:                            t <= 32
        print('It is freezing!')
```

However, explicitly making the conditions mutually exclusive can make the code unnecessarily complicated. Another way to fix the wrong implementation is by *implicitly* making the conditions mutually exclusive, as we did in the original implementation of function `temperature()`. Let's explain this.

The `temperature()` application should have three distinct code blocks, each corresponding to a particular temperature range: $t > 86°$, $32° < t \leq 86°$, and $t \leq 32°$. One of these ranges must become the first condition of the three-way `if` statement, say `t > 86`.

Any subsequent condition in a three-way `if` statement will be tested only if the first condition fails (i.e., the value of t is no more than 86). Therefore, any subsequent condition includes, implicitly, condition `t <= 86`. So, the explicit second condition `t > 32` is really `32 < t <= 86`. Similarly, the implicit condition for the `else` statement is `t <= 32` because it is executed only if t is at most 32.

**Practice Problem
5.1**

Implement function `myBMI()` that takes as input a person's height (in inches) and weight (in pounds) and computes the person's Body Mass Index (BMI). The BMI formula is:

$$bmi = \frac{weight * 703}{height^2}$$

Your functions should *print* the string `'Underweight'` if bmi < 18.5, `'Normal'` if 18.5 <= bmi < 25, and `Overweight` if bmi >= 25.

```
>>> myBMI(190, 75)
Normal
>>> myBMI(140, 75)
Underweight
```

5.2 `for` Loop and Iteration Patterns

In Chapter 3, we introduced the `for` loop. In general, the `for` loop has this structure:

```
for <variable> in <sequence>:
    <indented code block>
<non-indented statement>
```

The variable `<sequence>` must refer to an object that is a string, list, range, or any container type *that can be iterated over*—we will see what this means in Chapter 8. When Python runs the `for` loop, it assigns successive values in `<sequence>` to `<variable>` and executes the `<indented code block>` for every value of `<variable>`. After the `<indented code block>` has been executed for the last value in `<sequence>`, execution resumes with statement `<non-indented statement>` that is below the indented block and has the same indentation as the first line of the `for` loop statement.

The `for` loop, and loops in general, have many uses in programming, and there are different ways to use loops. In this section, we describe several basic loop usage patterns.

Loop Pattern: Iteration Loop

So far in this book, we have used the `for` loop to iterate over the items of a list:

```
>>> l = ['cat', 'dog', 'chicken']
>>> for animal in l:
        print(animal)

cat
dog
chicken
```

We have used it to iterate over the characters of a string:

```
>>> s = 'cupcake'
>>> for c in s:
        if c in 'aeiou':
                print(c)

u
a
e
```

Iterating through an explicit sequence of values and performing some action on each value represents the simplest usage pattern for a `for` loop. We call this usage pattern the *iteration loop pattern*. This is the loop pattern we have used most so far in this book. We include, as our final example of an iteration loop pattern, the code from Chapter 4 that reads a file line by line and prints each line in the interactive shell:

```
>>> infile = open('test.txt', 'r')
>>> for line in infile:
        print(line, end='')
```

In this example, the iteration is not over characters of a string or items of a list but over the lines of the file-like object `infile`. Even though the container is different, the basic iteration pattern is the same.

Loop Pattern: Counter Loop

Another loop pattern we have been using is iterating over a sequence of integers specified with the function `range()`:

```
>>> for i in range(10):
        print(i, end=' ')

0 1 2 3 4 5 6 7 8 9
```

We use this pattern, which we name the counter loop pattern, when we need to execute a block of code for every integer in some range. For example, we may want to find (and print) all even numbers from 0 up to some integer n:

```
>>> n = 10
>>> for i in range(n):
        if i % 2 == 0:
            print(i, end = ' ')

0 2 4 6 8
```

Practice Problem 5.2

Write a function named `powers()` that takes a positive integer n as input and prints, on the screen, all the powers of 2 from 2^1 to 2^n.

```
>>> powers(6)
2 4 8 16 32 64
```

A very common reason to iterate over a sequence of consecutive integers is to generate the indexes of a sequence, whether the sequence is a list, string, or other. We illustrate this with a new `pets` list.

```
>>> pets = ['cat', 'dog', 'fish', 'bird']
```

We can print the animals in the list using the iteration loop pattern:

```
>>> for animal in pets:
        print(animal)

cat
dog
fish
bird
```

Instead of iterating through *the items* of list `pets`, we could also iterate through *the indexes* of list `pets` and achieve the same result:

```
>>> for i in range(len(pets)): # i is assigned 0, 1, 2, . . .
        print(pets[i])         # print object at index i

cat
dog
fish
bird
```

Note how the `range()` and `len()` functions work in tandem to generate the indexes 0, 1, 2, and 3 of list `pets`. The execution of the loop is illustrated in Figure 5.2.

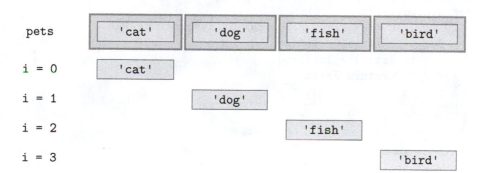

Figure 5.2 Counter pattern. In the for loop, variable i is successively assigned values 0, 1, 2, and 3. For every value of i, the list object pets[i] is printed: string 'cat' when i is 0, 'dog' when i is 1, and so on.

The second approach, using iteration through list indexes, is more complicated and less intuitive than the approach that iterates through list items. Why would one use it?

Well, there are situations when it is necessary to iterate through a sequence by index rather than by value. For example, consider the problem of checking whether a list `lst` of numbers is sorted in increasing order. To do this it suffices to check that each number in the list is smaller than the next one—if there is a next one. Let's try to implement this approach by iterating through the items of the list:

```
for item in lst:
    # now compare item with the next object in list lst
```

We're stuck. How do we compare a list item with the one following it? The problem is that we do not really have a way to access the object in list `lst` that is after object `item`.

If we iterate through the list by list *index* rather than by list *item*, we do have a way: The object that follows the item at index i must be at index $i + 1$:

```
for i in range(len(lst)):
    # compare lst[i] and lst[i+1]
```

The next question to resolve is how to compare `lst[i]` and `lst[i+1]`. If condition `lst[i] < lst[i+1]` is true, we do not need to do anything but go check the next adjacent pair in the next iteration of the loop. If the condition is false—that is, `lst[i] >= lst[i+1]` is true—then we know that list `lst` cannot be in increasing order and we can immediately return false. So, we only need a one-way `if` statement inside the loop:

```
for i in range(len(lst)):
    if lst[i] >= lst[i+1]:
        return False
```

In this loop, variable `i` gets assigned indexes of list `lst`. For every value of `i`, we check whether the object at position `i` is greater than or equal to the object at position `i+1`. If that is the case, we can return `False`. If the `for` loop terminates, that means that every consecutive pair of objects in list `lst` is in increasing order and therefore the whole list is increasing.

It turns out that we have made a mistake in this code. Note that we compare list items at index 0 and 1, 1 and 2, 2 and 3, all the way to items at index `len(lst)-1` and `len(lst)`. But there is no item at index `len(lst)`. In other words, we do not need to compare the last list item with the "next item" in the list. What we need to do is shorten the range over which the `for` loop iterates by 1.

Here is our final solution in the form of a function that takes as input a list and returns `True` if the list is sorted in increasing order and `False` otherwise:

Module: ch5.py

```
1  def sorted(lst):
2      'returns True if sequence lst is increasing, False otherwise'
3      for i in range(0, len(lst)-1): # i = 0, 1, 2, ..., len(lst)-2
4          if lst[i] > lst[i+1]:
5              return False
6      return True
```

Practice Problem 5.3

Write function `arithmetic()` that takes a list of integers as input and returns `True` if they form an arithmetic sequence. (A sequence of integers is an *arithmetic sequence* if the difference between consecutive items of the list is always the same.)

```
>>> arithmetic([3, 6, 9, 12, 15])
True
>>> arithmetic([3, 6, 9, 11, 14])
False
>>> arithmetic([3])
True
```

Loop Pattern: Accumulator Loop

A common pattern in loops is to accumulate "something" in every iteration of the loop. Given a list of numbers `numList`, for example, we might want to sum the numbers up. To do this using a `for` loop, we first need to introduce a variable `mySum` that will hold the sum. This variable is initialized to 0; then a `for` loop can be used to iterate through the numbers in `numList` and add them to `mySum`. For example:

```
>>> numList = [3, 2, 7, -1, 9]
>>> mySum = 0                    # initializing the accumulator
>>> for num in numList:
        mySum = mySum + num     # adding to the accumulator

>>> mySum                        # the sum of numbers in numList
20
```

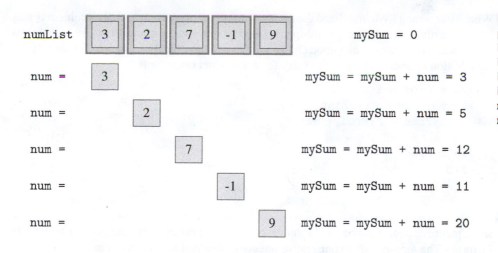

The execution of the previous for loop example is illustrated in Figure 5.3. The variable mySum serves as the *accumulator*. In this case, it is an integer accumulator initialized to 0 because we are summing integers and 0 is the identity for addition (i.e., 0 doesn't affect addition). Every value of num is added to the accumulator with the assignment

```
mySum = mySum + num
```

In the expression to the right of the assignment operator =, the value of num and the current value of the accumulator mySum are added together. The assignment then puts the result of this addition back into the accumulator mySum. We say that mySum is *incremented by* the value of num. This operation is so common that there is a shortcut for it:

```
mySum += num
```

Let's recompute the sum using this shortcut:

```
>>> mySum = 0
>>> for num in numList:
        mySum += num
```

We refer to the pattern of this for loop as the *accumulator loop pattern*.

Accumulating Different Types

We illustrate the accumulator pattern with several more examples. Recall that in Chapter 2 we introduced the built-in function sum() that can be used to add up the values in a list:

```
>>> sum(numList)
20
```

So, writing a for loop to sum up the numbers in a list was not really necessary. Usually, however, a built-in function is not available. What if, for example, we wanted to multiply all the numbers in the list? An approach similar to the one we used for the sum might work:

```
>>> myProd = 0                    # initializing the product
>>> for num in numList:           # num gets values from numList
        myProd = myProd * num     # myProd is multiplied by num
>>> myProd                        # what went wrong?
0
```

What went wrong? We initialized the accumulator product `myProd` to 0; the problem is that 0 times anything is 0. When we multiply `myProd` by every value in `numList`, we will always get 0 back. The value 0 was a good choice for initializing a sum because 0 is the identity for the addition operator. The identity value for the product operator is 1:

```
>>> myProd = 1
>>> for num in numList:
        myProd = myProd * num

>>> myProd
-378
```

Practice Problem 5.4

Implement function `factorial()` that takes as input a nonnegative integer and returns its factorial. The *factorial* of a nonnegative integer n, denoted $n!$, is defined in this way:

$$n! = \begin{cases} 1 & \text{if } n = 0 \\ n \times (n-1) \times (n-2) \times \dots \times 2 \times 1 & \text{if } n > 0 \end{cases}$$

So, $0! = 1$, $3! = 6$, and $5! = 120$.

```
>>> factorial(0)
1
>>> factorial(3)
6
>>> factorial(5)
120
```

In our first two examples of accumulator patterns, the accumulators were of a number type. If we accumulate (concatenate) characters into a string, the accumulator should be a string. What string value should the accumulator be initialized to? It has to be a value that is the identity for string concatenation (i.e., has the property: When concatenated with some character, the resulting string should just be the character). The empty string `' '` (not the blank space!) is thus the identity for string concatenation.

Practice Problem 5.5

An *acronym* is a word formed by taking the first letters of the words in a phrase and then making a word from them. For example, RAM is an acronym for random access memory. Write a function `acronym()` that takes a phrase (i.e., a string) as input and then returns the acronym for that phrase. *Note:* The acronym should be all uppercase, even if the words in the phrase are not capitalized.

```
>>> acronym('Random access memory')
'RAM'
>>> acronym('central processing unit')
'CPU'
```

If we accumulate objects into a list, the accumulator should be a list. What is the identity for list concatenation? It is the empty list `[]`.

Write function `divisors()` that takes a positive integer n as input and returns the list of all positive divisors of n.

Practice Problem
5.6

```
>>> divisors(1)
[1]
>>> divisors(6)
[1, 2, 3, 6]
>>> divisors(11)
[1, 11]
```

Loop Patterns: Nested Loop

Suppose we would like to develop a function `nested()` that takes one positive integer n as input and prints, on the screen, these n lines:

```
0 1 2 3 ... n-1
0 1 2 3 ... n-1
0 1 2 3 ... n-1
...
0 1 2 3 ... n-1
```

For example:

```
>>> n = 5
>>> nested(n)
0 1 2 3 4
0 1 2 3 4
0 1 2 3 4
0 1 2 3 4
0 1 2 3 4
```

As we have seen, in order to print one line, it suffices to do:

```
>>> for i in range(n):
        print(i,end=' ')

0 1 2 3 4
```

In order to get n such lines (or 5 lines in this case), all we need to do is repeat the loop n times (or 5 times in this case). We can do that with an additional outer `for` loop, which will repeatedly execute the `for` loop:

```
>>> for j in range(n):          # outer loop iterates 5 times
        for i in range(n):          # inner loop prints 0 1 2 3 4
            print(i, end = ' ')

0 1 2 3 4 0 1 2 3 4 0 1 2 3 4 0 1 2 3 4 0 1 2 3 4
```

Oops, this is not what we wanted. The statement `print(i, end=' ')` forces *all* the numbers in one line. What we want is to start a new line *after* each sequence 0 1 2 3 4 has been printed. In other words, we need to call function `print()` with no arguments every time the inner loop

```
for i in range(n):
    print(i, end = ' ')
```

has been executed. Here is our final solution:

Module: ch5.py

```
1  def nested(n):
2      'prints n lines each containing values 0 1 2 ... n-1'
3      for j in range(n):          # repeat n times:
4          for i in range(n):           # print 0, 1, ..., n-1
5              print(i, end = ' ')
6          print()                 # move cursor to next line
```

Note that we needed to use a variable name in the outer `for` loop different from the variable name in the inner for loop (`i`).

In this program, a loop statement is contained inside another loop statement. We refer to this type of loop pattern as a *nested loop pattern*. A nested loop pattern may contain more than two nested loops.

Practice Problem 5.7

Write a function `xmult()` that takes two lists of integers as input and returns a list containing all products of integers from the first list with the integers from the second list.

```
>>> xmult([2], [1, 5])
[2, 10]
>>> xmult([2, 3], [1, 5])
[2, 10, 3, 15]
>>> xmult([3, 4, 1], [2, 0])
[6, 0, 8, 0, 2, 0]
```

Suppose now we would like to write another function, `nested2()`, that takes one positive integer n and prints, on the screen, these n lines:

```
0
0 1
0 1 2
0 1 2 3
...
0 1 2 3 ... n-1
```

For example:

```
>>> nested2(5)
0
0 1
0 1 2
0 1 2 3
0 1 2 3 4
```

What needs to be changed in function `nested()` to create this output? In `nested()`, the complete line 0 1 2 3 ... n-1 is printed for every value of variable j. What we now want is to:

- Print 0 when j is 0.
- Print 0 1 when j is 1.
- Print 0 1 2 when j is 2, and so on.

Inner loop variable i needs to iterate not over `range(n)` but over values 0, 1, 2, . . . , j, that is, over `range(j+1)`. This suggests this solution:

Module: ch5.py

```
1  def nested2(n):
2      'prints n lines 0 1 2 ... j for j = 0, 1, ..., n-1'
3      for j in range(n):        # j = 0, 1, ..., n-1
4          for i in range(j+1):    # print 0 1 2 ... j
5              print(i, end=' ')
6          print()                  # move to next line
```

One way to sort a list of n *different* numbers in increasing order is to execute $n-1$ passes over the numbers in the list. Each pass compares all adjacent numbers in the list and swaps them if they are out of order. At the end of the first pass, the largest item will be the last in the list (at index $n-1$). Therefore, the second pass can stop before reaching the last element, as it is already in the right position; the second pass will place the second largest item in the next to last position. In general, pass i will compare pairs at indexes 0 and 1, 1 and 2, 2 and 3, . . . , and $i-1$ and i; at the end of the pass, the ith largest item will be at index $n-i$. Therefore, after pass $n-1$, the list will be in increasing order.

Write a function `bubbleSort()` that takes a list of numbers as input and sorts the list using this approach.

Practice Problem 5.8

```
>>> lst = [3, 1, 7, 4, 9, 2, 5]
>>> bubblesort(lst)
>>> lst
[1, 2, 3, 4, 5, 7, 9]
```

5.3 More on Lists: Two-Dimensional Lists

Lists we have seen so far can be viewed as one-dimensional tables. For example, the list

```
>>> l = [3, 5, 7]
```

can be viewed as the table

3	5	7

A one-dimensional table can easily be represented in Python as a list. But what about two-dimensional tables like the next one?

4	7	2	5
5	1	9	2
8	3	6	6

A two-dimensional table such as this is represented in Python as a list of lists, also referred to as a two-dimensional list.

Two-Dimensional Lists

A two-dimensional table can be viewed as consisting of a bunch of rows (or one-dimensional tables). That is exactly how two-dimensional tables are represented in Python: a list of list elements, with each list element corresponding to a row of the table. For example, the preceding two-dimensional table is represented in Python as:

```
>>> t = [[4, 7, 2, 5], [5, 1, 9, 2], [8, 3, 6, 6]]
>>> t
[[4, 7, 2, 5], [5, 1, 9, 2], [8, 3, 6, 6]]
```

List `t` is illustrated in Figure 5.4; note that `t[0]` corresponds to the first row of the table, `t[1]` corresponds to the second row, and `t[2]` corresponds to the third row. We check this:

```
>>> t[0]
[4, 7, 2, 2]
>>> t[1]
[5, 1, 9, 2]
```

So far there really is nothing new here: We knew that a list could contain another list. What is special here is that each list element is of the same size. Now, how do we access (read or write) individual table items? An item in a two-dimensional table is typically accessed by using its "coordinates" (i.e., its row index and column index). For example, the value 8 in the table is in row 2 (counting from the topmost row and starting with index 0) and column 0 (counting from the leftmost column). In other words, 8 is located at index 0 of of list `t[2]`, or at `t[2][0]` (see Figure 5.4). In general, the item located in row i and column

Figure 5.4
Two-dimensional list. List t represents a 2D table. The first row of the table is t[0], the second is t[1], and the third is t[2]. The items in the first row are t[0][0], t[0][1], t[0][2], and t[0][3]. The items in the second row are t[1][0], t[1][1], t[1][2], t[1][3], and so on.

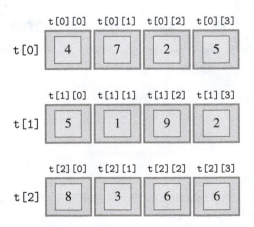

j of a two-dimensional list t is accessed with the expression t[i][j]:

```
>>> t[2][0]          # the element in row 2, column 0
8
>>> t[0][0]          # the element in row 0, column 0
4
>>> t[1][2]          # the element in row 1, column 2
9
```

To assign a value to the entry in row i and column j, we simply use the assignment statement. For example:

```
>>> t[2][3] = 7
```

The entry in row 2 and column 3 of t is now 7:

```
>>> t
[[4, 7, 2, 5], [5, 1, 9, 2], [8, 3, 6, 7]]
```

Sometimes we need to access *all* entries of a two-dimensional list in some order and not just a single entry at a specified row and column. To visit entries of a two-dimensional list systematically, the nested loop pattern is used.

Two-Dimensional Lists and the Nested Loop Pattern

When we printed the value of two-dimensional list t, the output we got was a list of lists rather than a table with rows in different lines. Often it is nice to print the content of a two-dimensional list so it looks like a table. The next approach uses the iteration pattern to print each row of the table in a separate line:

```
>>> for row in t:
        print(row)

[4, 7, 2, 5]
[5, 1, 9, 2]
[8, 3, 6, 7]
```

Suppose that instead of printing each row of the table as a list, we would like to have a function print2D() that prints the items in t as shown next:

```
>>> print2D(t)
4 7 2 5
5 1 9 2
8 3 6 7
```

We use the nested loop pattern to implement this function. The outer for loop is used to generate the rows, while the inner for loop iterates over the items in a row and prints them:

Module: ch5.py

```
1  def print2D(t):
2      'prints values in 2D list t as a 2D table'
3      for row in t:
4          for item in row:          # print item followed by
5              print(item, end=' ')      # a blank space
6          print()                   # move to next line
```

Let's consider one more example. Suppose we need to develop function `incr2D()` that increments the value of every number in a two-dimensional list of numbers:

```
>>> print2D(t)
4 7 2 5
5 1 9 2
8 3 6 7
>>> incr2D(t)
>>> print2D(t)
5 8 3 6
6 2 10 3
9 4 7 8
```

Clearly, the function `incr2D()` will need to execute:

```
t[i][j] += 1
```

for every row index `i` and column index `j` of an input two-dimensional list `t`. We can use the nested loop pattern to generate all combinations of row and column index.

The outer loop should generate the row indexes of `t`. To do this we need to know the number of rows in `t`. It is simply `len(t)`. The inner loop should generate the column indexes of `t`. We are hitting a snag here. How do we find out how many columns `t` has? Well, it is actually the number of items in a row, and since we assume that all rows have the same number of items, we can arbitrarily pick the first row to obtain the number of columns: `len(t[0])`. Now we can implement the function:

Module: ch5.py

```
1  def incr2D(t):
2      'increments each number in 2D list of numbers t'
3      nrows = len(t)                      # number of rows
4      ncols = len(t[0])                   # number of columns
5
6      for i in range(nrows):              # i is the row index
7          for j in range(ncols):             # j is the column index
8              t[i][j] += 1
```

The nested loop pattern is used in this program to access the items of two-dimensional list `t` row by row, from left to right, top to bottom. First accessed are the items in row 0—`t[0][0]`, `t[0][1]`, `t[0][2]`, and `t[0][3]`, in that order—as illustrated in Figure 5.5. After that, items in row 1 are accessed, from left to right, and then items in row 2, and so on.

Figure 5.5 Nested loop pattern. The outer `for` loop generates row indexes. The inner `for` loop generates column indexes. The arrow illustrates the execution of the inner for loop for the first-row index (0).

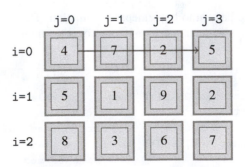

Write a function add2D() that takes two two-dimensional lists of same size (i.e., same number of rows and columns) as input arguments and increments every entry in the first list with the value of the corresponding entry in the second list.

```
>>> t = [[4, 7, 2, 5], [5, 1, 9, 2], [8, 3, 6, 6]]
>>> s = [[0, 1, 2, 0], [0, 1, 1, 1], [0, 1, 0, 0]]
>>> add2D(t,s)
>>> for row in t:
        print(row)

[4, 8, 4, 5]
[5, 2, 10, 3]
[8, 4, 6, 6]
```

5.4 while **Loop**

In addition to for loops, there is another, more general iteration control structure in Python: the while loop. In order to understand how the while loop works, we start by reviewing how a one-way if statement works:

```
if <condition>:
    <indented code block>
<non-indented statement>
```

Recall that the `<indented code block>` is executed when `<condition>` is true; after the `<indented code block>` has been executed, the program execution continues with `<non-indented statement>`. If `<condition>` is false, program execution goes straight to `<non-indented statement>`.

The *format* of a while statement is similar to the format of a one-way if statement:

```
while <condition>:
    <indented code block>
<non-indented statement>
```

Just as for an if statement, in a while statement, the `<indented code block>` is executed if `<condition>` is true. But after the `<indented code block>` has been executed, program execution goes back to checking whether `<condition>` is true. If so, then the `<indented code block>` is executed again. As long as `<condition>` is true, the `<indented code block>` keeps getting executed, again and again. When `<condition>` evaluates to false, then the execution jumps to the `<non-indented statement>`. The while loop flowchart in Figure 5.6 illustrates the possible execution paths.

while **Loop Usage**

When is the while loop useful? We illustrate that with the next problem. Suppose we have the silly idea to compute the first multiple of 73 that is greater than 3, 951. One way to solve this problem is to successively generate positive multiples of 73 until we get to a number greater than 3, 951. A for loop implementation of this idea would start with:

```
for multiple in range(73, ???, 73)}:
    ...
```

Figure 5.6 `while`
statement flowchart.
The conditional block will
repeatedly get executed,
as long as the condition
evaluates to true. When the
condition evaluates to false,
the statement that follows
the `while` loop gets
executed.

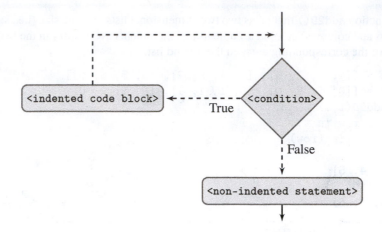

We are trying to use function `range()` to generate the sequence of multiples of 73: 73, 146, 219, . . . But when do we stop? In other words, what do we replace ??? with?

A `while` loop is perfect for situations in which we need to iterate but we do not know how many times. In our case, we need to keep generating multiples of 73 as long as the multiples are $\leq 3,951$. In other words, *while multiple $\leq$ 73, we generate the next multiple.* Let's translate that into Python:

```
while multiple <= 3951:
    multiple += 73
```

The variable `multiple` needs to be initialized before the `while` loop. We can initialize it to the first positive multiple of 73, which is 73. In every iteration of the `while` loop, the condition `multiple <= 3951` is checked. If true, `multiple` is incremented to the next multiple of 73:

```
>>> bound = 3951
>>> multiple = 73
>>> while multiple <= bound:
        multiple += 73

>>> multiple
4015
```

When the `while` loop condition evaluates to `False`, the execution of the loop stops. The value of `multiple` is then greater than bound. Since the previous value of `multiple` was not greater, it will have the value we want: the smallest multiple greater than bound.

**Practice Problem
5.10**

Write a function `interest()` that takes one input, a floating-point interest rate (e.g., 0.06 which corresponds to a 6% interest rate). Your function should compute and return how long (in years) it will take for an investment to double in value. *Note:* The number of years it takes for an investment to double does not depend on the value of the initial investment.

```
>>> interest(0.07)
11
```

5.5 More Loop Patterns

With the `while` loop in hand, as well as a few additional loop control structures we will introduce, we can develop a few more useful loop patterns.

Iteration Patterns: Sequence Loop

Some problems, particularly coming from science, engineering, and finance, can be solved by generating a sequence of numbers that eventually reaches a desired number. We illustrate this pattern on the well-known Fibonacci number sequence:

$$1, 1, 2, 3, 5, 8, 13, 21, 34, 55, 89, \ldots$$

The Fibonacci number sequence starts with integers 1 and 1 and goes on forever by applying this rule: The current number in the sequence is the sum of the previous two numbers in the sequence.

DETOUR

Fibonacci Numbers

The Fibonacci sequence is named after Leonardo of Pisa, known as Fibonacci, who introduced it to the Western world. The sequence was actually known much earlier among Indian mathematicians.

Fibonacci developed the sequence as a model for the growth of an idealized rabbit population. He assumed that (1) rabbits are able to mate at the age of one month and (2) it takes one month for baby rabbits to be born. The number of rabbit pairs at the end of month i is described by the ith Fibonacci number in this way:

- Initially, at the beginning of month 1, there is only one 1 pair.
- At the end of the month 1, the pair mates but there is still just 1 pair.
- At the end of month 2, the original pair produces a pair of rabbits and mates again, so now there are 2 pairs.
- At the end of month 3, the original pair produces a pair of rabbits again and mates again. The second pair mates but has no offspring yet. Now there are 3 pairs.
- At the end of month 4, the original pair and the second pair produces a pair of rabbits each, so now there are 5 pairs.

A natural problem is to compute the ith Fibonacci number. Problem 5.32 at the end of this chapter asks you to do just that. Right now we are going to solve a slightly different problem. We would like to compute the first Fibonacci number greater than some given integer bound. We will do that by generating the sequence of Fibonacci numbers and stopping when we reach a number greater than bound. So, if our current Fibonacci number is `current`, our `while` loop condition will be

```
while current <= bound:
```

If the condition is true, we need to generate the next Fibonacci number or, in other words, the next value of `current`. To do this, we need keep track of the Fibonacci number that comes before `current`. So we need to have another variable, say, `previous`, in addition to a variable `current` for the current Fibonacci number. Before the `while` loop, we initialize `previous` and `current` to the first and second Fibonacci numbers:

Module: ch5.py

```
1   def fibonacci(bound):
2       'returns the smallest Fibonacci number greater than bound'
3       previous = 1          # first Fibonacci number
4       current = 1           # second Fibonacci number
5       while current <= bound:
6           # current becomes previous, and new current is computed
7           previous, current = current, previous+current
8       return current
```

Note the use of the multiple assignment statement to compute the new values for `current` and `previous`.

In function `fibonacci()`, the loop is used to generate a sequence of numbers until a condition is satisfied. We refer to this loop pattern as the *sequence loop pattern*. In the next problem, we apply the sequence loop pattern to approximate the value of the mathematical constant e, called the Euler constant.

Practice Problem 5.11

It is known that the precise value of e is equal to this infinite sum:

$$\frac{1}{0!} + \frac{1}{1!} + \frac{1}{2!} + \frac{1}{3!} + \frac{1}{4!} + \frac{1}{5!} + \cdots$$

An infinite sum is impossible to compute. We can get an approximation of e by computing the sum of the first few terms in the infinite sum. For example, $e_o = \frac{1}{0!} = 1$ is a (lousy) approximation for e. The next sum, $e_1 = \frac{1}{0!} + \frac{1}{1!} = 2$, is better but still quite bad. The next one, $e_2 = \frac{1}{0!} + \frac{1}{1!} + \frac{1}{2!} = 2.5$, looks better. The next few sums show that we are heading in the right direction:

$$e_3 = \frac{1}{0!} + \frac{1}{1!} + \frac{1}{2!} + \frac{1}{3!} = 2.6666\ldots$$

$$e_4 = \frac{1}{0!} + \frac{1}{1!} + \frac{1}{2!} + \frac{1}{3!} + \frac{1}{4!} = 2.7083\ldots$$

Now, because, $e_4 - e_3 = \frac{1}{4!} > \frac{1}{5!} + \frac{1}{6!} + \frac{1}{7!} + \ldots$, we know that e_4 is within $\frac{1}{4!}$ of the actual value for e. This gives us a way to compute an approximation of e that is guaranteed to be within a given range of the true value of e.

Write a function `approxE()` that takes as input a float value `error` and returns a value that approximates constant e to within `error`. You will do this by generating the sequence of approximation $e_0, e_1, e_2, \ldots$ until the difference between the current approximation and the previous one is no greater than `error`.

```
>>> approxE(0.01)
2.7166666666666663
>>> approxE(0.000000001)
2.7182818284467594
```

Loop Pattern: Infinite Loop

The while loop can be used to create an *infinite* loop, which is a loop that runs "forever":

```
while True:
    <indented code block>
```

Because True is always true, `<indented code block>` will get executed again and again.

Infinite loops are useful when the program is meant to provide a service indefinitely. A web server (i.e., a program that serves web pages) is an example of a program that provides a service. It repeatedly receives web page requests from your—and other people's—web browser and sends back the requested web page. The next example illustrates the use of the infinite loop pattern in a much simpler "greeting service."

We would like to write a function `hello2()` that repeatedly requests users to input their name and then, when users have done so and pressed Return, greets them:

```
>>> hello2()
What is your name? Sam
Hello Sam
What is your name? Tim
Hello Tim
```

Here is a straightforward implementation that uses the *infinite loop pattern*:

Module: ch5.py

```
1  def hello2():
2      '''a greeting service; it repeatedly requests the name
3         of the user and then greets the user'''
4      while True:
5          name = input('What is your name? ')
6          print('Hello {}'.format(name))
```

How do you stop a program that uses the infinite loop pattern? Any running program, including one that runs an infinite loop, can be broken—more precisely, interrupted—from outside the program (externally) by typing (simultaneously) Ctrl - C on the keyboard. That is how you should stop the execution of the above `hello2()` function.

Loop Pattern: Loop and a Half

A while loop should also be used when a program must repeatedly process some input values until a *flag* is reached. (A flag is an arbitrary value that is chosen to indicate the end of the input.)

More specifically, consider the problem of developing a function `cities()` that repeatedly requests city names (i.e., strings) from the user and accumulates them in a list. The user indicates the end of the input by entering the empty string, at which point the function should return the list of all cities entered by the user. Here is the behavior we expect to see:

```
>>> cities()
Enter city: Lisbon
Enter city: San Francisco
Enter city: Hong Kong
Enter city:
['Lisbon', 'San Francisco', 'Hong Kong']
>>>
```

If the user enters no city, the empty list should be returned:

```
>>> cities()
Enter city:
[]
```

Clearly, function `cities()` should be implemented using a loop that interactively asks the user to enter a city in every iteration. Since the number of iterations is not known, we need to use a `while` loop. The condition of this `while` loop should check whether the user entered the empty string. That means that the user should be asked to enter the first city *before* even entering the `while` loop. We will, of course, also need to ask the user to enter a city in every iteration of the `while` loop:

Module: ch5.py

```
 1  def cities():
 2      '''returns the list of cities that are interactively entered
 3         by the user; the empty string ends the interactive input'''
 4      lst = []
 5
 6      city = input('Enter city: ')   # ask user to enter first city
 7
 8      while city != '':              # if city is not the flag value
 9          lst.append(city)           # append city to list
10          city = input('Enter city: ') # and ask user once again
11
12      return lst
```

Note that the function uses the accumulator loop pattern to accumulate the cities into a list.

In function `cities()`, there are two `input()` function calls: one before the `while` loop statement and one inside the `while` loop code block. A way to eliminate one of those "redundant" statements and make the code more intuitive is to use an infinite loop and an `if` statement inside the body of the `while` loop. The `if` statement would test whether the user entered the flag value:

Module: ch5.py

```
 1  def cities2():
 2      '''returns the list of cities that are interactively entered
 3         by the user; the empty string ends the interactive input'''
 4      lst = []
 5
 6      while True:                    # forever repeat:
 7          city = input('Enter city: ') # ask user to enter city
 8
 9          if city == '':             # if city is the flag value
10              return lst             # return list
11
12          lst.append(city)           # append city to list
```

When executing function `cities2()`, the last iteration of the `while` loop is the one during which the user enters the empty string. In this iteration, only "half" of the body of the `for` loop is executed; the statement `lst.append(city)` is skipped. For this reason, the loop pattern in `cities2()` is commonly referred to as the *loop-and-a-half* pattern.

DETOUR

More Loop Patterns

In this book we describe the core loop patterns only. Other loop patterns have been proposed. If you want to see more, this website keeps track of loop patterns proposed by various computer scientists:

http://max.cs.kzoo.edu/patterns/Repetition.shtml

5.6 Additional Iteration Control Statements

We end this chapter by introducing several Python statements that provide further control over iteration. We use simple examples so that we can clearly illustrate how they work.

break **Statement**

The break statement can be added to the code block of a loop (whether a for loop or a while loop). When it is executed, the current loop iteration is stopped and the loop is exited. Execution then resumes with the statement that follows the loop statement. If the break statement appears in the code block of a loop of a nested loop pattern, only the innermost loop containing the break is exited.

To illustrate the usage of the break statement, we start with another implementation of the function that prints the numbers in a two-dimensional list of numbers in a 2D table format:

Module: ch5.py

```
1  def print2D2(table):
2      'prints values in 2D list of numbers t as a 2D table'
3      for row in table:
4          for num in row:
5              print(num, end=' ')
6          print()
```

Let's test the code:

```
>>> table = [[2, 3, 0, 6], [0, 3, 4, 5], [4, 5, 6, 0]]
>>> print2D2(table)
2 3 0 6
0 3 4 5
4 5 6 0
```

Suppose that instead of printing the complete row, we want to print only those numbers in the row up to, and not including, the first 0 entry in the row. A function before0() doing this would behave as follows:

```
>>> before0(table)
2 3

4 5 6
```

To implement `before0()`, we modify the implementation of `print2D()` by adding an `if` statement, inside the inner `for` loop code block, that checks whether the current value of num is 0. If so, the `break` statement is executed. This will terminate the inner `for` loop. Note that the `break` statement does not terminate the outer `for` loop; execution thus resumes at the next row of the table.

Module: ch5.py

```
1   def before0(table):
2       '''prints values in 2D list of numbers t as a 2D table;
3          only values in row up to first 0 are printed'''
4       for row in table:
5
6           for num in row:      # inner for loop
7               if num == 0:         # if num is 0
8                   break            # terminate inner for loop
9               print(num, end=' ') # otherwise print num
10
11          print()              # move cursor to next line
```

The `break` statement does not affect the outer `for` loop, which will iterate through all the rows of the table regardless of whether the `break` statement has been executed.

`continue` **Statement**

The `continue` statement can be added to the code block of a loop, just like the `break` statement. When the `continue` statement is executed, the current, innermost loop iteration is stopped, and execution resumes with the *next* iteration of the current, innermost loop statement. Unlike the `break` statement, the `continue` statement does not terminate the innermost loop; it only terminates the current iteration of the innermost loop.

To illustrate the usage of the `continue` statement, we modify the `print2D2()` function to skip the printing of 0 values in the table. The modified function, which we call `ignore0()`, should behave like this:

```
>>> table = [[2, 3, 0, 6], [0, 3, 4, 5], [4, 5, 6, 0]]
>>> ignore0(table)
2 3 6
3 4 5
4 5 6
```

Note that the 0 values in the table are ignored. Let's implement `ignore0()`:

Module: ch5.py

```
1   def ignore0(table):
2       '''prints values in 2D list of numbers t as a 2D table;
3          0 values are no printed'''
4       for row in table:
5
6           for num in row:      # inner for loop
7               if num == 0:         # if num is 0, terminate
8                   continue         # current inner loop iteration
9               print(num, end=' ') # otherwise print num
10
11          print()              # move cursor to next line
```

pass **Statement**

In Python, every function definition `def` statement, `if` statement, or `for` or `while` loop statement must have a body (i.e., a nonempty indented code block). A syntax error while parsing the program would occur if the code block is missing. In the rare occasion when the code in the blocks really doesn't have to do anything, we still have to put some code in it. For this reason Python provides the `pass` statement, which does nothing but is still a valid statement.

In the next example we illustrate its usage, in a code fragment that prints the value of `n` only if the value of `n` is odd.

```
if n % 2 == 0:
    pass         # do nothing for even number n
else:
    print(n)   # print odd number n only
```

If the value of `n` is even, the first code block is executed. The block is just a `pass statement`, which does nothing.

The `pass` statement is used when the Python syntax requires code (bodies of functions and execution control statements). The `pass` statement is also useful when a code body has not yet been implemented.

E-Book Case Study: Image Processing

In the Chapter 4 case study we learned how to process images using Python. We saw, in particular, how to copy, rotate, crop, and blur an image. In this case study, we take a look underneath the hood and see how such image-processing tools can be implemented.

Chapter Summary

This key chapter covers the Python control flow structures in depth.

We start by revisiting the `if` control flow construct introduced in Chapter 2. We describe its most general format, the multiway decision structure that uses the `elif` statement. While one- and two-way conditional structures are defined with only one condition, multiway conditional structures have, in general, multiple conditions. If the conditions are not mutually exclusive, the order in which the conditions appear in the multiway `if` statement is important, and care must be taken to ensure that the order will give the desired behavior.

The bulk of this chapter describes the different ways that iteration structures are used. First covered are the fundamental iteration, counter, accumulator, and nested loop patterns. These are not only the most common loop patterns, but they are also the building blocks for more advanced loop patterns. The nested loop pattern is particularly useful for processing two-dimensional lists, which we introduce in this chapter.

Before describing more advanced iteration patterns, we introduce another Python loop construct, the `while` loop. It is more general than the `for` loop construct and can be used to implement loops that would be awkward to implement using the `for` loop. Using the `while` loop construct, we describe the sequence, infinite, interactive, and loop-and-a-half loop patterns.

At the end of the chapter, we introduce several more iteration control statements (`break`, `continue`, and `pass`) that give a bit more control over iteration structures and code development.

The decision and iteration control flow structures are the building blocks used to describe algorithmic solutions to problems. How to effectively apply these structures when solving a problem is one of the fundamental skills of a computing professional. Mastering multiway conditional structures and understanding when and how to apply the iteration patterns described in this chapter are the first steps toward developing this skill.

Solutions to Practice Problems

5.1 After computing the BMI, we use a multiway `if` statement to decide what to print:

```python
def myBMI(weight, height):
  'prints BMI report'
  bmi = weight * 703 / height**2
  if bmi < 18.5:
    print('Underweight')
  elif bmi < 25:
    print('Normal')
  else:                      # bmi >= 25
    print('Overweight')
```

5.2 We need to print $2^1, 2^2, 2^3, \ldots, 2^n$ (i.e., 2^i for all integers i from 1 to n). To iterate over the range from 1 up to (and including) n, we use function call `range(1, n+1)`:

```python
def powers(n):
  'prints 2**i for i = 1, 2, ..., n'
  for i in range(1, n+1):
    print(2**i, end=' ')
```

5.3 We need to check that the difference between adjacent list values are all the same. One way to do this is to check that they are all equal to the difference between the first two list items, `l[0]` and `l[1]`. So, we need to check that `l[2]-l[1]`, `l[3]-l[2]`, ..., `l[n-1]-l[n-2]`, where n is the size of list `l`, are all equal to `diff = l[1] - l[0]`. Or, to put it another way, we need to check that `l[i+1] - l[i] = diff` for $i = 1, 2, \ldots, n - 2$, values obtained by iterating through `range(1, len(l)-1)`:

```python
def arithmetic(lst):
    '''returns True if list lst contains an arithmetic sequence,
      False otherwise'''
    if len(lst) < 2: # a sequence of length < 2 is arithmetic
        return True
    # checking that difference between successive items is equal
    # to the difference between the first two numbers
    diff = lst[1] - lst[0]
    for i in range(1, len(lst)-1):
        if lst[i+1] - lst[i] != diff:
            return False
    return True
```

5.4 We need to multiply (accumulate) integers $1, 2, 3, \ldots, n$. The accumulator `res` is initialized to 1, the identity for multiplication. Then we iterate over sequence $2, 3, 4, \ldots, n$

and multiply `res` by each number in the sequence:

```
def factorial(n):
    'returns n!'
    res = 1
    for i in range(2, n+1):
        res *= i
    return res
```

5.5 In this problem we would like to iterate over the words of the phrase and *accumulate* the first letter in every word. So we need to break the phrase into a list of words using the string `split()` method and then iterate over the words in this list. We will add the first letter of every word to the accumulator string `res`.

```
def acronym(phrase):
    'returns the acronym of the input string phrase'
    # splits phrase into a list of words
    words = phrase.split()
    # accumulate first character, as an uppercase, of every word
    res = ''
    for w in words:
        res = res + w[0].upper()
    return res
```

5.6 Divisors of n include 1, n, and perhaps more numbers in between. To find them, we can iterate over *all* integers given by `range(1, n+1)` and check each integer whether it is a divisor of n.

```
def divisors(n):
    'returns the list of divisors of n'
    res = []
    for i in range(1, n+1):
        if n % i == 0:
            res.append(i)
    return res
```

5.7 We will use the nested loop pattern to multiply every integer in the first list with every integer in the second list. The outer for loop will iterate over the integers in the first list. Then, for every such integer `i`, the inner for loop will iterate over the integers of the second list, and each such integer is multiplied by `i`; the product is accumulated into a list accumulator.

```
def xmult(l1, l2):
    '''returns the list of products of items in list l1
       with items in list l2'''
    l = []
    for i in l1:
        for j in l2:
            l.append(i*j)
    return l
```

5.8 As discussed in the problem statement, in the first pass you need to successively compare items at indexes 0 and 1, 1 and 2, 2 and 3, ..., up to `len(lst)-2` and `len(lst)-1`. We can do this by generating the sequence of integers from 0 up to but not including `len(lst)-1`.

In the second pass, we can stop the pairwise comparisons with the pair of items at indexes `len(lst)-3` and `len(lst)-2`, so the indexes we need in the second pass go from 0 up to but not including `len(lst)-2`. This suggests that we should use the outer loop to generate the upper bounds `len(lst)-1` for pass 1, `len(lst)-2` for pass 2, down to 1 (when the final comparison between the first two list items is made).

The inner loop implements a pass that compares adjacent list items up to items at indexes `i-1` and `i` and swaps improperly ordered items:

```python
def bubblesort(lst):
    'sorts list lst in nondecreasing order'
    for i in range(len(lst)-1, 0, -1):
        # perform pass that ends at
        # i = len(lst)-1, len(lst)-2, ..., 1
        for j in range(i):
            # compare items at index j and j+1
            # for every j = 0, 1, ..., i-1
            if lst[j] > lst[j+1]:
                # swap numbers at index j and j+1
                lst[j], lst[j+1] = lst[j+1], lst[j]
```

5.9 We use the nested loop pattern to generate all pairs of column and row indexes and add up the corresponding entries:

```python
def add2D(t1, t2):
    '''t1 and t2 are 2D lists with the same number of rows and
       same number of equal sized columns

       add2D increments every item t1[i][j] by t2[i][j]'''
    nrows = len(t1)                     # number of rows
    ncols = len(t1[0])                  # number of columns
    for i in range(nrows):              # for every row index i
        for j in range(ncols):              # for every column index j
            t1[i][j] += t2[i][j]
```

5.10 First note that the number of years required for an investment to double in value does not depend on the amount invested. So we can assume the original investment is $100. We use a `while` loop to add the yearly interest to the investment x. The `while` loop condition will check whether x < 200. What the problem asks is how many times we have executed the `while` loop. To count it, we use the counter loop pattern:

```python
def interest(rate):
    '''returns the number of years for investment
       to double for the given rate'''
    amount = 100                    # initial account balance
    count = 0
    while amount < 200:
        # while investment not doubled in value
        count += 1                  # add one more year
        amount += amount*rate       # add interest
    return count
```

5.11 We start by assigning the first approximation (1) to prev and the second (2) to current. The while loop condition is then current - prev > error. If the condition is true, then we need to generate new values for prev and current. The value of current becomes previous, and the new current value is then previous + 1/factorial(???). What should ??? be? In the first iteration, it should be 2 because the third approximation is the value of the second $+\frac{1}{2!}$. In the next iteration, it should be 3, then 4, and so on. We obtain this solution:

```
def approxE(error):
    'returns approximation of e within error'
    prev = 1                        # approximation 0
    current = 2                     # approximation 1
    i = 2                           # index of next approximation
    while current-prev > error:
        # while difference between current and previous
        # approximation is too large
                                    # current approximation
        prev = current             # becomes previous
                                    # compute new approximation
        current = prev + 1/factorial(i)  # based on index i
        i += 1                      # index of next approximation
    return current
```

Exercises

5.12 Implement function test() that takes as input one integer and prints 'Negative', 'Zero', or 'Positive' depending on its value.

```
>>> test(-3)
Negative
>>> test(0)
Zero
>>> test(3)
Positive
```

5.13 Read every exercise 5.14 to 5.22 and decide what loop pattern should be used in each.

5.14 Write function mult3() that takes as input a list of integers and prints only the multiples of 3, one per line.

```
>>> mult3([3, 1, 6, 2, 3, 9, 7, 9, 5, 4, 5])
3
6
3
9
9
```

5.15 Implement the function vowels() that takes as input a string and prints the indexes of all vowels in the string. *Hint:* A vowel can be defined as any character in string 'aeiouAEIOU'

```
>>> vowels('Hello WORLD')
1
4
7
```

5.16 Implement function `indexes()` that takes as input a word (as a string) and a one-character letter (as a string) and returns a list of indexes at which the letter occurs in the word.

```
>>> indexes('mississippi', 's')
[2, 3, 5, 6]
>>> indexes('mississippi', 'i')
[1, 4, 7, 10]
>>> indexes('mississippi', 'a')
[]
```

5.17 Write function `doubles()` that takes as input a list of integers and outputs the integers in the list that are exactly twice the previous integer in the list, one per line.

```
>>> doubles([3, 0, 1, 2, 3, 6, 2, 4, 5, 6, 5])
2
6
4
```

5.18 Implement function `four_letter()` that takes as input a list of words (i.e., strings) and returns the sublist of all four letter words in the list.

```
>>> four_letter(['dog', 'letter', 'stop', 'door', 'bus', 'dust'])
['stop', 'door', 'dust']
```

5.19 Write a function `inBoth()` that takes two lists and returns `True` if there is an item that is common to both lists and `False` otherwise.

```
>>> inBoth([3, 2, 5, 4, 7], [9, 0, 1, 3])
True
```

5.20 Write a function `intersect()` that takes two lists, each containing no duplicate values, and returns a list containing values that are present in both lists (i.e., the intersection of the two input lists).

```
>>> intersect([3, 5, 1, 7, 9], [4, 2, 6, 3, 9])
[3, 9]
```

5.21 Implement the function `pair()` that takes as input two lists of integers and one integer n and prints the pairs of integers, one from the first input list and the other from the second input list, that add up to n. Each pair should be printed.

```
>>> pair([2, 3, 4], [5, 7, 9, 12], 9)
2 7
4 5
```

5.22 Implement the function `pairSum()` that takes as input a list of distinct integers `lst` and an integer n, and prints the indexes of all pairs of values in `lst` that sum up to n.

```
>>> pairSum([7, 8, 5, 3, 4, 6], 11)
0 4
1 3
2 5
```

Problems

5.23 Write function `pay()` that takes as input an hourly wage and the number of hours an employee worked in the last week. The function should compute and return the employee's pay. Overtime work should be paid in this way: Any hours beyond 40 but less than or equal 60 should be paid at 1.5 times the regular hourly wage. Any hours beyond 60 should be paid at 2 times the regular hourly wage.

```
>>> pay(10, 35)
350
>>> pay(10, 45)
475.0
>>> pay(10, 61)
720.0
```

5.24 Write function `case()` that takes a string as input and returns `'capitalized'`, `'not capitalized'`, or `'unknown'`, depending on whether the string starts with an uppercase letter, lowercase letter, or something other than a letter in the English alphabet, respectively.

```
>>> case('Android')
'capitalized'
>>> case('3M')
'unknown'
```

5.25 Implement function `leap()` that takes one input argument—a year—and returns `True` if the year is a leap year and `False` otherwise. (A year is a leap year if it is divisible by 4 but not by 100, unless it is divisible by 400 in which case it is a leap year. For example, 1700, 1800 and 1900 are not leap years but 1600 and 2000 are.)

```
>>> leap(2008)
True
>>> leap(1900)
False
>>> leap(2000)
True
```

5.26 Rock, Paper, Scissors is a two-player game in which each player chooses one of three items. If both players choose the same item, the game is tied. Otherwise, the rules that determine the winner are:

 (a) Rock always beats Scissors (Rock crushes Scissors)

 (b) Scissors always beats Paper (Scissors cut Paper)

 (c) Paper always beats Rock (Paper covers Rock)

Implement function `rps()` that takes the choice (`'R'`, `'P'`, or `'S'`) of player 1 and the choice of player 2, and returns −1 if player 1 wins, 1 if player 2 wins, or 0 if there is a tie.

```
>>> rps('R', 'P')
1
>>> rps('R', 'S')
-1
>>> rps('S', 'S')
0
```

5.27 Write function `letter2number()` that takes as input a letter grade (A, B, C, D, F, possibly with a − or +) and returns the corresponding number grade. The numeric values for A, B, C, D, and F are 4, 3, 2, 1, 0. A + increases the number grade value by 0.3 and a − decreases it by 0.3.

```
>>> letter2number('A-')
3.7
>>> letter2number('B+')
3.3
>>> letter2number('D')
1.0
```

5.28 Write function `geometric()` that takes a list of integers as input and returns True if the integers in the list form a geometric sequence. A sequence $a_0, a_1, a_2, a_3, a_4, \ldots, a_n - 2, a_n - 1$ is a geometric sequence if the ratios $a_1/a_0, a_2/a_1, a_3/a_2, a_4/a_3, \ldots, a_{n-1}/a_{n-2}$ are all equal.

```
>>> geometric([2, 4, 8, 16, 32, 64, 128, 256])
True
>>> geometric([2, 4, 6, 8])
False
```

5.29 Write function `lastfirst()` that takes one argument—a list of strings of the format <LastName, FirstName>—and returns a list consisting two lists:

(a) A list of all the first names

(b) A list of all the last names

```
>>> lastfirst(['Gerber, Len', 'Fox, Kate', 'Dunn, Bob'])
[['Len', 'Kate', 'Bob'], ['Gerber', 'Fox', 'Dunn']]
```

5.30 Develop the function `many()` that takes as input the name of a file in the current directory (as a string) and outputs the number of words of length 1, 2, 3, and 4. Test your function on file sample.txt.

File: sample.txt

```
>>> many('sample.txt')
Words of length 1 : 2
Words of length 2 : 5
Words of length 3 : 1
Words of length 4 : 10
```

5.31 Write a function `subsetSum()` that takes as input a list of positive numbers and a positive number `target`. Your function should return True if there are three numbers in the list that add up to `target`. For example, if the input list is [5, 4, 10, 20, 15, 19] and `target` is 38, then True should be returned since $4 + 15 + 19 = 38$. However, if the input list is the same but the target value is 10, then the returned value should be False because 10 is not the sum of any three numbers in the given list.

```
>>> subsetSum([5, 4, 10, 20, 15, 19], 38)
True
>>> subsetSum([5, 4, 10, 20, 15, 19], 10)
False
```

5.32 Implement function `fib()` that takes a nonnegative integer n as input and returns the nth Fibonacci number.

```
>>> fib(0)
1
>>> fib(4)
5
>>> fib(8)
34
```

5.33 Implement a function `mystery()` that takes as input a positive integer n and answers this question: How many times can n be halved (using integer division) before reaching 1? This value should returned.

```
>>> mystery(4)
2
>>> mystery(11)
3
>>> mystery(25)
4
```

5.34 Write a function `statement()` that takes as input a list of floating-point numbers, with positive numbers representing deposits to and negative numbers representing withdrawals from a bank account. Your function should return a list of two floating-point numbers; the first will be the sum of the deposits, and the second (a negative number) will be the sum of the withdrawals.

```
>>> statement([30.95, -15.67, 45.56, -55.00, 43.78])
[120.29, -70.67]
```

5.35 Implement function `pixels()` that takes as input a two-dimensional list of nonnegative integer entries (representing the values of pixels of an image) and returns the number of entries that are positive (i.e., the number of pixels that are not dark). Your function should work on two-dimensional lists of any size.

```
>>> l = [[0, 156, 0, 0], [34, 0, 0, 0], [23, 123, 0, 34]]
>>> pixels(l)
5
>>> l = [[123, 56, 255], [34, 0, 0], [23, 123, 0], [3, 0, 0]]
>>> pixels(l)
7
```

5.36 Implement function `prime()` that takes a positive integer as input and returns `True` if it is a prime number and `False` otherwise.

```
>>> prime(2)
True
>>> prime(17)
True
>>> prime(21)
False
```

5.37 Write function `mssl()` (minimum sum sublist) that takes as input a list of integers. It then computes and returns the sum of the maximum sum sublist of the input list. The maximum sum sublist is a sublist (slice) of the input list whose sum of entries is largest. The empty sublist is defined to have sum 0. For example, the maximum sum sublist of the list

    [4, -2, -8, 5, -2, 7, 7, 2, -6, 5]

is [5, -2, 7, 7, 2] and the sum of its entries is 19.

```
>>> l = [4, -2, -8, 5, -2, 7, 7, 2, -6, 5]
>>> mssl(l)
19
>>> mssl([3,4,5])
12
>>> mssl([-2,-3,-5])
0
```

In the last example, the maximum sum sublist is the empty sublist because all list items are negative.

5.38 Write function `collatz()` that takes a positive integer x as input and prints the Collatz sequence starting at x. A Collatz sequence is obtained by repeatedly applying this rule to the previous number x in the sequence:

$$x = \begin{cases} x/2 & \text{if } x \text{ is even} \\ 3x+1 & \text{if } x \text{ is odd.} \end{cases}$$

Your function should stop when the sequence gets to number 1. *Note:* It is an open question whether the Collatz sequence of every positive integer always ends at 1.

```
>>> collatz(10)
10
5
16
8
4
2
1
```

5.39 Write function `exclamation()` that takes as input a string and returns it with this modification: Every vowel is replaced by four consecutive copies of itself and an exclamation mark (!) is added at the end.

```
>>> exclamation('argh')
'aaaargh!'
>>> exclamation('hello')
'heeeelloooo!'
```

5.40 The constant π is an irrational number with value approximately 3.1415928 . . . The precise value of π is equal to this infinite sum:

$$\pi = 4/1 - 4/3 + 4/5 - 4/7 + 4/9 - 4/11 + \ldots$$

We can get a good approximation of π by computing the sum of the first few terms. Write a function `approxPi()` that takes as input a float-value `error` and approximates constant π within `error` by computing the preceding sum, term by term, until the difference between the current sum and the previous sum (with one less term) is no greater than `error`. The function should return the new sum.

```
>>> approxPi(0.01)
3.1465677471829556
>>> approxPi(0.0000001)
3.1415927035898146
```

5.41 A polynomial of degree n with coefficients $a_0, a_1, a_2, a_3, \ldots, a_n$ is the function

$$p(x) = a_0 + a_1 x + a_2 x^2 + a_3 * x^3 + \ldots + a_n * x^n$$

This function can be evaluated at different values of x. For example, if $p(x) = 1 + 2x + x^2$, then $p(2) = 1 + 2*2 + 2^2 = 9$. If $p(x) = 1 + x^2 + x^4$, then $p(2) = 21$ and $p(3) = 91$.

Write a function `poly()` that takes as input a list of coefficients $a_0, a_1, a_2, a_3, \ldots, a_n$ of a polynomial $p(x)$ and a value x. The function will return $p(x)$, which is the value of the polynomial when evaluated at x. Note that the usage below is for the three examples shown.

```
>>> poly([1, 2, 1], 2)
9
>>> poly([1, 0, 1, 0, 1], 2)
21
>>> poly([1, 0, 1, 0, 1], 3)
91
```

5.42 Implement function `primeFac()` that takes as input a positive integer n and returns a list containing all the numbers in the prime factorization of n. (The prime factorization of a positive integer n is the unique list of prime numbers whose product is n.)

```
>>> primeFac(5)
[5]
>>> primeFac(72)
[2, 2, 2, 3, 3]
```

5.43 Implement function `evenrow()` that takes a two-dimensional list of integers and returns `True` if each row of the table sums up to an even number and `False` otherwise (i.e., if some row sums up to an odd number).

```
>>> evenrow([[1, 3], [2, 4], [0, 6]])
True
>>> evenrow([[1, 3, 2], [3, 4, 7], [0, 6, 2]])
True
>>> evenrow([[1, 3, 2], [3, 4, 7], [0, 5, 2]])
False
```

5.44 A substitution cipher for the digits 0, 1, 2, 3, . . . , 9 substitutes each digit in 0, 1, 2, 3, . . . , 9 with another digit in 0, 1, 2, 3, . . . , 9. It can be represented as a 10-digit string specifying how each digit in 0, 1, 2, 3, . . . , 9 is substituted. For example, the 10-digit string '3941068257' specifies a substitution cipher in which digit 0 is substituted with digit 3, 1 with 9, 2 with 4, and so on. To encrypt a nonnegative integer, substitute each of its digits with the digit specified by the encryption key.

Implement function `cipher()` that takes as input a 10-digit string key and a digit string (i.e., the clear text to be encrypted) and returns the encryption of the clear text.

```
>>> encrypt('3941068257', '132')
'914'
>>> encrypt('3941068257', '111')
'999'
```

5.45 The function `avgavg()` takes as input a list whose items are lists of three numbers. Each three-number list represents the three grades a particular student received for a course. For example, here is an input list for a class of four students:

```
[[95,92,86], [66,75,54],[89, 72,100],[34,0,0]]
```

The function `avgavg()` should print, on the screen, two lines. The first line will contain a list containing every student's average grade. The second line will contain just one number: the average class grade, defined as the average of all student average grades.

```
>>> avgavg([[95, 92, 86], [66, 75, 54],[89, 72, 100], [34, 0, 0]])
[91.0, 65.0, 87.0, 11.333333333333334]
63.5833333333
```

5.46 An inversion in a sequence is a pair of entries that are out of order. For example, the characters F and D form an inversion in string 'ABBFHDL' because F appears before D; so do characters H and D. The total number of inversions in a sequence (i.e., the number of pairs that are out of order) is a measure of how *unsorted* the sequence is. The total number of inversions in 'ABBFHDL' is 2. Implement function `inversions()` that takes a sequence (i.e., a string) of uppercase characters A through Z and returns the number of inversions in the sequence.

```
>>> inversions('ABBFHDL')
2
>>> inversions('ABCD')
0
>>> inversions('DCBA')
6
```

5.47 Write function `d2x()` that takes as input a nonnegative integer n (in the standard decimal representation) and an integer x between 2 and 9 and returns a string of digits that represents the base-x representation of n.

```
>>> d2x(10, 2)
'1010'
>>> d2x(10, 3)
'101'
>>> d2x(10, 8)
'12'
```

5.48 Let `list1` and `list2` be two lists of integers. We say that `list1` is a sublist of `list2` if the elements in `list1` appear in `list2` in the same order as they appear in `list1`, but not necessarily consecutively. For example, if `list1` is defined as

```
[15, 1, 100]
```

and `list2` is defined as

```
[20, 15, 30, 50, 1, 100]
```

then `list1` is a sublist of `list2` because the numbers in `list1` (15, 1, and 100) appear in `list2` in the same order. However, list

```
[15, 50, 20]
```

is not a sublist of `list2`.

Implement function `sublist()` that takes as input lists `list1` and `list2` and returns True if `list1` is a sublist of `list2`, and False otherwise.

```
>>> sublist([15, 1, 100], [20, 15, 30, 50, 1, 100])
True
>>> sublist([15, 50, 20], [20, 15, 30, 50, 1, 100])
False
```

5.49 The Heron method is a method the ancient Greeks used to compute the square root of a number n. The method generates a sequence of numbers that represent better and better approximations for $\sqrt{n}$. The first number in the sequence is an arbitrary guess; every other number in the sequence is obtained from the previous number *prev* using the formula

$$\frac{1}{2}\left(\text{prev} + \frac{n}{\text{prev}}\right)$$

Write function `heron()` that takes as input two numbers: n and *error*. The function should start with an initial guess of 1.0 for $\sqrt{n}$ and then repeatedly generate better approximations until the difference (more precisely, the absolute value of the difference) between successive approximations is at most *error*.

```
>>> heron(4.0, 0.5)
2.05
>>> heron(4.0, 0.1)
2.000609756097561
```

Containers and Randomness

6.1 Dictionaries   166

6.2 Sets   177

6.3 Character Encodings and Strings   181

6.4 Module `random`   186

E-Book Case Study: Games of Chance   190

Chapter Summary   190

Solutions to Practice Problems   190

Exercises   194

Problems   195

THE FOCUS OF THIS CHAPTER is on the *other* built-in container classes available in Python. While lists are useful general-purpose containers, there are situations when they are awkward or inefficient to use. For this reason, Python provides other built-in container classes.

In a dictionary container, values stored in the container can be indexed using user-specified indexes we call *keys*. Dictionaries have many different uses, including counting, and they are general-purpose containers just as list containers are. In addition to dictionaries, we also explain when and how to use the `set` built-in container classes.

We also come back to strings one more time and look at them as containers of characters. In today's interconnected world, text is created in one place and read in another, and computers have to be able to deal with encoding and decoding characters from different writing systems. We introduce Unicode as the current standard for encoding characters.

In order to introduce a whole new class of problems and applications, including computer games, we end this chapter with a discussion of how to generate "random" numbers.

6.1 Dictionaries

We start the chapter by introducing the very important dictionary container built-in type.

User-Defined Indexes as Motivation for Dictionaries

Suppose we need to somehow store employee records for a company with 50,000 employees. Ideally, we would like to be able to access each employee's record using only the employee's Social Security Number (SSN) or ID number, like this:

```
>>> employee[987654321]
['Yu', 'Tsun']
>>> employee[864209753]
['Anna', 'Karenina']
>>> employee[100010010]
['Hans', 'Castorp']
```

At index 987654321 of the container named `employee` is stored the first and last name of the employee with SSN 987-65-4321, Yu Tsun. The first and last name are stored in a list, which could contain additional information, such as address, date of birth, position, and so on. At index 864209753 and 100010010 will be stored the records for `['Anna', 'Karenina']` and `['Hans', 'Castorp']`. In general, stored at index i will be the record (first and last name) of the employee with SSN i.

If `employee` were a `list`, it would have to be a very big list. It would need to be larger than the integer value of the largest employee SSN. Since SSNs are 9-digit numbers, `employee` would need to be as large as $1,000,000,000$. That's big. Even if our system can accommodate a list so large, it would be a huge waste: Most of the list will be empty. Only $50,000$ list positions will be used. There is one more problem with lists: SSNs are not really integer values since they are typically denoted using dashes, such as 987-65-4321, and can start with a 0, such as 012-34-5678. Values like 987-65-4321 and 012-34-5678 are better represented as string values `'012-34-5678'` or `'987-65-4321'`.

The issue is that list items are meant to be accessed using an integer index that represents the item's position in a collection. What we want is something else: We would like to access items using "user-defined indexes," such as `'012-34-5678'` or `'987-65-4321'`, as illustrated in Figure 6.1.

Figure 6.1 Motivation for a dictionary. A dictionary is a container that stores items that are accessible using "user-specified" indexes.

index	'987-65-4321'	'864-20-9753'	'100-01-0010'
item	['Anna','Karenina']	['Yu','Tsun']	['Hans','Castorp']

Python has a built-in container type called a *dictionary* that enables us to use "user-defined indexes". Here is how we can define a dictionary named `employee` that behaves as we would like:

```
>>> employee = {
        '864-20-9753': ['Anna', 'Karenina'],
        '987-65-4321': ['Yu', 'Tsun'],
        '100-01-0010': ['Hans', 'Castorp']}
```

We wrote the assignment statement using multiple lines to clearly emphasize that "index" `'864-20-9753'` corresponds to value `['Anna', 'Karenina']`, index `'987-65-4321'` corresponds to value `['Yu', 'Tsun']`, and so on. Let's check that the dictionary `employee` works as we want:

```
>>> employee['987-65-4321']
['Yu', 'Tsun']
>>> employee['864-20-9753']
['Anna', 'Karenina']
```

The dictionary `employee` differs from a list in that an item in a dictionary is accessed using a user-specified "index" rather than the index representing the items position in the container. We discuss this more precisely next.

Dictionary Class Properties

The Python dictionary type, denoted `dict`, is a container type, just like `list` and `str`. A dictionary contains *(key, value)* pairs. The general format of the expression that evaluates to a dictionary object is:

```
{<key 1>:<value 1>, <key 2>:<value 2>, ..., <key i>:<value i>}
```

This expression defines a dictionary containing i *key:value pairs*. The *key* and the *value* are both objects. The *key* is the "index" that is used to access the *value*. So, in our dictionary `employee`, `'100-01-0010'` is the key and `['Hans', 'Castorp']` is the value.

The (key, value) pairs in a dictionary expression are separated by commas and enclosed in curly braces (as opposed to square brackets, `[]`, used for lists.) The key and value in each (key, value) pair are separated by a colon (`:`) with the key being to the left and the value to the right of the colon. Keys can be of any type as long as the type is immutable. So string and number objects can be keys, whereas objects of type `list` cannot. The value can be of any type.

We often say that a key *maps* to its value or is the index of the value. Because dictionaries can be viewed as a mapping from keys to values, they are often referred to as *maps*. For example, here is a dictionary mapping day abbreviations `'Mo'`, `'Tu'`, `'We'`, and `'Th'` (the keys) to the corresponding days `'Monday'`, `'Tuesday'`, `'Wednesday'`, and `'Thursday'` (the values):

```
>>> days = {'Mo':'Monday', 'Tu':'Tuesday', 'We':'Wednesday',
            'Th':'Thursday'}
```

The variable `days` refers to a dictionary, illustrated in Figure 6.2, with four (key, value) pairs. The (key, value) pair `'Mo':'Monday'` has key `'Mo'` and value `'Monday'`, the (key, value) pair `'Tu':'Tuesday'` has key `'Tu'` and value `'Tuesday'`, etc.

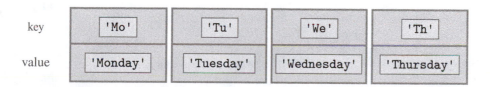

Figure 6.2 Dictionary `days`. The dictionary maps string keys `'Mo'`, `'Tu'`, `'We'`, and `'Th'` to string values `'Monday'`, `'Tuesday'`, and so on.

Values in the dictionary are accessed by key, not index (or offset). To access value `'Wednesday'` in dictionary `days`, we use key `'We'`

```
>>> days['We']
'Wednesday'
```

and not index 2

```
>>> days[2]
Traceback (most recent call last):
  File "<pyshell#27>", line 1, in <module>
    days[2]
KeyError: 2
```

The KeyError exception tells us that we are using an illegal, in this case undefined, key.

The (key, value) pairs in the dictionary are not ordered, and no ordering assumption can be made. For example, we could define a dictionary d as:

```
>>> d = {'b':23, 'a':34, 'c':12}
```

However, when we evaluate d, we may not get the (key, value) pairs in the order in which they were defined:

```
>>> d
{'a': 34, 'c': 12, 'b': 23}
```

Dictionaries are mutable, like lists. A dictionary can be modified to contain a new (key, value) pair:

```
>>> days['Fr'] = 'friday'
>>> days
{'Fr': 'friday', 'Mo': 'Monday', 'Tu': 'Tuesday',
'We': 'Wednesday', 'Th': 'Thursday'}
```

This implies that dictionaries have dynamic size. The dictionary can also be modified so that an existing key refers to a new value:

```
>>> days['Fr'] = 'Friday'
>>> days
{'Fr': 'Friday', 'Mo': 'Monday', 'Tu': 'Tuesday',
'We': 'Wednesday', 'Th': 'Thursday'}
```

An empty dictionary can be defined using the default dict() constructor or simply as:

```
>>> d = {}
```

Practice Problem 6.1

Write a function birthState() that takes as input the full name of a recent U.S. president (as a string) and returns his birth state. You should use this dictionary to store the birth state for each recent president:

```
{'Barack Hussein Obama II':'Hawaii',
 'George Walker Bush':'Connecticut',
 'William Jefferson Clinton':'Arkansas',
 'George Herbert Walker Bush':'Massachussetts',
 'Ronald Wilson Reagan':'Illinois',
 'James Earl Carter, Jr':'Georgia'}

>>> birthState('Ronald Wilson Reagan')
'Illinois'
```

Dictionary Operators

The dictionary class supports some of the same operators that the list class supports. We already saw that the indexing operator (`[]`) can be used to access a value using the key as the index:

```
>>> days['Fr']
'Friday'
```

The indexing operator can also be used to change the value corresponding to a key or to add a new (key, value) pair to the dictionary:

```
>>> days
{'Fr': 'Friday', 'Mo': 'Monday', 'Tu': 'Tuesday',
'We': 'Wednesday', 'Th': 'Thursday'}
>>> days['Sa'] = 'Sat'
>>> days
{'Fr': 'Friday', 'Mo': 'Monday', 'Tu': 'Tuesday',
'We': 'Wednesday', 'Th': 'Thursday', 'Sa': 'Sat'}
```

The length of a dictionary (i.e., the number of (key, value) pairs in it) can be obtained using the `len` function:

```
>>> len(days)
6
```

The `in` and `not in` operators are used to check whether an object is a key in the dictionary:

```
>>> 'Fr' in days
True
>>> 'Su' in days
False
>>> 'Su' not in days
True
```

Table 6.1 shows some of the operators that can be used with dictionaries.

Operation	Explanation
k in d	True if k is a key in dictionary d, else False
k not in d	False if k is a key in dictionary d, else True
d[k]	Value corresponding to key k in dictionary d
len(d)	Number of (key, value) pairs in dictionary d

Table 6.1 **Class** `dict` **operators.** The usage and explanation for commonly used dictionary operators are shown.

There are operators that the `list` class supports but the class `dict` does not. For example, the indexing operator `[]` cannot be used to get a *slice* of a dictionary. This makes sense: A slice implies an order, and there is no order in a dictionary. Also not supported are operators + and *, among others.

Implement function `rlookup()` that provides the reverse lookup feature of a phone book. Your function takes, as input, a dictionary representing a phone book. In the dictionary, phone numbers (keys) are mapped to individuals (values). Your function should provide a simple user interface through which a user can enter a phone number and obtain the first and last name of the individual assigned that number.

Practice Problem 6.2

```
>>> rphonebook = {'(123)456-78-90':['Anna','Karenina'],
                  '(901)234-56-78':['Yu', 'Tsun'],
                  '(321)908-76-54':['Hans', 'Castorp']}
>>> rlookup(rphonebook)
Enter phone number in the format (xxx)xxx-xx-xx: (123)456-78-90
('Anna', 'Karenina')
Enter phone number in the format (xxx)xxx-xx-xx: (453)454-55-00
The number you entered is not in use.
Enter phone number in the format (xxx)xxx-xx-xx:
```

Dictionary Methods

While the `list` and `dict` class share quite a few *operators*, there is only one *method* that they share: `pop()`. This method takes a key, and if the key is in the dictionary, it removes the associated (key, value) pair from the dictionary and returns the value:

```
>>> days
{'Fr': 'Friday', 'Mo': 'Monday', 'Tu': 'Tuesday',
'We': 'Wednesday', 'Th': 'Thursday', 'Sa': 'Sat'}
>>> days.pop('Tu')
'Tuesday'
>>> days.pop('Fr')
'Friday'
>>> days
{'Mo': 'Monday', 'We': 'Wednesday', 'Th': 'Thursday',
'Sa': 'Sat'}
```

We now introduce some more dictionary methods. When dictionary d1 calls method `update()` with input argument dictionary d2, all the (key, value) pairs of d2 are added to d1, possibly writing over (key, value) pairs of d1. For example, suppose we have a dictionary of our favorite days of the week:

```
>>> favorites = {'Th':'Thursday', 'Fr':'Friday','Sa':'Saturday'}
```

We can add those days to our `days` dictionary:

```
>>> days.update(favorites)
>>> days
{'Fr': 'Friday', 'Mo': 'Monday', 'We': 'Wednesday',
'Th': 'Thursday', 'Sa': 'Saturday'}
```

The (key, value) pair `'Fr':'Friday'` has been added to days and the (key, value) pair `'Sa':'Saturday'` has replaced the pair `'Sa':'Sat'`, originally in dictionary days. Note that only one copy of (key, value) pair `'Th':'Thursday'` can be in the dictionary.

Particularly useful dictionary methods are `keys()`, `values()`, and `items()`: They return the keys, values, and (key, value) pairs, respectively, in the dictionary. To illustrate how to use these methods, we use dictionary days defined as:

```
>>> days
{'Fr': 'Friday', 'Mo': 'Monday', 'We': 'Wednesday',
'Th': 'Thursday', 'Sa': 'Saturday'}
```

The method `keys()` returns the keys of the dictionary:

```
>>> keys = days.keys()
>>> keys
dict_keys(['Fr', 'Mo', 'We', 'Th', 'Sa'])
```

The container object returned by method `keys()` is not a list. Let's check its type:

```
>>> type(days.keys())
<class 'dict_keys'>
```

OK, it's a type we have not seen before. Do we really *have to* learn everything there is to know about this new type? At this point, not necessarily. We only really need to understand its usage. So, how is the object returned by the `keys()` method used? It is typically used to iterate over the keys of the dictionary, for example:

```
>>> for key in days.keys():
        print(key, end=' ')


Fr Mo We Th Sa
```

Thus, the `dict_keys` class supports iteration. In fact, when we iterate directly over a dictionary, as in:

```
>>> for key in days:
        print(key, end=' ')


Fr Mo We Th Sa
```

the Python interpreter translates the statement `for key in days` to the statement `for key in days.keys()` before executing it.

Table 6.2 lists some of the commonly used methods that the dictionary class supports; as usual, you can learn more by looking at the online documentation or by typing

```
>>> help(dict)
...
```

in the interpreter shell. The dictionary methods `values()` and `items()` shown in Table 6.2 also return objects that we can iterate over. The method `values()` is typically used to iterate over the values of a dictionary:

```
>>> for value in days.values():
        print(value, end=', ')


Friday, Monday, Wednesday, Thursday, Saturday,
```

Operation	Explanation
`d.items()`	Returns a view of the (key, value) pairs in d as tuples
`d.get(k)`	Returns the value of key k, equivalent to d[k]
`d.keys()`	Returns a view of the keys of d
`d.pop(k)`	Removes the (key, value) pair with key k from d and returns the value
`d.update(d2)`	Adds the (key, value) pairs of dictionary d2 to d
`d.values()`	Returns a view of the values of d

Table 6.2 **Methods of the** dict **class.** Listed are some commonly used methods of the dictionary class. d refers to a dictionary.

The method `items()` returns a container that contains `tuple` objects, one for each (key, value) pair:

```
>>> days.items()
dict_items([('We', 'Wednesday'), ('Mo', 'Monday'),
            ('Th', 'Thursday'), ('Tu', 'Tuesday')])
```

This method is typically used to iterate over the (key, value) pairs of the dictionary:

```
>>> for item in days.items():
        print(item, end='; ')

('Fr', 'Friday'); ('Mo', 'Monday'); ('We', 'Wednesday');
('Th', 'Thursday'); ('Sa', 'Saturday');
```

DETOUR

View Objects

The objects returned by methods `keys()`, `values()`, and `items()` are referred to as *view objects*. View objects provide a *dynamic view* of the dictionary's keys, values, and (key, value) pairs, respectively. What this means is that when the dictionary changes, the view reflects these changes.

For example, suppose we define dictionary days and view keys as:

```
>>> days
{'Fr': 'Friday', 'Mo': 'Monday', 'We': 'Wednesday',
 'Th': 'Thursday', 'Sa': 'Saturday'}
>>> keys = days.keys()
>>> keys
dict_keys(['Fr', 'Mo', 'We', 'Th', 'Sa'])
```

The name keys refers to a view of the keys of dictionary days. Now let's delete a key (and associated value) in dictionary days:

```
>>> del(days['Mo'])
>>> days
{'Fr': 'Friday', 'We': 'Wednesday', 'Th': 'Thursday',
 'Sa': 'Saturday'}
```

Note that the view keys has changed as well:

```
>>> keys
dict_keys(['Fr', 'We', 'Th', 'Sa'])
```

The container objects returned by `keys()`, `value()`, and `items()` have types that also support various setlike operations, like union and intersection. These operations allow us to, say, combine the keys of two dictionaries or find the values common to both dictionaries. We discuss those operations in more detail in Section 6.2, when we cover the `set` built-in type.

A Dictionary as a Substitute for the Multiway `if` Statement

When we introduced dictionaries at the start of this section, our motivation was the need for a container with user-defined indexes. We now show alternate uses for dictionaries.

Suppose we would like to develop a small function, named `complete()`, that takes the abbreviation of a day of week, such as `'Tu'`, and returns the corresponding day, which for input `'Tu'` would be `'Tuesday'`:

```
>>> complete('Tu')
'Tuesday'
```

One way to implement the function would be to use a multiway `if` statement:

```
def complete(abbreviation):
    'returns day of the week corresponding to abbreviation'
    if abbreviation == 'Mo':
        return 'Monday'
    elif abbreviation == 'Tu':
        return 'Tuesday'
    elif ...
        ...
    else: # abbreviation must be Su
        return 'Sunday'
```

We omit part of the implementation, because it is long, because you should be able to finish it, and also because it is tedious to read and write. We also omit it because it is not an effective way to implement the function.

The main problem with the implementation is that it is simply overkill to use a seven-way `if` statement to implement what is really a "mapping" from day abbreviations to the corresponding days. We now know how to implement such a mapping using a dictionary. Here is a better implementation of function `complete()`:

```
1  def complete(abbreviation):
2      'returns day of the week corresponding to abbreviation'
3
4      days = {'Mo': 'Monday', 'Tu':'Tuesday', 'We': 'Wednesday',
5              'Th': 'Thursday', 'Fr': 'Friday', 'Sa': 'Saturday',
6              'Su':'Sunday'}
7
8      return days[abbreviation]
```

Module: ch6.py

Dictionary as a Collection of Counters

An important application of the dictionary type is its use in computing the number of occurrences of "things" in a larger set. A search engine, for example, may need to compute the frequency of each word in a web page in order to calculate its relevance with respect to search engine queries.

On a smaller scale, suppose that we would like to count the frequency of each name in a list of student names such as:

```
>>> students = ['Cindy', 'John', 'Cindy', 'Adam', 'Adam',
                'Jimmy', 'Joan', 'Cindy', 'Joan']
```

Figure 6.3 Dynamically created counters.
Counters are created dynamically, in the course of iterating over the list `students`. When the first item, `'Cindy'`, is visited, a counter for string `'Cindy'` is created. When the second item, `'John'`, is visited, a counter for `'John'` is created. When the third item, `'Cindy'`, is visited, the counter corresponding to `'Cindy'` is incremented.

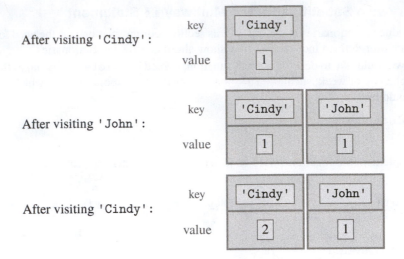

More precisely, we would like to implement a function `frequency()` that takes a list such as `students` as input and computes the number of occurrences of each distinct list item.

As usual, there are different ways to implement function `frequency()`. However, the best way is to have a counter for each distinct item in the list and then iterate over the items in the list: For each visited item, the corresponding counter is incremented. In order for this to work, we need to answer three questions:

1. How do we know how many counters we need?
2. How do we store all the counters?
3. How do we associate a counter with a list item?

The answer to the first question is not to worry about how many counters we need but to create them dynamically, as needed. In other words, we create a counter for an item only when, in the course of iterating over the list, we encounter the item for the first time. Figure 6.3 illustrates the states of the counters after visiting the first, second, and third name in list `students`.

Practice Problem 6.3

Draw the state of the counters after visiting the next three names in list `students`. Make a drawing after visiting `'Adam'`, another after visiting the second `'Adam'`, and still another after visiting `'Jimmy'` using Figure 6.3 as your model.

Figure 6.3 gives us an insight on how to answer the second question: We can use a dictionary to store the counters. Each item counter will be a value in the dictionary, and the item itself will be the key corresponding to the value. For example, the string `'Cindy'` would be the key and the corresponding value would be its counter. The dictionary mapping of keys to values also answers the third question.

Now we can also decide what the function `frequency()` should return: a dictionary mapping each distinct item in the list to the number of times it occurs in the list. Here is an example usage of this function:

```
>>> students = ['Cindy', 'John', 'Cindy', 'Adam', 'Adam',
                'Jimmy', 'Joan', 'Cindy', 'Joan']
```

```
>>> frequency(students)
{'John': 1, 'Joan': 2, 'Adam': 2, 'Cindy': 3, 'Jimmy': 1}
```

In the dictionary returned by the call `frequency(students)`, shown in Figure 6.4, the keys are the distinct names in the list `students` and the values are the corresponding frequencies: so `'John'` occurs once, `'Joan'` occurs twice, and so on.

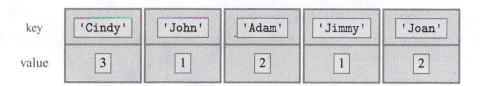

Figure 6.4 Dictionary as a container of counters. This dictionary is the output of running function `frequency()` on list `students`.

With all the pieces of the puzzle in place, we can now implement the function:

Module: ch6.py

```
 1  def frequency(itemList):
 2      'returns frequency of items in itemList'
 3      counters = {}               # initialize dictionary of counters
 4
 5      for item in itemList:
 6
 7          if item in counters:    # counter for item already exists
 8              counters[item] += 1     # so increment it
 9          else:                   # counter for item is created
10              counters[item] = 1     # an initialized to 1
11
12      return counters
```

The dictionary `counters` is initialized to an empty dictionary in line 3. The `for` loop iterates through the list of items `itemList`, and for every item:

- Either the counter corresponding to the item is incremented,
- Or, if no counter exists yet for the item, a counter corresponding to the item is created and initialized to 1.

Note the use of an accumulator pattern to accumulate frequency counts.

Implement function `wordcount()` that takes as input a text—as a string— and prints the frequency of each word in the text. You may assume that the text has no punctuation and words are separated by blank spaces.

Practice Problem 6.4

```
>>> text = 'all animals are equal but some \
animals are more equal than others'
>>> wordCount(text)
all        appears 1 time.
animals    appears 2 times.
some       appears 1 time.
equal      appears 2 times.
but        appears 1 time.
are        appears 2 times.
```

```
others    appears 1 time.
than      appears 1 time.
more      appears 1 time.
```

---

tuple **Objects Can Be Dictionary Keys**

In Practice Problem 6.2, we defined a dictionary that maps phone numbers to (the first and last name of) individuals:

```
>>> rphonebook = {'(123)456-78-90':['Anna','Karenina'],
                  '(901)234-56-78':['Yu', 'Tsun'],
                  '(321)908-76-54':['Hans', 'Castorp']}
```

We used this dictionary to implement a reverse phone book lookup application: Given a phone number, the app returns the individual that number is assigned to. What if, instead, we wanted to build an app that implements a standard phone book lookup: Given a person's first and last name, the app would return the phone number assigned to that individual.

For the standard lookup app, a dictionary such as rphonebook is not appropriate. What we need is a mapping *from* individuals *to* phone numbers. So let's define a new dictionary that is, effectively, the inverse of the mapping of rphonebook:

```
>>> phonebook = {['Anna','Karenina']:'(123)456-78-90',
                 ['Yu', 'Tsun']:'(901)234-56-78',
                 ['Hans', 'Castorp']:'(321)908-76-54'}
Traceback (most recent call last):
  File "<pyshell#242>", line 1, in <module>
    phonebook = {['Anna','Karenina']:'(123)456-78-90',
TypeError: unhashable type: 'list'
```

Oops, we have a problem. The problem is that we are trying to define a dictionary whose keys are list objects. Recall that the list type is mutable and that dictionary keys must be of a type that is immutable.

To the rescue comes the built-in tuple class. Because tuple objects are immutable, they can be used as dictionary keys. Let's get back to our original goal of constructing a dictionary that maps (the first and last name of) individuals to phone numbers. We can now use tuple objects as keys, instead of list objects:

```
>>> phonebook = {('Anna','Karenina'):'(123)456-78-90',
                 ('Yu', 'Tsun'):'(901)234-56-78',
                 ('Hans', 'Castorp'):'(321)908-76-54'}
>>> phonebook
{('Hans', 'Castorp'): '(321)908-76-54',
('Yu', 'Tsun'): '(901)234-56-78',
('Anna', 'Karenina'): '(123)456-78-90'}
```

Let's check that the indexing operator works as we want:

```
>>> phonebook[('Hans', 'Castorp')]
'(321)908-76-54'
```

Now you can implement the standard phone book lookup tool.

Implement function `lookup()` that implements a phone book lookup application. Your function takes, as input, a dictionary representing a phone book. In the dictionary, tuples containing first and last names of individual (the keys) are mapped to strings containing phone numbers (the values). Here is an example:

Practice Problem
6.5

```
>>> phonebook = {('Anna','Karenina'):'(123)456-78-90',
                 ('Yu', 'Tsun'):'(901)234-56-78',
                 ('Hans', 'Castorp'):'(321)908-76-54'}
```

Your function should provide a simple user interface through which a user can enter the first and last name of an individual and obtain the phone number assigned to that individual.

```
>>> lookup(phonebook)
Enter the first name: Anna
Enter the last name: Karenina
(123)456-78-90
Enter the first name: Yu
Enter the last name: Tsun
(901)234-56-78
```

6.2 Sets

In this section, we introduce another built-in Python container type. The `set` class has all the properties of a mathematical set. It is used to store an unordered collection of items, with no duplicate items allowed. The items must be immutable objects. The `set` type supports operators that implement the classical set operations: set membership, intersection, union, symmetric difference, and so on. It is thus useful whenever a collection of items is modeled as a mathematical set. It is also useful for duplicate removal.

A set is defined using the same notation that is used for mathematical sets: a sequence of items separated by commas and enclosed in curly braces: { }. Here is how we would assign the set of three phone numbers (as strings) to variable `phonebook1`:

```
>>> phonebook1 = {'123-45-67', '234-56-78', '345-67-89'}
```

We check the value and type of `phonebook1`:

```
>>> phonebook1
{'123-45-67', '234-56-78', '345-67-89'}
>>> type(phonebook1)
<class 'set'>
```

If we had defined a set with duplicate items, they would be ignored:

```
>>> phonebook1 = {'123-45-67', '234-56-78', '345-67-89',
                  '123-45-67', '345-67-89'}
>>> phonebook1
{'123-45-67', '234-56-78', '345-67-89'}
```

Using the `set` Constructor to Remove Duplicates

The fact that sets cannot have duplicates gives us the first great application for sets: removing duplicates from a list. Suppose we have a list with duplicates, such as this list of ages of students in a class:

```
>>> ages = [23, 19, 18, 21, 18, 20, 21, 23, 22, 23, 19, 20]
```

To remove duplicates from this list, we can convert the list to a set, using the set constructor. The set constructor will eliminate all duplicates because a set is not supposed to have them. By converting the set back to a list, we get a list with no duplicates:

```
>>> ages = list(set(ages))
>>> ages
[18, 19, 20, 21, 22, 23]
```

There is, however, *one major caveat*: The elements have been reordered.

CAUTION

Empty Sets

To instantiate an empty set, we may be tempted to do this:

```
>>> phonebook2 = {}
```

When we check the type of phonebook2, however, we get a dictionary type:

```
>>> type(phonebook2)
<class 'dict'>
```

The problem here is that curly braces ({}) are used to define dictionaries as well, and {} represents an empty dictionary. If that is that case, then two questions are raised:

1. How does Python then differentiate between set and dictionary notation?

2. How do we create an empty set?

The answer to the first question is this: Even though both sets and dictionaries are denoted using curly braces enclosing a comma-separated sequence of items, the items in dictionaries are (key, value) pairs of objects separated by colons (:), whereas the items in sets are not separated by colons.

The answer to the second question is that we have to use the set constructor explicitly when creating an empty set:

```
>>> phonebook2 = set()
```

We check the value and type of phonebook2 to make sure that we have an empty set:

```
>>> phonebook2
set()
>>> type(phonebook2)
<class 'set'>
```

set **Operators**

The set class supports operators that correspond to the usual mathematical set operations. Some are operators that can also be used with list, string, and dictionary types. For example, the in and not in operators are used to test set membership:

```
>>> '123-45-67' in phonebook1
True
>>> '456-78-90' in phonebook1
False
>>> '456-78-90' not in phonebook1
True
```

The len() operator returns the size of the set:

```
>>> len(phonebook1)
3
```

Comparison operators ==, !=, <, <=, >, and >= are supported as well, but their meaning is set-specific. Two sets are "equal" if and only if they have the same elements:

```
>>> phonebook3 = {'345-67-89','456-78-90'}
>>> phonebook1 == phonebook3
False
>>> phonebook1 != phonebook3
True
```

As shown in Figure 6.5, sets phonebook1 and phonebook3 do not contain the same elements.

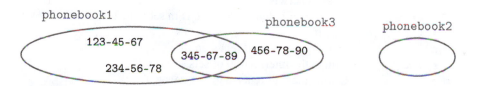

Figure 6.5 Three phone book sets. The Venn diagram of sets phonebook1, phonebook2, and phonebook3 is shown.

A set is "less than or equal to" another set if it is a subset of it, and a set is "less than another set" if it is a proper subset of it. So, for example:

```
>>> {'123-45-67', '345-67-89'} <= phonebook1
True
```

As Figure 6.5 shows, the set {'123-45-67', '345-67-89'} is a subset of set phonebook1. However, phonebook1 is not a proper subset of phonebook1:

```
>>> phonebook1 < phonebook1
False
```

The mathematical set operations union, intersection, difference, and symmetric difference are implemented as set operators |, &, -, and ^, respectively. Each set operation takes two sets and returns a new set. The union of two sets contains all elements that are in either set:

```
>>> phonebook1 | phonebook3
{'123-45-67', '234-56-78', '345-67-89', '456-78-90'}
```

The intersection of two sets contains all elements that are in both sets:

```
>>> phonebook1 & phonebook3
{'345-67-89'}
```

The difference between two sets contains all elements that are in the first set but not the second one:

```
>>> phonebook1 - phonebook3
{'123-45-67', '234-56-78'}
```

The symmetric difference of two sets contains all elements that are either in the first set or in the second set, but not both:

```
>>> phonebook1 ^ phonebook3
{'123-45-67', '234-56-78', '456-78-90'}
```

Use Figure 6.5 to check that the `set` operators work as expected.

Before we move on to discussing the `set` class methods, we summarize in Table 6.3 the commonly used `set` operators that we just covered.

Table 6.3 Class `set` **operators.** Shown are the usage and explanation for commonly used set operators.

Operation	Explanation
`x in s`	True if `x` is in set `s`, else `False`
`x not in s`	`False` if `x` is in set `s`, else `True`
`len(s)`	Returns the size of set `s`
`s == t`	True if sets `s` and `t` contain the same elements, `False` otherwise
`s != t`	True if sets `s` and `t` do not contain the same elements, `False` otherwise
`s <= t`	True if every element of set `s` is in set `t`, `False` otherwise
`s < t`	True if `s <= t` and `s != t`
`s	t`	Returns the union of sets `s` and `t`
`s & t`	Returns the intersection of sets `s` and `t`
`s - t`	Returns the difference between sets `s` and `t`
`s ^ t`	Returns the symmetric difference of sets `s` and `t`

`set` **Methods**

In addition to operators, the `set` class supports a number of methods. The `set` method `add()` is used to add an item to a set:

```
>>> phonebook3.add('123-45-67')
>>> phonebook3
{'123-45-67', '345-67-89', '456-78-90'}
```

The method `remove()` is used to remove an item from a set:

```
>>> phonebook3.remove('123-45-67')
>>> phonebook3
{'345-67-89', '456-78-90'}
```

Finally, the method `clear()` is used to empty a set:

```
>>> phonebook3.clear()
```

We check that `phonebook3` is indeed empty:

```
>>> phonebook3
set()
```

To learn more about the `set` class, read the online documentation or use the `help()` documentation function.

Implement function `sync()` that takes a list of phone books (where each phone book is a set of phone numbers) as input and returns a phone book (as a set) containing the union of all the phone books.

Practice Problem 6.6

```
>>> phonebook4 = {'234-56-78', '456-78-90'}
>>> phonebooks = [phonebook1, phonebook2, phonebook3, phonebook4]
>>> sync(phonebooks)
{'234-56-78', '456-78-90', '123-45-67', '345-67-89'}
```

6.3 Character Encodings and Strings

The string type, `str`, is the Python type for storing text values. In Chapters 2 and 4, we have seen how to create string objects and manipulate them using string operators and methods. The assumption then was that we were dealing with string objects containing English text. That assumption helped make string processing intuitive, but it also hid the complexity and richness of string representations. We now discuss the complexity of text representations that is due to the huge number of symbols and characters in the world languages we speak and write. We discuss specifically what kind of characters strings can contain.

Character Encodings

String objects are used to store text, that is, a sequence of characters. The characters could be upper- and lowercase letters from the alphabet, digits, punctuation marks, and possibly symbols like the dollar sign ($). As we saw in Chapter 2, in order to create a variable whose value is the text 'An apple costs $0.99!', we just need to do:

```
>>> text = 'An apple costs $0.99!'
```

The variable `text` then evaluates to the text:

```
>>> text
'An apple costs $0.99!'
```

While all this may sound very clean and straightforward, strings *are* somewhat messy. The problem is that computers deal with bits and bytes, and string values need to be somehow encoded with bits and bytes. In other words, each character of a string value needs to be mapped to a specific bit encoding, and this encoding should map back to the character.

But why should we care about this encoding? As we saw in Chapters 2 and 4, manipulating strings is quite intuitive, and we certainly did not worry about how strings are encoded. Most of the time, we do *not* have to worry about it. However, in a global Internet, documents created in one location may need to be read in another. We need to know how to work with characters from other writing systems, whether they are characters from other languages, such as French, Greek, Arabic, or Chinese, or symbols from various domains, such as math, science, or engineering. As importantly, we need to understand how strings are represented because, as computer scientists, we do like to know what is below the hood.

ASCII

For many years, the standard encoding for characters in the English language was ASCII encoding. The American Standard Code for Information Interchange (ASCII) was developed in the 1960s. It defines a numeric code for 128 characters, punctuation, and a few other symbols common in the American English language. Table 6.4 shows the decimal ASCII codes for the printable characters.

Let's explain what the entries of this table mean. The decimal ASCII code for lowercase a is 97. The & sign is encoded with decimal ASCII code 38. ASCII codes 0 through 32 and 127 include nonprintable characters, such as backspace (decimal code 8), horizontal tab (decimal code 9), and line feed (decimal code 10). You can explore the ASCII encodings using the Python function ord(), which returns the decimal ASCII code of a character:

```
>>> ord('a')
97
```

The sequence of characters of a string value (such as 'dad') is encoded as a sequence of ASCII codes 100, 97, and 100. What is stored in memory is exactly this sequence of codes. Of course, each code is stored in binary. As ASCII decimal codes go from 0 to 127, they can be encoded with seven bits; because a byte (eight bits) is the smallest memory storage unit, each code is stored in one byte.

For example, the decimal ASCII code for lowercase a is 97, which corresponds to binary ASCII code 1100001. So, in the ASCII encoding, character a is encoded in a single byte with the first bit being a 0 and the remaining bits being 1100001. The resulting byte 01100001 can be described more succinctly using a two-digit hex number 0x61 (6 for the leftmost four bits, 0110, and 1 for the rightmost 4 bits, 0001). In fact, it it common to use hex ASCII codes (as a shorthand for ASCII binary codes).

Table 6.4 ASCII encoding. Printable ASCII characters and their corresponding decimal codes are shown. The character for decimal code 43, for example, is the operator +. The character for decimal code 32 is the blank space, which is displayed as a blank space.

32		48	0	64	@	80	P	96	`	112	p
33	!	49	1	65	A	81	Q	97	a	113	q
34	"	50	2	66	B	82	R	98	b	114	r
35	#	51	3	67	C	83	S	99	c	115	s
36	$	52	4	68	D	84	T	100	d	116	t
37	%	53	5	69	E	85	U	101	e	117	u
38	&	54	6	70	F	86	V	102	f	118	v
39	'	55	7	71	G	87	W	103	g	119	w
40	(	56	8	72	H	88	X	104	h	120	x
41	)	57	9	73	I	89	Y	105	i	121	y
42	*	58	:	74	J	90	Z	106	j	122	z
43	+	59	;	75	K	91	[	107	k	123	{
44	,	60	<	76	L	92	\	108	l	124	|
45	-	61	=	77	M	93	]	109	m	125	}
46	.	62	>	78	N	94	^	110	n	126	~
47	/	63	?	79	O	95	_	111	o		

The symbol &, for example, is encoded with decimal ASCII code 38, which corresponds to binary code 0100110 or hex code 0x26.

Write a function `encoding()` that takes a string as input and *prints* the ASCII code—in decimal, hex, and binary notation—of every character in it.

Practice Problem
6.7

```
>>> encoding('dad')
Char Decimal  Hex   Binary
 d        100   64  1100100
 a         97   61  1100001
 d        100   64  1100100
```

The function `chr()` is the inverse of function `ord()`. It takes a numeric code and returns the character corresponding to it.

```
>>> chr(97)
'a'
```

Write function `char(low, high)` that prints the characters corresponding to ASCII decimal codes i for all values of i from `low` up to and including `high`.

Practice Problem
6.8

```
>>> char(62, 67)
62 : >
63 : ?
64 : @
65 : A
66 : B
67 : C
```

Unicode

ASCII is an *American* standard. As such, it does not provide for characters not in the American English language. There is no French 'é', Greek 'Δ', or Chinese '世' in ASCII encoding. Encodings other than ASCII were developed to handle different languages or groups of languages. This raises a problem, however: With the existence of different encodings, it is likely that some encodings are not installed on a computer. In a globally interconnected world, a text document that was created on one computer will often need to be read on another, a continent away. What if the computer reading the document does not have the right encoding installed?

Unicode was developed to be the universal character-encoding scheme. It covers all characters in all written languages, modern or ancient, and includes technical symbols from science, engineering, and mathematics, punctuation, and so on. In Unicode, every character is represented by an integer *code point*. The code point is not necessarily the actual byte representation of the character, however; it is just the identifier for the particular character.

For example, the code point for lowercase 'k' is the integer with hex value 0x006B, which corresponds to decimal value 107. As you can see in Table 6.4, 107 is also the ASCII code for letter 'k'. Unicode conveniently uses a code point for ASCII characters that is equal to their ASCII code.

How do you incorporate Unicode characters into a string? To include character 'k', for example, you would use the Python escape sequence \u006B:

```
>>> '\u006B'
'k'
```

In the next example, the escape sequence \u0020 is used to denote the Unicode character with code point 0x0020 (in hex, corresponding to decimal 32). This is, of course, the blank space (see Table 6.4):

```
>>> 'Hello\u0020World !'
'Hello World !'
```

We now try a few examples in several different languages. Let's start with my name in Cyrillic:

```
>>> '\u0409\u0443\u0431\u043e\u043c\u0438\u0440'
'Љубомир'
```

Here is 'Hello World!' in Greek:

```
>>> '\u0393\u03b5\u03b9\u03b1\u0020\u03c3\u03b1\u03c2
     \u0020\u03ba\u03cc\u03c3\u03bc\u03bf!'
'Γεια σας κόσμο!'
```

Finally, let's write 'Hello World!' in Chinese:

```
>>> chinese = '\u4e16\u754c\u60a8\u597d!'
>>> chinese
'世界您好!'
```

DETOUR

String Comparisons, Revisited

Now that we know how strings are represented, we can understand how string comparison works. First, the Unicode code points, being integers, give a natural ordering to all the characters representable in Unicode. So, for example, the blank space ' ' is earlier in this ordering than Cyrillic character 'Љ' because the Unicode code point for ' ' (which is 0x0020) is a smaller integer than the Unicode code point for 'Љ' (which is 0x0409):

```
>>> '\u0020' > '\u0409'
False
>>> '\u0020' < '\u0409'
True
```

Unicode was designed so that for any pair of characters from the same alphabet, one that is earlier in the alphabet than the other will have a smaller Unicode code point. For example, 'a' is before 'd' in the alphabet, and the code point for 'a' is smaller than the code point for 'd'. In this way, the Unicode characters form an ordered set of characters that is consistent with all the alphabets Unicode covers.

When two strings are compared, we have said that the comparison is done using dictionary order. Another name for dictionary order is *lexicographic order*. This order can be precisely defined, now that we understand that characters come from an ordered set (Unicode). The word

$$a_1 a_2 a_3 \ldots a_k$$

appears earlier in the lexicographic order than word

$$b_1 b_2 b_3 \ldots b_l$$

if either:

- $a_1 = b_1$, $a_2 = b_2$, $\ldots$, $a_k = b_k$, and $k < l$, or
- for the smallest index i for which a_i and b_i are different, the Unicode code point for a_i is smaller than the Unicode code point for b_i.

Let's check that the basic string operators work on this string.

```
>>> len(chinese)
5
>>> chinese[0]
'世'
```

String operators work regardless of the alphabet used in the string. Now let's see whether the `ord()` and `chr()` functions extend from ASCII to Unicode:

```
>>> ord(chinese[0])
19990
>>> chr(19990)
'世'
```

They do! Note that 19990 is the decimal value of hex value 0x4e16, which is of course the Unicode code point of character 世. Thus, the built-in function `ord()` really takes a Unicode character and outputs the decimal value of its Unicode code point, and `chr()` does the inverse. The reason they both also work for ASCII characters is that the Unicode code points for ASCII characters are, by design and as noted, the ASCII codes.

UTF-8 Encoding for Unicode Characters

A Unicode string is a sequence of code points that are numbers from 0 to 0x10FFFF. Unlike ASCII codes, however, Unicode code points are not what is stored in memory. The rule for translating a Unicode character or code point into a sequence of bytes is called an *encoding*.

There is not just one but several Unicode encodings: UTF-8, UTF-16, and UTF-32. UTF stands for Unicode Transformation Format, and each UTF-x defines a different way to map a Unicode code point to a byte sequence. UTF-8 has become the preferred encoding for e-mail, web pages, and other applications where characters are stored or sent across a network. In fact, the default encoding when you write Python 3 programs is UTF-8. One of the features of UTF-8 is: Every ASCII character (i.e., every symbol in Table 6.4) has a UTF-8 encoding that is exactly the 8-bit (1-byte) ASCII encoding. This means that an

ASCII text is a Unicode text encoded with the UTF-8 encoding.

In some situations, your Python program will receive text without a specified encoding. This happens, for example, when the program downloads a text document from the World Wide Web (as we will see in Chapter 11). In that case, Python has no choice but to treat the "text" as a sequence of raw bytes stored in an object of type `bytes`. This is because files downloaded from the web could be images, video, audio, and not just text.

Consider this content of a text file downloaded from the web:

```
>>> content
b'This is a text document\nposted on the\nWWW.\n'
```

Variable `content` refers to an object of type `bytes`. As you can verify, the letter b in the front of the "string" indicates that:

```
>>> type(content)
<class 'bytes'>
```

To decode it to a string encoded using the UTF-8 Unicode encoding, we need to use the `decode()` method of the `bytes` class:

```
>>> content.decode('utf-8')
'This is a text document\nposted on the\nWWW.\n'
```

If the method `decode()` is called without arguments, the default, platform-dependent encoding is used, which is UTF-8 for Python 3 (or ASCII for Python 2).

DETOUR

Files and Encodings

The third, optional, argument to the `open()` function, used to open a file, is the encoding to use when reading, or writing, the text file. If not specified, the default platform-dependent encoding will be used. This argument should be used only in text mode; an error will occur if used for binary files. Let's open file `chinese.txt` by explicitly specifying the UTF-8 encoding:

```
>>> infile = open('chinese.txt', 'r', encoding='utf-8')
>>> print(infile.read())
你好世界!

(translation: Hello World!)
```

6.4 Module `random`

Random numbers are useful for running simulations in science, engineering, and finance. They are needed in modern cryptographic protocols that provide computer security, communication privacy, and authentication. They also are a necessary component in games of chance, such as poker or blackjack, and help make computer games less predictable.

Truly random numbers are not easy to obtain. Most computer applications that require random numbers use numbers generated by a *pseudorandom number generator* instead. The "pseudo" in "pseudorandom" means fake, or not real. Pseudorandom number generators are programs that produce a sequence of numbers that "look" random and are good enough for most applications that need random numbers.

In Python, pseudorandom number generators and associated tools are available through the `random` module. As usual, if we need to use functions in the `random` module, we need to import it first:

```
>>> import random
```

Next we describe a few functions in the `random` module that are particularly useful.

Choosing a Random Integer

We start with function `randrange()`, which takes a pair of integers a and b and returns some number in the range from—and including—a up to—and *not* including—b with each number in the range equally likely. Here is how we would use this function to simulate several (six-sided) die tosses:

```
>>> random.randrange(1,7)
2
>>> random.randrange(1,7)
6
>>> random.randrange(1,7)
5
>>> random.randrange(1,7)
1
>>> random.randrange(1,7)
2
```

Implement function `guess()` that takes as input an integer n and implements a simple, interactive number guessing game. The function should start by choosing a random number in the range from 0 up to but not including n. The function will then repeatedly ask the user to guess the chosen number; When the user guesses correctly, the function should print a `'You got it.'` message and terminate. Each time the user guesses incorrectly, the function should help the user by printing message `'Too low.'`, or `'Too high.'`.

Practice Problem
6.9

```
>>> guess(100)
Enter your guess: 50
Too low.
Enter your guess: 75
Too high.
Enter your guess: 62
Too high.
Enter your guess: 56
Too low.
Enter your guess: 59
Too high.
Enter your guess: 57
You got it!
```

DETOUR

Randomness

We usually think of the result, heads or tails, of a coin toss as a random event. Most games of chance depend on the generation of random events (die tosses, card shuffling, roulette spins, etc.). The problem with these methods of generating random events is that they are not appropriate for generating randomness quickly enough for a running computer program. It is, in fact, not easy to get a computer program to generate truly random numbers. For this reason, computer scientists have developed deterministic algorithms called pseudorandom number generators that generate numbers that "appear" random.

Choosing a Random "Real"

Sometimes what we need in an application is not a random integer but a random number chosen from a given number interval. The function `uniform()` takes two numbers a and b and returns a `float` number x such that $a \leq x \leq b$ (assuming $a \leq b$), with each `float` value in the range equally likely. Here is how we would use it to obtain several random numbers between 0 and 1:

```
>>> random.uniform(0,1)
0.9896941090637834
>>> random.uniform(0,1)
0.3083484771618912
>>> random.uniform(0,1)
0.12374451518957152
```

Practice Problem 6.10

There is a way to estimate the value of mathematical constant π by throwing darts at a dartboard. It is not a good way to estimate π, but it is fun. Suppose that you have a dartboard of radius 1 inside a 2×2 square on the wall. Now throw darts at random and suppose that out of n darts that hit the square, k hit the dartboard (see Figure 6.6.)

Figure 6.6 Dartboard inside a square. Shown are 10 random dart hits with 8 lying inside the dartboard. In this case, the estimate for π would be: $\frac{4*8}{10} = 3.2$.

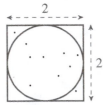

Because the darts were randomly thrown, the ratio k/n should approximate the ratio of the area of the dartboard ($\pi \times 1^2$) and the area of the square surrounding it (2^2). In other words, we should have:

$$\frac{k}{n} \approx \frac{\pi}{4}$$

The formula can be rewritten so that it can be used to estimate π:

$$\pi \approx \frac{4k}{n}$$

Implement function `approxPi()` that takes as input an integer n, simulates n random dart throws into the 2×2 square containing the dartboard, counts the number of darts hitting the dartboard, and returns an estimate of π based on the count and n. *Note:* In order to simulate a random dart hit into the square, you just need to obtain random x and y coordinates of the hit.

```
>>> approxPi(1000)
3.028
>>> approxPi(100000)
3.1409600000000002
>>> approxPi(1000000)
3.141702
>>>
```

Shuffling, Choosing, and Sampling at Random

Let's illustrate a few more functions from the `random` module. The function `shuffle()` shuffles, or permutes, the objects in a sequence not unlike how a deck of cards is shuffled prior to a card game like blackjack. Each possible permutation is equally likely. Here is how we can use this function to shuffle a list twice:

```
>>> lst = [1,2,3,4,5]
>>> random.shuffle(lst)
>>> lst
[3, 4, 1, 5, 2]
>>> random.shuffle(lst)
>>> lst
[1, 3, 2, 4, 5]
```

The function `choice()` allows us to choose an item from a container uniformly at random. Given list

```
>>> lst = ['cat', 'rat', 'bat', 'mat']
```

here is how we would choose a list item uniformly at random:

```
>>> random.choice(lst)
'mat'
>>> random.choice(lst)
'bat'
>>> random.choice(lst)
'rat'
>>> random.choice(lst)
'bat'
```

If, instead of needing just one item, we want to choose a sample of size k, with every sample equally likely, we would use the `sample()` function. It takes as input the container and the number k.

Here is how we would choose random samples of list `lst` of size 2 or 3:

```
>>> random.sample(lst, 2)
['mat', 'bat']
>>> random.sample(lst, 2)
['cat', 'rat']
>>> random.sample(lst, 3)
['rat', 'mat', 'bat']
```

E-Book Case Study: Games of Chance

Games of chance such as poker and blackjack have transitioned to the digital age very successfully. In this case study, we show how to develop a blackjack application. As we develop this application, we make use of several concepts introduced in this chapter: sets, dictionaries, Unicode characters, and of course randomness through card shuffling.

Chapter Summary

This chapter starts by introducing several built-in Python container classes that complement the string and list classes we have been using so far.

The dictionary class `dict` is a container of (key, value) pairs. One way to view a dictionary is to see it as as a container that stores values that are accessible through user-specified indexes called keys. Another is to see it as a mapping from keys to values. Dictionaries are as useful as lists in practice. A dictionary can be used, for example, as a substitute for a multiway conditional structure or as a collection of counters.

In some situations, the mutability of lists is a problem. For example, we cannot use lists as keys of a dictionary because lists are mutable. We introduce the built-in class `tuple`, which is essentially an immutable version of class `list`. We use `tuple` objects when we need an immutable version of a list.

The last built-in container class covered in this book is the class `set` that implements a mathematical set, that is, a container that supports mathematical set operations, such as union and intersection. As all elements of a set must be distinct, sets can be used to easily remove duplicates from other containers.

In this chapter, we also complete the coverage of Python's built-in string type `str` that we started in Chapter 2 and continued in Chapter 4. We describe the range of characters that a string object can contain. We introduce the Unicode character encoding scheme, the default in Python 3 (but not Python 2), which enables developers to work with strings that use non-American English characters.

Finally, this chapter introduces the Standard Library module `random`. The module supports functions that return pseudorandom numbers, which are needed in simulations and computer games. We also introduce `random` module functions `shuffle()`, `choice()`, and `sample()` that enable us to do shuffling and sampling on container objects.

Solutions to Practice Problems

6.1 The function takes a president's name (`president`) as input. This name maps to a state. The mapping of presidents' names to states is best described using a dictionary. After the dictionary is defined, the function simply returns the value corresponding to the key president:

```python
def birthState(president):
    'returns the birth state of the given president'

    states = {'Barack Hussein Obama II':'Hawaii',
              'George Walker Bush':'Connecticut',
              'William Jefferson Clinton':'Arkansas',
              'George Herbert Walker Bush':'Massachussetts',
              'Ronald Wilson Reagan':'Illinois',
              'James Earl Carter, Jr':'Georgia'}

    return states[president]
```

6.2 The reverse lookup service is implemented with an infinite, interactive loop pattern. In each iteration of this loop, the user is requested to enter a number. The phone number entered by the user is mapped, using the phone book, to a name. This name is then printed.

```python
def rlookup(phonebook):
    '''implements an interactive reverse phone book lookup service
       phonebook is a dictionary mapping phone numbers to names'''
    while True:
        number = input('Enter phone number in the\
                        format (xxx)xxx-xx-xx: ')
        if number in phonebook:
            print(phonebook[number])
        else:
            print('The number you entered is not in use.')
```

6.3 See Figure 6.7.

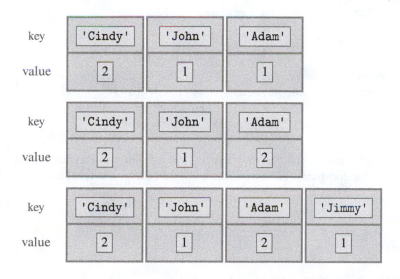

Figure 6.7 Counters states. When string `'Adam'` is visited, (key, value) pair (`'Adam'`, 1) is added to the dictionary. When another string `'Adam'` is visited, the value in this same (key, value) pair is incremented by one. Another (key, value) pair is added when visiting string `'Jimmy'`.

6.4 The first thing to do is split the text and obtain a list of words. Then the standard pattern for counting using a dictionary of counter is used.

```
def wordCount(text):
    'prints frequency of each word in text'

    wordList = text.split()    # split text into list of words
    counters = {}              # dictionary of counters

    for word in wordList:
        if word in counters:   # counter for word exists
            counters[word] += 1
        else:                  # counter for word doesn't exist
            counters[word] = 1

    for word in counters:      # print word counts
        if counters[word] == 1:
            print('{:8} appears {} time.'.format(word,\
                                        counters[word]))

        else:
            print('{:8} appears {} times.'.format(word,\
                                        counters[word]))
```

6.5 The infinite loop pattern is used to provide a long-running service. In every iteration, the user is asked to enter a first and a last name, which are then used to build a `tuple` object. This object is used as a key for the phone book dictionary. If the dictionary contains a value corresponding to this key, the value is printed; otherwise, an error message is printed.

```
def lookup(phonebook):
    '''implements interactive phone book service using the input
        phonebook dictionary'''
    while True:
        first = input('Enter the first name: ')
        last = input('Enter the last name: ')

        person = (first, last)     # construct the key

        if person in phonebook:    # if key is in dictionary
            print(phonebook[person])  # print value
        else:                      # if key not in dictionary
            print('The name you entered is not known.')
```

6.6 The goal is to obtain the union of all the sets appearing in a list. The accumulator pattern is the right loop pattern for doing this. The accumulator should be a set that is initialized to be empty:

```
def sync(phonebooks):
    'returns the union of sets in phonebooks'
    res = set()  # initialize the accumulator

    for phonebook in phonebooks:
        res = res | phonebook     # accumulate phonebook into res
    return res
```

6.7 The iteration pattern is used to iterate over the characters of the string. In each iteration, the ASCII code of the current character is printed:

```python
def encoding(text):
    'prints ASCII codes of characters in S, one per line'
    print('Char Decimal  Hex   Binary') # print column headings

    for c in text:
        code = ord(c)    # compute ASCII code
        # print character and its code in decimal, hex, and binary
        print(' {}    {:7} {:4x}  {:7b}'.format(c,code,code,code))
```

6.8 We use a counter loop pattern to generate integers from `low` to `high`. The character corresponding to each integer is printed:

```python
def char(low, high):
    '''prints the characters with ASCII codes
       in the range from low to high'''
    for i in range(low, high+1):
        # print integer ASCII code and corresponding character
        print('{} : {}'.format(i, chr(i)))
```

6.9 The `randrange()` function of the `random` module is used to generate the secret number to be guessed. An infinite loop and a loop-and-a-half pattern are used to implement the interactive service:

```python
import random
def guess(n):
    'an interactive number guessing game'
    secret = random.randrange(0,n)   # generate secret number

    while True:
        # user enters a guess
        guess = eval(input('Enter you guess: '))
        if guess == secret:
            print('You got it!')
            break
        elif guess < secret:
            print('Too low.')
        else: # guess > secret
            print('Too high.')
```

6.10 Each random dart throw hit is simulated by choosing, uniformly at random, an x and a y coordinate between -1 and 1. If the resulting point (x, y) is within distance 1 from the origin $(0, 0)$ (i.e., the center of the dartboard), the point represents a hit. An accumulator loop pattern is used to add up all the "hits."

```python
import random
def approxPi(total):
    'return approximate value of pi based on "dart throwing"'
    count = 0                 # counts darts hitting dartboard
    for i in range(total):
```

```
        x = random.uniform(-1,1) # x-coordinate of dart
        y = random.uniform(-1,1) # y coordinate of dart
        if x**2+y**2 <= 1:        # if dart hit dartboard
            count += 1                # increment count
    return 4*count/total
```

Exercises

6.11 Implement function `easyCrypto()` that takes as input a string and prints its encryption defined as follows: Every character at an odd position i in the alphabet will be encrypted with the character at position $i + 1$, and every character at an even position i will be encrypted with the character at position $i - 1$. In other words, 'a' is encrypted with 'b', 'b' with 'a', 'c' with 'd', 'd' with 'c', and so on. Lowercase characters should remain lowercase, and uppercase characters should remain uppercase.

```
>>> easyCrypto('abc')
bad
>>> easyCrypto('ZOO')
YPP
```

6.12 Redo Problem 5.27 using a dictionary instead of a multiway `if` statement.

6.13 Define a dictionary called `agencies` that stores a mapping of acronyms CCC, FCC, FDIC, SSB, WPA (the keys) to the federal government agencies 'Civilian Conservation Corps', 'Federal Communications Commission', 'Federal Deposit Insurance Corporation', 'Social Security Board', and 'Works Progress Administration' (the values) created by President Roosevelt during the New Deal. Then:

(a) Add the map of acronym SEC to 'Securities and Exchange Commission'.

(b) Change the value of key SSB to 'Social Security Administration'.

(c) Remove the (key, value) pairs with keys CCC and WPA.

6.14 Repeat Exercise 6.13 with this change: Before making changes to `agencies`, define `acronyms` to be the view of its keys. After making the changes, evaluate `acronyms`.

6.15 The dictionary used in Practice Problem 6.5 assumes that only one person can have a certain first and last name. In a typical phone book, however, there can be more than one person with the same first and last name. A modified dictionary that maps a (last name, first name) tuple to a *list* of phone numbers could be used to implement a more realistic phone book. Reimplement the `lookup()` function from Practice Problem 6.5 so that it can take such a dictionary (i.e., with list values) as input and return all the numbers that a (last name, first name) tuple maps to.

6.16 Using a counter loop pattern, construct sets `mult3`, `mult5`, and `mult7` of nonnegative multiples of 3, 5, and 7, respectively, less than 100. Then, using these three sets, write set expressions that return

(a) Multiples of 35

(b) Multiples of 105

(c) Multiples of 3 or 7

(d) Multiples of 3 or 7, but not both

(e) Multiples of 7 that are not multiples of 3

6.17 Write a function `hexASCII()` that prints the correspondence between the lowercase characters in the alphabet and the hexadecimal representation of their ASCII code. *Note:* A format string and the `format` string method can be used to represent a number value in hex notation.

```
>>> hexASCII()
a:61 b:62 c:63 d:64 e:65 f:66 g:67 h:68 i:69 j:6a k:6b l:6c m:6d
n:6e o:6f p:70 q:71 r:72 s:73 t:74 u:75 v:76 w:77 x:78 y:79 z:7a
```

6.18 Implement function `coin()` that returns `'Heads'` or `'Tails'` with equal probability.

```
>>> coin()
'Heads'
>>> coin()
'Heads'
>>> coin()
'Tails'
```

6.19 Using an online translator such as Google Translate, translate the phrase 'My name is Ada' into Arabic, Japanese, and Serbian. Then copy and paste the translations into your interactive shell and assign them as strings to variable names `arabic`, `japanese`, and `serbian`. Finally, for each string, print the Unicode code point of each character in the string using an iteration loop pattern.

Problems

6.20 Write function `reverse()` that takes as input a phone book, that is, a dictionary mapping names (the keys) to phone numbers (the values). The function should return another dictionary representing the reverse phone book mapping phone numbers (the keys) to the names (the values).

```
>>> phonebook = {'Smith, Jane':'123-45-67',
            'Doe, John':'987-65-43','Baker,David':'567-89-01'}
>>> reverse(phonebook)
{'123-45-67': 'Smith, Jane', '567-89-01': 'Baker,David',
'987-65-43': 'Doe, John'}
```

6.21 Write function `ticker()` that takes a string (the name of a file) as input. The file will contain company names and stock (ticker) symbols. In this file, a company name will occupy a line, and its stock symbol will be in the next line. Following this line will be a line with another company name, and so on. Your program will read the file and store the name and stock symbol in a dictionary. Then it will provide an interface to the user so that the user can obtain the stock symbol for a given company. Test your code on the NASDAQ 100 list of stock given in file `nasdaq.txt`.

```
>>> ticker('nasdaq.txt')
Enter Company name: YAHOO
```

File: nasdaq.txt

```
Ticker symbol: YHOO
Enter Company name: GOOGLE INC
Ticker symbol: GOOG
...
```

6.22 The mirror image of string vow is string wov, and the mirror image wood is string boow. The mirror image of string bed cannot be represented as a string, however, because the mirror image of e is not a valid character.

Develop function mirror() that takes a string and returns its mirror image but only if the mirror image can be represented using letters in the alphabet.

```
>>> mirror('vow')
'wov'
>>> mirror('wood')
'boow'
>>> mirror('bed')
'INVALID'
```

6.23 You would like to produce a unique scary dictionary but have a hard time finding the thousands of words that should go into such a dictionary. Your brilliant idea is to write a function scaryDict() that reads in an electronic version of a scary book, say *Frankenstein* by Mary Wollstonecraft Shelley, picks up all the words in it, writes them in alphabetical order in a new file called dictionary.txt, and prints them as well. You can eliminate one- and two-letter words because none of them are scary.

You will notice that punctuation in the text makes this exercise a bit more complicated. You can handle it by replacing punctuation with blanks or empty strings.

File: frankenstein.txt

```
>>> scaryDict('frankenstein.txt')
abandon
abandoned
abbey
abhor
abhorred
abhorrence
abhorrent
...
```

6.24 Implement function names() that takes no input and repeatedly asks the user to enter the first name of a student in a class. When the user enters the empty string, the function should print for every name the number of students with that name.

```
>>> names()
Enter next name: Valerie
Enter next name: Bob
Enter next name: Valerie
Enter next name: Amelia
Enter next name: Bob
Enter next name:
There is 1 student named Amelia
There are 2 students named Bob
There are 2 students named Valerie
```

6.25 Write function `different()` that takes a two-dimensional table as input and returns the number of distinct entries in the table.

```
>>> t = [[1,0,1],[0,1,0]]
>>> different(t)
2
>>> t = [[32,12,52,63],[32,64,67,52],[64,64,17,34],[34,17,76,98]]
>>> different(t)
10
```

6.26 Write function week() that takes no arguments. It will repeatedly ask the user to enter an abbreviation for a day of the week (Mo, Tu, We, Th, Fr, Sa, or Su) and then print the corresponding day.

```
>>> week()
Enter day abbreviation: Tu
Tuesday
Enter day abbreviation: Su
Sunday
Enter day abbreviation: Sa
Saturday
Enter day abbreviation:
```

6.27 At the end of this and other textbooks, there usually is an index that lists the pages where a certain word appears. In this problem, you will create an index for a text but, instead of page number, you will use the line numbers.

You will implement function `index()` that takes as input the name of a text file and a list of words. For every word in the list, your function will find the lines in the text file where the word occurs and print the corresponding line numbers (where the numbering starts at 1). You should open and read the file only once.

```
>>> index('raven.txt', ['raven', 'mortal', 'dying', 'ghost',
          'ghastly', 'evil','demon'])
ghost       9
dying       9
demon       122
evil        99, 106
ghastly     82
mortal      30
raven       44, 53, 55, 64, 78, 97, 104, 111, 118, 120
```

File: raven.txt

6.28 Implement function `translate()` that provides a rudimentary translation service. The function input is a dictionary mapping words in one language (the first language) to corresponding words in another (the second language). The function provides a service that lets users type a phrase in the first language interactively and then obtain a translation into the second language, by pressing the Enter/Return key. Words not in the dictionary should be translated as ____.

6.29 In your class, many students are friends. Let's assume that two students sharing a friend must be friends themselves; in other words, if students 0 and 1 are friends and students 1 and 2 are friends, then students 0 and 2 must be friends. Using this rule, we can partition the students into circles of friends.

To do this, implement a function `networks()` that takes two input arguments. The first is the number n of students in the class. We assume students are identified using integers 0 through $n - 1$. The second input argument is a list of tuple objects that define friends. For example, tuple $(0, 2)$ defines students 0 and 2 as friends. Function `networks()` should print the partition of students into circles of friends as illustrated:

```
>>> networks(5, [(0, 1), (1, 2), (3, 4)])
Social network 0 is {0, 1, 2}
Social network 1 is {3, 4}
```

6.30 Implement function `simul()` that takes as input an integer n and simulates n rounds of Rock, Paper, Scissors between players Player 1 and Player 2. The player who wins the most rounds wins the n-round game, with ties possible. Your function should print the result of the game as shown. (You may want to use your solution to Problem 5.26.)

```
>>> simul(1)
Player 1
>>> simul(1)
Tie
>>> simul(100)
Player 2
```

6.31 Craps is a dice-based game played in many casinos. Like blackjack, a player plays against the house. The game starts with the player throwing a pair of standard, six-sided dice. If the player rolls a total of 7 or 11, the player wins. If the player rolls a total of 2, 3, or 12, the player loses. For all other roll values, the player will repeatedly roll the pair of dice until either she rolls the initial value again (in which case she wins) or 7 (in which case she loses)

(a) Implement function `craps()` that takes no argument, simulates one game of craps, and returns 1 if the player won and 0 if the player lost.

```
>>> craps()
0
>>> craps()
1
>>> craps()
1
```

(b) Implement function `testCraps()` that takes a positive integer n as input, simulates n games of craps, and returns the fraction of games the player won.

```
>>> testCraps(10000)
0.4844
>>> testCraps(10000)
0.492
```

6.32 You may know that the streets and avenues of Manhattan form a grid. A random walk through the grid (i.e., Manhattan) is a walk in which a random direction (N, E, S, or W) is chosen with equal probability at every intersection. For example, a random walk on a 5×11 grid starting $(5, 2)$ could visit grid points $(6, 2)$, $(7, 2)$, $(8, 2)$, $(9, 2)$, $(10, 2)$, back to $(9, 2)$ and then back to $(10, 2)$ before leaving the grid.

Write function `manhattan()` that takes the number of rows and columns in the grid, simulates a random walk starting in the center of the grid, and computes the number of times each intersection has been visited by the random walk. Your function should print the table line by line once the random walk moves outside the grid.

```
>>> manhattan(5, 11)
[0, 0, 0, 0, 0, 0, 0, 0, 0, 0, 0]
[0, 0, 0, 0, 0, 0, 0, 0, 0, 0, 0]
[0, 0, 0, 0, 0, 1, 1, 1, 1, 2, 2]
[0, 0, 0, 0, 0, 0, 0, 0, 0, 0, 0]
[0, 0, 0, 0, 0, 0, 0, 0, 0, 0, 0]
```

6.33 Write function `diceprob()` that takes as input a possible result r of a roll of pair of dice (i.e. an integer between 2 and 12) and simulates repeated rolls of a pair of dice until 100 rolls of r have been obtained. Your function should print how many rolls it took to obtain 100 rolls of r.

```
>>> diceprob(2)
It took 4007 rolls to get 100 rolls of 2
>>> diceprob(3)
It took 1762 rolls to get 100 rolls of 3
>>> diceprob(4)
It took 1058 rolls to get 100 rolls of 4
>>> diceprob(5)
It took 1075 rolls to get 100 rolls of 5
>>> diceprob(6)
It took 760 rolls to get 100 rolls of 6
>>> diceprob(7)
It took 560 rolls to get 100 rolls of 7
```

6.34 The two-player card game War is played with a standard deck of 52 cards. A shuffled deck is evenly split among the two players who keep their decks face-down. The game consists of battles until one of the players runs out of cards. In a battle, each player reveals the card on top of their deck; the player with the higher card takes both cards and adds them face-down to the bottom of her stack. If both cards have the same value, a war occurs.

In a war, each player lays, face-down, their top three cards and picks one of them. The player who picks the higher valued card adds all eight cards to the bottom of her deck. In case of another tie, wars are repeated until a player wins and collects all cards on the table. If a player runs out of cards before laying down three cards in a war, he is allowed to complete the war, using his last card as his pick.

In War, the value of a number card is its rank, and the values of cards with rank A, K, Q, and J are 14, 13, 12, and 11, respectively.

(a) Write a function `war()` that simulates one game of war and returns a tuple containing the number of battles, wars, and two-round wars in the game. *Note:* When adding cards to the bottom of a player's deck, make sure to shuffle the cards first to add additional randomness to the simulation.

(b) Write a function `warStats()` that takes a positive integer n as input, simulates n games of war, and computes the average number of battles, wars, and two-round wars.

6.35 Develop a simple game that teaches kindergartners how to add single-digit numbers.

Your function `game()` will take an integer n as input and then ask n single-digit addition questions. The numbers to be added should be chosen randomly from the range $[0, 9]$ (i.e., 0 to 9 inclusive). The user will enter the answer when prompted. Your function should print `'Correct'` for correct answers and `'Incorrect'` for incorrect answers. After n questions, your function should print the number of correct answers.

```
>>> game(3)
8 + 2 =
Enter answer: 10
Correct.
6 + 7 =
Enter answer: 12
Incorrect.
7 + 7 =
Enter answer: 14
Correct.
You got 2 correct answers out of 3
```

6.36 The *Caesar cipher* is an encryption technique in which every letter of the message is replaced by the letter that is a fixed number of positions down the alphabet. This "fixed number" is referred to as the *key*, which can have any value from 1 to 25. If the key is 4, for example, then letter A would be replaced by E, B by F, C by G, and so on. Characters at the end of the alphabet, W, X, Y, and Z would be replaced by A, B, C, and D.

Write function `caesar` that takes as input a key between 1 and 25 and the name (i.e., a string) of a text file. Your function should encode the file content with a Caesar cipher using the input key and write the encrypted content into a new file `cipher.txt` (and return the encrypted content as well).

File: clear.txt

```
>>> caesar(3,'clear.txt')
"Vsb Pdqxdo (Wrs vhfuhw)\n\n1. Dozdbv zhdu d gdun frdw.\n2. Dozdbv
zhdu brxu djhqfb'v edgjh rq brxu frdw.\n"
```

6.37 George Kingsley Zipf (1902–1950) observed that the frequency of the kth most common word in a text is roughly proportional to $1/k$. This means that there is a constant value C such that *for most* words w in the text the following is true:

$$\text{If word } w \text{ is } k\text{th most common then freq}(w) * k \approx C$$

Here, by frequency of word w, freq(w), we mean the number of times the word occurs in the text divided by the total number of words in the text.

Implement function `zipf()` that takes a file name as input and verifies Zipf's observation by printing the value freq$(w) * k$ for the first 10 most frequent words w in the file. Ignore capitalization and punctuation when processing the file.

File: frankenstein.txt

```
>>> zipf('frankenstein.txt')
0.0557319552019
0.0790477076165
0.113270715149
0.140452498306
0.139097394747
0.141648177917
0.129359248582
```

0.119993091629
0.122078888284
0.134978942754

Namespaces

7.1 Encapsulation in Functions   204

7.2 Global versus Local Namespaces   211

7.3 Exceptional Control Flow   215

7.4 Modules as Namespaces   223

7.5 Classes as Namespaces   230

E-Book Case Study: Debugging with a debugger   231

Chapter Summary   232

Solutions to Practice Problems   232

Exercises   233

Problems   236

THIS CHAPTER presents namespaces as a fundamental construct for managing program complexity. As computer programs increase in complexity, it becomes necessary to adopt a modular approach and develop them using several smaller components that are developed, tested, and debugged individually. These components—whether they are functions, modules, or classes—must work together as a program but they also should not interfere, in unintended ways, with each other.

Modularity and "noninterference" (usually called *encapsulation*) are made possible thanks to the fact that each component has its own *namespace*. Namespaces organize the naming scheme in functions, modules, and classes so that names defined inside a component are not visible to other components. Namespaces play a key role in the execution of function calls and the normal control flow of a program. We contrast this with the exceptional control flow that is caused by a raised exception. We introduce exception handling as a way to control this control flow.

This chapter covers concepts and techniques that fundamentally deal with program design. We apply them in Chapter 8 to create new classes and in Chapter 10 to understand how recursive functions execute.

7.1 Encapsulation in Functions

In Chapter 3, we introduced functions as wrappers that package a fragment of code. To recall the reasons for wrapping code into functions—and then using those functions—we take as an example the function jump() from the Chapter 3 case study:

Module: turtlefunctions.py

```
1  def jump(t, x, y):
2      'makes turtle t jump to coordinates (x, y)'
3      t.penup()
4      t.goto(x, y)
5      t.pendown()
```

The function jump() provides a succinct way to make the turtle object t (i.e., the pen) move to a new location (on the drawingg surface) without leaving a trace. In Chapter 3, we used jump() multiple times in the function emoticon() that draws a smiley face:

Module: turtlefunctions.py

```
1  def emoticon(t, x, y):
2      'directs turtle t to draw a smiley face with chin at (x, y)'
3      t.pensize(3)              # set turtle heading and pen size
4      t.setheading(0)
5      jump(t, x, y)             # move to (x, y) and draw head
6      t.circle(100)
7      jump(t, x+35, y+120)      # move and draw right eye
8      t.dot(25)
9      jump(t, x-35, y+120)      # move and draw left eye
10     t.dot(25)
11     jump(t, x-60.62, y+65)    # move and draw smile
12     t.setheading(-60)
13     t.circle(70, 120)         # 120 degree section of a circle
```

The functions jump() and emoticon() illustrate some of the benefits of functions: code reuse, encapsulation, and modularity. We explain each in more detail.

Code Reuse

A fragment of code that is used multiple times in a program—or by multiple programs—can be packaged in a function. That way, the programmer types the code fragment only once, inside a function definition, and then calls the function wherever the code fragment is needed. The program ends up being shorter, with a single function call replacing a code fragment, and clearer, because the name of the function can be more descriptive of the action being performed by the code fragment. Debugging also becomes easier because a bug in the code fragment will need to be fixed only once.

In function emoticon(), we use function jump() four times, making the emoticon() function shorter and more readable. We also make it easier to modify: Any change to how the jump should be done will need to be implemented only once, inside the jump() function. In fact, the function emoticon() would not even need to be modified.

We saw another example of code reuse in the Chapter 6 case study, where we developed a blackjack application. Because shuffling a standard deck of 52 cards and dealing a card to a game participant is common to most card games, we implemented each action in a separate, reusable function (shuffledDeck() and dealCard()).

Modularity (or Procedural Decomposition)

The complexity of developing a large program can be dealt with by breaking down the program into smaller, simpler, self-contained pieces. Each smaller piece (e.g., function) can be designed, implemented, tested, and debugged independently.

For example, we broke the problem of drawing a smiley face into two functions. The function `jump()` is independent of the function `emoticon()` and can be tested and debugged independently. Once function `jump()` has been developed, the function `emoticon()` is easier to implement. We also used the modular approach to develop the blackjack application using five functions in the Chapter 6 case study.

Encapsulation (or Information Hiding)

When using a function in a program, typically the developer does not need to know its implementation details, but only what it does. In fact, removing the implementation details from the developer's radar makes her job easier.

The developer of the function `emoticon()` does not need to know how function `jump()` works, just that it lifts turtle (i.e., pen) t and drops it at coordinates (x, y). This simplifies the process of developing function `emoticon()`. Another benefit of encapsulation is that if the implementation of function `jump()` changes (and is made more efficient, for example), the function `emoticon()` would not have to change.

In the blackjack application, the functions that shuffle the deck and compute the value of a hand encapsulate the code doing the actual work. The benefit here is that the main blackjack program contains meaningful function calls, such as

```
deck = shuffledDeck()      # get shuffled deck
```

and

```
dealCard(deck, player)     # deal to player first
```

rather than code that is harder to read.

Local Variables

There is a potential danger when the developer using a function does not know its implementation details. What if, somehow, the execution of the function inadvertently affects the calling program (i.e., the program that made the function call)? For example, the developer could accidentally use a variable name in the calling program that happens to be defined and used in the executing function. In order to achieve encapsulation, those two variables should be separate. Variable names defined (i.e., assigned) inside a function should be "invisible" to the calling program: They should be variables that exist only locally, in the context of the execution of the function, and they should not affect variables of the same name in the calling program. This invisibility is achieved thanks to the fact that variables defined inside functions are *local variables*.

We illustrate this with the next function:

Module: ch7.py

```
1  def double(y):
2      x = 2
3      print('x = {}, y = {}'.format(x,y))
4      return x*y
```

After running the module ch7, we check that names x and y have not been defined in the interpreter shell:

```
>>> x
Traceback (most recent call last):
  File "<pyshell#37>", line 1, in <module>
    x
NameError: name 'x' is not defined
>>> y
Traceback (most recent call last):
  File "<pyshell#38>", line 1, in <module>
    y
NameError: name 'y' is not defined
```

Now let's execute double():

```
>>> res = double(3)
x = 2, y = 3
```

During the execution of the function, variables x and y exist: y is assigned 3, and then x is assigned 2. However, after the execution of the function, the names x and y do not exist in the interpreter shell:

```
>>> x
Traceback (most recent call last):
  File "<pyshell#40>", line 1, in <module>
    x
NameError: name 'x' is not defined
>>> y
Traceback (most recent call last):
  File "<pyshell#41>", line 1, in <module>
    y
NameError: name 'y' is not defined
```

Clearly x and y exist only during the execution of the function.

Namespaces Associated with Function Calls

Actually, something even stronger is true: The names x and y that are defined during the execution of double() are invisible to the calling program (the interpreter shell in our example) even during the execution of the function. To convince ourselves of this, let's define values x and y in the shell and then execute function double() again:

```
>>> x,y = 20,30
>>> res = double(4)
x = 2, y = 4
```

Let's check whether the variables x and y (defined in the interpreter shell) have changed:

```
>>> x,y
(20, 30)
```

No, they have not. This example shows that there are two separate pairs of variable names x and y: the pair defined in the interpreter shell and the pair defined during the execution of the function. Figure 7.1 illustrates that the interpreter shell and the executing function double()

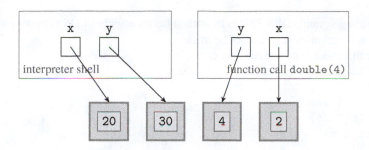

Figure 7.1 Namespaces. Variable names x and y are defined in the interpreter shell. During the execution of `double(4)`, separate local variables y and x get defined in the namespace of the function call.

each has its own, separate space for names. Each space is called a *namespace*. The interpreter shell has its namespace. Each function call creates a new namespace. Different function calls will have different corresponding namespaces. The net effect is that each function call has its own "execution area" so it does not interfere with the execution of the calling program or other functions.

Names that are assigned during the execution of a function call are said to be *local names*, and they are local with respect to a function call. Names that are local to a function exist only in the namespace associated with the function call. They:

- Are only visible to the code inside the function.

- Do not interfere with names defined outside of the function, even if they are the same.

- Exist only during the execution of the function; they do not exist before the function starts execution and they no longer exist after the function completes execution.

Define functions `f()` and `g()` in this way:

```
>>> def f(y):
        x = 2
        print('In f(): x = {}, y = {}'.format(x,y))
        g(3)
        print('In f(): x = {}, y = {}'.format(x,y))

>>> def g(y):
        x = 4
        print('In g(): x = {}, y = {}'.format(x,y))
```

Using Figure 7.1 as your model, show graphically the variables names, their values, and the namespaces of functions `f()` and `g()` during the execution of function `g()` when this call is made:

```
>>> f(1)
```

Practice Problem 7.1

Namespaces and the Program Stack

We know that a new namespace is created for every function call. If we call a function that in turn calls a second function that in turn calls a third function, there would be three namespaces, one for each function call. We now discuss how these namespaces are managed by the operating system (OS). This is important because without OS support for managing namespaces, function calls could not be made.

We use this module as our running example:

Module: stack.py

```
1   def h(n):
2       print('Start h')
3       print(1/n)
4       print(n)
5
6   def g(n):
7       print('Start g')
8       h(n-1)
9       print(n)
10
11  def f(n):
12      print('Start f')
13      g(n-1)
14      print(n)
```

After we run the module, we make the function call `f(4)` from the shell:

```
>>> f(4)
Start f
Start g
Start h
0.5
2
3
4
```

Figure 7.2 illustrates the execution of `f(4)`.

Figure 7.2 Execution of
`f(4)`. The execution starts in the namespace of function call `f(4)`, where n is 4. Function call `g(3)` creates a new namespace in which n is 3; function `g()` executes using that value of n. Function call `h(2)` creates another namespace in which n is 2; function `h()` uses that value of n. When the execution of `h(2)` terminates, the execution of `g(3)` and its corresponding namespace, in which n is 3, is restored. When `g(3)` terminates, the execution of `f(4)` is restored.

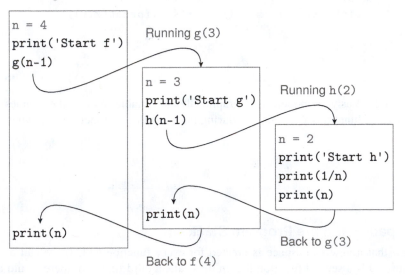

Figure 7.2 shows the three different namespaces and the different value that n has in each. To understand how these namespaces are managed, we go through the execution of f(4) carefully.

When we start executing f(4), the value of n is 4. When the function call g(3) is made, the value of n in the namespace of the function call g(3) is 3. However, the old value of n, 4, is still needed because the execution of f(4) is not complete; line 14 will need to be executed after g(3) is done.

Before the execution of g(3) gets started, the underlying OS stores all the information necessary to complete the execution of f(4):

- The value of variable n (in this case, the value n = 4)

- The line of code where the execution of f(4) should resume (in this case, line 14)

This information is stored by the OS in an area of main memory called the *program stack*. It is referred to as a stack because the OS will *push* the information on *top* of the program stack before executing g(3), as shown in Figure 7.3.

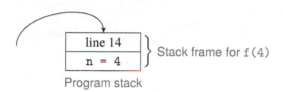

Program stack

Figure 7.3 Stack frame. A function call stores its local variables in its stack frame; if another function is called, then the line to be executed next is stored too.

The program stack area storing the information related to a specific unfinished function call is called the *stack frame*.

When function call g(3) starts executing, the value of n is 3. During the execution of g(3), function h() is called on input n-1 = 2. Before the call is made, the stack frame corresponding to g(3) is pushed onto the program stack, as shown in Figure 7.4.

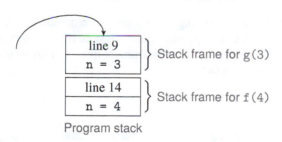

Program stack

Figure 7.4 Program stack. If a function is called inside another function, the stack frame for the called function is stored on top of the stack frame of the calling function.

In Figure 7.5, we again illustrate the execution of function call f(4), but this time we also show how the OS uses the program stack to store the namespace of an unfinished function call so that it can restore the namespace when the function call resumes. In the top half of Figure 7.5, the sequence of function calls is illustrated with black arrows. Each call has a corresponding "push" of a frame to the program stack, shown with blue arrows.

Now let's resume our careful analysis of the execution of f(4). When h(2) executes, n is 2 and values 1/n = 0.5 and n = 2 are printed. Then h(2) terminates. At this point, the execution should return to function call g(3). So the namespace associated with g(3) needs to get restored and the execution of g(3) should continue from where it left off. The

Figure 7.5 Execution of f(4), part 2. The function call f(4) executes in its own namespace. When function call g(3) is made, the namespace of f(4) is pushed onto the program stack. The call g(3) runs in its own namespace. When the call h(2) is made, the namespace of g(3) is also pushed onto the program stack. When function call h(2) terminates, the namespace of g(3) is restored by popping the top stack frame of the program stack; its execution continues from the line stored in the stack frame (i.e., line 9). When g(3) terminates, the namespace of f(4) and its execution are restored by popping the program stack again.

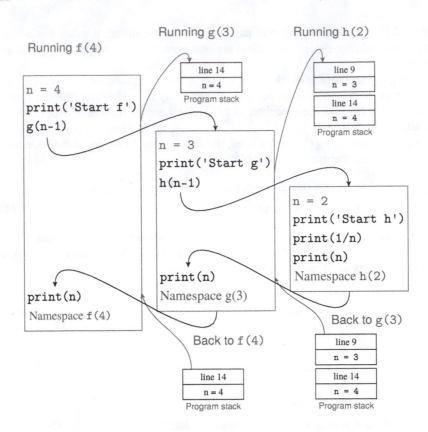

OS will do this by *popping* a frame from the top of the program stack and using the values in the frame to:

- Restore the value of n to 3 (i.e., restore the namespace).
- Continue the execution of g(3) starting with line 9.

Executing line 9 will result in the printing of n = 3 and the termination of g(3). As shown in Figure 7.5, the program stack is then popped again to restore the namespace of function call f(4) and to continue the execution of f(4) starting at line 14. This results in the printing of n = 4 and the termination of f(4).

DETOUR

Program Stacks and Buffer Overflow Attacks

The program stack is an essential component of an OS's main memory. The program stack contains a stack frame for every function call. A stack frame is used to store variables (like n) that are local with respect to the function call. Also, when a call to another function is made, the stack frame is used to store the line number (i.e., memory address) of the instruction where execution should be resumed, once that other function terminates.

The program stack also presents a vulnerability in a computer system, one that is often exploited in a type of computer system attack known as the *buffer overflow attack*. The vulnerability is that the input argument of a function call, say the 4 in `f(4)`, may be written into the program stack, as illustrated in Figure 7.5. In other words, the OS allocates a small space in the program stack to store the expected input argument (in our case, an integer value).

A malicious user could call the function with an argument that is much larger than the allocated space. This argument could contain nefarious code and would also overwrite one of the existing line numbers in the program stack with a new line number. This new line number would, of course, point to the nefarious code.

Eventually, the executing program will pop the stack frame containing the overwritten line number and start executing instructions starting from that line.

7.2 Global versus Local Namespaces

We have seen that every function call has a namespace associated with it. This namespace is where names defined during the execution of the function live. We say that the *scope* of these names (i.e., the space where they live) is the namespace of the function call.

Every name (whether a variable name, function name, or type name—and not just a local name) in a Python program has a scope, that is, a namespace where it lives. Outside of its scope, the name does not exist, and any reference to it will result in an error. Names assigned inside (the body of) a function are said to have *local scope* (local with respect to a function call), which means that their namespace is the one associated with the function call.

Names assigned in the interpreter shell or in a module outside of any function are said to have *global scope*. Their scope is the namespace associated with the shell or the whole module. Variables with global scope are referred to as *global variables*.

Global Variables

When you execute a Python statement in the interpreter shell, you are doing so in a namespace associated with the shell. In this context, this namespace is the global namespace, and the variables defined in it, such as `a` in

```
>>> a = 0
>>> a
0
```

are global variables whose scope is global.

When you execute a module, whether from within or from outside your integrated development environment, there is a namespace associated with the executing module. This namespace is the global namespace during the execution of the module. Any variable that is defined in the module outside of any function, such as `a` in the one-line module `scope.py`

Module: scope.py

```
1  # a really small module
2  a = 0
```

is a global variable.

Variables with Local Scope

We use a sequence of examples to illustrate the difference between global and local scopes. Our first example is this strange module:

Module: scope1.py

```
1  def f(b):          # f has global scope, b has local scope
2      a = 6          # this a has scope local to function call f()
3      return a*b     # this a is the local a
4
5  a = 0              # this a has global scope
6  print('f(3) = {}'.format(f(3)))
7  print('a is {}'.format(a))        # global a is still 0
```

When we run this module, the function definition is executed first, and then the last three lines of the module are executed in succession. Names f and a have global scope. When function f(3) is called in line 6, local variables b and then a get defined in the namespace of the function call f(3). The local variable a is unrelated to the global name a, as shown in Figure 7.6.

Figure 7.6 Local variables. In line 5, integer 0 is assigned to global variable name a. During execution of function call f(3) in line 6, a separate variable a, local with respect to the function call, gets defined and is assigned integer 3.

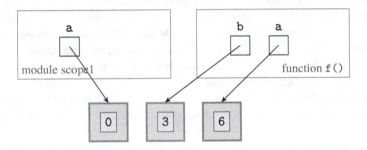

This is printed when the module executes:

```
>>>
f(3) = 18
a is 0
```

Note that when evaluating the product a*b while executing f(3), the local name a is used.

Variables with Global Scope

To get our next example, we remove line 2 from module scope1:

Module: scope2.py

```
1  def f(b):
2      return a*b                    # this a is the global a
3
4  a = 0                             # this a has global scope
5  print('f(3) = {}'.format(f(3)))
6  print('a is {}'.format(a)) # global a is still 0
```

When we run the module scope2, function call f(3) will be made. Figure 7.7 shows the variable names, and the namespaces they are defined in, when function call f(3) executes.

When the product a*b is evaluated during the execution of f(3), no local variable a exists in the namespace associated with function call f(3). The variable a that is used is

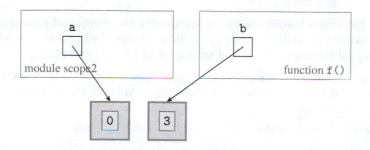

Figure 7.7 Global variables. During the execution of function call f(3) in line 5, variable a is evaluated when computing the product a*b. Because no name a exists in the function call namespace, the name a defined in the global namespace is used.

now the global variable a, whose value is 0. When you run this example, you get:

```
>>>
f(3) = 0
a is 0
```

How does the Python interpreter decide whether to evaluate a name as a local or as a global name?

Whenever the Python interpreter needs to evaluate a name (of a variable, function, etc.), it searches for the name definition in this order:

1. First the enclosing function call namespace
2. Then the global (module) namespace
3. Finally the namespace of module builtins

In our first example, module scope1, name a in product a*b evaluated to a local name; in the second example, module scope2, because no name a was defined in the local namespace of the function call, a evaluates to the global name a.

Built-in names (such as sum(), len(), print(), etc.) are names that are predefined in the module builtins that Python automatically imports upon start-up. (We discuss this built-in module in more detail in Section 7.4.) Figure 7.8 shows the different namespaces that exist when the function call f(3) gets executed in module scope2.

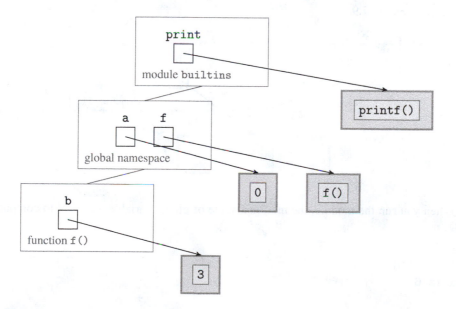

Figure 7.8 Searching for a name definition. Three namespaces exist during the execution of f(3) when running module scope2. Whenever the Python interpreter needs to evaluate a name, it starts the search for the name in the local namespace. If the name is not found there, it continues the search in the global namespace. If the name is not found there either, the name search then moves to the builtins namespace.

Figure 7.8 illustrates how names are evaluated during the execution of statement `print(a*b)` in line 2 of function `f()` while executing `f(3)`. The execution of `print(a*b)` involves three name searches, all starting with the local namespace of function call `f(3)`:

1. The Python interpreter first searches for name a. First, it looks in the local namespace of function `f(3)`. Since it is not there, it looks next in the global namespace, where it finds name a.

2. The search for name b starts and ends in the local namespace.

3. The search for (function) name `print` starts in the local namespace, continues through the global namespace, and ends, successfully, in the namespace of module `builtins`.

Changing Global Variables Inside a Function

In our last example, we consider this situation: Suppose that in function `f()` of module `scope1`, the intention of statement a = 0 was to *modify* the global variable a. As we saw in module `scope1`, the statement a = 0 inside function `f()` will instead create a new local variable of the same name. If our intention was to have the function *change the value of a global variable*, then we must use the `global` reserved keyword to indicate that a name is global. We use this module to explain the keyword `global`:

Module: scope3.py

```
1   def f(b):
2       global a      # all references to a in f() are to the global a
3       a = 6         # global a is changed
4       return a*b    # this a is the global a
5
6   a = 0             # this a has global scope
7   print('f(3) = {}'.format(f(3)))
8   print('a is {}'.format(a))          # global a has been changed to 6
```

In line 3, the assignment a = 6 changes the value of the global variable a because the statement `global a` specifies that the name a is global rather than local. This concept is illustrated in Figure 7.9.

Figure 7.9 Keyword
`global`. During execution
of `f(3)`, the assignment
a = 6 is executed. Because
name a is defined to refer to
the global name a, it is the
global a that gets assigned.
No name a is created in the
local namespace of the
function call.

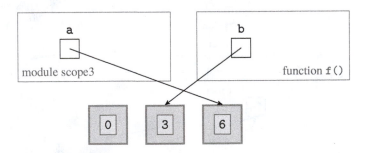

When you run the module, the modified value of global variable a is used to compute `f(3)`:

```
>>>
f(3) = 18
a is 6
```

Practice Problem 7.2

Module: fandg.py

For each name in the next module, indicate whether it is a global name or whether it is local in f(x) or local in g(x).

```
1   def f(y):
2       x = 2
3       return g(x)
4
5   def g(y):
6       global x
7       x = 4
8       return x*y
9
10  x = 0
11  res = f(x)
12  print('x = {}, f(0) = {}'.format(x, res))
```

7.3 Exceptional Control Flow

While the focus of the discussion in this chapter has been on namespaces, we have also touched on another fundamental topic: how the operating system and namespaces support the "normal" execution control flow of a program, especially function calls. We consider, in this section, what happens when the "normal" execution control flow gets interrupted by an exception and ways to control this exceptional control flow. This section also continues the discussion of exceptions we started in Section 4.4.

Exceptions and Exceptional Control Flow

Error objects are called *exceptions* because when they are created, the normal execution flow of the program (as described by, say, the program's flowchart) is interrupted, and the execution switches to the so called *exceptional control flow* (which the flowchart typically does not show as it is not part of the normal program execution). The default exceptional control flow is to stop the program and print the error message contained in the exception object.

We illustrate this using the functions f(), g(), and h() we defined in Section 7.1. In Figure 7.2, we illustrated the normal flow of execution of function call f(4). In Figure 7.10, we illustrate what happens when we make the function call f(2) from the shell.

The execution runs normally all the way to function call h(0). During the execution of h(0), the value of n is 0. Therefore, an error state occurs when the expression 1/n is evaluated. The interpreter raises a ZeroDivisionError exception and creates a ZeroDivisionError exception object that contains information about the error.

The default behavior when an exception is raised is to interrupt the function call in which the error occurred. Because the error occurred while executing h(0), the execution of h(0) is interrupted. However, the error also occurred during the execution of function calls g(1) and f(2), and the execution of both is interrupted as well. Thus, statements shown in gray in Figure 7.10 are never executed.

Figure 7.10 Execution of
`f(2)`. The normal execution
control flow of function
call `f(2)` from the shell is
shown with black arrows:
`f(2)` calls `g(1)`, which, in
turn, calla `h(0)`. When the
evaluation of expression
`1/n = 1/0` is attempted,
a `ZeroDivisionError`
exception is raised. The
normal execution control
flow is interrupted: Function
call `h(0)` does not run to
completion, and neither
do `g(1)` or `f(2)`. The
exceptional control flow is
shown with a dashed arrow.
Statements that are not
executed are shown in
gray. Since call `f(2)` is
interrupted, the error
information is output in
the shell.

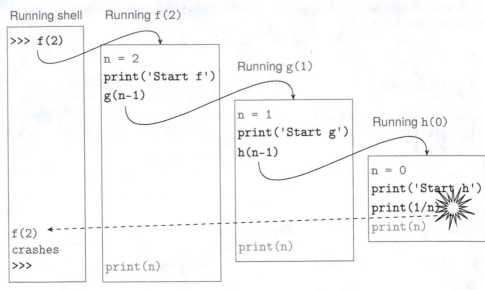

When execution returns to the shell, the information contained in the exception object
is printed in the shell:

```
Traceback (most recent call last):
  File "<pyshell#116>", line 1, in <module>
    f(2)
  File "/Users/me/ch7.py", line 13, in f
    g(n-1)
  File "/Users/me/ch7.py", line 8, in g
    h(n-1)
  File "/Users/me/ch7.py", line 3, in h
    print(1/n)
ZeroDivisionError: division by zero
```

In addition to the type of error and a friendly error message, the output also includes a
traceback, which consists of all the function calls that got interrupted by the error.

Catching and Handling Exceptions

Some programs should not terminate when an exception is raised: server programs, shell
programs, and pretty much any program that handles requests. Since these programs receive
requests from outside the program (interactively from the user or from a file), it is difficult
to ensure that the program will not enter an erroneous state because of malformed input.
These programs need to continue providing their service even if internal errors occur. What
this means is that the default behavior of stopping the program when an error occurs and
printing an error message must be changed.

We can change the default exceptional control flow by specifying an alternate behavior
when an exception is raised. We do this using the `try`/`except` pair of statements. The next

small application illustrates how to use them:

Module: age1.py

```
1  strAge = input('Enter your age: ')
2  intAge = int(strAge)
3  print('You are {} years old.'.format(intAge))
```

The application asks the user to interactively enter her age. The value entered by the user is a string. This value is converted to an integer before being printed. Try it!

This program works fine as long as the user enters her age in a way that makes the conversion to an integer possible. But what if the user types "fifteen" instead?

```
>>>
Enter your age: fifteen
Traceback (most recent call last):
  File "/Users/me/age1.py", line 2, in <module>
    intAge = int(strAge)
ValueError: invalid literal for int() with base 10: 'fifteen'
```

A ValueError exception is raised because string 'fifteen' cannot be converted to an integer.

Instead of "crashing" while executing the statement age = int(strAge), wouldn't it be nicer if we could tell users that they were supposed to enter their age using decimal digits. We can achieve this using the next try and except pair of statements:

Module: age2.py

```
1   try:
2       # try block --- executed first; if an exception is
3       # raised, the execution of the try block is interrupted
4       strAge = input('Enter your age: ')
5       intAge = int(strAge)
6       print('You are {} years old.'.format(intAge))
7   except:
8       # except block --- executed only if an exception
9       # is raised while executing the try block
10      print('Enter your age using digits 0-9!')
```

The try and except statements work in tandem. Each has an indented code block below it. The code block below the try statement, from line 2 to line 6, is executed first. If no errors occur, then the code block below except is ignored:

```
>>>
Enter your age: 22
You are 22 years old.
```

If, however, an exception is raised during the execution of a try code block (say, strAge cannot be converted to an integer), the Python interpreter will skip the execution of the remaining statements in the try code block and execute the code block of the except statement (i.e., line 9) instead:

```
>>>
Enter your age: fifteen
Enter your age using digits 0-9!
```

Note that the first line of the try block got executed but not the last.

The format of a `try`/`except` pair of statements is:

```
try:
    <indented code block 1>
except:
    <indented code block 2>
<non-indented statement>
```

The execution of `<indented code block 1>` is attempted first. If it goes through without any raised exceptions, then `<indented code block 2>` is ignored and execution continues with `<non-indented statement>`. If, however, an exception is raised during the execution of `<indented code block 1>`, then the remaining statements in `<indented code block 1>` are not executed; instead `<indented code block 2>` is executed. If `<indented code block 2>` runs to completion without a new exception being raised, then the execution continues with `<non-indented statement>`.

The code block `<indented code block 2>` is referred to as the *exception handler* because it handles a raised exception. We will also say that an `except` statement *catches* an exception.

The Default Exception Handler

If a raised exception is not caught by an `except` statement (and thus not handled by a user-defined exception handler), the executing program will be interrupted and the traceback and information about the error are output. We saw this behavior when we ran module `age1.py` and entered the age as a string:

```
>>>
Enter your age: fifteen
Traceback (most recent call last):
  File "/Users/me/age1.py", line 2, in <module>
    intAge = int(strAge)
ValueError: invalid literal for int() with base 10: 'fifteen'
```

This default behavior is actually the work of Python's *default exception handler*. In other words, every raised exception will be caught and handled, if not by a user-defined handler then by the default exception handler.

Catching Exceptions of a Given Type

In the module `age2.py`, the `except` statement can catch an exception of any type. The `except` statement could also be written to catch only a certain type of exception, say `ValueError` exceptions:

Module: age3.py

```
1   try:
2       # try block
3       strAge = input('Enter your age: ')
4       intAge = int(strAge)
5       print('You are {} years old.'.format(intAge))
6   except ValueError:
7       # except block --- executed only if a ValueError
8       # exception is raised in the try block
9       print('Enter your age using digits 0-9!')
```

If an exception is raised while executing the `try` code block, then the exception handler is executed only if the type of the exception object matches the exception type specified in the corresponding `except` statement (`ValueError` in this case). If an exception is raised that does match the type specified in the `except` statement, then the `except` statement will not catch it. Instead, the default exception handler will handle it.

Multiple Exception Handlers

There could be not just one but several `except` statements following one `try` statement, each with its own exception handler. We illustrate this with the next function `readAge()`, which attempts to open a file, read the first line, and convert it to an integer in a single `try` code block.

Module: ch7.py

```
1   def readAge(filename):
2       '''converts first line of file filename to
3          an integer and prints it'''
4       try:
5           infile = open(filename)
6           strAge = infile.readline()
7           age = int(strAge)
8           print('age is', age)
9       except IOError:
10          # executed only if an IOError exception is raised
11          print('Input/Output error.')
12      except ValueError:
13          # executed only if a ValueError exception is raised
14          print('Value cannot be converted to integer.')
15      except:
16          # executed if an exception other than IOError
17          # or ValueError is raised
18          print('Other error.')
```

Several types of exceptions could be raised while executing the `try` code block in function `readAge`. The file might not exist:

```
>>> readAge('agg.txt')
Input/Output error.
```

In this case, what happened was that an `IOError` exception got raised while executing the first statement of the `try` code block; the remaining statements in the code section were skipped and the `IOError` exception handler got executed.

Another error could be that the first line of the file `age.txt` does not contain something that can be converted to an integer value:

```
>>> readAge('age.txt')
Value cannot be converted to integer
```

File: age.txt

The first line of file `age.txt` is `'fifteen\n'`, so a `ValueError` exception is raised when attempting to convert it to an integer. The associated exception handler prints the friendly message without interrupting the program.

The last `except` statement will catch any exception that the first two `except` statements did not catch.

DETOUR

Maiden Flight of Ariane 5

On June 4, 1996, the Ariane 5 rocket developed over many years by the European Space Agency flew its first test flight. Seconds after the launch, the rocket exploded.

The crash happened when an overflow exception got raised during a conversion from floating point to integer. The cause of the crash was not the unsuccessful conversion (it turns out that it was of no consequence); the real cause was that the exception was not handled. Because of this, the rocket control software crashed and shut the rocket computer down. Without its navigation system, the rocket started turning uncontrollably, and the onboard monitors made the rocket self-destruct.

This was probably one of the most expensive computer bugs in history.

Practice Problem 7.3

Create a "wrapper" function `safe-open()` for the `open()` function. Recall that when `open()` is called to open a file that doesn't exist in the current working directory, an exception is raised:

```
>>> open('ch7.px', 'r')

Traceback (most recent call last):
  File "<pyshell#19>", line 1, in <module>
    open('ch7.px', 'r')
IOError: [Errno 2] No such file or directory: 'ch7.px'
```

If the file exist, a reference to the opened file object is returned:

```
>>> open('ch7.py', 'r')
<_io.TextIOWrapper name='ch7.py' encoding='US-ASCII'>
```

When `safe-open()` is used to open a file, a reference to the opened file object should be returned if no exception is raised, just like for the `open()` function. If an exception is raised while trying to open the file, `safe-open()` should return `None`.

```
>>> safe-open('ch7.py', 'r')
<_io.TextIOWrapper name='ch7.py' encoding='US-ASCII'>
>>> safe-open('ch7.px', 'r')
>>>
```

Controlling the Exceptional Control Flow

We started this section with an example illustrating how a raised exception interrupts the normal flow of a program. We now look at ways to manage the exceptional flow using appropriately placed exception handlers. We again use the functions `f()`, `g()`, and `h()` defined in module `stack.py`, shown next, as our running example.

```
1   def h(n):
2       print('Start h')
3       print(1/n)
4       print(n)
5
6   def g(n):
7       print('Start g')
8       h(n-1)
9       print(n)
10
11  def f(n):
12      print('Start f')
13      g(n-1)
14      print(n)
```

Module: stack.py

In Figure 7.10, we showed how the evaluation of f(2) causes an exception to be raised. The ZeroDivisionError exception is raised when an attempt is made to evaluate 1/0 while executing h(0). Since the exception object is not caught in function calls h(0), g(1), and f(2), these function calls are interrupted, and the default exception handler handles the exception, as shown in Figure 7.10.

Suppose we would like to catch the raised exception and handle it by printing 'Caught!' and then continuing with the normal flow of the program. We have several choices where to write a try code block and catch the exception. One approach is to to put the outermost function call f(2) in a try block (see also Figure 7.11):

```
>>> try:
        f(2)
except:
        print('Caught!')
```

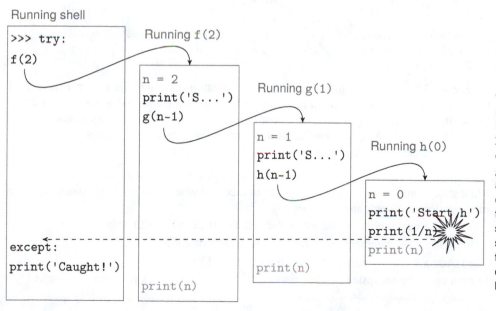

Running shell

Figure 7.11 Execution of f(2) with an exception handler. We run f(2) in a try code block. The execution runs normally until an exception is raised while executing h(0). The normal flow of execution is interrupted: Function call h(0) does not run to completion, and neither do g(1) or f(2). The dashed arrow shows the exceptional execution flow. Statements that are not executed are shown in gray. The except statement corresponding to the try block catches the exception, and the matching handler handles it.

The execution in Figure 7.11 parallels the one illustrated in Figure 7.10 until the point when function call f(2), made from the shell, is interrupted because of a raised exception. Because the function call was made in a try block, the exception is caught by the corresponding except statement and handled by its exception handler. The resulting output includes the string 'Caught!' printed by the handler:

```
Start f
Start g
Start h
Caught!
```

Compare this to the execution shown in Figure 7.10, when the default exception handler handled the exception.

In the previous example, we chose to implement an exception handler at the point where function f(2) is called. This represents a design decision by the developer of function f() that it is up to the function user to worry about handling exceptions.

In the next example, the developer of function h makes the design decision that function h() should handle any exception that occur during its execution. In this example, the function h() is modified so that its code is inside a try block:

Module: stack2.py

```
1  def h(n):
2      try:
3          print('Start h')
4          print(1/n)
5          print(n)
6      except:
7          print('Caught!')
```

(Functions f() and g() remain the same as in stack.py.) When we run f(2), we get:

```
>>> f(2)
Start f
Start g
Start h
Caught!
1
2
```

Figure 7.12 illustrates this execution. The execution parallels the one in Figure 7.11 until the exception is raised when evaluating 1/0. Since the evaluation is now inside a try block, the corresponding except statement catches the exception. The associated handler prints 'Caught!'. When the handler is done, the normal execution control flow resumes, and function call h(0) runs to completion as do g(1) and f(2).

Practice Problem 7.4

What statements in module stack.py are not executed when running f(2), assuming these modifications are made in stack.py:

(a) Add a try statement that wraps the line print(1/n) in h() only.

(b) Add a try statement that wraps the three lines of code in g().

(c) Add a try statement that wraps the line h(n-1) in g() only.

In each case, the exception handler associated with the try block just prints 'Caught!'.

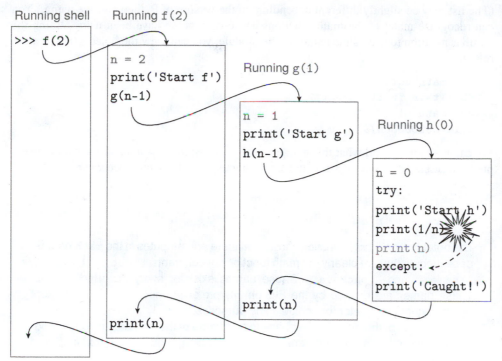

Figure 7.12 Execution of f(2) with an exception handler inside h(). The normal execution flow is shown with black arrows. When an attempt is made to evaluate 1/n = 1/0, a `ZeroDivisionError` exception is raised and the normal flow of execution is interrupted. The dashed arrow shows the exceptional flow of execution, and statements that are not executed are shown in gray. Since the exception occurred in a `try` block, the corresponding except statement catches the exception, and its associated handler handles it. The normal flow of execution then resumes, with h(0), g(1), and h(2) all running to completion.

7.4 Modules as Namespaces

So far, we have used the term *module* to describe a file containing Python code. When the module is executed (imported), then the module is (also) a namespace. This namespace has a name, which is the name of the module. In this namespace will live the names that are defined in the global scope of the module: the names of functions, values, and classes defined in the module. These names are all referred to as the module's *attributes*.

Module Attributes

As we have already seen, to get access to all the functions in the Standard Library module `math`, we import the module:

```
>>> import math
```

Once a module is imported, the Python built-in function `dir()` can be used to view all the module's attributes:

```
>>> dir(math)
['__doc__', '__file__', '__name__', '__package__', 'acos',
 'acosh', 'asin', 'asinh', 'atan', 'atan2', 'atanh', 'ceil',
 'copysign', 'cos', 'cosh', 'degrees', 'e', 'exp', 'fabs',
 'factorial', 'floor', 'fmod', 'frexp', 'fsum', 'hypot', 'isinf',
 'isnan', 'ldexp', 'log', 'log10', 'log1p', 'modf', 'pi', 'pow',
 'radians', 'sin', 'sinh', 'sqrt', 'tan', 'tanh', 'trunc']
```

(The list may be slightly different depending on the version of Python you are using.) You can recognize many of the math functions and constants we have been using. Using the familiar notation to access the names in the module, you can view the objects these names refer to:

```
>>> math.sqrt
<built-in function sqrt>
>>> math.pi
3.141592653589793
```

We can now understand what this notation really means: `math` is a namespace and the expression `math.pi`, for example, evaluates the name `pi` in the namespace `math`.

DETOUR

"Other" Imported Attributes

The output of the `dir()` function shows that there are attributes in the `math` namespace module that are clearly not math functions or constants: `__doc__`, `__file__`, `__name__`, and `__package__`. These names exist for every imported module. These names are defined by the Python interpreter at import time and are kept by the Python interpreter for bookkeeping purposes.

The name of the module, the absolute pathname of the file containing the module, and the module docstring are stored in variables `__name__`, `__file__`, and `__doc__`, respectively.

What Happens When Importing a Module

When the Python interpreter executes an `import` statement, it:

1. Looks for the file corresponding to the module.
2. Runs the module's code to create the objects defined in the module.
3. Creates a namespace where the names of these objects will live.

We discuss the first step in detail next. The second step consists of executing the code in the module. This means that all Python statements in the imported module are executed from top to bottom. All assignments, function definitions, class definitions, and import statements will create objects (whether integer or string objects, or functions, or modules, or classes) and generate the attributes (i.e., names) of the resulting objects. The names will be stored in a new namespace whose name is typically the name of the module.

Module Search Path

Now we look into how the interpreter finds the file corresponding to the module to be imported. An `import` statement only lists a name, the name of the module, without any directory information or .py suffix. Python uses a Python *search path* to locate the module. The search path is simply a list of directories (folders) where Python will look for modules. The variable name `path` defined in the Standard Library module `sys` refers to this list. You can thus see what the (current) search path is by executing this in the shell:

```
>>> import sys
>>> sys.path
['/Users/me/Documents', ...]
```

(We omit the long list of directories containing the Standard Library modules.) The module search path always contains the directory of the *top-level module*, which we discuss next, and also the directories containing the Standard Library modules. At every import statement, Python will search for the requested module in each directory in this list, from left to right. If Python cannot find the module, then an `ImportError` exception is raised.

For example, suppose we want to import the module `example.py` that is stored in home directory `/Users/me` (or whatever directory you saved the file `example.py` in):

Module: example.py

```
1   'an example module'
2   def f():
3       'function f'
4       print('Executing f()')
5
6   def g():
7       'function g'
8       print('Executing g()')
9
10  x = 0  # global var
```

Before we import the module, we run function `dir()` to check what names are defined in the shell namespace:

```
>>> dir()
['__builtins__', '__doc__', '__name__', '__package__']
```

The function `dir()`, when called without an argument, returns the names in the current namespace, which in this case is the shell namespace. It seems that only "bookkeeping" names are defined. (Read the next Detour about the name `__builtins__`.)

Now let's try to import the module `example.py`:

```
>>> import example
Traceback (most recent call last):
  File "<pyshell#24>", line 1, in <module>
    import example
ImportError: No module named example
```

It did not work because directory `/Users/me` is not in list `sys.path`. So let's append it:

```
>>> import sys
>>> sys.path.append('/Users/me')
```

and try again:

```
>>> import example
>>> example.f
<function f at 0x15e7d68>
>>> example.x
0
```

It worked. Let's run `dir()` again and check that the module `example` has been imported:

```
>>> dir()
['__builtins__', '__doc__', '__name__', '__package__', 'example',
 'sys']
```

DETOUR

Module `builtins`

The name `__builtins__` refers to the namespace of the `builtins` module, which we referred to in Figure 7.8.

The `builtins` module contains all the built-in types and functions and is usually imported automatically upon starting Python. You can check that by listing the attributes of module `builtins` using the `dir()` function:

```
>>> dir(__builtins__)
['ArithmeticError', 'AssertionError', ..., 'vars', 'zip']
```

Note: Use `dir(__builtins__)`, not `dir('__builtins__')`.

Practice Problem 7.5

Find the `random` module in one of the directories listed in `sys.path`, open it, and find the implementations of functions `randrange()`, `random()`, and `sample()`. Then import the module into the interpreter shell and view its attributes using the `dir()` function.

Top-Level Module

A computer application is a program that is typically split across multiple files (i.e., modules). In every Python program, one of the modules is special: It contains the "main program" by which we mean the code that starts the application. This module is referred to as the *top-level* module. The remaining modules are essentially "library" modules that are imported by the top-level module and contain functions and classes that are used by the application.

We have seen that when a module is imported, the Python interpreter creates a few "bookkeeping" variables in the module namespace. One of these is variable `__name__`. Python will set its value in this way:

- If the module is being run as a top-level module, attribute `__name__` is set to the string `__main__`.

- If the file is being imported by another module, whether the top-level or other, attribute `__name__` is set to the module's name.

We use the next module to illustrate how `__name__` is assigned:

Module: name.py

```
1  print('My name is {}'.format(__name__))
```

When this module is executed by running it from the shell (e.g., by hitting F5 in the IDLE shell), it is run as the main program (i.e., the top-level module):

```
>>>
My name is __main__
```

So the `__name__` attribute of the imported module is set to `__main__`.

DETOUR

> **Top-Level Module and the Module Search Path**
>
> In the last subsection, we mentioned that the directory containing the top-level module is listed in the search path. Let's check that this is indeed the case. First run the previous module `name.py` that was saved in, say, directory /Users/me. Then check the value of `sys.path`:
>
> ```
> >>> import sys
> >>> sys.path
> ['/Users/me', '/Users/me/Documents', ...]
> ```
>
> Note that directory /Users/me is in the search path.

The module `name` is also the top-level module when it is run at the command line:

```
> python name.py
My name is __main__
```

If, however, another module imports module `name`, then module `name` will not be top level. In the next import statement, the shell is the top-level program that imports the module `name.py`:

```
>>> import name
My name is name
```

Here is another example. The next module has only one statement, a statement that imports module `name.py`:

```
1  import name
```

Module: import.py

When module `import.py` is run from the shell, it is run as the main program that imports module `name.py`:

```
>>>
My name is name
```

In both cases, the `__name__` attribute of the imported module is set to the name of the module.

The `__name__` attribute of a module is useful for writing code that should be executed only when the module is run as the top-level module. This would be the case, for example, if the module is a "library" module that contains function definitions and we want to add to it debugging code that should be executed only when the module is run as the top-level module. All we need to do is make the debugging code a code block of this `if` statement:

```
if __name__ == '__main__':
    # code block
```

If the module is run as a top-level module, the code block will be executed; otherwise it will not.

Practice Problem 7.6

Add code to module `example.py` that calls the functions defined in the module and prints the values of variables defined in the module. The code should execute when the module is run as a top-level module only, such as when it is run from the shell:

```
>>>
Testing module example:
Executing f()
Executing g()
0
```

Different Ways to Import Module Attributes

We now describe three different ways to import a module and its attributes, and we discuss the relative benefits of each. We again use the module `example` as our running example:

Module: example.py

```
1  'an example module'
2  def f():
3      print('Executing f()')
4
5  def g():
6      print('Executing g()')
7
8  x = 0   # global var
```

One way to get access to functions `f()` or `g()`, or global variable x, is to:

```
>>> import example
```

This `import` statement will find the file `example.py` and run the code in it. This will instantiate two function objects and one integer object and create a namespace, called `example`, where the names of the created objected will be stored. In order to access and use the module attributes, we need to specify the module namespace:

```
>>> example.f()
Executing f()
```

As we have seen, calling `f()` directly would result in an error. Therefore, the `import` statement did not bring name f into the namespace of module `__main__` (the module that imported `example`); it only brings the name of the module `example`, as illustrated in Figure 7.13.

Figure 7.13 Importing a module. The statement `import example` creates name example in the calling module namespace which will refer to the namespace associated with the imported module `example`.

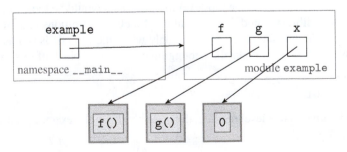

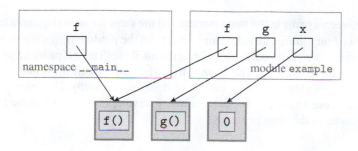

Figure 7.14 **Importing a module attribute.** Module attributes can be imported into the calling module namespace. The statement `from example import f` creates name `f` in the calling module namespace that refers to the appropriate function object.

Instead of importing the name of the module, it is also possible to import the names of the needed attributes themselves using the `from` command:

```
>>> from example import f
```

As illustrated in Figure 7.14, `from` copies the name of attribute `f` to the scope of the main program, the module doing the import, so that `f` can be referred to directly, without having to specify the module name.

```
>>> f()
Executing f()
```

Note that this code copies only the name of attribute `f`, not that of attribute `g` (see Figure 7.14). Referring to `g` directly results in an error:

```
>>> g()
Traceback (most recent call last):
  File "<pyshell#7>", line 1, in <module>
    g()
NameError: name 'g' is not defined
```

Finally, is is also possible to use `from` to import all the attributes of a module using the wild card `*`:

```
>>> from example import *
>>> f()
Executing f()
>>> x
0
```

Figure 7.15 shows that all the attributes of `example` are copied to the namespace `__main__`.

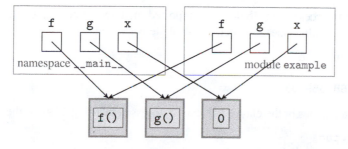

Figure 7.15 **Importing all the module's attributes.** The statement `from example import *` imports all the attributes of `example` into the calling module namespace.

Which way is best? That might not be the right question. Each of the three approaches has some benefits. Just importing the module name has the benefit of keeping the names in the module in a namespace separate from the main module. This guarantees that there will be no clash between a name in the main module and the same name in the imported module.

The benefit of importing individual attributes from the module is that we do not have to use the namespace as a prefix when we refer to the attribute. This helps make the code less verbose and thus more readable. The same is true when *all* module attributes are imported using `import *`, with the additional benefit of doing it succinctly. However, it is usually not a good idea to use `import *` because we may inadvertently import a name that clashes with a global name in the main program.

7.5 Classes as Namespaces

In Python, a namespace is associated with every class. In this section we explain what that means. We discuss, in particular, how Python uses namespaces in a clever way to implement classes and class methods.

But first, why should we care *how* Python implements classes? We have been using Python's built-in classes without ever needing to look below the hood. There will be times, however, when we will want to have a class that does not exist in Python. Chapter 8 explains how to develop new classes. There it will be very useful to know how Python uses namespaces to implement classes.

A Class Is a Namespace

Underneath the hood, a Python class is essentially a plain old namespace. The name of the namespace is the name of the class, and the names stored in the namespace are the class attributes (e.g., the class methods). For example, the class `list` is a namespace called `list` that contains the names of the methods and operators of the `list` class, as shown in Figure 7.16.

Figure 7.16 The namespace `list` and its attributes. The class `list` defines a namespace that contains the names of all list operators and methods. Each name refers to the appropriate function object.

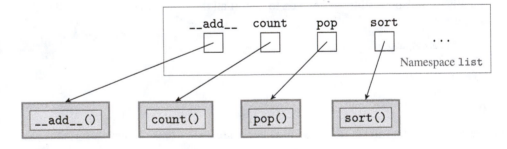

Recall that to access an attribute of an imported module, we need to specify the namespace (i.e., the module name) in which the attribute is defined:

```
>>> import math
>>> math.pi
3.141592653589793
```

Similarly, the attributes of the class `list` can be accessed by using `list` as the namespace:

```
>>> list.pop
<method 'pop' of 'list' objects>
>>> list.sort
<method 'sort' of 'list' objects>
```

Just as for any other namespace, you can use the built-in function `dir()` to find out all the names defined in the `list` namespace:

```
>>> dir(list)
['__add__', '__class__', '__contains__', '__delattr__',
...,
    'index', 'insert', 'pop', 'remove', 'reverse', 'sort']
```

These are names of the operators and methods of the list class.

Class Methods Are Functions Defined in the Class Namespace

We now look at how class methods are implemented in Python. We continue to use the class `list` as our running example. Suppose, for example, that you would like to sort this list:

```
>>> lst = [5,2,8,1,3,6,4,7]
```

In Chapter 2, we learned how to do this:

```
>>> lst.sort()
```

We know now that function `sort()` is really a function defined in the namespace `list`. In fact, when the Python interpreter executes the statement

```
>>> lst.sort()
```

the first thing it will do is translate the statement to

```
>>> list.sort(lst)
```

Try executing both statements and you will see that the result is the same!

When method `sort()` is invoked on the list object `lst`, what really happens is that the function `sort()`, defined in namespace `list`, is called on list object `lst`. More generally, Python automatically maps the invocation of a method by an instance of a class, such as

```
instance.method(arg1, arg2, ...)
```

to a call to a function defined in the class namespace and using the instance as the first argument:

```
class.method(instance, arg1, arg2, ...)
```

where `class` is the type of `instance`. This last statement is the statement that is actually executed.

Let's illustrate this with a few more examples. The method invocation `lst.append(9)` on list `lst` gets translated by the Python interpreter to function call `list.append(lst, 9)`. The method invocation `d.keys()` by dictionary `d` gets translated to `dict.keys(d)`.

From these examples, you can see that the *implementation* of every class method must include an additional input argument, corresponding to the instance calling the method.

E-Book Case Study: Debugging with a debugger

In this case study, we show how to use a debugger to find bugs in a program or, more generally, to analyze the execution of the program. To do this, the debugger provides a way to stop the execution of a program at any program statement and to inspect the value of the program variables at that point. This includes, in particular, the variables stored in the frames of the program stack.

Chapter Summary

This chapter covers programming language concepts and constructs that are key to managing program complexity. The chapter builds on the introductory material on functions and parameter passing from Sections 3.3 and 3.5 and sets up a framework that will be useful when learning how to develop new Python classes in Chapter 8 and when learning how recursive functions execute in Chapter 10.

One of the main benefits of functions—encapsulation—follows from the black box property of functions: Functions do not interfere with the calling program other than through the input arguments (if any) and returned values (if any). This property of functions holds because a separate namespace is associated with each function call, and thus a variable name defined during the execution of the function call is not visible outside of that function call.

The normal execution control flow of a program, in which functions call other functions, requires the management of function call namespaces by the OS through a program stack. The program stack is used to keep track of the namespaces of active function calls. When an exception is raised, the normal control flow of the program is interrupted and replaced by the exceptional control flow. The default exceptional control flow is to interrupt every active function call and output an error message. In this chapter, we introduce exception handling, using the `try`/`except` pair of statements, as a way to manage the exceptional control flow and, when it makes sense, use it as part of the program.

Namespaces are associated with imported modules as well as classes and, as shown in Chapter 8, objects as well. The reason for this is the same as for functions: Components of a program are easier to manage if they behave like black boxes that do not interfere with each other in unintended ways. Understanding Python classes as namespaces is particularly useful in the next chapter, where we learn how to develop new classes.

Solutions to Practice Problems

7.1 During the execution of `g(3)`, function call `f(1)` has not terminated yet and has a namespace associated with it; in this namespace, local variable names y and x are defined, with values 1 and 2, respectively. Function call `g(3)` also has a namespace associated with it, containing different variable names y and x, referring to values 3 and 4, respectively.

The namespaces are shown graphically in the following figure.

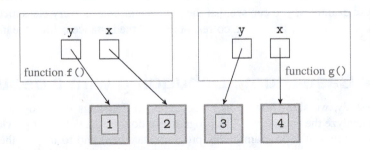

7.2 The answers are shown as inline comments:

```
def f(y):          # f is global, y is local to f()
    x = 2          # x is local to f()
    return g(x)    # g is global, x is local to f()

def g(y):          # g is global, y is local to g()
    global x        # x is global
    x = 4          # x is global
    return x*y     # x is global, y is local to g()

x = 0              # x is global
res = f(x)         # res, f and x are global
print('x = {}, f(0) = {}'.format(x, res)) # same here
```

7.3 The function should take the same arguments as the `open()` function. The statements that open the file and return the reference to the opened file should be in the `try` code section. The exception handler should just return `None`.

```
def safe-open(filename, mode):
    'returns handle to file filename, or None if error occurred'
    try:
        # try block
        infile = open(filename, mode)
        return infile
    except:
        # exept block
        return None
```

7.4 These statements are not executed:
(a) Every statement is executed.
(b) The last statements in `h()` and `g()`.
(c) The last statements in `h()`.

7.5 On Windows, the folder containing the module `random` is `C:\\Python3x\lib`, where x can be 1, 2, or other digit, depending on the version of Python 3 you are using; on a Mac, it is `/Library/Frameworks/Python.Framework/Versions/3.x/lib/python31`.

7.6 This code is added at the end of file `example.py`:

```
if __name__ == '__main__':
    print('Testing module example:')
    f()
    g()
    print(x)
```

Exercises

7.7 Using Figure 7.5 as your model, illustrate the execution of function call `f(1)` as well as the state of the program stack. Function `f()` is defined in module `stack.py`.

7.8 What is the problem with the next program?

Module: probA.py

```
1  print(f(3))
2  def f(x):
3      return 2*x+1
```

Does the next program exhibit the same problem?

Module: probB.py

```
1  def g(x):
2      print(f(x))
3
4  def f(x):
5      return 2*x+1
6
7  g(3)
```

7.9 The blackjack application developed in the Chapter 6 case study consists of five functions. Therefore, all variables defined in the program are local. However, some of the local variables are passed as arguments to other functions, and the objects they refer to are therefore (intentionally) shared. For each such object, indicate in which function the object was created and which functions have access to it.

7.10 This exercise relates to modules one, two, and three:

Module: one.py

```
1  import two
2
3  def f1():
4      two.f2()
5
6  def f4():
7      print('Hello!')
```

Module: two.py

```
1  import three
2
3  def f2():
4      three.f3()
```

Module: three.py

```
1  import one
2
3  def f3():
4      one.f4()
```

When module one is imported into the interpreter shell, we can execute `f1()`:

```
>>> import one
>>> one.f1()
Hello!
```

(For this to work, list sys.path should include the folder containing the three modules.) Using Figure 7.13 as your model, draw the namespaces corresponding to the three imported modules and also the shell namespace. Show all the names defined in the three imported namespaces as well as the objects they refer to.

7.11 After importing one in the previous problem, we can view the attributes of one:

```
>>> dir(one)
['__builtins__', '__doc__', '__file__', '__name__', '__package__',
'f1', 'f4', 'two']
```

However, we cannot view the attributes of two in the same way:

```
>>> dir(two)
Traceback (most recent call last):
  File "<pyshell#202>", line 1, in <module>
    dir(two)
NameError: name 'two' is not defined
```

Why is that? Note that importing module one forces the importing of modules two and three. How can we view their attributes using function dir()?

7.12 Using Figure 7.2 as your model, illustrate the execution of function call one.f1(). Function f1() is defined in module one.py.

7.13 Modify the module blackjack.py from the Chapter 6 case study so that when the module is run as the top module, the function blackjack() is called (in other words, a blackjack game starts). Test your solution by running the program from your system's command-line shell:

```
> python blackjack.py
House:    7 ♣    8 ◇
  You:   10 ♣    J ♠
Hit or stand? (default: hit):
```

7.14 Let list lst be:

```
>>> lst = [2,3,4,5]
```

Translate the next list method invocations to appropriate calls to functions in namespace list:

(a) lst.sort()

(b) lst.append(3)

(c) lst.count(3)

(d) lst.insert(2, 1)

7.15 Translate the following string method invocations to functions calls in namespace str:

(a) 'error'.upper()

(b) '2,3,4,5'.split(',')

(c) 'mississippi'.count('i')

(d) 'bell'.replace('e', 'a')

(e) ' '.format(1, 2, 3)

Problems

7.16 The first input argument of function `index()` in Problem 6.27 is supposed to be the name of a text file. If the file cannot be found by the interpreter or if it cannot be read as a text file, an exception will be raised. Reimplement function `index()` so that the message shown here is printed instead:

```
>>> index('rven.txt', ['raven', 'mortal', 'dying', 'ghost'])
File 'rven.txt' not found.
```

7.17 In Problem 6.35, you were asked to develop an application that asks users to solve addition problems. Users were required to enter their answers using digits 0 through 9.

Reimplement the function `game()` so that it handles nondigit user input by printing a friendly message like "Please write your answer using digits 0 though 9. Try again!" and then giving the user another opportunity to enter an answer.

```
>>> game(3)
8 + 2 =
Enter answer: ten
Please write your answer using digits 0 though 9. Try again!
Enter answer: 10
Correct.
```

7.18 The blackjack application developed in the Chapter 6 case study includes the `dealCard()` function that pops the top card from the deck and passes it to a game participant. The deck is implemented as a list of cards, and popping the top card from the deck corresponds to popping the list. If the function is called on an empty deck, an attempt to pop an empty list is made, and an `IndexError` exception is raised.

Modify the blackjack application by handling the exception raised when trying to deal a card from an empty deck. Your handler should create a new shuffled deck and deal a card from the top of this new deck.

7.19 Implement function `inValues()` that asks the user to input a set of nonzero floating-point values. When the user enters a value that is not a number, give the user a second chance to enter the value. After two mistakes in a row, quit the program. When the user enters 0, the function should return the sum of all correctly entered values. Use exception handling to detect improper inputs.

```
>>> inValues()
Please enter a number: 4.75
Please enter a number: 2,25
Error. Please re-enter the value.
Please enter a number: 2.25
Please enter a number: 0
7.0
>>> inValues()
Please enter a number: 3.4
Please enter a number: 3,4
Error. Please re-enter the value.
Please enter a number: 3,4
Two errors in a row. Quitting ...
```

7.20 In Problem 7.19, the program quits only when the user makes two mistakes *in a row*. Implement the alternative version of the program that quits when the user makes the second mistake, even if it follows a correct entry by the user.

7.21 If you type ⌐Ctrl⌐C⌐ while the shell is executing the input() function, a KeyboardInterrupt exception will be raised. For example:

```
>>> x = input()          # Typing Ctrl-C
Traceback (most recent call last):
  File "<stdin>", line 1, in <module>
KeyboardInterrupt
```

Create a wrapper function safe_input() which works just like function input() except that it returns nothing when an exception is raised.

```
>>> x = safe_input()    # Typing Ctrl-C
>>> x                    # x is None
>>> x = safe_input()    # Typing 34
34
>>> x                    # x is 34
'34'
```

Object-Oriented Programming

8.1 Defining a New Python Class   240

8.2 Examples of User-Defined Classes   248

8.3 Designing New Container Classes   251

8.4 Overloaded Operators   256

8.5 Inheritance   264

8.6 User-Defined Exceptions   272

E-Book Case Study: Indexing and Iterators   275

Chapter Summary   275

Solutions to Practice Problems   276

Exercises   279

Problems   281

THIS CHAPTER DESCRIBES how to implement new Python classes and introduces object-oriented programming (OOP).

There are several reasons why programming languages such as Python enable developers to define new classes. Classes that are custom-built for a particular application will make the application program more intuitive and easier to develop, debug, read, and maintain.

The ability to create new classes also enables a new approach to structuring application programs. A function exposes to the user its behavior but encapsulates (i.e., hides) its implementation. Similarly, a class exposes to the user the methods that can be applied to objects of the class but encapsulates how the data contained in the objects is stored and how the class methods are implemented. This property of classes is achieved thanks to fine-grained, customized namespaces that are associated with every class and object. OOP is a software development paradigm that achieves modularity and code portability by organizing application programs around components that are classes and objects.

8.1 Defining a New Python Class

We now explain how to define a new class in Python. The first class we develop is the class Point, a class that represents points in the plane or, if you prefer, on a map. More precisely, an object of type Point corresponds to a point in the two-dimensional plane. Recall that each point in the plane can be specified by its x-axis and y-axis coordinates as shown in Figure 8.1.

Figure 8.1 A point in the plane. An object of type Point represents a point in the plane. A point is defined by its x and y coordinates.

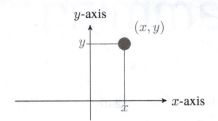

Before we implement the class Point, we need to decide how it should behave, that is, what methods it should support.

Methods of Class Point

Let's describe how we would like to use the class Point. To create a Point object, we would use the default constructor of the Point class. This is no different from using the list() or int() default constructors to create a list or integer object.

```
>>> point = Point()
```

(Just a reminder: We have not implemented the class Point yet; the code here is only meant to illustrate how we want the class Point to behave.)

Once we have a Point object, we would set its coordinates using the methods setx() and sety():

```
>>> point.setx(3)
>>> point.sety(4)
```

At this point, Point object point should have its coordinates set. We could check this using method get():

```
>>> point.get()
(3, 4)
```

The method get() would return the coordinates of point as a tuple object. Now, to move point down by three units, we would use method move():

```
>>> point.move(0,-3)
>>> point.get()
(3, 1)
```

We should also be able to change the coordinates of point:

```
>>> point.sety(-2)
>>> point.get()
(3, -2)
```

We summarize the methods we want class Point to support in Table 8.1.

Usage	Explanation
`point.setx(xcoord)`	Sets the x coordinate of `point` to `xcoord`
`point.sety(ycoord)`	Sets the y coordinate of `point` to `ycoord`
`point.get()`	Returns the x and y coordinates of `point` as a tuple `(x, y)`
`point.move(dx, dy)`	Changes the coordinates of `point` from the current `(x, y)` to `(x+dx, y+dy)`

Table 8.1 Methods of class Point. The usage for the four methods of class `Point` is shown; `point` refers to an object of type `Point`.

A Class and Its Namespace

As we learned in Chapter 7, a namespace is associated with every Python class, and the name of the namespace is the name of the class. The purpose of the namespace is to store the names of the class attributes. The class `Point` should have an associated namespace called `Point`. This namespace would contain the names of class `Point` methods, as shown in Figure 8.2.

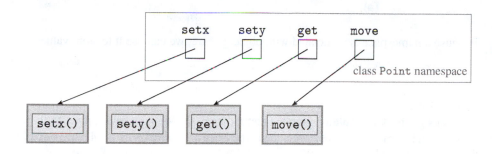

Figure 8.2 Class Point **and its attributes.** When class `Point` is defined, a namespace associated with the class is defined too; this namespace contains the class attributes.

Figure 8.2 shows how each name in namespace `Point` refers to the implementation of a function. Let's consider the implementation of function `setx()`.

In Chapter 7, we learned that Python translates a method invocation like

```
>>> point.setx(3)
```

to

```
>>> Point.setx(point, 3)
```

So function `setx()` is a function that is defined in the namespace `Point`. It takes not one but two arguments: the `Point` object that is invoking the method and an x-coordinate. Therefore, the implementation of `setx()` would have to be something like:

```
def setx(point, xcoord):
    # implementation of setx
```

Function `setx()` would somehow have to store the x-coordinate `xcoord` so that it can later be retrieved by, say, method `get()`. Unfortunately, the next code will not work

```
def setx(point, xcoord):
    x = xcoord
```

because `x` is a local variable that will disappear as soon as function call `setx()` terminates. Where should the value of `xcoord` be stored so that it can be retrieved later?

Every Object Has an Associated Namespace

We know that a namespace is associated with every class. It turns out that not only classes but *every* Python object has its own, separate namespace. When we instantiate a new object of type Point and give it name point, as in

```
>>> point = Point()
```

a new namespace called point gets created, as shown in Figure 8.3(a).

Figure 8.3 The namespace of an object. (a) Every Point object has a namespace. (b) The statement point.x = 3 assigns 3 to variable x defined in namespace point.

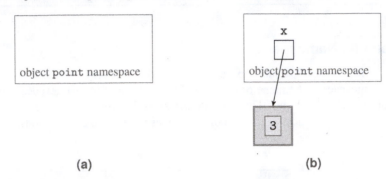

(a)   (b)

Because a namespace is associated with object point, we can use it to store values:

```
>>> point.x = 3
```

This statement creates name x in namespace point and assigns it integer object 3, as shown in Figure 8.3(b).

Now let's get back to implementing the method setx(). We now have a place to the *x*-coordinate of a Point object. We store it the namespace associated with it. Method setx() would be implemented in this way:

```
def setx(point, xcoord):
    point.x = xcoord
```

Implementation of Class Point

We are now ready to write the implementation of class Point:

Module: ch8.py

```
1  class Point:
2      'class that represents points in the plane'
3      def setx(self, xcoord):
4          'set x coordinate of point to xcoord'
5          self.x = xcoord
6      def sety(self, ycoord):
7          'set y coordinate of point to ycoord'
8          self.y = ycoord
9      def get(self):
10         'return a tuple with x and y coordinates of the point'
11         return (self.x, self.y)
12     def move(self, dx, dy):
13         'change the x and y coordinates by dx and dy'
14         self.x += dx
15         self.y += dy
```

The reserved keyword `class` is used to define a new Python class. The `class` statement is very much like the `def` statement. A `def` statement defines a new *function* and gives the function a name; a `class` statement defines a new *type* and gives the type a name. (They are both also similar to the assignment statement that gives a name to an object.)

Following the `class` keyword is the name of the class, just as the function name follows the `def` statement. Another similarity with function definitions is the docstring below the `class` statement: It will be processed by the Python interpreter as part of the documentation for the class, just as for functions.

A class is defined by its attributes. The class attributes (i.e., the four methods of class `Point`) are defined in an indented code block just below the line

```
class Point:
```

The first input argument of each class method refers to the object invoking the method. We have already figured out the implementation of method `setx()`:

```
def setx(self, xcoord):
    'sets x coordinate of point'
    self.x = xcoord
```

We made one change to the implementation. The first argument that refers to the `Point` object invoking method `setx()` is named `self` rather than `point`. The name of the first argument can be anything really; the important thing is that it always refers to the object invoking the method. However, the convention among Python developers is to use name `self` for the object that the method is invoked on, and we follow that convention.

The method `sety()` is similar to `setx()`: It stores the *y*-coordinate in variable y, which is also defined in the namespace of the invoking object. Method `get()` returns the values of names x and y defined in the namespace of the invoking object. Finally, method `move()` changes the values of variables x and y associated with the invoking object.

You should now test your new class `Point`. First execute the class definition by running module `ch8.py`. Then try this, for example:

```
>>> a = Point()
>>> a.setx(3)
>>> a.sety(4)
>>> a.get()
(3, 4)
```

Add method `getx()` to the class `Point`; this method takes no input and returns the *x* coordinate of the `Point` object invoking the method.

```
>>> a.getx()
3
```

Practice Problem 8.1

Instance Variables

Variables defined in the namespace of an object, such as variables x and y in the `Point` object a, are called *instance variables*. Every instance (object) of a class will have its own namespace and therefore its own separate copy of an instance variable.

For example, suppose we create a second `Point` object b as follows:

```
>>> b = Point()
>>> b.setx(5)
>>> b.sety(-2)
```

Instances a and b will each have its own copies of instance variables x and y, as shown in Figure 8.4.

Figure 8.4 Instance variables. Each object of type `Point` has its own instance variables x and y, stored in the namespace associated with the object.

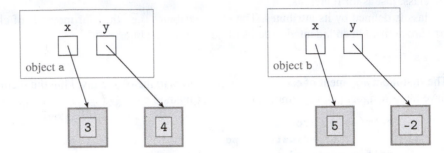

In fact, instance variables x and y can be accessed by specifying the appropriate instance:

```
>>> a.x
3
>>> b.x
5
```

They can, of course, be changed directly as well:

```
>>> a.x = 7
>>> a.x
7
```

Instances Inherit Class Attributes

Names a and b refer to objects of type `Point`, so the namespaces of a and b should have some relationship with the namespace `Point` that contains the class methods that can be invoked on objects a and b. We can check this, using Python's function `dir()`, which we introduced in Chapter 7 and which takes a namespace and returns a list of names defined in it:

```
>>> dir(a)
['__class__', '__delattr__', '__dict__', '__doc__', '__eq__',
  ...
  '__weakref__', 'get', 'move', 'setx', 'sety', 'x', 'y']
```

(We omit a few lines of output.)

As expected, instance variable names x and y appear in the list. But so do the methods of the Point class: `setx`, `sety`, `get`, and `move`. We will say that object a *inherits* all the attributes of class `Point`, just as a child inherits attributes from a parent. Therefore, all the attributes of class `Point` are accessible from namespace a. Let's check this:

```
>>> a.setx
<bound method Point.setx of <__main__.Point object at 0x14b7ef0>>
```

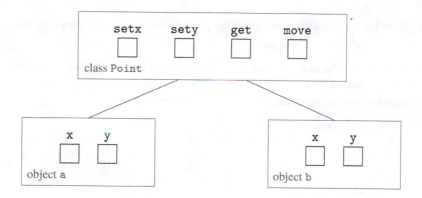

Figure 8.5 Instance and class attributes. Each object of type `Point` has its own instance attributes `x` and `y`. They all inherit the attributes of class `Point`.

The relationship between namespaces a, b, and `Point` is illustrated in Figure 8.5. It is important to understand that the method names `setx`, `sety`, `get`, and `move` are defined in namespace `Point`, not in namespace a or b. Thus, the Python interpreter uses this procedure when it evaluates expression `a.setx`:

1. It first attempts to find name `setx` in object (namespace) a.
2. If name `setx` does not exist in namespace a, then it attempts to find `setx` in namespace `Point` (where it will find it).

Class Definition, More Generally

The format of the class definition statement is:

```
class <Class Name>:
    <class variable 1> = <value>
    <class variable 2> = <value>
    ...
    def <class method 1>(self, arg11, arg12, ...):
        <implementation of class method 1>
    def <class method 2>(self, arg21, arg22, ...):
        <implementation of class method 2>
    ...
```

(We will see a more general version in later sections.)

The first line of a class definition consists of the `class` keyword followed by `<Class Name>`, the name of the class. In our example, the name was `Point`.

The definitions of the class attributes follow the first line. Each definition is indented with respect to the first line. Class attributes can be class methods or class variables. In class `Point`, four class methods were defined, but no class variable. A class variable is one whose name is defined in the namespace of the class.

Start by defining the class `Test` and then creating two instances of `Test` in your interpreter shell:

```
>>> class Test:
        version = 1.02

>>> a = Test()
>>> b = Test()
```

Practice Problem 8.2

The class `Test` has only one attribute, the class variable `version` that refers to `float` value 1.02.

(a) Draw the namespaces associated with the class and the two objects, the names—if any—contained in them, and the value(s) the name(s) refer to.

(b) Execute these statements and fill in the question marks:

```
>>> a.version
???
>>> b.version
???
>>> Test.version
???
>>> Test.version=1.03
>>> a.version
???
>>> Point.version
???
>>> a.version = 'Latest!!'
>>> Point.version
???
>>> b.version
???
>>> a.version
???
```

(c) Draw the state of the namespaces after this execution. Explain why the last three expressions evaluate the way they did.

Documenting a Class

In order to get usable documentation from the `help()` tool, it is important to document a new class properly. The class `Point` we defined has a docstring for the class and also one for every method:

```
>>> help(Point)
Help on class Point in module __main__:

class Point(builtins.object)
 |  class that represents a point in the plane
 |
 |  Methods defined here:
 |
 |  get(self)
 |      returns the x and y coordinates of the point as a tuple
 |
 ...
```

(We omit the rest of the output.)

Class Animal

Before we move on to the next section, let's put into practice everything we have learned so far and develop a new class called Animal that abstracts animals and supports three methods:

- setSpecies(species): Sets the species of the animal object to species.

- setLanguage(language): Sets the language of the animal object to language.

- speak(): Prints a message from the animal as shown below.

Here is how we want the class to behave:

```
>>> snoopy = Animal()
>>> snoopy.setpecies('dog')
>>> snoopy.setLanguage('bark')
>>> snoopy.speak()
I am a dog and I bark.
```

We start the class definition with the first line:

```
class Animal:
```

Now, in an indented code block, we define the three class methods, starting with method setSpecies(). Even though the method setSpecies() is *used* with one argument (the animal species), it must be *defined* as a function that takes two arguments: the argument self that refers to the object invoking the method and the species argument:

```
def setSpecies(self, species):
    self.species = species
```

Note that we named the instance variable species the same as the local variable species. Because the instance variable is defined in the namespace self and the local variable is defined in the local namespace of the function call, there is no name conflict.

The implementation of method setLanguage() is similar to the implementation of setSpecies. The method speak() is *used* without input arguments; therefore, it must be defined with just input argument self. Here is the final implementation:

Module: ch8.py

```
1  class Animal:
2      'represents an animal'
3
4      def setSpecies(self, species):
5          'sets the animal species'
6          self.spec = species
7
8      def setLanguage(self, language):
9          'sets the animal language'
10         self.lang = language
11
12     def speak(self):
13         'prints a sentence by the animal'
14         print('I am a {} and I {}.'.format(self.spec, self.lang))
```

Practice Problem
8.3

Implement class `Rectangle` that represents rectangles. The class should support methods:

- `setSize(width, length)`: Takes two number values as input and sets the length and the width of the rectangle
- `perimeter()`: Returns the perimeter of the rectangle
- `area()`: Returns the area of the rectangle

```
>>> rectangle = Rectangle(3,4)
>>> rectangle.perimeter()
14
>>> rectangle.area()
12
```

8.2 Examples of User-Defined Classes

In order to get more comfortable with the process of designing and implementing a new class, in this section we work through the implementation of several more classes. But first, we explain how to make it easier to create and initialize new objects.

Overloaded Constructor Operator

We take another look at the class `Point` we developed in the previous section. To create a `Point` object at (x, y)-coordinates $(3, 4)$, we need to execute three separate statements:

```
>>> a = Point()
>>> a.setx(3)
>>> a.sety(4)
```

The first statement creates an instance of `Point`; the remaining two lines initialize the point's x- and y-coordinates. That's quite a few steps to create a point at a certain location. It would be nicer if we could fold the instantiation and the initialization into one step:

```
>>> a = Point(3,4)
```

We have already seen types that allow an object to be initialized when created. Integers can be initialized when created:

```
>>> x = int(93)
>>> x
93
```

So can objects of type `Fraction` from the built-in `fractions` module:

```
>>> import fractions
>>> x = fractions.Fraction(3,4)
>>> x
Fraction(3, 4)
```

Constructors that take input arguments are useful because they can initialize the state of the object at the moment the object is instantiated.

In order to be able to use a `Point()` constructor with input arguments, we must explicitly add a method called `__init__()` to the implementation of class `Point`. When added to a class, it will be automatically called by the Python interpreter whenever an object is created. In other words, when Python executes

        Point(3,4)

it will create a "blank" `Point` object first and then execute

        self.__init__(3, 4)

where `self` refers to the newly created `Point` object. Note that since `__init__()` is a method of the class `Point` that takes two input arguments, the function `__init__()` will need to be defined to take two input arguments as well, *plus* the obligatory argument `self`:

```
1   class Point:
2       'represents points in the plane'
3       def __init__(self, xcoord, ycoord):
4           'initializes point coordinates to (xcoord, ycoord)'
5           self.x = xcoord
6           self.y = ycoord
7
8       # implementations of methods setx(), sety(), get(), and move()
```

Module: ch8.py

Function `__init__()` Is Called *Every Time* an Object Is Created

Because the `__init__()` method is called every time an object is instantiated, the `Point()` constructor must now be called with two arguments. This means that calling the constructor without an argument will result in an error:

```
>>> a = Point()
Traceback (most recent call last):
  File "<pyshell#23>", line 1, in <module>
    a = Point()
TypeError: __init__() takes exactly 3 positional arguments
(1 given)
```

It *is* possible to rewrite the `__init__()` function so that it can handle two arguments, or none, or one. Read on.

CAUTION

Default Constructor

We know that constructors of built-in classes can be used with or without arguments:

```
>>> int(3)
3
>>> int()
0
```

We can do the same with user-defined classes. All we need to do is specify the default values of the input arguments `xcoord` and `ycoord` *if* input arguments are not provided. In the next reimplementation of the `__init__()` method, we specify default values of 0:

Module: ch8.py

```
1  class Point:
2      'represents points in the plane'
3
4      def __init__(self, xcoord=0, ycoord=0):
5          'initializes point coordinates to (xcoord, ycoord)'
6          self.x = xcoord
7          self.y = ycoord
8
9      # implementations of methods setx(), sety(), get(), and move()
```

This `Point` constructor can now take two input arguments

```
>>> a = Point(3,4)
>>> a.get()
(3, 4)
```

or none

```
>>> b = Point()
>>> b.get()
(0, 0)
```

or even just one

```
>>> c = Point(2)
>>> c.get()
(2, 0)
```

The Python interpreter will assign the constructor arguments to the local variables `xcoord` and `ycoord` from left to right.

Playing Card Class

In Chapter 6, we developed a blackjack application. We used strings such as `'3 ♠'` to represent playing cards. Now that we know how to develop new types, it makes sense to develop a `Card` class to represent playing cards.

This class should support a two-argument constructor to create `Card` objects:

```
>>> card = Card('3', '\u2660')
```

The string `'\u2660'` is the escape sequence that represents Unicode character ♠. The class should also support methods to retrieve the rank and suit of the `Card` object:

```
>>> card.getRank()
'3'
>>> card.getSuit()
'♠'
```

That should be enough. We want the class `Card` to support these methods:

- `Card(rank, suit)`: Constructor that initializes the rank and suit of the card
- `getRank()`: Returns the card's rank
- `getSuit()`: Returns the card's suit

Note that the constructor is specified to take exactly two input arguments. We choose not to provide default values for the rank and suit because it is not clear what a default playing card would really be. Let's implement the class:

Module: cards.py

```
1   class Card:
2       'represents a playing card'
3
4       def __init__(self, rank, suit):
5           'initialize rank and suit of playing card'
6           self.rank = rank
7           self.suit = suit
8
9       def getRank(self):
10          'return rank'
11          return self.rank
12
13      def getSuit(self):
14          'return suit'
15          return self.suit
```

Note that the method `__init__()` is implemented to take two arguments, which are the rank and suit of the card to be created.

Modify the class `Animal` we developed in the previous section so that it supports a two, one, or no input argument constructor:

```
>>> snoopy = Animal('dog', 'bark')
>>> snoopy.speak()
I am a dog and I bark.
>>> tweety = Animal('canary')
>>> tweety.speak()
I am a canary and I make sounds.
>>> animal = Animal()
>>> animal.speak()
I am a animal and I make sounds.
```

Practice Problem 8.4

8.3 Designing New Container Classes

Although Python provides a diverse set of container classes, there will always be a need to develop container classes tailored for specific applications. We illustrate this with a class that represents a deck of playing cards and also with the classic queue container class.

Designing a Class Representing a Deck of Playing Cards

We again use the blackjack application from Chapter 6 to motivate our next class. In the blackjack program, the deck of cards was implemented using a list. To shuffle the deck, we used the `shuffle()` method from the `random` module, and to deal a card, we used the `list` method `pop()`. In short, the blackjack application was written using nonapplication-specific terminology and operations.

The blackjack program would have been more readable if the list container and operations were hidden and the program was written using a Deck class and Deck methods. So let's develop such a class. But first, how would we want the Deck class to behave?

First, we should be able to obtain a standard deck of 52 cards using a default constructor:

```
>>> deck = Deck()
```

The class should support a method to shuffle the deck:

```
>>> deck.shuffle()
```

The class should also support a method to deal the top card from the deck.

```
>>> card = deck.dealCard()
>>> (card.getRank(), card.getSuit())
('9', '♠')
>>> card = deck.dealCard()
>>> (card.getRank(), card.getSuit())
('J', '◇')
>>> card = deck.dealCard()
>>> (card.getRank(), card.getSuit())
('10', '◇')
```

The methods that the Deck class should support are:

- `Deck()`: Constructor that initializes the deck to a standard deck of 52 playing cards

- `shuffle()`: Shuffles the deck

- `dealCard()`: Pops and returns the card at the *top* of the deck

Implementing the Deck (of Cards) Class

Let's implement the Deck class, starting with the Deck constructor. Unlike the two examples from the previous section (classes `Point` and `Card`), the Deck constructor does not take input arguments. It still needs to be implemented because its job is to create the 52 playing cards of a deck and store them somewhere.

To create the list of the 52 standard playing cards, we can use a nested loop that is similar to the one we used in function `shuffledDeck()` of the blackjack application. There we created a set of suits and a set of ranks

```
suits = {'\u2660', '\u2661', '\u2662', '\u2663'}
ranks = {'2','3','4','5','6','7','8','9','10','J','Q','K','A'}
```

and then used a nested `for` loop to create every combination of rank and suit

```
for suit in suits:
    for rank in ranks:
        # create card with given rank and suit and add to deck
```

We need a container to store all the generated playing cards. Because the ordering of cards in a deck is relevant and the deck should be allowed to change, we choose a list just as we did in the blackjack application in Chapter 6.

Now we have some design decisions to make. First, should the list containing the playing cards be an instance or class variable? Because every Deck object should have its own list of playing cards, the list clearly should be an instance variable.

We have another design question to resolve: Where should the sets suits and ranks be defined? They could be local variables of the __init__() function. They could also be class variables of the class Deck. Or they could be instance variables. Because the sets will not be modified and they are shared by all Deck instances, we decide to make them class variables.

Take a look at the implementation of the method __init__() in module cards.py. Because the sets suits and ranks are class variables of the class Deck, they are defined in namespace Deck. Therefore, in order to access them in lines 12 and 13, you must specify a namespace:

```
for suit in Deck.suits:
    for rank in Deck.ranks:
        # add Card with given rank and suit to deck
```

We now turn our attention to the implementation of the two remaining methods of class Deck. The method shuffle() should just call random module function shuffle() on instance variable self.deck.

For method dealCard(), we need to decide where the top of the deck is. Is it at the beginning of list self.deck or at the end of it? We decide to go for the end. The complete class Deck is:

Module: cards.py

```python
1   from random import shuffle
2   class Deck:
3       'represents a deck of 52 cards'
4
5       # ranks and suits are Deck class variables
6       ranks = {'2','3','4','5','6','7','8','9','10','J','Q','K','A'}
7
8       # suits is a set of 4 Unicode symbols representing the 4 suits
9       suits = {'\u2660', '\u2661', '\u2662', '\u2663'}
10
11      def __init__(self):
12          'initialize deck of 52 cards'
13          self.deck = []           # deck is initially empty
14
15          for suit in Deck.suits: # suits and ranks are Deck
16              for rank in Deck.ranks: # class variables
17                  # add Card with given rank and suit to deck
18                  self.deck.append(Card(rank, suit))
19
20      def dealCard(self):
21          'deal (pop and return) card from the top of the deck'
22          return self.deck.pop()
23
24      def shuffle(self):
25          'shuffle the deck'
26          shuffle(self.deck)
```

Practice Problem 8.5

Modify the constructor of the class Deck so that the class can also be used for card games that do not use the standard deck of 52 cards. For such games, we would need to provide the list of cards explicitly in the constructor. Here is a somewhat artificial example:

```
>>> deck = Deck(['1', '2', '3', '4'])
>>> deck.shuffle()
>>> deck.dealCard()
'3'
>>> deck.dealCard()
'1'
```

Container Class Queue

A queue is a container type that abstracts a queue, such as a queue of shoppers in a supermarket waiting at the cashier's. In a checkout queue, shoppers are served in a first-in first-out (FIFO) fashion. A shopper will put himself at the end of the queue and the first person in the queue is the next one served by the cashier. More generally, all insertions must be at the rear of the queue, and all removals must be from the front.

We now develop a basic Queue class that abstracts a queue. It will support very restrictive accesses to the items in the queue: method enqueue() to add an item to the rear of the queue and method dequeue() to remove an item from the front of the queue. As shown in Table 8.2, the Queue class will also support method isEmpty() that returns true or false depending on whether the queue is empty or not. The Queue class is said to be a FIFO container type because the item removed is the item that entered the queue earliest.

Before we implement the Queue class, we illustrate its usage. We start by instantiating a Queue object:

```
>>> fruit = Queue()
```

We then insert a fruit (as a string) into it:

```
>>> fruit.enqueue('apple')
```

Let's insert a few more fruits:

```
>>> fruit.enqueue('banana')
>>> fruit.enqueue('coconut')
```

We can then dequeue the queue:

```
>>> fruit.dequeue()
'apple'
```

The method dequeue() should both remove *and* return the item at the front of the queue.

Table 8.2 Queue methods. A queue is a container of a sequence of items; the only accesses to the sequence are enqueue(item) and dequeue().

Method	Description
enqueue(item)	Add item to the end of the queue
dequeue()	Remove and return the element at the front of the queue
isEmpty()	Returns True if the queue is empty, False otherwise

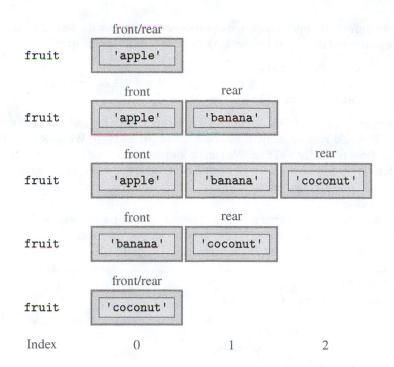

Figure 8.6 Queue operations. Shown is the state of the queue `fruit` after the statements:
`fruit.enqueue('apple')`
`fruit.enqueue('banana')`
`fruit.enqueue('coconut')`
`fruit.dequeue()`
`fruit.dequeue()`

We dequeue two more times to get back an empty queue:

```
>>> fruit.dequeue()
'banana'
>>> fruit.dequeue()
'coconut'
>>> fruit.isEmpty()
True
```

Figure 8.6 shows the sequence of states the queue `fruit` went through as we executed the previous commands.

Implementing a Queue Class

Let's discuss the implementation of the `Queue` class. The most important question we need to answer is how are we going to store the items in the queue. The queue can be empty or contain an unbounded number of items. It also has to maintain the order of items, as that is essential for a (fair) queue. What built-in type can be used to store, in order, an arbitrary number of items and allow insertions on one end and deletions from the other?

The `list` type certainly satisfies these constraints, and we go with it. The next question is: When and where in the `Queue` class implementation should this list be created? In our example, it is clear that we expect that the default `Queue` constructor gives us an empty queue. This means that we need to create the list as soon as the `Queue` object is created—that is, in an `__init__()` method:

```
def __init__(self):
    'instantiates an empty list that will contain queue items'
    self.q = []
... # remainder of class definition
```

Now we move to the implementation of the three Queue methods. The method `isEmpty()` can be implemented easily just by checking the length of list `self.q`:

```
def isEmpty(self):
    'returns True if queue is empty, False otherwise'
    return (len(self.q) == 0)
```

The method `enqueue()` should put items into the rear of list `self.q`, and the method `dequeue()` should remove items from the front of list `self.q`. We now need to decide what is the front of the list `self.q`. We can choose the front to be the leftmost list element (i.e., at index 0) or the rightmost one (at index −1). Both will work, and the benefit of each depends on the underlying implementation of the built-in class `list`—which is beyond the scope of this chapter.

In Figure 8.6, the first element of the queue is shown on the left, which we usually associate with index 0, and we thus do the same in our implementation. Once we make this decision, the Queue class can be implemented:

Module: ch8.py

```
1   class Queue:
2       'a classic queue class'
3
4       def __init__(self):
5           'instantiates an empty list'
6           self.q = []
7
8       def isEmpty(self):
9           'returns True if queue is empty, False otherwise'
10          return (len(self.q) == 0)
11
12      def enqueue (self, item):
13          'insert item at rear of queue'
14          return self.q.append(item)
15
16      def dequeue(self):
17          'remove and return item at front of queue'
18          return self.q.pop(0)
```

8.4 Overloaded Operators

There are a few inconveniences with the user-defined classes we have developed so far. For example, suppose you created a `Point` object:

```
>>> point = Point(3,5)
```

and then tried to evaluate it:

```
>>> point
<__main__.Point object at 0x15e5410>
```

Not very user-friendly, is it? By the way, the code says that `point` refers to an object of type `Point`—where `Point` is defined in the namespace of the top module—and that its object ID—memory address, effectively—is 0x15e5410, in hex. In any case, probably that is not the information we wanted to get when we evaluated `point`.

Here is another problem. To obtain the number of characters in a string or the number of items in a list, dictionary, tuple, or set, we use the `len()` function. It seems natural to use the same function to obtain the number of items in a `Queue` container object. Unfortunately, we do not get that:

```
>>> fruit = Queue()
>>> fruit.enqueue('apple')
>>> fruit.enqueue('banana')
>>> fruit.enqueue('coconut')
>>> len(fruit)
Traceback (most recent call last):
  File "<pyshell#356>", line 1, in <module>
    len(fruit)
TypeError: object of type 'Queue' has no len()
```

The point we are making is this: The classes we have developed so far do not behave like built-in classes. For user-defined classes to be useful and easy to use, it is important to make them more more familiar (i.e., more like built-in classes). Fortunately, Python supports *operator overloading*, which makes this possible.

Operators Are Class Methods

Consider the operator +. It can be used to add numbers:

```
>>> 2 + 4
6
```

It can also be used to concatenate lists and strings:

```
>>> [4, 5, 6] + [7]
[4, 5, 6, 7]
>>> 'strin' + 'g'
'string'
```

The + operator is said to be an *overloaded operator*. An overloaded operator is an operator that has been defined for multiple classes. For each class, the definition—and thus the meaning—of the operator is different. So, for example, the + operator has been defined for the `int`, `list`, and `str` classes. It implements integer addition for the `int` class, list concatenation for the `list` class, and string concatenation for the `str` class. The question now is: How is operator + defined for a particular class?

Python is an object-oriented language, and, as we have said, any "evaluation," including the evaluation of an arithmetic expression like `2 + 4`, is really a method invocation. To see what method exactly, you need to use the `help()` documentation tool. Whether you type `help(int)`, `help(str)`, or `help(list)`, you will see that the documentation for the + operator is:

```
...
|  __add__(...)
|      x.__add__(y) <==> x+y
...
```

This means that whenever Python evaluates expression `x + y`, it first substitutes it with expression `x.__add__(y)`, a method invocation by object x with object y as input argument, and then evaluates the new, method invocation, expression. This is true no matter what x and y are. So you can actually evaluate 2 + 3, [4, 5, 6] + [7] and 'strin'+ 'g' using invocations to method `__add__()` instead:

```
>>> int(2).__add__(4)
6
>>> [4, 5, 6].__add__([7])
[4, 5, 6, 7]
>>> 'strin'.__add__('g')
'string'
```

DETOUR

Addition Is Just a Function, After All

The algebraic expression

```
>>> x+y
```

gets translated by the Python interpreter to

```
>>> x.__add__(y)
```

which is a method invocation. In Chapter 7, we learned that this method invocation gets translated by the interpreter to

```
>>> type(x).__add__(x,y)
```

(Recall that `type(x)` evaluates to the class of object x.) This last expression is the one that really gets evaluated.

This is true, of course, for all operators: Any expression or method invocation is really a call by a function defined in the namespace of the class of the first operand.

The + operator is just one of the Python overloaded operators; Table 8.3 shows some others. For each operator, the corresponding function is shown as well as an explanation of the operator behavior for the number types, the `list` type, and the `str` type. All the operators listed are also defined for other built-in types (dict, set, etc.) and can also be defined for user-defined types, as shown next.

Note that the last operator listed is the *overloaded constructor operator*, which maps to function `__init__()`. We have already seen how we can implement an overloaded constructor in a user-defined class. We will see that implementing other overloaded operators is very similar.

Making the Class `Point` User Friendly

Recall the example we started this section with:

```
>>> point = Point(3,5)
>>> point
<__main__.Point object at 0x15e5410>
```

What would we prefer `point` to evaluate to instead? Suppose that we want:

```
>>> point
Point(3, 5)
```

Operator	Method	Number	List and String
x + y	x.__add__(y)	Addition	Concatenation
x - y	x.__sub__(y)	Subtraction	—
x * y	x.__mul__(y)	Multiplication	Self-concatenation
x / y	x.__truediv__(y)	Division	—
x // y	x.__floordiv__(y)	Integer division	—
x % y	x.__mod__(y)	Modulus	—
x == y	x.__eq__(y)	Equal to	
x != y	x.__ne__(y)	Unequal to	
x > y	x.__gt__(y)	Greater than	
x >= y	x.__ge__(y)	Greater than or equal to	
x < y	x.__lt__(y)	Less than	
x <= y	x.__le__(y)	Less than or equal to	
repr(x)	x.__repr__()	Canonical string representation	
str(x)	x.__str__()	Informal string representation	
len(x)	x.__len__()	—	Collection size
<type>(x)	<type>.__init__(x)	Constructor	

Table 8.3 **Overloaded operators.** Some of the commonly used overloaded operators are listed, along with the corresponding methods and behaviors for the number, list, and string types.

To understand how we can achieve this, we first need to understand that when we evaluate point in the shell, Python will display the *string representation* of the object. The default string representation of an object is its type and address, as in

```
<__main__.Point object at 0x15e5410>
```

To modify the string representation for a class, we need to implement the overloaded operator repr() for the class. The operator repr() is called automatically by the interpreter whenever the object must be represented as a string. One example of when that is the case is when the object needs to be displayed in the interpreter shell. So the familiar representation [3, 4, 5] of a list lst containing numbers 3, 4, and 5

```
>>> lst
[3, 4, 5]
```

is really the display of the string output by the call repr(lst)

```
>>> repr(lst)
'[3, 4, 5]'
```

All built-in classes implement overloaded operator repr() for this purpose. To modify the default string representation of objects of user-defined classes, we need to do the same. We do so by implementing the method corresponding to operator repr() in Table 8.3, method __repr__().

To get a Point object displayed in the format Point(<x>, <y>), all we need to do is add the next method to the class Point:

Module: ch8.py

```
1  class Point:
2
3      # other Point methods
4
5      def __repr__(self):
6          'return canonical string representation Point(x, y)'
7          return 'Point({}, {})'.format(self.x, self.y)
```

Now, when we evaluate a `Point` object in the shell, we get what we want:

```
>>> point = Point(3,5)
>>> point
Point(3, 5)
```

CAUTION

String Representations of Objects

There are actually two ways to get a string representation of an object: the over-loaded operator `repr()` and the string constructor `str()`.

The operator `repr()` is supposed to return the *canonical string representation* of the object. Ideally, but not necessarily, this is the string representation you would use to construct the object, such as `'[2, 3, 4]'` or `'Point(3, 5)'`.

In other words, the expression `eval(repr(o))` should give back the original object o. The method `repr()` is automatically called when an expression evaluates to an object in the interpreter shell and this object needs to be displayed in the shell window.

The string constructor `str()` returns an informal, ideally very readable, string representation of the object. This string representation is obtained by method call `o.__str__()`, if method `__str__()` is implemented. The Python interpreter calls the string constructor instead of the overloaded operator `repr()` whenever the object is to be "pretty printed" using function `print()`. We illustrate the difference with this class:

```
class Representation:
    def __repr__(self):
        return 'canonical string representation'
    def __str__(self):
        return 'Pretty string representation.'
```

Let's test it:

```
>>> rep = Representation()
>>> rep
canonical string representation
>>> print(rep)
Pretty string representation.
```

Contract between the Constructor and the `repr()` Operator

The last caution box stated that the output of the overloaded operator `repr()` should be the canonical string representation of the object. The canonical string representation of `Point` object `Point(3, 5)` is `'Point(3, 5)'`. The output of the `repr()` operator for the same `Point` object is:

```
>>> repr(Point(3, 5))
'Point(3, 5)'
```

It seems we have satisfied the *contract* between the constructor and the representation operator repr(): They are the same. Let's check:

```
>>> Point(3, 5) == eval(repr(Point(3, 5)))
False
```

What did we do wrong?

The problem is not with the constructor or operator repr() but with the operator ==: It does not consider two points with the same coordinates necessarily equal. Let's check:

```
>>> Point(3, 5) == Point(3, 5)
False
```

The reason for this somewhat strange behavior is that for user-defined classes the default behavior for operator == is to return True only when the two objects we are comparing are the same object. Let's show that this is indeed the case:

```
>>> point = Point(3,5)
>>> point == point
True
```

As shown in Table 8.3, the method corresponding to the overloaded operator == is method __eq__(). To change the behavior of overloaded operator ==, we need to implement method __eq__() in class Point. We do so in this final version of class Point:

Module: ch8.py

```
1   class Point:
2       'class that represents a point in the plane'
3
4       def __init__(self, xcoord=0, ycoord=0):
5           'initializes point coordinates to (xcoord, ycoord)'
6           self.x = xcoord
7           self.y = ycoord
8       def setx(self, xcoord):
9           'sets x coordinate of point to xcoord'
10          self.x = xcoord
11      def sety(self, ycoord):
12          'sets y coordinate of point to ycoord'
13          self.y = ycoord
14      def get(self):
15          'returns the x and y coordinates of the point as a tuple'
16          return (self.x, self.y)
17      def move(self, dx, dy):
18          'changes the x and y coordinates by i and j, respectively'
19          self.x += dx
20          self.y += dy
21      def __eq__(self, other):
22          'self == other is they have the same coordinates'
23          return self.x == other.x and self.y == other.y
24      def __repr__(self):
25          'return canonical string representation Point(x, y)'
26          return 'Point({}, {})'.format(self.x, self.y)
```

The new implementation of class `Point` supports the `==` operator in a way that makes sense

```
>>> Point(3, 5) == Point(3, 5)
True
```

and also ensures that the contract between the constructor and the operator `repr()` is satisfied:

```
>>> Point(3, 5) == eval(repr(Point(3, 5)))
True
```

Practice Problem 8.6

Implement overloaded operators `repr()` and `==` for the `Card` class. Your new `Card` class should behave as shown:

```
>>> Card('3', '♠') == Card('3', '♠')
True
>>> Card('3', '♠') == eval(repr(Card('3', '♠')))
True
```

Making the Queue Class User Friendly

We now make the class `Queue` from the previous section friendlier by overloading operators `repr()`, `==`, and `len()`. In the process we find it useful to extend the constructor.

We start with this implementation of `Queue`:

Module: ch8.py

```
1   class Queue:
2       'a classic queue class'
3
4       def __init__(self):
5           'instantiates an empty list'
6           self.q = []
7
8       def isEmpty(self):
9           'returns True if queue is empty, False otherwise'
10          return (len(self.q) == 0)
11
12      def enqueue (self, item):
13          'insert item at rear of queue'
14          return self.q.append(item)
15
16      def dequeue(self):
17          'remove and return item at front of queue'
18          return self.q.pop(0)
```

Let's first take care of the "easy" operators. What does it mean for two queues to be equal? It means that they have the same elements in the same order. In other words, the lists that contain the items of the two queues are the same. Therefore, the implementation of operator `__eq__()` for class `Queue` should consist of a comparison between the lists corresponding to the two `Queue` objects we are comparing:

```
def __eq__(self, other):
    '''returns True if queues self and other contain
       the same items in the same order'''
    return self.q == other.q
```

The overloaded operator function `len()` returns the number of items in a container. To enable its use on `Queue` objects, we need to implement the corresponding method `__len__()` (see Table 8.3) in the `Queue` class. The length of the queue is of course the length of the underlying list `self.q`:

```
def __len__(self):
    'return number of items in queue'
    return len(self.q)
```

Let's now tackle the implementation of the `repr()` operator. Suppose we construct a queue like this:

```
>>> fruit = Queue()
>>> fruit.enqueue('apple')
>>> fruit.enqueue('banana')
>>> fruit.enqueue('coconut')
```

What do we want the canonical string representation to look like? How about:

```
>>> fruit
Queue(['apple', 'banana', 'coconut'])
```

Recall that when implementing the overloaded operator `repr()`, ideally we should satisfy the contract between it and the constructor. To satisfy it, we should be able to construct the queue as shown:

```
>>> Queue(['apple', 'banana', 'coconut'])
Traceback (most recent call last):
  File "<pyshell#404>", line 1, in <module>
    Queue(['apple', 'banana', 'coconut'])
TypeError: __init__() takes exactly 1 positional argument (2 given)
```

We cannot because we have implemented the `Queue` constructor so it does not take any input arguments. So, we decide to change the constructor, as shown next. The two benefits of doing this are that (1) the contract between the constructor and `repr()` is satisfied and (2) newly created `Queue` objects can now be initialized at instantiation time.

Module: ch8.py

```
1  class Queue:
2      'a classic queue class'
3
4      def __init__(self, q=None):
5          'initialize queue based on list q, default is empty queue'
6          if q == None:
7              self.q = []
8          else:
9              self.q = q
10
11     # methods enqueue, dequeue, and isEmpty defined here
```

```
12
13      def __eq__(self, other):
14          '''return True if queues self and other contain
15              the same items in the same order'''
16          return self.q == other.q
17
18      def __len__(self):
19          'returns number of items in queue'
20          return len(self.q)
21
22      def __repr__(self):
23          'return canonical string representation of queue'
24          return 'Queue({})'.format(self.q)
```

Practice Problem 8.7

Implement overloaded operators len(), repr(), and == for the Deck class. Your new Deck class should behave as shown:

```
>>> len(Deck()))
52
>>> Deck() == Deck()
True
>>> Deck() == eval(repr(Deck()))
True
```

8.5 Inheritance

Code reuse is a fundamental software engineering goal. One of the main reasons for wrapping code into functions is to more easily reuse the code. Similarly, a major benefit of organizing code into user-defined classes is that the classes can then be reused in other programs, just as it is possible to use a function in the development of another. A class can be (re)used as is, something we have been doing since Chapter 2. A class can also be "extended" into a new class through *class inheritance*. In this section, we introduce the second approach.

Inheriting Attributes of a Class

Suppose that in the process of developing an application, we find that it would be very convenient to have a class that behaves just like the built-in class list but also supports a method called choice() that returns an item from the list, chosen uniformly at random.

More precisely, this class, which we refer to as MyList, would support the same methods as the class list and in the same way. For example, we would be able to create a MyList container object:

```
>>> mylst = MyList()
```

We also would be able to append items to it using list method append(), compute the number of items in it using overloaded operator len(), and count the number of occurrences of an item using `list` method `count()`:

```
>>> mylst.append(2)
>>> mylst.append(3)
>>> mylst.append(5)
>>> mylst.append(3)
>>> len(mylst)
4
>>> mylst.count(3)
2
```

In addition to supporting the same methods that the class `list` supports, the class `MyList` should also support method `choice()` that returns an item from the list, with each item in the list equally likely to be chosen:

```
>>> mylst.choice()
5
>>> mylst.choice()
2
>>> mylst.choice()
5
```

One way to implement the class `MyList` is the approach we took when developing classes `Deck` and `Queue`. A list instance variable `self.lst` would be used to store the items of `MyList`:

```
import random
class MyList:
    def __init__(self, initial = []):
        self.lst = initial
    def __len__(self):
        return len(self.lst)
    def append(self, item):
        self.lst.append(self, item)
    # implementations of remaining "list" methods

    def choice(self):
        return random.choice(self.lst)
```

This approach to developing class `MyList` would require us to write more than 30 methods. It would take a while and be tedious. Wouldn't it be nicer if we could define class `MyList` in a much shorter way, one that essentially says that class `MyList` is an "extension" of class `list` with method `choice()` as an additional method? It turns out that we can:

```
1  import random
2  class MyList(list):
3      'a subclass of list that implements method choice'
4
5      def choice(self):
6          'return item from list chosen uniformly at random'
7          return random.choice(self)
```

Module: ch8.py

This class definition specifies that class `MyList` is a *subclass* of the class `list` and thus supports all the methods that class `list` supports. This is indicated in the first line

```
class MyList(list):
```

The hierarchical structure between classes `list` and `MyList` is illustrated in Figure 8.7.

Figure 8.7 Hierarchy of classes `list` **and** `MyList`. Some of the attributes of class `list` are listed, all of which refer to appropriate functions. Class `MyList` is a subclass of class `list` and inherits all the attributes of class `list`. It also defines an additional attribute, method `choice()`. The object referred to by `mylst` inherits all the class attributes from its class, `MyList`, which includes the attributes from class `list`.

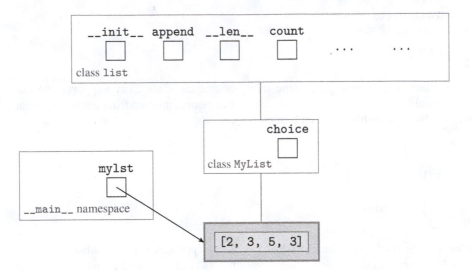

Figure 8.7 shows a `MyList` container object called `mylst` that is created in the interpreter shell (i.e., in the `__main__` namespace):

```
>>> mylst = MyList([2, 3, 5, 3])
```

The object `mylst` is shown as a "child" of class `MyList`. This hierarchical representation illustrates that object `mylst` inherits all the attributes of class `MyList`. We saw that objects inherit the attributes of their class in Section 8.1.

Figure 8.7 also shows class `MyList` as a "child" of class `list`. This hierarchical representation illustrates that class `MyList` *inherits* all the attributes of `list`. You can check that using the built-in function `dir()`:

```
>>> dir(MyList)
['__add__', '__class__', '__contains__', '__delattr__',
 ...
 'append', 'choice', 'count', 'extend', 'index', 'insert',
 'pop', 'remove', 'reverse', 'sort']
```

What this means is that object `mylst` will inherit not only method `choice()` from class `MyList` but also all the attributes of `list`. You can, again, check that:

```
>>> dir(mylst)
['__add__', '__class__', '__contains__', '__delattr__',
 ...
 'append', 'choice', 'count', 'extend', 'index', 'insert',
 'pop', 'remove', 'reverse', 'sort']
```

The class `MyList` is said to be a *subclass* of class `list`. The class `list` is the *superclass* of class `MyList`.

Class Definition, in General

When we implemented classes `Point`, `Animal`, `Card`, `Deck`, and `Queue`, we used this format for the first line of the class definition statement:

```
class <Class Name>:
```

To define a class that inherits attributes from an existing class `<Super Class>`, the first line of the class definition should be:

```
class <Class Name>(<Super Class>):
```

It is also possible to define a class that inherits attributes from more than just one existing class. In that case, the first line of the class definition statement is:

```
class <Class Name>(<Super Class 1>, <Super Class 2>, ...):
```

Overriding Superclass Methods

We illustrate class inheritance using another simple example. Suppose that we need a class `Bird` that is similar to the class `Animal` from Section 8.1. The class `Bird` should support methods `setSpecies()` and `setLanguage()`, just like class `Animal`:

```
>>> tweety = Bird()
>>> tweety.setSpecies('canary')
>>> tweety.setLanguage('tweet')
```

The class `Bird` should also support a method called `speak()`. However, its behavior differs from the behavior of the `Animal` method `speak()`:

```
>>> tweety.speak()
tweet! tweet! tweet!
```

Here is another example of the behavior we expect from class `Bird`:

```
>>> daffy = Bird()
>>> daffy.setSpecies('duck')
>>> daffy.setLanguage('quack')
>>> daffy.speak()
quack! quack! quack!
```

Let's discuss how to implement class `Bird`. Because class `Bird` shares attributes with existing class `Animal` (birds are animals, after all), we develop it as a subclass of `Animal`. Let's first recall the definition of class `Animal` from Section 8.1:

Module: ch8.py

```
1   class Animal:
2       'represents an animal'
3
4       def setSpecies(self, species):
5           'sets the animal species'
6           self.spec = species
7
8       def setLanguage(self, language):
9           'sets the animal language'
10          self.lang = language
11
```

```
12    def speak(self):
13        'prints a sentence by the animal'
14        print('I am a {} and I {}.'.format(self.spec, self.lang))
```

If we define class `Bird` as a subclass of class `Animal`, it will have the wrong behavior for method `speak()`. So the question is this: Is there a way to define `Bird` as a subclass of `Animal` *and* change the behavior of method `speak()` in class `Bird`?

There is, and it is simply to implement a new method `speak()` in class `Bird`:

Module: ch8.py

```
1    class Bird(Animal):
2        'represents a bird'
3
4        def speak(self):
5            'prints bird sounds'
6            print('{}! '.format(self.language) * 3)
```

Class `Bird` is defined to be a subclass of `Animal`. Therefore, it inherits all the attributes of class `Animal`, including the `Animal` method `speak()`. There is a method `speak()` defined in class `Bird`, however; this method *replaces* the inherited `Animal` method. We say that the `Bird` method *overrides* the superclass method `speak()`.

Now, when method `speak()` is invoked on a `Bird` object like `daffy`, how does the Python interpreter decide which method `speak()` to invoke? We use Figure 8.8 to illustrate how the Python interpreter searches for attribute definitions.

Figure 8.8 Namespaces associated with classes `Animal` **and** `Bird`, **object** `daffy`, **and the shell.** Omitted are the values of instance variables and implementations of class methods.

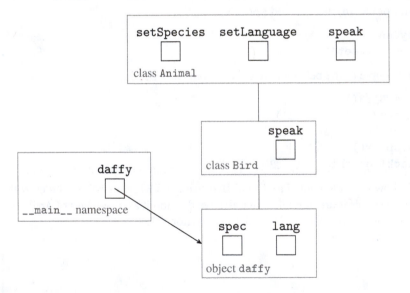

When the interpreter executes

```
>>> daffy = Bird()
```

it creates a `Bird` object named `daffy` and a namespace, initially empty, associated with it. Now let's consider how the Python interpreter finds the definition of `setSpecies()` in:

```
>>> daffy.setSpecies('duck')
```

The interpreter looks for the definition of attribute `setSpecies` starting with the namespace associated with object `daffy` and continuing up the class hierarchy. It does not find the definition in the namespace associated with object `daffy` or in the namespace associated with class `Bird`. Eventually, it does find the definition of `setSpecies` in the namespace associated with class `Animal`.

The search for the method definition when the interpreter evaluates

```
>>> daffy.setLanguage('quack')
```

also ends with the namespace of class `Animal`.

However, when the Python interpreter executes

```
>>> daffy.speak()
quack! quack! quack!
```

the interpreter finds the definition of method `speak()` in class `Bird`. In other words, the search for attribute `speak` never reaches the class `Animal`. It is the `Bird` method `speak()` that is executed.

Attribute Names Issues

Now that we understand how object attributes are evaluated by the Python interpreter, we can discuss the problems that can arise with carelessly chosen attribute names. Consider, for example, this class definition

```
class Problem:
    def value(self, v):
        self.value = v
```

and try:

```
>>> p = Problem()
>>> p.value(9)
>>> p.value
9
```

So far, so good. When executing `p.value(9)`, the object `p` does not have an instance variable `value`, and the attribute search ends with the function `value()` in class `Problem`. An instance variable `value` is then created in the object itself, and that is confirmed by the evaluation of the statement that follows, `p.value`.

Now suppose we try:

```
>>> p.value(3)
Traceback (most recent call last):
  File "<pyshell#324>", line 1, in <module>
    p.value(9)
TypeError: 'int' object is not callable
```

What happened? The search for attribute `value` started and ended with the object `p`: The object has an attribute called `value`. That attribute refers to an integer object, 9, which cannot be called like a function.

Extending Superclass Methods

We have seen that a subclass can *inherit* a method from a superclass or *override* it. It is also possible to *extend* a superclass method. We illustrate this using an example that compares the three inheritance patterns.

When designing a class as a subclass of another class, inherited attributes are handled in several ways. They can be inherited as is, they can be replaced, or they can be extended. The next module shows three subclasses of class Super. Each illustrates one of the ways an inherited attribute is handled.

Module: ch8.py

```
1   class Super:
2       'a generic class with one method'
3       def method(self):                    # the Super method
4           print('in Super.method')
5
6   class Inheritor(Super):
7       'class that inherits method'
8       pass
9
10  class Replacer(Super):
11      'class that overrides method'
12      def method(self):
13          print('in Replacer.method')
14
15  class Extender(Super):
16      'class that extends method'
17      def method(self):
18          print('starting Extender.method')
19          Super.method(self)               # calling Super method
20          print('ending Extender.method')
```

In class Inheritor, attribute method() is inherited as is. In class Replacer, it is completely replaced. In Extender, attribute method() is overridden, but the implementation of method() in class Extender calls the original method() from class Super. Effectively, class Extender adds additional behavior to the superclass attribute.

In most cases, a subclass will inherit different attributes in different ways, but each inherited attribute will follow one of these patterns.

Practice Problem 8.8

Implement a class Vector that supports the same methods as the class Point we developed in Section 8.4. The class Vector should also support vector addition and product operations. The addition of two vectors

```
>>> v1 = Vector(1, 3)
>>> v2 = Vector(-2, 4)
```

is a new vector whose coordinates are the sum of the corresponding coordinates of v1 and v2:

```
>>> v1 + v2
Vector(-1, 7)
```

The product of v1 and v2 is the sum of the products of the corresponding coordinates:

```
>>> v1 * v2
10
```

In order for a `Vector` object to be displayed as `Vector(., .)` instead of `Point(., .)`, you will need to override method `__repr__()`.

Implementing a Queue Class by Inheriting from `list`

The class `Queue` we developed in Sections 8.3 and 8.4 is just one way to design and implement a queue class. Another implementation becomes natural after we recognize that every `Queue` object is just a "thin wrapper" for a `list` object. So why not design the `Queue` class so that every `Queue` object *is* a `list` object? In other words, why not design the `Queue` class as a subclass of `list`? So let's do it:

Module: ch8.py

```
1   class Queue2(list):
2       'a queue class, subclass of list'
3
4       def isEmpty(self):
5           'returns True if queue is empty, False otherwise'
6           return (len(self) == 0)
7
8       def dequeue(self):
9           'remove and return item at front of queue'
10          return self.pop(0)
11
12      def enqueue (self, item):
13          'insert item at rear of queue'
14          return self.append(item)
```

Note that because variable `self` refers to a `Queue2` object, which is a subclass of `list`, it follows that `self` is also a `list` object. So `list` methods like `pop()` and `append()` are invoked directly on `self`. Note also that methods `__repr__()` and `__len__()` do not need to be implemented because they are inherited from the `list` superclass.

Developing class `Queue2` involved a lot less work than developing the original class `Queue`. Does that make it better?

CAUTION

Inheriting Too Much

While inheriting a lot is desirable in real life, there is such a thing as too much inheritance in OOP. While straightforward to implement, class `Queue2` has the problem of inheriting *all* the `list` attributes, including methods that violate the spirit of a queue. To see this, consider this `Queue2` object:

```
>>> q2
[5, 7, 9]
```

The implementation of `Queue2` allows us to remove items from the middle of the queue:

```
>>> q2.pop(1)
7
>>> q2
[5, 9]
```

It also allows us to insert items into the middle of the queue:

```
>>> q2.insert(1,11)
>>> q2
[5, 11, 9]
```

So 7 got served before 5 and 11 got into the queue in front of 9, violating queue rules. Due to all the inherited `list` methods, we cannot say that class `Queue2` behaves in the spirit of a queue.

8.6 User-Defined Exceptions

There is one problem with the implementation of class Queue we developed in Section 8.4. What happens when we try to dequeue an empty queue? Let's check. We first create an empty queue:

```
>>> queue = Queue()
```

Next, we attempt to dequeue it:

```
>>> queue.dequeue()
Traceback (most recent call last):
  File "<pyshell#185>", line 1, in <module>
    queue.dequeue()
  File "/Users/me/ch8.py",
    line 156, in dequeue
    return self.q.pop(0)
IndexError: pop from empty list
```

An `IndexError` exception is raised because we are trying to remove the item at index 0 from empty list `self.q`. What is the problem?

The issue is not the exception: Just as for popping an empty list, there is no other sensible thing to do when we are trying to dequeue an empty queue. The issue is the type of exception. An `IndexError` exception and the associated message `'pop from empty list'` are of little use to the developer who is using the `Queue` class and who may not know that `Queue` containers use `list` instance variables.

Much more useful to the developer would be an exception called `EmptyQueueError` with a message like `'dequeue from empty queue'`. In general, often it is a good idea to define your own exception type rather than rely on a generic, built-in exception class like `IndexError`. A user-defined class can, for example, be used to customize handling and the reporting of errors.

In order to obtain more useful error messages, we need to learn two things:

1. How to define a new exception class
2. How to raise an exception in a program

We discuss how to do the latter first.

Raising an Exception

In our experience so far, when an exception is raised during the execution of a program, it is raised by the Python interpreter because an error condition occurred. We have seen one type of exception not caused by an error: It is the `KeyboardInterrupt` exception, which typically is raised by the user. The user would raise this exception by simultaneously clicking keys `Ctrl`–`c` to terminate an infinite loop, for example:

```
>>> while True:
        pass


Traceback (most recent call last):
  File "<pyshell#210>", line 2, in <module>
    pass
KeyboardInterrupt
```

(The infinite loop is interrupted by a `KeyboardInterrupt` exception.)

In fact, the user can raise all types of exceptions, not just `KeyboardInterrupt` exceptions. The `raise` Python statement forces an exception of a given type to be raised. Here is how we would raise a `ValueError` exception in the interpreter shell:

```
>>> raise ValueError()
Traceback (most recent call last):
  File "<pyshell#24>", line 1, in <module>
    raise ValueError()
ValueError
```

Recall that `ValueError` is just a class that happens to be an exception class. The `raise` statement consists of the keyword `raise` followed by an exception constructor such as `ValueError()`. Executing the statement raises an exception. If it is not handled by the `try`/`except` clauses, the program is interrupted and the default exception handler prints the error message in the shell.

The exception constructor can take an input argument that can be used to provide information about the cause of the error:

```
>>> raise ValueError('Just joking ...')
Traceback (most recent call last):
  File "<pyshell#198>", line 1, in <module>
    raise ValueError('Just joking ...')
ValueError: Just joking ...
```

The optional argument is a string message that will be associated with the object: It is, in fact, the *informal string representation* of the object, that is, the one returned by the `__str__()` method and printed by the `print()` function.

In our two examples, we have shown that an exception can be raised regardless of whether it makes sense or not. We make this point again in the next Practice Problem.

Reimplement method dequeue() of class Queue so that a KeyboardInterrupt exception (an inappropriate exception type in this case) with message 'dequeue from empty queue' (an appropriate error message, actually) is raised if an attempt to dequeue an empty queue is made:

```
>>> queue = Queue()
>>> queue.dequeue()
Traceback (most recent call last):
  File "<pyshell#30>", line 1, in <module>
    queue.dequeue()
  File "/Users/me/ch8.py", line 183, in dequeue
    raise KeyboardInterrupt('dequeue from empty queue')
KeyboardInterrupt: dequeue from empty queue
```

User-Defined Exception Classes

We now describe how to define our own exception classes.

Every built-in exception type is a subclass of class Exception. In fact, all we have to do to define a new exception class is to define it as a subclass, either directly or indirectly, of Exception. That's it.

As an example, here is how we could define a new exception class MyError that behaves exactly like the Exception class:

```
>>> class MyError(Exception):
        pass
```

(This class only has attributes that are inherited from Exception; the pass statement is required because the class statement expects an indented code block.) Let's check that we can raise a MyError exception:

```
>>> raise MyError('test message')
Traceback (most recent call last):
  File "<pyshell#247>", line 1, in <module>
    raise MyError('test message')
MyError: test message
```

Note that we were also able to associate error message 'test message' with the exception object.

Improving the Encapsulation of Class Queue

We started this section by pointing out that dequeueing an empty queue will raise an exception and print an error message that has nothing to do with queues. We now define a new exception class EmptyQueueError and reimplement method dequeue() so that it raises an exception of that type if it is invoked on an empty queue.

We choose to implement the new exception class without any additional methods:

Module: ch8.py

```
1  class EmptyQueueError(Exception):
2      pass
```

Shown next is the new implementation of class `Queue`, with a new version of method `dequeue()`; no other `Queue` method is modified.

```
1  class Queue:
2      'a classic queue class'
3      # methods __init__(), enqueue(), isEmpty(), __repr__(),
4      # __len__(), __eq__() implemented here
5
6      def dequeue(self):
7          if len(self) == 0:
8              raise EmptyQueueError('dequeue from empty queue')
9          return self.q.pop(0)
```

With this new `Queue` class, we get a more meaningful error message when attempting to dequeue an empty queue:

```
>>> queue = Queue()
>>> queue.dequeue()
Traceback (most recent call last):
  File "<pyshell#34>", line 1, in <module>
    queue.dequeue()
  File "/Users/me/ch8.py", line 186, in dequeue
    raise EmptyQueueError('dequeue from empty queue')
EmptyQueueError: dequeue from empty queue
```

We have effectively hidden away the implementation details of class `Queue`.

E-Book Case Study: Indexing and Iterators

In this case study, we will learn how to make a container class feel more like a built-in class. We will see how to enable indexing of items in the container and how to enable iteration, using a `for` loop, over the items in the container.

Chapter Summary

In this chapter, we describe how to develop new Python classes. We also explain the benefits of the object-oriented programming (OOP) paradigm and discuss core OOP concepts that we will make use of in this chapter and in the chapters that follow.

A new class in Python is defined with the `class` statement. The body of the class statement contains the definitions of the attributes of the class. The attributes are the class methods and variables that specify the class properties and what can be done with instances of the class. The idea that a class object can be manipulated by users through method invocations alone and without knowledge of the implementation of these methods is called *abstraction*. Abstraction facilitates software development because the programmer works with objects abstractly (i.e., through "abstract" method names rather than "concrete" code).

In order for abstraction to be beneficial, the "concrete" code and data associated with objects must be *encapsulated* (i.e., made "invisible" to the program using the object). *Encapsulation* is achieved thanks to the fact that (1) every class defines a namespace in which class attributes (variables and methods) live, and (2) every object has a namespace that inherits the class attributes and in which instance attributes live.

In order to complete the encapsulation of a new, user-defined class, it may be necessary to define class-specific exceptions for it. The reason is that if an exception is thrown when invoking a method on an object of the class, the exception type and error message should be meaningful to the user of the class. For this reason, we introduce user-defined exceptions in this chapter as well.

OOP is an approach to programming that achieves modular code through the use of objects and by structuring code into user-defined classes. While we have been working with objects since Chapter 2, this chapter finally shows the benefits of the OOP approach.

In Python, it is possible to implement operators such as + and == for user-defined classes. The OOP property that operators can have different, and new, meanings depending on the type of the operands is called *operator overloading* (and is a special case of the OOP concept of *polymorphism*). Operator overloading facilitates software development because (well-defined) operators have intuitive meanings and make the code look sparser and cleaner.

A new, user-defined class can be defined to inherit the attributes of an already existing class. This OOP property is referred to as *class inheritance*. Code reuse is, of course, the ultimate benefit of class inheritance. We will make heavy use of class inheritance when developing graphical user interfaces in Chapter 9 and HTML parsers in Chapter 11.

Solutions to Practice Problems

8.1 The method `getx()` takes no argument, other than `self` and returns `xcoord`, defined in namespace `self`.

```
def getx(self):
    'return x coordinate'
    return self.xcoord
```

8.2 The drawing for part (a) is shown in Figure 8.9(a). For part (b), you can fill in the question marks by just executing the commands. The drawing for part (c) is shown in Figure 8.9(c). The last statement `a.version` returns string `'test'`. This is because the assignment `a.version` creates name `version` in namespace `a`.

Figure 8.9 Solution for Practice Problem 8.2.

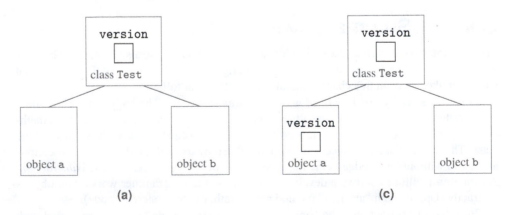

(a)　　　　　　　　　　　　　(c)

8.3 When created, a `Rectangle` object has no instance variables. The method `setSize()` should create and initialize instance variables to store the width and length of the rectangle.

These instance variables are then used by methods `perimeter()` and `area()`. Shown next is the implementation of class `Rectangle`.

```python
class Rectangle:
    'class that represents rectangles'
    def setSize(self, xcoord, ycoord):
        'constructor'
        self.x = xcoord
        self.y = ycoord

    def perimeter(self):
        'returns perimeter of rectangle'
        return 2 * (self.x + self.y)

    def area(self):
        'returns area of rectangle'
        return self.x * self.y
```

8.4 An `__init__()` method is added to the class. It includes default values for input arguments `species` and `language`:

```python
def __init__(self, species='animal', language='make sounds'):
    'constructor'
    self.spec = species
    self.lang = language
```

8.5 Since we allow the constructor to be used with or without a list of cards, we need to implement the function `__init__()` with one argument and have a default value for it. This default value should really be a list containing the standard 52 playing cards, but this list has not been created yet. We choose instead to set the default value to `None`, a value of type `NoneType` and used to represent no value. We can thus start implementing the `__init__()` as shown:

```python
def __init__(self, cardList=None):
    'constructor'
    if cardList != None:      # input deck provided
        self.deck = cardList
    else:                     # no input deck
        # self.deck is a list of 52 standard playing cards
```

8.6 The string returned by operator `repr()` must look like a statement that constructs a `Card` object. Operator `==` returns `True` if and only if the two cards being compared have the same rank and suit.

```python
class Card:

    # other Card methods

    def __repr__(self):
        'return formal representation'
        return "Card('{}', '{}')".format(self.rank, self.suit)
```

```
    def __eq__(self, other):
        'self = other if rank and suit are the same'
        return self.rank == other.rank and self.suit == other.suit
```

8.7 The implementations are shown next. The operator == decides that two decks are equal if they have the same cards and in the same order.

```
class Deck:
    # other Deck methods
    def __len__(self):
        'returns size of deck'
        return len(self.deck)

    def __repr__(self):
        'returns canonical string representation'
        return 'Deck({})'.format(self.deck)

    def __eq__(self, other):
        '''returns True if decks have the same cards
           in the same order'''
        return self.deck == other.deck
```

8.8 The complete implementation of the Vector class is:

```
class Vector(Point):
    'a 2D vector class'
    def __mul__(self, v):
        'vector product'
        return self.x * v.x + self.y * v.y

    def __add__(self, v):
        'vector addition'
        return Vector(self.x+v.x, self.y+v.y)

    def __repr__(self):
        'returns canonical string representation'
        return 'Vector{}'.format(self.get())
```

8.9 If the length of the Queue object (i.e., self) is 0, a KeyboardInterrupt exception is raised:

```
def dequeue(self):
    '''removes and returns item at front of the queue
       raises KeyboardInterrupt exception if queue is empty'''
    if len(self) == 0:
        raise KeyboardInterrupt('dequeue from empty queue')

    return self.q.pop(0)
```

Exercises

8.10 Add method `distance()` to the class `Point`. It takes another `Point` object as input and returns the distance to that point (from the point invoking the method).

```
>>> c = Point()
>>> c.setx(0)
>>> c.sety(1)
>>> d = Point()
>>> d.setx(1)
>>> d.sety(0)
>>> c.distance(d)
1.4142135623730951
```

8.11 Add to class `Animal` methods `setAge()` and `getAge()` to set and retrieve the age of the `Animal` object.

```
>>> flipper = Animal()
>>> flipper.setSpecies('dolphin')
>>> flipper.setAge(3)
>>> flipper.getAge()
3
```

8.12 Add to class `Point` methods `up()`, `down()`, `left()`, and `right()` that move the `Point` object by 1 unit in the appropriate direction. The implementation of each should not modify instance variables x and y directly but rather indirectly by calling existing method `move()`.

```
>>> a = Point(3, 4)
>>> a.left()
>>> a.get()
(2, 4)
```

8.13 Add a constructor to class `Rectangle` so that the length and width of the rectangle can be set at the time the `Rectangle` object is created. Use default values of 1 if the length or width is not specified.

```
>>> rectangle = Rectangle(2, 4)
>>> rectange.perimeter()
12
>>> rectangle = Rectangle()
>>> rectangle.area()
1
```

8.14 Translate these overloaded operator expressions to appropriate method calls:

(a) x > y

(b) x != y

(c) x % y

(d) x // y

(e) x or y

8.15 Overload appropriate operators for class `Card` so that you can compare cards based on rank:

```
>>> Card('3', '♠') < Card('8', '◇')
True
>>> Card('3', '♠') > Card('8', '◇')
False
>>> Card('3', '♠') <= Card('8', '◇')
True
>>> Card('3', '♠') >= Card('8', '◇')
False
```

8.16 Implement a class `myInt` that behaves almost the same as the class `int`, except when trying to add an object of type `myInt`. Then, this strange behavior occurs:

```
>>> x = myInt(5)
>>> x * 4
20
>>> x * (4 + 6)
50
>>> x + 6
'Whatever ...'
```

8.17 Implement your own string class `myStr` that behaves like class `str` except that:

- The addition (+) operator returns the sum of the lengths of the two strings (instead of the concatenation).

- The multiplication (*) operator returns the product of the lengths of the two strings.

The two operands, for both operators, are assumed to be strings; the behavior of your implementation can be undefined if the second operand is not a string.

```
>>> x = myStr('hello')
>>> x + 'universe'
13
>>> x * 'universe'
40
```

8.18 Develop a class `myList` that is a subclass of the built-in `list` class. The only difference between `myList` and `list` is that the `sort` method is overridden. `myList` containers should behave just like regular lists, except as shown next:

```
>>> x = myList([1, 2, 3])
>>> x
[1, 2, 3]
>>> x.reverse()
>>> x
[3, 2, 1]
>>> x[2]
1
>>> x.sort()
You wish...
```

8.19 Suppose you execute the next statements using class Queue2 from Section 8.5:

```
>>> queue2 = Queue2(['a', 'b', 'c'])
>>> duplicate = eval(repr(queue2))
>>> duplicate
['a', 'b', 'c']
>>> duplicate.enqueue('d')
Traceback (most recent call last):
  File "<pyshell#22>", line 1, in <module>
    duplicate.enqueue('d')
AttributeError: 'list' object has no attribute 'enqueue'
```

Explain what happened and offer a solution.

Problems

8.20 Develop a class BankAccount that supports these methods:

- __init__(): Initializes the bank account balance to the value of the input argument, or to 0 if no input argument is given

- withdraw(): Takes an amount as input and withdraws it from the balance

- deposit(): Takes an amount as input and adds it to the balance

- balance(): Returns the balance on the account

```
>>> x = BankAccount(700)
>>> x.balance()
700.00
>>> x.withdraw(70)
>>> x.balance()
630.00
>>> x.deposit(7)
>>> x.balance()
637.00
```

8.21 Implement a class Polygon that abstracts regular polygons and supports class methods:

- __init__(): A constructor that takes as input the number of sides and the side length of a regular n-gon (n-sided polygon) object

- perimeter(): Returns the perimeter of n-gon object

- area(): returns the area of the n-gon object

Note: The area of a regular polygon with n sides of length s is

$$\frac{s^2 n}{4 \tan(\frac{\pi}{n})}$$

```
>>> p2 = Polygon(6, 1)
>>> p2.perimeter()
6
>>> p2.area()
2.5980762113533165
```

8.22 Implement class `Worker` that supports methods:

- `__init__()`: Constructor that takes as input the worker's name (as a string) and the hourly pay rate (as a number)
- `changeRate()`: Takes the new pay rate as input and changes the worker's pay rate to the new hourly rate
- `pay()`: Takes the number of hours worked as input and prints `'Not Implemented'`

Next develop classes `HourlyWorker` and `SalariedWorker` as subclasses of `Worker`. Each overloads the inherited method `pay()` to compute the weekly pay for the worker. Hourly workers are paid the hourly rate for the actual hours worked; any overtime hours above 40 are paid double. Salaried workers are paid for 40 hours regardless of the number of hours worked. Because the number of hours is not relevant, the method `pay()` for salaried workers should also be callable without an input argument.

```
>>> w1 = Worker('Joe', 15)
>>> w1.pay(35)
Not implemented
>>> w2 = SalariedWorker('Sue', 14.50)
>>> w2.pay()
580.0
>>> w2.pay(60)
580.0
>>> w3 = HourlyWorker('Dana', 20)
>>> w3.pay(25)
500
>>> w3.changeRate(35)
>>> w3.pay(25)
875
```

8.23 Create a class `Segment` that represents a line segment in the plane and supports methods:

- `__init__()`: Constructor that takes as input a pair of `Point` objects that represent the endpoints of the line segment
- `length()`: Returns the length of the segment
- `slope()`: Returns the slope of the segment or `None` if the slope is unbounded

```
>>> p1 = Point(3,4)
>>> p2 = Point()
>>> s = Segment(p1, p2)
>>> s.length()
5.0
>>> s.slope()
0.75
```

8.24 Implement a class `Person` that supports these methods:

- `__init__()`: A constructor that takes as input a person's name (as a string) and birth year (as an integer)
- `age()`: Returns the age of the person
- `name()`: Returns the name of the person

Use function `localtime()` from the Standard Library module `time` to compute the age.

8.25 Develop a class `Textfile` that provides methods to analyze a text file. The class `Textfile` will support a constructor that takes as input a file name (as a string) and instantiates a `Textfile` object associated with the corresponding text file. The `Textfile` class should support methods `nchars()`, `nwords()`, and `nlines()` that return the number of characters, words, and lines, respectively, in the associated text file. The class should also support methods `read()` and `readlines()` that return the content of the text file as a string or as a list of lines, respectively, just as we would expect for file objects.

Finally, the class should support method `grep()` that takes a target string as input and searches for lines in the text file that contain the target string. The method returns the lines in the file containing the target string; in addition, the method should print the line number, where line numbering starts with 0.

```
>>> t = Textfile('raven.txt')
>>> t.nchars()
6299
>>> t.nwords()
1125
>>> t.nlines()
126
>>> print(t.read())
Once upon a midnight dreary, while I pondered weak and weary,
...
Shall be lifted - nevermore!
>>> t.grep('nevermore')
75: Of `Never-nevermore.`
89: She shall press, ah, nevermore!
124: Shall be lifted - nevermore!
```

File: raven.txt

8.26 Add method `words()` to class `Textfile` from Problem 8.25. It takes no input and returns a list, without duplicates, of words in the file.

8.27 Add method `occurrences()` to class `Textfile` from Problem 8.25. It takes no input and returns a dictionary mapping each word in the file (the key) to the number of times it occurs in the file (the value).

8.28 Add method `average()` to class `Textfile` from Problem 8.25. It takes no input and returns, in a `tuple` object, (1) the average number of words per sentence in the file, (2) the number of words in the sentence with the most words, and (3) the number of words in the sentence with the fewest words. You may assume that the symbols delimiting a sentence are in `'!?.'`.

8.29 Implement class `Hand` that represents a hand of playing cards. The class should have a constructor that takes as input the player ID (a string). It should support method `addCard()`

that takes a card as input and adds it to the hand and method `showHand()` that displays the player's hand in the format shown.

```
>>> hand = Hand('House')
>>> deck = Deck()
>>> deck.shuffle()
>>> hand.addCard(deck.dealCard())
>>> hand.addCard(deck.dealCard())
>>> hand.addCard(deck.dealCard())
>>> hand.showHand()
House:   10 ♡   8 ♠   2 ♠
```

8.30 Reimplement the blackjack application from the Chapter 6 case study (Games of Chance) using classes `Card` and `Deck` developed in this chapter and class `Hand` from Problem 8.29.

8.31 Implement class `Date` that support methods:

- `__init__()`: Constructor that takes no input and initializes the `Date` object to the current date

- `display()`: Takes a format argument and displays the date in the requested format

Use function `localtime()` from the Standard Library module `time` to obtain the current date. The format argument is a string

- 'MDY' : MM/DD/YY (e.g., 02/18/09)

- 'MDYY' : MM/DD/YYYY (e.g., 02/18/2009)

- 'DMY' : DD/MM/YY (e.g., 18/02/09)

- 'DMYY' : DD/MM/YYYY (e.g., 18/02/2009)

- 'MODY' : Mon DD, YYYY (e.g., Feb 18, 2009)

You should use methods `localtime()` and `strftime()` from Standard Library module `time`.

```
>>> x = Date()
>>> x.display('MDY')
'02/18/09'
>>> x.display('MODY')
'Feb 18, 2009'
```

8.32 Develop a class `Craps` that allows you to play craps on your computer. (The craps rules are described in Problem 6.31.) Your class will support methods:

- `__init__()`: Starts by rolling a pair of dice. If the value of the roll (i.e., the sum of the two dice) is 7 or 11, then a winning message is printed. If the value of the roll is 2, 3, or 12, then a losing message is printed. For all other roll values, a message telling the user to throw for point is printed.

- `forPoint()`: Generates a roll of a pair of dice and, depending on the value of the roll, prints one of three messages as appropriate (and as shown):

```
>>> c = Craps()
Throw total: 11. You won!
>>> c = Craps()
Throw total: 2. You lost!
>>> c = Craps()
Throw total: 5. Throw for Point.
>>> c.forPoint()
Throw total: 6. Throw for Point.
>>> c.forPoint()
Throw total: 5. You won!
>>> c = Craps()
Throw total: 4. Throw for Point.
>>> c.forPoint()
Throw total: 7. You lost!
```

8.33 Implement class Pseudorandom that is used to generate a sequence of pseudorandom integers using a *linear congruential generator*. The linear congruential method generates a sequence of numbers starting from a given seed number x. Each number in the sequence will be obtained by applying a (math) function $f(x)$ on the previous number x in the sequence. The precise function $f(x)$ is defined by three numbers: a (the multiplier), c (the increment), and m (the modulus):

$$f(x) = (ax + c) \bmod m$$

For example, if $m = 31$, $a = 17$, and $c = 7$, the linear congruential method would generate the next sequence of numbers starting from seed $x = 12$:

$$12, 25, 29, 4, 13, 11, 8, 19, 20, \ldots$$

because $f(12) = 25$, $f(25) = 29$, $f(29) = 4$, and so on. The class Pseudorandom should support methods:

- __init__(): Constructor that takes as input the values a, x, c, and m and initializes the Pseudorandom object

- next(): Generates and returns the next number in the pseudorandom sequence

```
>> x = pseudorandom(17, 12, 7, 31)
>>> x.next()
25
>>> x.next()
29
>>> x.next()
4
```

8.34 Implement the container class Stat that stores a sequence of numbers and provides statistical information about the numbers. It supports an overloaded constructor that initializes the container and the methods shown.

```
>>> s = Stat()
>>> s.add(2)        # adds 2 to the Stat container
>>> s.add(4)
```

```
>>> s.add(6)
>>> s.add(8)
>>> s.min()        # returns minimum value in container
2
>>> s.max()        # returns maximum value in container
8
>>> s.sum()        # returns sum of values in container
20
>>> len(s)         # returns number of items in container
4
>>> s.mean()       # returns average of items in container
5.0
>>> 4 in s         # returns True if in the container
True
>>> s.clear()      # Empties the sequence
```

8.35 A stack is a sequence container type that, like a queue, supports very restrictive access methods: All insertions and removals are from one end of the stack, typically referred to as the top of the stack. Implement container class `Stack` that implements a stack. It should be a subclass of `object`, support the `len()` overloaded operator, and support the methods:

- `push()`: Take an item as input and push it on top of the stack
- `pop()`: Remove and return the item at the top of the stack
- `isEmpty()`: Return True if the stack is empty, False otherwise

You should also insure that the stack can be printed as shown. A stack is often referred to as a last-in first-out (LIFO) container because the last item inserted is the first removed.

```
>>> s = Stack()
>>> s.push('plate 1')
>>> s.push('plate 2')
>>> s.push('plate 3')
>>> s
['plate 1', 'plate 2', 'plate 3']
>>> len(s)
3
>>> s.pop()
'plate 3'
>>> s.pop()
'plate 2'
>>> s.pop()
'plate 1'
>>> s.isEmpty()
True
```

8.36 Write a container class called `PriorityQueue`. The class should support methods:

- `insert()`: Takes a number as input and adds it to the container
- `min()`: Returns the smallest number in the container
- `removeMin()`: Removes the smallest number in the container

- isEmpty(): Returns True if container is empty, False otherwise

The overloaded operator len() should also be supported.

```
>>> pq = PriorityQueue()
>>> pq.insert(3)
>>> pq.insert(1)
>>> pq.insert(5)
>>> pq.insert(2)
>>> pq.min()
1
>>> pq.removeMin()
>>> pq.min()
2
>>> len(pq)
3
>>> pq.isEmpty()
False
```

8.37 Implement classes Square and Triangle as subclasses of class Polygon from Problem 8.21. Each will overload the constructor method __init__ so it takes only one argument l (the side length), and each will override method area() that computes the area using a simpler implementation. The method __init__ should make use of the superclass __init__ method, so no instance variables (l and n) are defined in subclasses. *Note:* The area of an equilateral triangle of side length s is $s^2 * \sqrt{3}/4$.

```
>>> s = Square(2)
>>> s.perimeter()
8
>>> s.area()
4
>>> t = Triangle(3)
>>> t.perimeter()
9
>>> t.area()
6.3639610306789285
```

8.38 Implement two subclasses of class Person described in Problem 8.24. The class Instructor supports methods:

- __init__(): Constructor that takes the person's degree in addition to name and birth year

- degree(): Returns the degree of the instructor

The class Student, also a subclass of class Person, supports:

- __init__(): Constructor that takes the person's major in addition to name and birth year

- major(): Returns the major of the student

Your implementation of the three classes should behave as shown in the next code:

```
>>> x = Instructor('Smith', 1963, 'PhD')
>>> x.age()
45
>>> y = Student('Jones', 1987, 'Computer Science')
>>> y.age()
21
>>> y.major()
'Computer Science'
>>> x.degree()
'PhD'
```

8.39 Consider the class tree hierarchy:

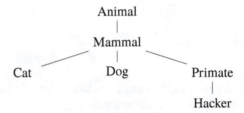

Implement six classes to model this taxonomy with Python inheritance. In class `Animal`, implement method `speak()` that will be inherited by the descendant classes of `Animal`. Complete the implementation of the six classes so that they exhibit this behavior:

```
>>> garfield = Cat()
>>> garfield.speak()
Meeow
>>> dude = Hacker()
>>> dude.speak( )
Hello world!
```

8.40 In Problem 8.20, there are some problems with the implementation of the class `BankAccount`, and they are illustrated here:

```
>>> x = BankAccount(-700)
>>> x.balance()
-700
>>> x.withdraw(70)
>>> x.balance()
-770
>>> x.deposit(-7)
>>> x.balance()
Balance:  -777
```

The problems are: (1) a bank account with a negative balance can be created, (2) the withdrawal amount is greater than the balance, and (3) the deposit amount is negative. Modify the code for the `BankAccount` class so that a `ValueError` exception is thrown for any of these violations, together with an appropriate message: `'Illegal balance'`, `'Overdraft'`, or `'Negative deposit'`.

```
>>> x = BankAccount2(-700)
Traceback (most recent call last):
...
ValueError: Illegal balance
```

8.41 In Problem 8.40, a generic `ValueError` exception is raised if any of the three violations occur. It would be more useful if a more specific, user-defined exception is raised instead. Define new exception classes `NegativeBalanceError`, `OverdraftError`, and `DepositError` that would be raised instead. In addition, the informal string representation of the exception object should contain the balance that would result from the negative balance account creation, the overdraft, or the negative deposit.

For example, when trying to create a bank account with a negative balance, the error message should include the balance that would result if the bank account creation was allowed:

```
>>> x = BankAccount3(-5)
Traceback (most recent call last):
...
NegativeBalanceError: Account created with negative balance -5
```

When a withdrawal results in a negative balance, the error message should also include the balance that would result if the withdrawal was allowed:

```
>>> x = BankAccount3(5)
>>> x.withdraw(7)
Traceback (most recent call last):
...
OverdraftError: Operation would result in negative balance -2
```

If a negative deposit is attempted, the negative deposit amount should be included in the error message:

```
>>> x.deposit(-3)
Traceback (most recent call last):
...
DepositError: Negative deposit -3
```

Finally, reimplement the class `BankAccount` to use these new exception classes instead of `ValueError`.

Graphical User Interfaces

9.1 Basics of `tkinter` GUI Development 292

9.2 Event-Based `tkinter` Widgets 299

9.3 Designing GUIs 308

9.4 OOP for GUIs 313

E-Book Case Study: Developing a Calculator 318

Chapter Summary 319

Solutions to Practice Problems 319

Exercises 323

Problems 324

THIS CHAPTER INTRODUCES graphical user interface (GUI) development.

When you use a computer application—whether it is a web browser, an email client, a computer game, or your Python integrated development environment (IDE)—you typically do so through a GUI, using a mouse and a keyboard. There are two reasons for using a GUI: A GUI gives a better overview of what an application does, and it makes it easier to use the application.

In order to develop GUIs, a developer will require a GUI application programming interface (API) that provides the necessary GUI toolkit. There are several GUI APIs for Python; in this text we use `tkinter`, a module that is part of Python's Standard Library.

Beyond the development of GUIs using `tkinter`, this chapter also covers fundamental software development techniques that are naturally used in GUI development. We introduce *event-driven programming*, an approach for developing applications in which tasks are executed in response to events (such as button clicks). We also learn that GUIs are ideally developed as user-defined classes, and we take the opportunity to once again showcase the benefit of object-oriented programming (OOP).

9.1 Basics of `tkinter` GUI Development

A graphical user interface (GUI) consists of basic visual building blocks such as buttons, labels, text entry forms, menus, check boxes, and scroll bars, among others, all packed inside a standard window. The building blocks are commonly referred to as *widgets*. In order to develop GUIs, a developer will require a module that makes such widgets available. We will use the module `tkinter` that is included in the Standard Library.

In this section, we explain the basics of GUI development using `tkinter`: how to create a window, how to add text or images to it, and how to manipulate the look and location of widgets.

Widget Tk: The GUI Window

In our first GUI example, we build a bare-bones GUI that consists of a window and nothing else. To do this we import the class Tk from module `tkinter` and instantiate an object of type Tk:

```
>>> from tkinter import Tk
>>> root = Tk()
```

A Tk object is a GUI widget that represents the GUI window; it is created without arguments.

If you execute the preceding code, you will notice that creating a Tk() widget did not get you a window on the screen. To get the window to appear, the Tk method `mainloop()` needs to be invoked on the widget:

```
>>> root.mainloop()
```

You should now see a window like the one in Figure 9.1.

Figure 9.1 A `tkinter` GUI window. The window can be minimized and closed, and looks and feels like any other window in the underlying operating system.

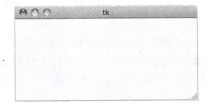

This GUI window is just that: a window and nothing else. To display text or pictures inside this window, we need to use the `tkinter` widget Label.

Widget Label for Displaying Text

The widget Label can be used to display text inside a window. Let's illustrate its usage by developing a GUI version of the classic "Hello World!" application. To get started, we need to import the class Label in addition to class Tk from `tkinter`:

```
>>> from tkinter import Tk, Label
>>> root = Tk()
```

We then create a Label object that displays the text "Hello GUI world!":

```
>>> hello = Label(master = root, text = 'Hello GUI world!')
```

The first argument in this `Label` constructor, named `master`, specifies that the `Label` widget will live inside widget `root`. A GUI typically contains many widgets organized in a hierarchical fashion. When a widget X is defined to live inside widget Y, widget Y is said to be the *master* of widget X.

The second argument, named `text`, refers to the text displayed by the `Label` widget. The `text` argument is one of about two dozen *optional* constructor arguments that specify the look of a `Label` widget (and of other `tkinter` widgets as well). We list some of those optional arguments in Table 9.1 and show their usage in this section.

While the `Label` constructor specifies that the label widget lives inside widget `root`, it does not specify *where* in the widget `root` the label should be placed. There are several ways to specify the geometry of the GUI (i.e., the placement of the widgets inside their master); we discuss them in more detail later in this section. One simple way to specify the placement of a widget inside its master is to invoke method `pack()` on the widget. The method `pack()` can take arguments that specify the desired position of the widget inside its master; without any arguments, it will use the default position, which is to place the widget centered and against the top boundary of its master:

```
>>> hello.pack() # hello is placed against top boundary of master
>>> root.mainloop()
```

Just as in our first example, the `mainloop()` method will get the GUI shown in Figure 9.2 started:

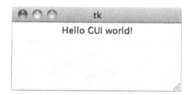

Figure 9.2 A text label.
The `Label` widget created with the `text` argument will display a text label. Note that the label is packed against the top boundary of its master, the window itself.

As Table 9.1 illustrates, the `text` argument is only one of a number of optional widget constructor arguments that define the look of a widget. We showcase some of the other options in the next three GUI examples.

Option	Description
`text`	Text to display
`image`	Image to display
`width`	Width of widget in pixels (for images) or characters (for text); if omitted, size is calculated based on content
`height`	Height of widget in pixels (for images) or characters (for text); if omitted, size is calculated based on content
`relief`	Border style; possibilities are FLAT (default), GROOVE, RAISED, RIDGE, and SUNKEN, all defined in `tkinter`
`borderwidth`	Width of border, default is 0 (no border)
`background`	Background color name (as a string)
`foreground`	Foreground color name (as a string)
`font`	Font descriptor (as a tuple with font family name, font size, and—optionally—a font style)
`padx,pady`	Padding added to the widget along the x- or y-axis

Table 9.1 `tkinter` widget options. Shown are some of the `tkinter` widget options that can be used to specify the look of the widget. The values for the options are passed as input arguments to the widget constructor. The options can be used to specify the look of all `tkinter` widgets, not just widget `Label`. The usage of the options in this table is illustrated throughout this section.

Displaying Images

A Label widget can be used to display more than just text. To display an image, an argument named `image` should be used in the Label constructor instead of a `text` argument. The next example program places a GIF image inside a GUI window. (The example uses file `peace.gif`, which should be in the same folder as module `peace.py`.)

File: peace.gif

Module: peace.py

```
1  from tkinter import Tk, Label, PhotoImage
2  root = Tk()                           # the window
3  # transform GIF image to a format tkinter can display
4  photo = PhotoImage(file='peace.gif')
5
6  peace = Label(master=root,
7                image=photo,
8                width=300,             # width of label, in pixels
9                height=180)            # height of label, in pixels
10 peace.pack()
11 root.mainloop()
```

The resulting GUI is shown in Figure 9.3. The constructor argument `image` must refer to an image in a format that `tkinter` can display. The `PhotoImage` class, defined in the module `tkinter`, is used to transform a GIF image into an object with such a format. Arguments `width` and `height` specify the width and height of the label in pixels.

Figure 9.3 An image label.
With the `image` argument, a
Label widget displays an
image. Options `width` and
`height` specify the width
and height of the label, in
pixels. If the image is
smaller than the label, white
padding is added around it.

DETOUR

GIF and Other Image Formats

GIF is just one among many image file formats that have been defined. You are probably familiar with the Joint Photographic Experts Group (JPEG) format used primarily for photographs. Other commonly used image formats include Bitmap Image File (BMP), Portable Document Format (PDF), and Tagged Image File Format (TIFF).

In order to display images in formats other than GIF, the Python Imaging Library (PIL) can be used. It contains classes that load images in one of 30+ formats and convert them to `tkinter`-compatible image object. The PIL also contains tools for processing images. For more information, go to

    www.pythonware.com/products/pil/

Note: At the time of writing, the PIL was not updated to support Python 3.

Packing Widgets

The `tkinter` geometry manager is responsible for the placement of widgets within their master. If multiple widgets must be laid out, the placement will be computed by the geometry manager using sophisticated layout algorithms (that attempt to ensure that the layout looks good) and using directives given by the programmer. The size of a master widget containing one or more widgets is based on their size and placement. Furthermore, the size and layout will be dynamically adjusted as the GUI window is resized by the user.

The method `pack()` is one of the three methods that can be used to provide directives to the geometry manager. (We will see another one, method `grid()`, later in this section.) The directives specify the relative position of widgets within their master.

To illustrate how to use the directives and also to show additional widget constructor options, we develop a GUI with with two image labels and a text label, shown in Figure 9.4:

Figure 9.4 Multiple widgets GUI. Three `Label` widgets are packed inside the GUI window; the peace image is pushed left, the smiley face is pushed right, and the text is pushed down.

The optional argument `side` of method `pack()` is used to direct the `tkinter` geometry manager to push a widget against a particular border of its master. The value of `side` can be TOP, BOTTOM, LEFT, or RIGHT, which are constants defined in module `tkinter`; the default value for `side` is TOP. In the implementation of the preceding GUI, we use the `side` option to appropriately pack the three widgets:

```
1  from tkinter import Tk,Label,PhotoImage,BOTTOM,LEFT,RIGHT,RIDGE
2  # GUI illustrates widget constructor options and method pack()
3  root = Tk()
4
5  # label with text "Peace begins with a smile."
6  text = Label(root,
7               font = ('Helvetica', 16, 'bold italic'),
8               foreground='white',   # letter color
9               background='black',   # background color
10              padx=25,   # widen label 25 pixels left and right
11              pady=10,   # widen label 10 pixels up and down
12              text='Peace begins with a smile.')
13 text.pack(side=BOTTOM)                # push label down
14
15 # label with peace symbol image
16 peace = PhotoImage(file='peace.gif')
17 peaceLabel = Label(root,
18                    borderwidth=3,   # label border width
19                    relief=RIDGE,    # label border style
20                    image=peace)
21 peaceLabel.pack(side=LEFT)              # push label left
```

File: peace.gif,smiley.gif

Module: smileyPeace.py

```
22   # label with smiley face image
23   smiley = PhotoImage(file='smiley.gif')
24   smileyLabel = Label(root,
25                          image=smiley)
26   smileyLabel.pack(side=RIGHT)              # push label right
27
28   root.mainloop()
```

Table 9.2 lists two other options for method pack(). The option expand, which can be set to True or False, specifies whether the widget should be allowed to expand to fill any extra space inside the master. If option expand is set to True, option fill can be used to specify whether the expansion should be along the x-axis, the y-axis, or both.

Table 9.2 Some packing options. In addition to option side, method pack() can take options fill and expand.

Option	Description
side	Specifies the side (using constants TOP, BOTTOM, LEFT, or RIGHT defined in tkinter) the widget will be pushed against; the default is TOP
fill	Specifies whether the widget should fill the width or height of the space given to it by the master; options include 'both', 'x', 'y', and 'none' (the default)
expand	Specifies whether the widget should expand to fill the space given to it; the default is False, no expansion

The GUI program smileyPeace.py also showcases a few widget constructor options we have not seen yet. A RIDGE-style border of width 3 around the peace symbol is specified using options borderwith and relief. Also, the text label (a quote by Mother Theresa) is constructed with options that specify white lettering (option foreground) on a black background (option background) with extra padding of 10 pixels up and down (option pady) and of 25 pixels left and right (option padx). The font option specifies that the text font should be a bold, italic, Helvetica font of size 16 points.

Practice Problem 9.1

File: peace.gif

Write a program peaceandlove.py that creates this GUI:

The "Peace & Love" text label should be pushed to the left and have a black background of size to fit 5 rows of 20 characters. If the user expands the window, the label should remain right next to the left border of the window. The peace symbol image label should be pushed to the right. However, when the user expands the window, white padding should fill the space created. The picture shows the GUI *after* the user manually expanded it.

CAUTION

Forgetting the Geometry Specification

It's a common mistake to forget to specify the placement of the widgets. A widget appears in a GUI window only after it has been packed in its master. This is achieved by invoking, on the widget, the method pack(), the method grid(), which we discuss shortly, or the method place(), which we do not go over.

Arranging Widgets in a Grid

We now consider a GUI that has more than just a couple of labels. How would you go about developing the phone dial GUI shown in Figure 9.5?

Figure 9.5 Phone dial GUI. This GUI's labels are stored in a 4 × 3 grid. Method grid() is more suitable than pack() for placing widgets in a grid. Rows (resp. columns) are indexed top to bottom (resp. left to right) starting from index 0.

We already know how to create each individual phone dial "button" using a Label widget. What is not clear at all is how to get all 12 of them arranged in a grid.

If we need to place several widgets in a gridlike fashion, method grid() is more appropriate than method pack(). When using method grid(), the master widget is split into rows and columns, and each cell of the resulting grid can store a widget. To place a widget in row r and column c, method grid() is invoked on the widget with the row r and column c as input arguments, as shown in this implementation of the phone dial GUI:

Module: phone.py

```
1  from tkinter import Tk, Label, RAISED
2  root = Tk()
3  labels = [['1', '2', '3'],        # phone dial label texts
4            ['4', '5', '6'],        # organized in a grid
5            ['7', '8', '9'],
6            ['*', '0', '#']]
7
8  for r in range(4):         # for every row r = 0, 1, 2, 3
9      for c in range(3):        # for every row c = 0, 1, 2
10         # create label for row r and column c
11         label = Label(root,
12                       relief=RAISED,      # raised border
13                       padx=10,            # make label wide
14                       text=labels[r][c])  # label text
15         # place label in row r and column c
16         label.grid(row=r, column=c)
17
18  root.mainloop()
```

In lines 5 through 8, we define a two-dimensional list that stores in row r and column c the text that will be put on the label in row r and column c of the phone dial. Doing this facilitates the creation and proper placement of the labels in the nested for loop in lines 10 through 19. Note the use of the method `grid()` with row and column input arguments.

Table 9.3 shows some options that can be used with the `grid()` method.

Table 9.3 Some `grid()` method options. The `columnspan` (i.e., `rowspan`) option is used to place a widget across multiple columns (i.e., rows).

Option	Description
`column`	Specifies the column for the widget; default is column 0
`columnspan`	Specifies how many columns the widgets should occupy
`row`	Specifies the row for the widget; default is row 0
`rowspan`	Specifies how many rows the widgets should occupy

CAUTION

Mixing `pack()` and `grid()`

The methods `pack()` and `grid()` use different methods to compute the layout of the widgets. Those methods do *not* work well together, and each will try to optimize the layout in its own way, trying to undo the other algorithm's choices. The result is that the program may never complete execution.

The short story is this: You must use one or the other for *all* widgets with the same master.

Practice Problem 9.2

Implement function `cal()` that takes as input a year and a month (a number between 1 and 12) and starts up a GUI that shows the corresponding calendar. For example, the calendar shown is obtained using:

```
>>> cal(2012, 2)
```

Mon	Tue	Wed	Thu	Fri	Sat	Sun
		1	2	3	4	5
6	7	8	9	10	11	12
13	14	15	16	17	18	19
20	21	22	23	24	25	26
27	28	29				

To do this, you will need to compute (1) the day of the week (Monday, Tuesday, . . .) on which the first day of the month falls and (2) the number of days in the month (taking into account leap years). The function `monthrange()` defined in the module `calendar` returns exactly those two values:

```
>>> from calendar import monthrange
>>> monthrange(2012, 2)     # year 2012, month 2 (February)
(2, 29)
```

The returned value is a tuple. The first value in the tuple, 2, corresponds to Wednesday (Monday is 0, Tuesday is 1, etc.). The second value, 29, is the number of days in February of year 2012, a leap year.

DETOUR

Do You Want to Learn More?

This chapter is only an introduction to GUI development using `tkinter`. A comprehensive overview of GUI development and `tkinter` would fill a whole textbook. If you want to learn more, start with the Python documentation at

    http://docs.python.org/py3k/library/tkinter.html

There are also other free, online resources that you can use to learn more. The "official" list of these resources is at

    http://wiki.python.org/moin/TkInter

Two particularly useful resources (although they use Python 2) are at

    http://www.pythonware.com/library/tkinter/introduction/
    http://infohost.nmt.edu/tcc/help/pubs/tkinter/

9.2 Event-Based `tkinter` Widgets

We now explore the different types of widgets available in `tkinter`. In particular, we study those widgets that respond to mouse clicks and keyboard inputs by the user. Such widgets have an interactive behavior that needs to be programmed using a style of programming called *event-driven programming*. In addition to GUI development, event-driven programming is also used in the development of computer games and distributed client/server applications, among others.

`Button` Widget and Event Handlers

Let's start with the classic button widget. The class `Button` from module `tkinter` represents GUI buttons. To illustrate its usage, we develop a simple GUI application, shown in Figure 9.6, that contains just one button.

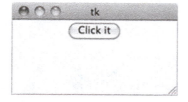

Figure 9.6 **GUI with one** `Button` **widget.** The text "Click it" is displayed on top of the button. When the button is clicked, the day and time information is printed.

The application works in this way: When you press the button "Click it", the day and time of the button click is printed in the interpreter shell:

```
>>>
Day:  07 Jul 2011
Time: 23:42:47 PM
```

You can click the button again (and again) if you like:

```
>>>
Day:  07 Jul 2011
Time: 23:42:47 PM

Day:  07 Jul 2011
Time: 23:42:50 PM
```

Let's implement this GUI. To construct a button widget, we use the Button constructor. Just as for the Label constructor, the first argument of the Button constructor must refer to the button's master. To specify the text that will be displayed on top of the button, the text argument is used, again just as for a Label widget. In fact, all the options for customizing widgets shown in Table 9.1 can be used for Button widgets as well.

The one difference between a button and a label is that a button is an interactive widget. Every time a button is clicked, an action is performed. This "action" is actually implemented as a function, which gets called every time the button is clicked. We can specify the name of this function using a command option in the Button constructor. Here is how we would create the button widget for the GUI just shown:

```
root = Tk()
button = Button(root, text='Click it', command=clicked)
```

When the button is clicked, the function clicked() will be executed. Now we need to implement this function. When called, the function should print the current day and time information. We use the module time, covered in Section 4.2, to obtain and print the local time. The complete GUI program is then:

Module: clickit.py

```
1   from tkinter import Tk, Button
2   from time import strftime, localtime
3
4   def clicked():
5       'prints day and time info'
6       time = strftime('Day:  %d %b %Y\nTime: %H:%M:%S %p\n',
7                        localtime())
8       print(time)
9
10  root = Tk()
11
12  # create button labeled 'Click it' and event handler clicked()
13  button = Button(root,
14                  text='Click it',    # text on top of button
15                  command=clicked)     # button click event handler
16  button.pack()
17  root.mainloop()
```

The function clicked() is said to be an *event handler*; what it *handles* is the *event* of the button "Click it" being clicked.

In the first implementation of clicked(), the day and time information is printed in the shell. Suppose we prefer to print the message in its own little GUI window, as shown in Figure 9.7, instead of the shell.

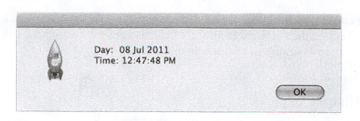

Figure 9.7 Window
`showinfo()`. The function
`showinfo()` from module
`tkinter.messagebox`
displays a message in a
separate window. Clicking
the "OK" button makes the
window disappear.

In module `tkinter.messagebox`, there is a function named `showinfo` that prints a string in a separate window. So, we can just replace the original function `clicked()` with:

Module: clickit.py

```
1  from tkinter.messagebox import showinfo
2
3  def clicked():
4      'prints day and time info'
5      time = strftime('Day:  %d %b %Y\nTime: %H:%M:%S %p\n',
6                      localtime())
7      showinfo(message=time)
```

Implement a GUI app that contains two buttons labeled "Local time" and "Greenwich time". When the first button is pressed, the local time should be printed in the shell. When the second button is pressed, the Greenwich Mean Time should be printed.

Practice Problem 9.3

```
>>>
Local time
Day:  08 Jul 2011
Time: 13:19:43 PM

Greenwich time
Day:  08 Jul 2011
Time: 18:19:46 PM
```

You can obtain the current Greenwich Mean Time using the function `gmtime()` from module `time`.

Events, Event Handlers, and `mainloop()`

Having seen the workings of the interactive `Button` widget, it is now a good time to explain how a GUI processes user-generated events, such as button clicks. When a GUI is started with the `mainloop()` method call, Python starts an infinite loop called an *event loop*. The event loop is best described using pseudocode:

```
while True:
    wait for a an event to occur
    run the associated event handler function
```

In other words, at any point in time, the GUI is waiting for an event. When an event such as a button click occurs, the GUI executes the function that is specified to handle the event. When the handler terminates, the GUI goes back to waiting for the next event.

A button click is just one type of event that can occur in a GUI. Movements of the mouse and pressing keys on the keyboard in an entry field also generate events the can be handled by the GUI. We see examples of this later in this section.

DETOUR

Short History of GUIs

The first computer system with a GUI was the Xerox Alto computer developed in 1973 by researchers at Xerox PARC (Palo Alto Research Center) in Palo Alto, California. Founded in 1970 as a research and development division of Xerox Corporation, Xerox PARC was responsible for developing many now-common computer technologies, such as laser printing, Ethernet, and the modern personal computer, in addition to GUIs.

The Xerox Alto GUI was inspired by the text-based hyperlinks clickable with a mouse in the On-Line System developed by researchers at Stanford Research Institute International in Menlo Park, California, led by Douglas Engelbart. The Xerox Alto GUI included graphical elements such as windows, menus, radio buttons, check boxes, and icons, all manipulated using a mouse and a keyboard.

In 1979, Apple Computer's cofounder Steve Jobs visited Xerox PARC, where he learned of the mouse-controlled GUI of the Xerox Alto. He promptly integrated it, first into the Apple Lisa in 1983 and then in the Macintosh in 1984. Since then, all major operating systems have supported GUIs.

The `Entry` Widget

In our next GUI example, we introduce the `Entry` widget class. It represents the classic, single-line text box you would find in a form. The GUI app we want to build asks the user to enter a date and then computes the weekday corresponding to it. The GUI should look as shown in Figure 9.8:

Figure 9.8 Weekday application. The app requests the user to type a data in the format MMM DD, YYYY, as in "Jan 21, 1967".

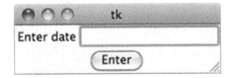

After the user types "Jan 21, 1967" in the entry box and clicks the button "Enter", a new window, shown in Figure 9.9, should pop up:

Figure 9.9 Pop-up window of the weekday app. When the user enters the date and presses button "Enter", the weekday corresponding to the date is shown in the pop-up window.

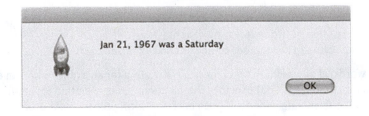

It is clear that the GUI should have a `Label` and a `Button` widget. For a text entry box, we need to use the `Entry` widget defined in `tkinter`. The `Entry` widget is appropriate for entering (and displaying) a single line of text. The user can enter text inside the widget using the keyboard. We can now start the implementation of the GUI:

Module: day.py

```
1   # import statements and
2   # event handler compute() that computes and displays the weekday
3
4   root = Tk()
5
6   # label
7   label = Label(root, text='Enter date')
8   label.grid(row=0, column=0)
9
10  # entry
11  dateEnt = Entry(root)
12  dateEnt.grid(row=0, column=1)
13
14  # button
15  button = Button(root, text='Enter', command=compute)
16  button.grid(row=1, column=0, columnspan=2)
17
18  root.mainloop()
```

In line 13, we create an `Entry` widget. Note that we are using method `grid()` to place the three widgets. The only thing left to do is to implement the event-handling function `compute()`. Let's first describe what this function needs to do:

1. Read the date from the entry `dateEnt`.
2. Compute the weekday corresponding to the date.
3. Display the weekday message in a pop-up window.
4. Erase the date from entry `dateEnt`.

The last step is a nice touch: We delete the date just typed in to make it easier to enter a new date.

To *read* the string that is inside an `Entry` widget, we can use the `Entry` method `get()`. It returns the string that is inside the entry. To *delete* the string inside an `Entry` widget, we need to use the `Entry` method `delete()`. In general, it is used to delete a substring of the string inside the `Entry` widget. Therefore, it takes two indexes `first` and `last`, and it deletes the substring starting at index `first` and ending *before* index `last`. Indexes 0 and `END` (a constant defined in `tkinter`) are used to delete the whole string inside an entry. Table 9.4 shows the usage of these and other `Entry` methods.

Method	Description
`e.get()`	Returns the string inside the entry e
`e.insert(index, text)`	Inserts text into entry e at the given index; if index is END, it appends the string
`e.delete(from, to)`	Deletes the substring in entry e from index from up to and not including index to; delete(0, END) deletes all the text in the entry

Table 9.4 **Some** `Entry` **methods.** Listed are three core methods of class `Entry`. The constant `END` is defined in `tkinter` and refers to the index *past* the last character in the entry.

Armed with the method of the Entry widget class, we can now implement the event-handling function `compute()`:

Module: day.py

```
1   from tkinter import Tk, Button, Entry, Label, END
2   from time import strptime, strftime
3   from tkinter.messagebox import showinfo
4
5   def compute():
6       '''display day of the week corresponding to date in dateEnt;
7          date must have format MMM DD, YYYY (e.g., Jan 21, 1967)'''
8
9       global dateEnt   # dateEnt is a global variable
10
11      # read date from entry dateEnt
12      date = dateEnt.get()
13
14      # compute weekday corresponding to date
15      weekday = strftime('%A', strptime(date, '%b %d, %Y'))
16
17      # display the weekday in a pop-up window
18      showinfo(message = '{} was a {}'.format(date, weekday))
19
20      # delete date from entry dateEnt
21      dateEnt.delete(0, END)
22
23  # rest of program
```

In line 9, we specify that `dateEnt` is a global variable. While that is not strictly necessary (we are not assigning to `dateEnt` inside function `compute()`), it is a warning so the programmer maintaining the code is aware that `dateEnt` is not a local variable.

In line 15, we use two functions from module `time` to compute the weekday corresponding to a date. Function `strptime()` takes as input a string containing a date (`date`) and a format string (`'%b %d, %Y'`), which uses directives from Table 4.3. The function returns the date in an object of type `time.struct_time`. Recall from Section 4.2 that function `strftime()` takes such an object and a format string (`'%A'`) and returns the date formatted according to the format string. Since the format string contains only the directive `%A` that specifies the date weekday, only the weekday is returned.

Practice Problem 9.4

Implement a variation of GUI program `day.py` called `day2.py`. Instead of displaying the weekday message in a separate pop-up window, insert it in front of the date in the entry box, as shown. Also add a button labeled "Clear" that erases the entry box.

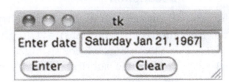

Text **Widget and Binding Events**

Next we introduce the `Text` widget, which is used to interactively enter multiple lines of text in a way similar to entering text in a text editor. The `Text` widget class supports the same methods `get()`, `insert()`, and `delete()` that class `Entry` does, albeit in a different format (see Table 9.5).

Method	Description
`t.insert(index, text)`	Insert `text` into `Text` widget `t` before index `index`
`t.get(from, to)`	Return the substring in `Text` widget `t` from index `from` up to but not including index `to`
`t.delete(from, to)`	Delete the substring in `Text` widget `t` between index `from` up to but not including index `to`

Table 9.5 Some Text methods. Unlike indexes used for `Entry` methods, indexes used in `Text` methods are of the form `row.column` (e.g., index 2.3 refers to the fourth character in the third row).

We use a `Text` widget to develop an application that looks like a text editor, but "secretly" records and prints every keystroke the user types in the `Text` widget. For example, suppose you were to type the sentence shown in Figure 9.10:

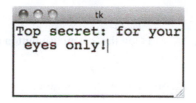

Figure 9.10 Key logger application. The key logger GUI consists of a `Text` widget. When the user types text inside the text box, the keystrokes are recorded and printed in the shell.

This would be printed in the shell:

```
>>>
char = Shift_L
char = T
char = o
char = p
char = space
char = s
char = e
char = c
char = r
char = e
char = t
...
```

(We omit the rest of the characters.) This application is often referred to as a *keylogger*.

We now develop this GUI app. To create a `Text` widget big enough to contain five rows of 20 characters, we use the `width` and `height` widget constructor options:

```
from tkinter import Text
t = Text(root, width=20, height=5)
```

In order to record every keystroke when we type inside the `Text` widget `text`, we need to somehow associate an event-handling function with keystrokes. We achieve this with the bind() method, whose purpose is to "bind" (or associate) an *event type* to an *event handler*. For example, the statement

```
text.bind('<KeyPress>', record)
```

binds a keystroke, an event type described with string `'<KeyPress>'`, to the event handler `record()`.

In order to complete the keylogger application, we need to learn a bit more about event patterns and the `tkinter` Event class.

Event Patterns and the `tkinter` Class `Event`

In general, the first argument of the `bind()` method is the type of event we want to bind. The type of event is described by a string that is the concatenation of one or more *event patterns*. An event pattern has the form

```
<modifier-modifier-type-detail>
```

Table 9.6 shows some possible values for the modifier, type, and detail. For our keylogger application, the event pattern will consist of just a type, `KeyPress`. Here are some other examples of event patterns and associated target events:

- `<Control-Button-1>`: Hitting $\boxed{\text{Ctrl}}$ and the left mouse button simultaneously
- `<Button-1><Button-3>`: Clicking the left mouse button and *then* the right one
- `<KeyPress-D><Return>`: Hitting the keyboard key $\boxed{\text{D}}$ and *then* $\boxed{\text{Enter/Return}}$
- `<Buttons1-Motion>`: Mouse motion while holding left mouse button

The second argument to method `bind()` is the event-handling function. This function must be defined by the developer to take exactly one argument, an object of type Event. The class Event is defined in `tkinter`. When an event (like a key press) occurs, the Python interpreter will create an object of type Event associated with the event and call the event-handling function with the Event object passed as the single argument.

An Event object has many attributes that store information about the event that caused its instantiation. For a key press event, for example, the Python interpreter will create an

Table 9.6 Some event pattern modifiers, types, and details. An event pattern is a string, delimited by symbols < and > consisting of up to two modifiers, one type, and up to one detail, in that order.

Modifier	Description
Control	$\boxed{\text{Ctrl}}$ key
Button1	Left mouse button
Button3	Right mouse button
Shift	$\boxed{\text{Shift}}$ key
Type	
Button	Mouse button
Return	$\boxed{\text{Enter/Return}}$ key
KeyPress	Press of a keyboard key
KeyRelease	Release of a keyboard key
Motion	Mouse motion
Detail	
<button number>	1, 2, or 3 for left, middle, and right button, respectively
<key symbol>	Key letter symbol

Event object and assign the pressed key symbol and (Unicode) number to attributes `keysym` and `keysum_num`.

Therefore, in our keyLogger application, the event-handling function `record()` should take this `Event` object as input, read the key symbol and number information stored in it, and display them in the shell. This will achieve the desired behavior of continuously displaying the keystrokes made by the GUI user.

```python
from tkinter import Tk, Text, BOTH

def record(event):
    '''event handling function for key press event;
       input event is of type tkinter.Event'''
    print('char = {}'.format(event.keysym)) # print key symbol

root = Tk()

text = Text(root,
            width=20,   # set width to 20 characters
            height=5)   # set height to 5 rows of characters

# Bind a key press event with the event handling function record()
text.bind('<KeyPress>', record)

# widget expands if the master does
text.pack(expand=True, fill=BOTH)

root.mainloop()
```

Module: keyLogger.py

Other Event object attributes are set by the Python interpreter, depending on the type of event. Table 9.7 shows some of the attributes. The table also shows, for each attribute, the type of event that will cause it to be defined. For example, the `num` attribute will be defined by a `ButtonPress` event, but not by a `KeyPress` or `KeyRelease` event.

Attribute	Event Type	Description
num	ButtonPress, ButtonRelease	Mouse button pressed
time	all	Time of event
x	all	x-coordinate of mouse
y	all	y-coordinate of mouse
keysym	KeyPress, KeyRelease	Key pressed as string
keysym_num	KeyPress, KeyRelease	Key pressed as Unicode number

Table 9.7 Some `Event` **attributes.** A few attributes of class `Event` are shown. The type of event that causes the attribute to be defined is also shown. All event types will set the `time` attribute, for example.

In the original `day.py` program, the user has to click button "Enter" after typing a date in the entry box. Requiring the user to use the mouse right after typing his name using the keyboard is an inconvenience. Modify the program `day.py` to allow the user just to press the ⎡Enter/Return⎤ keyboard key instead of clicking the button "Enter".

Practice Problem 9.5

CAUTION

Event-Handling Functions

There are two distinct types of event-handling functions in `tkinter`. A function `buttonHandler()` that handles clicks on a `Button` widget is one type:

> `Button(root, text='example', command=buttonHandler)`

Function `buttonhandler()` must be defined to take no input arguments.
   A function `eventHandler()` that handles an event type is:

> `widget.bind('<event type>', eventHandler)`

Function `eventHandler()` must be defined to take exactly one input argument that is of type `Event`.

9.3 Designing GUIs

In this section, we continue to introduce new types of interactive widgets. We discuss how to design GUIs that keep track of some values that are read or modified by event handlers. We also illustrate how to design GUIs that contain multiple widgets in a hierarchical fashion.

Widget `Canvas`

The `Canvas` widget is a fun widget that can display drawings consisting of lines and geometrical objects. You can think of it as a primitive version of `turtle` graphics. (In fact, `turtle` graphics is essentially a `tkinter` GUI.)

We illustrate the `Canvas` widget by building a very simple pen drawing application. The application consists of an initially empty canvas. The user can draw curves inside the canvas using the mouse. Pressing the left mouse button starts the drawing of the curve. Mouse motion while pressing the button moves the pen and draws the curve. The curve is complete when the button is released. A scribble done using this application is shown in Figure 9.11.

Figure 9.11 Pen drawing app. This GUI implements a pen drawing application. A left mouse button press starts the curve. You then draw the curve by moving the mouse while pressing the left mouse button. The drawing stops when the button is released.

We get started by first creating a `Canvas` widget of size 100×100 pixels. Since the drawing of the curve is to be started by pressing the left mouse button, we will need to bind the event type `<Button-1>` to an event-handling function. Furthermore, since mouse motion while holding down the left mouse button draws the curve, we will also need to bind the event type `<Button1-Motion>` to another event-handling function.

This is what we have so far:

Module: draw.py

```python
from tkinter import Tk, Canvas

# event handlers begin and draw here

root = Tk()

oldx, oldy = 0, 0    # mouse coordinates (global variables)

# canvas
canvas = Canvas(root, height=100, width=150)

# bind left mouse button click event to function begin()
canvas.bind("<Button-1>", begin)

# bind mouse motion while pressing left button event
canvas.bind("<Button1-Motion>", draw)

canvas.pack()
root.mainloop()
```

We now need to implement the handlers `begin()` and `draw()` that will actually draw the curve. Let's discuss the implementation of `draw()` first. Every time the mouse is moved while pressing the left mouse button, the handler `draw()` is called with an input argument that is an `Event` object storing the new mouse position. To continue drawing the curve, all we need to do is connect this new mouse position to the previous one with a straight line. The curve that is displayed will effectively be a sequence of *very* short straight line segments connecting successive mouse positions.

The `Canvas` method `create_line()` can be used to draw a straight line between points. In its general form, it takes as input a sequence of (x, y) coordinates (x1, y1, x2, y2, . . . , xn, yn) and draws a line segment from point (x1, y1) to point (x2, y2), another one from point (x2, y2) to point (x3, y3), and so on. So, to connect the old mouse position at coordinates (oldx, oldy) to the new one at coordinates (newx, newy), we just need to execute:

```python
canvas.create_line(oldx, oldy, newx, newy)
```

The curve is thus drawn by repeatedly connecting the new mouse position to the old (previous) mouse position. This means that there must be an "initial" old mouse position (i.e., the start of the curve). This position is set by the event handler `begin()` called when the left mouse button is pressed:

Module: draw.py

```python
def begin(event):
    'initializes the start of the curve to mouse position'

    global oldx, oldy
    oldx, oldy = event.x, event.y
```

In handler `begin()`, the variables `oldx` and `oldy` receive the coordinates of the mouse when the left mouse button is pressed. These global variables will be constantly updated inside handler `draw()` to keep track of the last recorded mouse position as the curve is drawn. We can now implement event handler `draw()`:

Module: draw.py

```
1  def draw(event):
2      'draws a line segment from old mouse position to new one'
3      global oldx, oldy, canvas        # x and y will be modified
4      newx, newy = event.x, event.y    # new mouse position
5
6      # connect previous mouse position to current one
7      canvas.create_line(oldx, oldy, newx, newy)
8
9      oldx, oldy = newx, newy          # new position becomes previous
```

Before we move on, we list in Table 9.8 some methods supported by widget `Canvas`.

Table 9.8 Some `Canvas` **methods.** Only a few methods of `tkinter` widget class `Canvas` are listed. Every object drawn in the canvas has a unique ID (which happens to be an integer).

Method	Description
`create_line(x1, y1, x2, y2, ...)`	Creates line segments connecting points `(x1,y1)`, `(x2,y2)`, ...; returns the ID of the item constructed
`create_rectangle(x1, y1, x2, y2)`	Creates a rectangle with vertexes at `(x1, y1)` and `(x2, y2)`; returns the ID of the item constructed
`create_oval(x1, y1, x2, y2)`	Creates an oval that is bounded by a rectangle with vertexes at `(x1, y1)` and `(x2, y2)`; returns the ID of the item constructed
`delete(ID)`	Deletes item identified with ID
`move(item, dx, dy)`	Moves `item` right dx units and down dy units

CAUTION

Storing State in a Global Variable

In program `draw.py`, the variables `oldx` and `oldy` store the coordinates of the mouse's last position. These variables are initially set by function `begin()` *and* then updated by function `draw()`. Therefore the variables `oldx`, `oldy` cannot be local variables to either function and have to be defined as global variables.

The use of global variables is problematic because the scope of global variables is the whole module. The larger the module and the more names it contains, the more likely it is that we inadvertently define a name twice in the module. This is even more likely when variables, functions, and classes are imported from another module. If a name is defined multiple times, all but one definition will be discarded, which then typically results in very strange bugs.

In the next section, we learn how to develop GUIs as new widget classes using OOP techniques. One of the benefits is that we will be able to store the GUI state in instance variables rather than in global variables.

Practice Problem
9.6

Implement program `draw2.py`, a modification of `draw.py` that supports deletion of the last curve drawn on the canvas by pressing Ctrl and the left mouse button simultaneously. In order to do this, you will need to delete all the short line segments created by `create_line()` that make up the last curve. This in turn means that you must store all the segments forming the last curve in some type of container.

Widget `Frame` as an Organizing Widget

We now introduce the `Frame` widget, an important widget whose primary purpose is to serve as the master of other widgets and facilitate the specification of the geometry of a GUI. We make use of it in another graphics GUI we call *plotter* shown in Figure 9.12. The plotter GUI allows the user to draw by moving a pen horizontally or vertically using the buttons to the right of the canvas. A button click should move the pen 10 pixels in the direction indicated on the button.

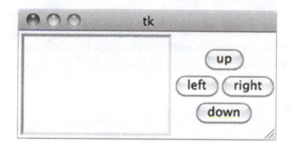

Figure 9.12 Plotter App. This GUI presents a canvas and four buttons controlling the pen moves. Each button will move the pen 10 units in the indicated direction.

It is clear that the plotter GUI consists of a `Canvas` widget and four `Button` widgets. What is less clear is how to specify the geometry of the widgets inside their master (i.e., the window itself). Neither the `pack()` method nor the `grid()` method can be used to pack the canvas and button widgets directly in the window so that they are displayed as shown in Figure 9.12.

To simplify the geometry specification, we can use a `Frame` widget whose sole purpose is to be the master of the four button widgets. The hierarchical packing of the widgets is then achieved in two steps. The first step is to pack the four button widgets into their `Frame` master using method `grid()`. Then we simply pack the `Canvas` and the `Frame` widgets next to each other.

Module: plotter.py

```
1  from tkinter import Tk, Canvas, Frame, Button, SUNKEN, LEFT, RIGHT
2
3  # event handlers up(), down(), left(), and right()
4
5  root = Tk()
6
7  # canvas with border of size 100 x 150
8  canvas = Canvas(root, height=100, width=150,
9                  relief=SUNKEN, borderwidth=3)
10 canvas.pack(side=LEFT)
11
```

```
12   # frame to hold the 4 buttons
13   box = Frame(root)
14   box.pack(side=RIGHT)
15
16   # the 4 button widgets have Frame widget box as their master
17   button = Button(box, text='up', command=up)
18   button.grid(row=0, column=0, columnspan=2)
19   button = Button(box, text='left',command=left)
20   button.grid(row=1, column=0)
21   button = Button(box, text='right', command=right)
22   button.grid(row=1, column=1)
23   button = Button(box, text='down', command=down)
24   button.grid(row=2, column=0, columnspan=2)
25
26   x, y = 50, 75 # pen position, initially in the middle
27
28   root.mainloop()
```

The four button event handlers are supposed to move the pen in the appropriate direction. We only show the handler for the up button, leaving the implementation of the remaining three handlers as an exercise:

Module: plotter.py

```
1   def up():
2       'move pen up 10 pixels'
3       global y, canvas              # y is modified
4       canvas.create_line(x, y, x, y-10)
5       y -= 10
```

DETOUR

Why Does the y Coordinate Decrease When Moving Up?

The function up() is supposed to move the pen at position (x, y) up by 10 units. In a typical coordinate system, that means that y should be increased by 10 units. Instead, the value of y is decreased by 10 units.

The reason for this is that the coordinate system in a canvas is not quite the same as the coordinate system we are used to. The origin, that is, the position at coordinates $(0, 0)$, is at the top left corner of the canvas. The x coordinates increase to the right and the y coordinates *increase to the bottom of the canvas*. Therefore, moving up means decreasing the y coordinate, which is what we do in function up().

While peculiar, the Canvas coordinate system follows the screen coordinate system. Every pixel on your screen has coordinates defined with respect to the upper left corner of the screen, which has coordinates $(0, 0)$. Why does the screen coordinate system use such a system?

It has to do with the order in which pixels are refreshed in a television set, the precursor of the computer monitor. The top line of pixels is refreshed first from left to right, and then the second, third, and so on.

Complete the implementation of functions `down()`, `left()`, and `right()` in program `plotter.py`.

Practice Problem 9.7

9.4 OOP for GUIs

So far in this chapter, the focus of our presentation has been on understanding how to use `tkinter` widgets. We developed GUI applications to illustrate the usage of the widgets. To keep matters simple, we have not concerned ourselves about whether our GUI apps can easily be reused.

To make a GUI app or any program reusable, it should be developed as a component (a function or a class) that encapsulates all the implementation details and all the references to data (and widgets) defined in the program. In this section, we introduce the OOP approach to designing GUIs. This approach will make our GUI applications far easier to reuse.

GUI OOP Basics

In order to illustrate the OOP approach to GUI development, we reimplement the application `clickit.py`. This application presents a GUI with a single button; when clicked, a window pops up and displays the current time. Here is our original code (with the import statements and comments removed so we can focus on the program structure):

Module: clickit.py

```
1  def clicked():
2      'prints day and time info'
3      time = strftime('Day:  %d %b %Y\nTime: %H:%M:%S %p\n',
4                      localtime())
5      showinfo(message=time)
6
7  root = Tk()
8  button = Button(root,
9                  text='Click it',
10                 command=clicked)    # button click event handler
11 button.pack()
12 root.mainloop()
```

This program has a few undesirable properties. The names `button` and `clicked` have global scope. (We ignore the window widget `root` as it is really "outside of the application," as we will see soon.) Also, the program is not encapsulated into a single named component (function or class) that can be cleanly referred to and incorporated into a larger GUI.

The key idea of the OOP approach to GUI development is to develop the GUI app as a new, user-defined widget class. Widgets are complicated beasts, and it would be an overwhelming task to implement a widget class from scratch. To the rescue comes OOP inheritance. We can ensure that our new class is a widget class simply by having it inherit attributes from an existing widget class. Because our new class has to contain another widget (the button), it should inherit from a widget class that can contain other widgets (i.e., the `Frame` class).

The reimplementation of the GUI `clickit.py` therefore consists of defining a new class, say `ClickIt`, that is a subclass of `Frame`. A `ClickIt` widget should contain inside of it just one button widget. Since the button must be part of the GUI from the GUI start-up, it will need to be created and packed at the time the ClickIt widget is instantiated. This means that the button widget must be created and packed in the ClickIt constructor.

Now, what will be the master of the button? Since the button should be contained in the instantiated ClickIt widget, its master is the widget itself (self).

Finally, recall that we have always specified a master when creating a widget. We also should be able to specify the master of a ClickIt widget, so we can create the GUI in this way:

```
>>> root = Tk()
>>> clickit = Clickit(root)   # create ClickIt widget inside root
>>> clickit.pack()
>>> root.mainloop()
```

Therefore, the ClickIt constructor should be defined to take one argument, its master widget. (By the way, this code shows why we chose not to encapsulate the window widget root inside the class ClickIt.)

With all the insights we have just made, we can start our implementation of the ClickIt widget class, in particular its constructor:

Module: ch9.py

```
1   from tkinter import Button, Frame
2   from tkinter.messagebox import showinfo
3   from time import strftime, localtime
4
5   class ClickIt(Frame):
6       'GUI that shows current time'
7
8       def __init__(self, master):
9           'constructor'
10          Frame.__init__(self, master)
11          self.pack()
12          button = Button(self,
13                          text='Click it',
14                          command=self.clicked)
15          button.pack()
16
17          # event handling function clicked()
```

There are three things to note about the constructor __init__(). First note in line 10 that the ClickIt __init__() constructor *extends* the Frame __init__() constructor. We are doing that for two reasons:

1. We want the ClickIt widget to get initialized just like a Frame widget so it is a full-fledged Frame widget.

2. We want the ClickIt widget to be assigned a master the same way any Frame widget is assigned a master; we thus pass the master input argument of the ClickIt constructor to the Frame constructor.

The next thing to note is that button is not a global variable, as it was in the original program clickit.py. It is simply a local variable, and it cannot affect names defined in the program that uses class ClickIt. Finally note that we defined the button event handler to be self.clicked, which means that clicked() is a method of class ClickIt. Here is its implementation:

Module: ch9.py

```
1    def clicked(self):
2        'prints day and time info'
3        time = strftime('Day:  %d %b %Y\nTime: %H:%M:%S %p\n',
4                        localtime())
5        showinfo(message=time)
```

Because it is a class method, the name `clicked` is not global, as it was in the original program `clickit.py`.

The class `ClickIt` therefore encapsulates the code and the names `clicked` and `button`. This means that neither of these names is visible to a program that uses a `ClickIt` widget, which relieves the developer from worrying about whether names in the program will clash with them. Furthermore, the developer will find it extremely easy to use and incorporate a `ClickIt` widget in a larger GUI. For example, the next code incorporates the `ClickIt` widget in a window and starts the GUI:

```
>>> root = Tk()
>>> app = Clickit(root)
>>> app.pack()
>>> root.mainloop()
```

Shared Widgets Are Assigned to Instance Variables

In our next example, we reimplement the GUI application `day.py` as a class. We use it to illustrate when to give widgets instance variable names. The original program `day.py` (again without import statements or comments) is:

Module: day.py

```
1    def compute():
2        global dateEnt   # dateEnt is a global variable
3
4        date = dateEnt.get()
5        weekday = strftime('%A', strptime(date, '%b %d, %Y'))
6        showinfo(message = '{} was a {}'.format(date, weekday))
7        dateEnt.delete(0, END)
8
9    root = Tk()
10
11   label = Label(root, text='Enter date')
12   label.grid(row=0, column=0)
13
14   dateEnt = Entry(root)
15   dateEnt.grid(row=0, column=1)
16
17   button = Button(root, text='Enter', command=compute)
18   button.grid(row=1, column=0, columnspan=2)
19
20   root.mainloop()
```

In this implementation, names `compute`, `label`, `dateEnt`, and `button` have global scope. We reimplement the application as a class called Day that will encapsulate those names and the code.

The Day constructor should be responsible for creating the label, entry, and button widgets, just as the `ClickIt` constructor was responsible for creating the button widget. There is one difference, though: The entry `dateEnt` is referred to in the event handler `compute()`. Because of that, `dateEnt` cannot just be a local variable of the Day constructor. Instead, we make it an instance variable that can be referred from the event handler:

Module: ch9.py

```
1   from tkinter import Tk, Button, Entry, Label, END
2   from time import strptime, strftime
3   from tkinter.messagebox import showinfo
4
5   class Day(Frame):
6       'an application that computes weekday corresponding to a date'
7
8       def __init__(self, master):
9           Frame.__init__(self, master)
10          self.pack()
11
12          label = Label(self, text='Enter date')
13          label.grid(row=0, column=0)
14
15          self.dateEnt = Entry(self)                  # instance variable
16          self.dateEnt.grid(row=0, column=1)
17
18          button = Button(self, text='Enter',
19                          command=self.compute)
20          button.grid(row=1, column=0, columnspan=2)
21
22      def compute(self):
23          '''display weekday corresponding to date in dateEnt; date
24             must have format MMM DD, YYYY (e.g., Jan 21, 1967)'''
25          date = self.dateEnt.get()
26          weekday = strftime('%A', strptime(date, '%b %d, %Y'))
27          showinfo(message = '{} was a {}'.format(date, weekday))
28          self.dateEnt.delete(0, END)
```

The Label and Button widgets do not need to be assigned to instance variables because they are never referenced by the event handler. They are simply given names that are local to the constructor. The event handler `compute()` is a class method just like `clicked()` in `ClickIt`. In fact, event handlers should always be class methods in a user-defined widget class.

The class Day therefore encapsulates the four names that were global in program `day.py`. Just as for the `ClickIt` class, it becomes very easy to incorporate a Day widget into a GUI. To make our point, let's run a GUI that incorporates both:

```
>>> root = Tk()
>>> day = Day(root)
>>> day.pack()
```

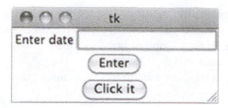

```
>>> clickit = ClickIt(root)
>>> clickit.pack()
>>> root.mainloop()
```

Figure 9.13 shows the resulting GUI, with a Day widget above a ClickIt widget.

Reimplement the GUI application keylogger.py as a new, user-defined widget class. You will need to decide whether it is necessary to assign the Text widget contained in this GUI to an instance variable or not.

Practice Problem 9.8

Shared Data Are Assigned to Instance Variables

To further showcase the encapsulation benefit of implementing a GUI as a user-defined widget class, we reimplement the GUI application draw.py. Recall that this application provides a canvas that the user can draw on using the mouse. The original implementation is this:

Module: draw.py

```python
1  from tkinter import Tk, Canvas
2
3  def begin(event):
4      'initializes the start of the curve to mouse position'
5      global oldx, oldy
6      oldx, oldy = event.x, event.y
7
8  def draw(event):
9      'draws a line segment from old mouse position to new one'
10     global oldx, oldy, canvas      # x and y will be modified
11     newx, newy = event.x, event.y  # new mouse position
12     canvas.create_line(oldx, oldy, newx, newy)
13     oldx, oldy = newx, newy    # new position becomes previous
14
15 root = Tk()
16
17 oldx, oldy = 0, 0    # mouse coordinates (global variables)
18
19 canvas = Canvas(root, height=100, width=150)
20 canvas.bind("<Button-1>", begin)
21 canvas.bind("<Button1-Motion>", draw)
22 canvas.pack()
23
24 root.mainloop()
```

In the original implementation draw.py, we needed to use global variables oldx and oldy to keep track of the mouse position. This was because event handlers begin() and draw() referred to them. In the reimplementation as a new widget class, we can store the mouse coordinates in instance variables instead.

Similarly, because canvas is referred to by event handler draw(), we must make it an instance variable as well:

Module: ch9.py

```
1   from tkinter import Canvas, Frame, BOTH
2   class Draw(Frame):
3       'a basic drawing application'
4
5       def __init__(self, parent):
6           Frame.__init__(self, parent)
7           self.pack()
8
9           # mouse coordinates are instance variables
10          self.oldx, self.oldy = 0, 0
11
12          # create canvas and bind mouse events to handlers
13          self.canvas = Canvas(self, height=100, width=150)
14          self.canvas.bind("<Button-1>", self.begin)
15          self.canvas.bind("<Button1-Motion>", self.draw)
16          self.canvas.pack(expand=True, fill=BOTH)
17
18      def begin(self,event):
19          'handles left button click by recording mouse position'
20          self.oldx, self.oldy = event.x, event.y
21
22      def draw(self, event):
23          '''handles mouse motion, while pressing left button, by
24             connecting previous mouse position to the new one'''
25          newx, newy = event.x, event.y
26          self.canvas.create_line(self.oldx, self.oldy, newx, newy)
27          self.oldx, self.oldy = newx, newy
```

Practice Problem 9.9

Reimplement the plotter GUI application as a user-defined widget class that encapsulates the state of the plotter (i.e., the pen position). Think carefully about which widgets need to be assigned to instance variables.

E-Book Case Study: Developing a Calculator

In this case study, we implement a basic calculator GUI. We use OOP techniques to implement it as a user-defined widget class, from scratch. In the process, we explain how to write a single event-handling function that handles many different buttons.

Chapter Summary

In this chapter, we introduce the development of GUIs in Python.

The specific Python GUI API we use is the Standard Library module `tkinter`. This module defines widgets that correspond to the typical components of a GUI, such as buttons, labels, text entry forms, and so on. In this chapter, we explicitly cover widget classes Tk, Label, Button, Text, Entry, Canvas, and Frame. To learn about other `tkinter` widget classes, we give pointers to online `tkinter` documentation.

There are several techniques for specifying the geometry (i.e., the placement) of widgets in a GUI. We introduce the widget class methods `pack()` and `grid()`. We also illustrate how to facilitate the geometry specification of more complex GUIs by organizing the widgets in a hierarchical fashion.

GUIs are interactive programs that react to user-generated events such as mouse button clicks, mouse motion, or keyboard key presses. We describe how to define the handlers that are executed in response to these events. Developing event handlers (i.e., functions that respond to events) is a style of programming called event-driven programming. We encounter it again when we discuss the parsing of HTML files in Chapter 11.

Finally, and perhaps most important, we use the context of GUI development to showcase the benefits of OOP. We describe how to develop GUI applications as new widget classes that can be easily incorporated into larger GUIs. In the process, we apply OOP concepts such class inheritance, modularity, abstraction, and encapsulation.

Solutions to Practice Problems

9.1 The `width` and `height` options can be used to specify the width and height of the text label. (Note that a width of 20 means that 20 characters can fit inside the label.) To allow padding to fill the available space around the peace symbol widget, the method `pack()` is called with options `expand = True` and `fill = BOTH`.

Module: peaceandlove.py

```
1  from tkinter import Tk, Label, PhotoImage, BOTH, RIGHT, LEFT
2  root = Tk()
3
4  label1 = Label(root, text="Peace & Love", background='black',
5                 width=20, height=5, foreground='white',
6                 font=('Helvetica', 18, 'italic'))
7  label1.pack(side=LEFT)
8
9  photo = PhotoImage(file='peace.gif')
10
11 label2 = Label(root, image=photo)
12 label2.pack(side=RIGHT, expand=True, fill=BOTH)
13
14 root.mainloop()
```

9.2 Using iteration makes the creation of all the labels manageable. The first row of "days of the week" labels can be best done by creating the list of days of the week, iterating over this list, creating a label widget for each, and placing it in the appropriate column of row 0. The relevant code fragment is shown next.

Module: ch9.py

```
1    days = ['Mon', 'Tue', 'Wed', 'Thu', 'Fri', 'Sat', 'Sun']
2    # create and place weekday labels
3    for i in range(7):
4        label = Label(root, text=days[i])
5        label.grid(row=0, column=i)
```

Iteration is also used to create and place the number labels. Variables week and weekday keep track of the row and column, respectively.

Module: ch9.py

```
1    # obtain the day of the week for the first of the month and
2    # the number of days in the month
3    weekday, numDays = monthrange(year, month)
4    # create calendar starting at week (row) 1 and day (column) 1
5    week = 1
6    for i in range(1, numDays+1): # for i = 1, 2, ..., numDays
7        # create label i and place it in row week, column weekday
8        label = Label(root, text=str(i))
9        label.grid(row=week, column=weekday)
10
11       # update weekday (column) and week (row)
12       weekday += 1
13       if weekday > 6:
14           week += 1
15           weekday = 0
```

9.3 Two buttons should be created instead of one. The next code fragment shows the separate event-handling functions for each button.

Module: twotimes.py

```
1    def greenwich():
2        'prints Greenwich day and time info'
3        time = strftime('Day:  %d %b %Y\nTime: %H:%M:%S %p\n',
4                         gmtime())
5        print('Greenwich time\n' + time)
6
7    def local():
8        'prints local day and time info'
9        time = strftime('Day:  %d %b %Y\nTime: %H:%M:%S %p\n',
10                        localtime())
11       print('Local time\n' + time)
12
13   # Local time button
14   buttonl = Button(root, text='Local time', command=local)
15   buttonl.pack(side=LEFT)
16
17   # Greenwich mean time button
18   buttong = Button(root,text='Greenwich time', command=greenwich)
19   buttong.pack(side=RIGHT)
```

9.4   We only describe the changes from program `day.py`. The event-handling function `compute()` for button "Enter" should be modified to:

```
def compute():
    global dateEnt     # warning that dateEnt is a global variable
    # read date from entry dateEnt
    date = dateEnt.get()
    # compute weekday corresponding to date
    weekday = strftime('%A', strptime(date, '%b %d, %Y'))
    # display the weekday in a pop-up window
    dateEnt.insert(0, weekday+' ')
```

The event-handling function for button "Clear" should be:

```
def clear():
    'clears entry datEnt'
    global dateEnt
    dateEnt.delete(0, END)
```

Finally, the buttons should be defined as shown:

```
# Enter button
button = Button(root, text='Enter', command=compute)
button.grid(row=1, column=0)

# Clear button
button = Button(root, text='Clear', command=clear)
button.grid(row=1, column=1)
```

9.5   We need to bind the Enter/Return key press to an event-handling function that takes an Event object as input. All this function really has to do is call the handler `compute()`. So we only need to add to `day.py`:

```
def compute2(event):
    compute()


dateEnt.bind('<Return>', compute2)
```

9.6   The key is to store the items returned by `canvas.create_line(x,y,newX,newY)` in some container, say list `curve`. This container should be initialized to an empty list every time we start drawing:

```
1  def begin(event):
2      'initializes the start of the curve to mouse position'
3      global oldx, oldy, curve
4      oldx, oldy = event.x, event.y
5      curve = []
```

Module: draw2.py

As we move the mouse, the IDs of line segments created by `Canvas` method `create_line()` need to be appended to list `curve`. This is shown in the reimplementation of event-handling function `draw()`, shown next.

Module: draw2.py

```
1  def draw(event):
2      'draws a line segment from old mouse position to new one'
3      global oldx, oldy, canvas, curve  # x and y will be modified
4      newx, newy = event.x, event.y      # new mouse position
5      # connect previous mouse position to current one
6      curve.append(canvas.create_line(oldx, oldy, newx, newy))
7      oldx, oldy = newx, newy          # new position becomes previous
8  def delete(event):
9      'delete last curve drawn'
10     global curve
11     for segment in curve:
12         canvas.delete(segment)
13 # bind Ctrl-Left button mouse click to delete()
14 canvas.bind('<Control-Button-1>', delete)
```

The event handler for the `<Control-Button-1>` event type, function `delete()`, should iterate over the line segment ID in `curve` and call `canvas.delete()` on each.

9.7 The implementations are similar to function `up()`:

Module: plotter.py

```
1  def down():
2      'move pen down 10 pixels'
3      global y, canvas                 # y is modified
4      canvas.create_line(x, y, x, y+10)
5      y += 10
6  def left():
7      'move pen left 10 pixels'
8      global x, canvas                 # x is modified
9      canvas.create_line(x, y, x-10, y)
10     x -= 10
11 def right():
12     'move pen right 10 pixels'
13     global x, canvas                 # x is modified
14     canvas.create_line(x, y, x+10, y)
15     x += 10
```

9.8 Because the Text widget is not used by the event handler, it is not necessary to assign it to an instance variable.

Module: ch9.py

```
1  from tkinter import Text, Frame, BOTH
2  class KeyLogger(Frame):
3      'a basic editor that logs keystrokes'
4      def __init__(self, master=None):
5          Frame.__init__(self, master)
6          self.pack()
7          text = Text(width=20, height=5)
8          text.bind('<KeyPress>', self.record)
9          text.pack(expand=True, fill=BOTH)
```

```
10        def record(self, event):
11            '''handles keystroke events by printing character
12               associated with key'''
13            print('char={}'.format(event.keysym))
```

9.9 Only the `Canvas` widget is referenced by the function `move()` that handles button clicks, so it is the only widget that needs to be assigned to an instance variable, `self.canvas`. The coordinates (i.e., state) of the pen will also need to be stored in instance variables `self.x` and `self.y`. The solutions is in module `ch9.py`. Next is the constructor code fragment that creates the button "up" and its handler; the remaining buttons are similar.

Module: ch9.py

```
1            # create up button
2            b = Button(buttons, text='up', command=self.up)
3            b.grid(row=0, column=0, columnspan=2)
4
5        def up(self):
6            'move pen up 10 pixels'
7            self.canvas.create_line(self.x, self.y, self.x, self.y-10)
8            self.y -= 10
```

Exercises

9.10 Develop a program that displays a GUI window with your picture on the left side and your first name, last name, and place and date of birth on the right. The picture has to be in the GIF format. If you do not have one, find a free online converter tool online and a JPEG picture to the GIF format.

9.11 Modify the solution to Practice Problem 9.3 so that the times are displayed in a separate pop-up window.

9.12 Modify the phone dial GUI from Section 9.1 so it has buttons instead of digits. When the user dials a number, the digits of the number should be printed in the interactive shell.

9.13 In program `plotter.py`, the user has to click one of the four buttons to move the pen. Modify the program to allow the user to use the arrow keys on the keyboard instead.

9.14 In the implementation of widget class `Plotter`, there are four very similar button event handlers: `up()`, `down()`, `left()`, and `right()`. Reimplement the class using just one function `move()` that takes two input arguments `dx` and `dy` and moves the pen from position `(x, y)` to `(x+dx, y+dx)`.

9.15 Add two more buttons to the `Plotter` widget. One, labeled "clear", should clear the canvas. The other, labeled "delete", should erase the last pen move.

Problems

9.16 Implement a GUI application that allows users to compute their body mass index (BMI), which we defined in Practice Problem 5.1. Your GUI should look as shown below.

After entering the weight and height and then clicking the button, a new window should pop up with the computed BMI. Make sure your GUI is user friendly by deleting the entered weight and height so that the user can enter new inputs without having to erase the old ones.

9.17 Develop a GUI application whose purpose is to compute the monthly mortgage payment given a loan amount (in $), the interest rate (in %), and the loan term (i.e., the number of months that it will take to repay the loan). The GUI should have three labels and three entry boxes for users to enter this information. It should also have a button labeled "Compute mortgage" that, when clicked, should compute and display the monthly mortgage in a fourth entry box.

The monthly mortgage m is computed from the loan amount a, interest rate r, and loan terms t as:

$$ m = \frac{a \times c \times (1+c)^t}{(1+c)^t - 1} $$

where $c = r/1200$.

9.18 Develop a GUI that contains just one `Frame` widget of size 480×640 that has this behavior: Every time the user clicks at some location in the frame, the location coordinates are printed in the interactive shell.

```
>>>
you clicked at (55, 227)
you clicked at (426, 600)
you clicked at (416, 208)
```

9.19 Modify the phone dial GUI from Section 9.1 so that it has buttons instead of digits and an entry box on top. When the user dials a number, the number should be displayed in the traditional U.S. phone number format. For example, if the user enters 1234567890, the entry box should display 123-456-7890.

9.20 Develop new widget `Game` that implements a number guessing game. When started, a secret random number between 0 and 9 is chosen. The user is then requested to enter number guesses. Your GUI should have an `Entry` widget for the user to type the number guess and a `Button` widget to enter the guess:

If the guess is correct, a separate window should inform the user of that. The user should be able to enter guesses until he makes the correct guess.

9.21 In Problem 9.20, pressing the ⟨Enter/Return⟩ key on your keyboard after entering a guess in the entry is ignored. Modify the `Game` GUI so that pressing the key is equivalent to pressing the button.

9.22 Modify the widget `Game` from Problem 9.21 so that a new game starts automatically when the user has guessed the number. The window informing the user that she made the correct guess should say something like "Let's do this again . . ." Note that a new random number would have to be chosen at the start of each game.

9.23 Implement GUI widget `Craps` that simulates the gambling game craps. The GUI should include a button that starts a new game by simulating the initial roll of a pair of dice. The result of the initial roll is then shown in an `Entry` widget, as shown.

If the initial roll is not a win or a loss, the user will have to click the button "Roll for point", and keep clicking it until she wins.

9.24 Develop an application with a text box that measures how fast you type. It should record the time when you type the first character. Then, every time you press the blank character, it should print (1) the time you took to type the preceding word and (2) an estimate of your typing speed in words per minute by averaging the time taken for typing the words so far and normalizing over 1 minute. So, if the average time per word is 2 seconds, the normalized measure is 30 words per minute.

9.25 Develop new GUI widget class `Ed` that can be used to teach first-graders addition and subtraction. The GUI should contain two `Entry` widgets and a `Button` widget labeled "Enter".

At start-up, your program should generate (1) two single-digit pseudorandom numbers a and b and (2) an operation o, which could be addition or subtraction—with equal likelihood—using the `randrange()` function in the `random` module. The expression a o b will then be displayed in the first `Entry` widget (unless a is less than b and the operation o is subtraction, in which case b o a is displayed, so the result is never negative). Expressions displayed could be, for example, 3+2, 4+7, 5-2, 3-3 but could not be 2-6.

The user will have to enter, in the second `Entry` widget, the result of evaluating the expression shown in the first `Entry` widget and click the "Enter" button (or the ⎡Return⎤ key on the keyboard). If the correct result is entered, a new window should say "You got it!".

9.26 Augment the GUI you developed in Problem 9.25 so that a new problem gets generated after the user answers a problem correctly. In addition, your app should keep track of the number of tries for each problem and include that information in the message displayed when the user gets the problem right.

9.27 Enhance the widget Ed from Problem 9.26 so that it does not repeat a problem given recently. More precisely, ensure that a new problem is always different from the previous 10 problems.

9.28 Develop widget class `Calendar` that implements a GUI-based calendar application. The `Calendar` constructor should take as input three arguments: the master widget, a year, and a month (using numbers 1 through 12). For example, `Calendar(root, 2012, 2)` should create a Calendar widget within the master widget `root`. The `Calendar` widget should display the calendar page for the given month and year, with a button for every day:

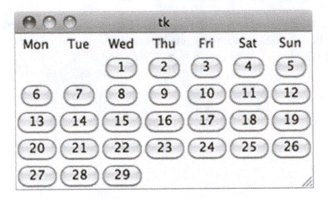

Then, when you click on a day, a dialog will appear:

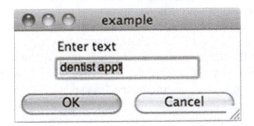

This dialog gives you an entry field to enter an appointment. When you click button "OK", the dialog window will disappear. However, when you click the same day button in the main calendar window again, the dialog window should reappear together with the appointment information.

You may use the `askstring` function from module `tkinter.simpledialog` for the dialog window. It takes the window title and label as input and returns whatever the user typed. For example, the last dialog window was created with the function call

```
askstring('example', 'Enter text')
```

When the user clicks OK, the string typed in the entry box is returned by this function call.

The function can also take an optional argument `initialvalue` that takes a string and puts it in the entry field:

```
askstring('example', ' Enter text', initialvalue='appt with John')
```

9.29 Modify class `Calendar` from Problem 9.28 so that it can be used for any month in any year. When started, it should display the calendar for the current month. It should also have two additional buttons labeled "previous" and "next" that, when clicked, switch the calendar to the previous or next month.

Recursion

10.1 Introduction to Recursion   330

10.2 Examples of Recursion   336

10.3 Run Time Analysis   347

10.4 Searching   354

E-Book Case Study: Tower of Hanoi   359

Chapter Summary   360

Solutions to Practice Problems   360

Exercises   362

Problems   363

IN THIS CHAPTER, we learn about recursion, a powerful problem-solving technique, and run time analysis.

Recursion is a problem-solving technique that expresses the solution to a problem in terms of solutions to subproblems of the original problem. Recursion can be used to solve problems that might otherwise be quite challenging. The functions developed by solving a problem recursively will naturally call themselves, and we refer to them as recursive functions. We also show how namespaces and the program stack support the execution of recursive functions.

We demonstrate the wide use of recursion in number patterns, fractals, virus scanners, and searching. We differentiate between linear and nonlinear recursion and illustrate the close relationship between iteration and linear recursion.

As we discuss when recursion should and should not be used, the issue of program run time comes up. So far we have not worried much about the efficiency of our programs. We now rectify this situation and use the opportunity to analyze several fundamental search tasks. We develop a tool that can be used to analyze experimentally the running time of functions with respect to the size of the input.

10.1 Introduction to Recursion

A *recursive* function is a function that calls itself. In this section we explain what this means and how recursive functions get executed. We also introduce *recursive thinking* as an approach to problem solving. In the next section, we apply recursive thinking and how to develop recursive functions.

Functions that Call Themselves

Here is an example that illustrates what we mean by a function that calls itself:

Module: ch10.py

```
1  def countdown(n):
2          print(n)
3          countdown(n-1)
```

In the implementation of function countdown(), the function countdown() is called. So, function countdown() calls itself. When a function calls itself, we say that it makes a *recursive call*.

Let's understand the behavior of this function by tracing the execution of function call countdown(3):

- When we execute countdown(3), the input 3 is printed and then countdown() is called on the input decremented by 1—that is, $3 - 1 = 2$. We have 3 printed on the screen, and we continue tracing the execution of countdown(2).

- When we execute countdown(2), the input 2 is printed and then countdown() is called on the input decremented by 1—that is, $2 - 1 = 1$. We now have 3 and 2 printed on the screen, and we continue tracing the execution of countdown(1).

- When we execute countdown(1), the input 1 is printed and then countdown() is called on the input decremented by 1—that is, $1 - 1 = 0$. We now have 3, 2, and 1 printed on the screen, and we continue tracing the execution of countdown(0).

- When we execute countdown(0), the input 0 is printed and then countdown() is called on the input, 0, decremented by 1—that is, $0 - 1 = -1$. We now have 3, 2, 1, and 0 printed on the screen, and we continue tracing the execution of countdown(-1).

- When we execute countdown(-1), . . .

It seems that the execution will never end. Let's check:

```
>>> countdown(3)
3
2
1
0
-1
-2
-3
. . .
```

The behavior of the function is to count down, starting with the original input number. If we let the function call countdown(3) execute for a while, we get:

. . .

```
-973
-974
Traceback (most recent call last):
  File "<pyshell#2>", line 1, in <module>
    countdown(3)
  File "/Users/me/ch10.py"...
    countdown(n-1)
  ...
```

And after getting many lines of error messages, we end up with:

```
RuntimeError: maximum recursion depth exceeded
```

OK, so the execution was going to go on forever, but the Python interpreter stopped it. We will explain why the Python VM does this soon. The main point to understand right now is that a recursive function will call itself forever unless we modify the function so there is a *stopping condition*.

Stopping Condition

To show this, suppose that the behavior we wanted to achieve with the `countdown()` function is really:

```
>>> countdown(3)
3
2
1
Blastoff!!!
```

or

```
>>> countdown(0)
Blastoff!!!
```

Function `countdown()` is supposed to count down to 0, starting from a given input n; when 0 is reached, `Blastoff!!!` should be printed.

To implement this version of `countdown()`, we consider two cases that depend on the value of the input n. When the input n is 0 or negative, all we need to do is print `'Blastoff!!!'`:

```
def countdown(n):
    'counts down to 0'
    if n <= 0:                    # base case
        print('Blastoff!!!')
    else:
... # remainder of function
```

We call this case the *base case* of the recursion; it is the condition that will ensure that the recursive function is not going to call itself forever.

The second case is when the input n is positive. In that case we do the same thing we did before:

```
        print(n)
        countdown(n-1)
```

How does this code implement the function `countdown()` for input value $n > 0$? The insight used in the code is this: *Counting down from (positive number) n can be done by printing n first and then counting down from $n - 1$.* This fragment of code is called *the recursive step*.

With the two cases resolved, we obtain the recursive function:

Module: ch10.py

```
1  def countdown(n):
2      'counts down from n to 0'
3      if n <= 0:                # base case
4          print('Blastoff!!!')
5      else:                     # n > 0: recursive step
6          print(n)              # print n first and then
7          countdown(n-1)        # count down from n-1 to 0
8                                # recursively
```

Properties of Recursive Functions

A recursive function that terminates will always have:

1. One or more base cases, which provide the stopping condition for the recursion. In function `countdown()`, the base case is the condition $n \leq 0$, where n is the input.

2. One or more recursive calls, which must be on arguments that are "closer" to the base case than the function input. In function `countdown()`, the sole recursive call is made on $n - 1$, which is "closer" to the base case than input n.

What is meant by "closer" depends on the problem solved by the recursive function. The idea is that each recursive call should be made on problem inputs that are closer to the base case; this will ensure that the recursive calls eventually will get to the base case that will stop the execution.

In the remainder of this section and the next, we present many more examples of recursion. The goal is to learn how to develop recursive functions. To do this, we need to learn how to think recursively—that is, to describe the solution to a problem in terms of solutions of its subproblems. Why do we need to bother? After all, function `countdown()` could have been implemented easily using iteration. (Do it!) The thing is that recursive functions provide us with an approach that is an alternative to the iterative approach we used in Chapter 5. For some problems, this alternative approach actually is the easier, and sometimes, much easier approach. When you start writing programs that search the Web, for example, you will appreciate having mastered recursion.

Recursive Thinking

We use recursive thinking to develop recursive function `vertical()` that takes a nonnegative integer as input and prints its digits stacked vertically. For example:

```
>>> vertical(3124)
3
1
2
4
```

To develop `vertical()` as a recursive function, the first thing we need to do is decide the base case of the recursion. This is typically done by answering the question: When is the problem of printing vertically easy? For what kind of nonnegative number?

The problem is certainly easy if the input n has only one digit. In that case, we just output n itself:

```
>>> vertical(6)
6
```

So we make the decision that the base case is when $n < 10$. Let's start the implementation of the function `vertical()`:

```
def vertical(n):
    'prints digits of n vertically'
    if n < 10:              # base case: n has 1 digit
        print(n)               # just print n
    else:                   # recursive step: n has 2 or more digits
        # remainder of function
```

Function `vertical()` prints n if n is less than 10 (i.e., n is a single digit number).

Now that we have a base case done, we consider the case when the input n has two or more digits. In that case, we would like to break up the problem of printing vertically number n into "easier" subproblems, involving the vertical printing of numbers "smaller" than n. In this problem, "smaller" should get us closer to the base case, a single-digit number. This suggests that our recursive call should be on a number that has fewer digits than n.

This insight leads to the following algorithm: Since n has at least two digits, we break the problem:

a. Print vertically the number obtained by removing the last digit of n; this number is "smaller" because it has one less digit. For $n = 3124$, this would mean calling function `vertical()` on 312.

b. Print the last digit. For $n = 3124$, this would mean printing 4.

The last thing to figure out is the math formulas for (1) the last digit of n and (2) the number obtained by removing the last digit. The last digit is obtained using the modulus (%) operator:

```
>>> n = 3124
>>> n%10
4
```

We can "remove" the last digit of n using the integer division operator (//):

```
>>> n//10
312
```

With all the pieces we have come up with, we can write the recursive function:

Module: ch10.py

```
1  def vertical(n):
2      'prints digits of n vertically'
3      if n < 10:              # base case: n has 1 digit
4          print(n)               # just print n
5      else:                   # recursive step: n has 2 or more digits
6          vertical(n//10)        # recursively print all but last digit
7          print(n%10)            # print last digit of n
```

Practice Problem 10.1	Implement recursive method `reverse()` that takes a nonnegative integer as input and prints its digits vertically, starting with the low-order digit.

```
>>> reverse(3124)
4
2
1
3
```

Let's summarize the process of solving a problem recursively:

1. First decide on the base case or cases of the problem that can be solved directly, without recursion.
2. Figure out how to break the problem into one or more subproblems that are closer to the base case; the subproblems are to be solved recursively. The solutions to the subproblems are used to construct the solution to the original problem.

Practice Problem 10.2	Use recursive thinking to implement recursive function `cheers()` that, on integer input n, outputs n strings `'Hip '` followed by `'Hurray!!! '`.

```
>>> cheers(0)
Hurray!!!
>>> cheers(1)
Hip Hurray!!!
>>> cheers(4)
Hip Hip Hip Hip Hurray!!!
```

The base case of the recursion should be when n is 0; your function should then print Hurrah. When $n > 1$, your function should print `'Hip '` and then recursively call itself on integer input $n - 1$.

Practice Problem 10.3	In Chapter 5, we implemented function `factorial()` iteratively. The factorial function $n!$ has a natural recursive definition:

$$n! = \begin{array}{ll} 1 & \text{if } n = 0 \\ n \cdot (n-1)! & \text{if } n > 0 \end{array}$$

Reimplement function `factorial()` function using recursion. Also, estimate how many calls to `factorial()` are made for some input value $n > 0$.

Recursive Function Calls and the Program Stack

Before we practice solving problems using recursion, we take a step back and take a closer look at what happens when a recursive function gets executed. Doing so should help us recognize that recursion does work.

We consider what happens when function `vertical()` is executed on input $n = 3124$. In Chapter 7, we saw how namespaces and the program stack support function calls and the normal execution control flow of a program. Figure 10.1 illustrates the sequence of recursive function calls, the associated namespaces, and the state of the program stack during the execution of `vertical(3124)`.

Module: ch10.py

```
1   def vertical(n):
2       'prints digits of n vertically'
3       if n < 10:              # base case: n has 1 digit
4           print(n)            #  just print n
5       else:                   # recursive step: n has 2 or more digits
6           vertical(n//10)      # recursively print all but last digit
7           print(n%10)          # print last digit of n
```

The difference between the execution shown in Figure 10.1 and Figure 7.5 in Chapter 7 is that in Figure 10.1, the same function gets called: function `vertical()` calls `vertical()`, which calls `vertical()`, which calls `vertical()`. In Figure 7.5, function `f()` calls `g()`, which calls `h()`. Figure 10.1 thus underlines that a namespace is associated with every function call rather than with the function itself.

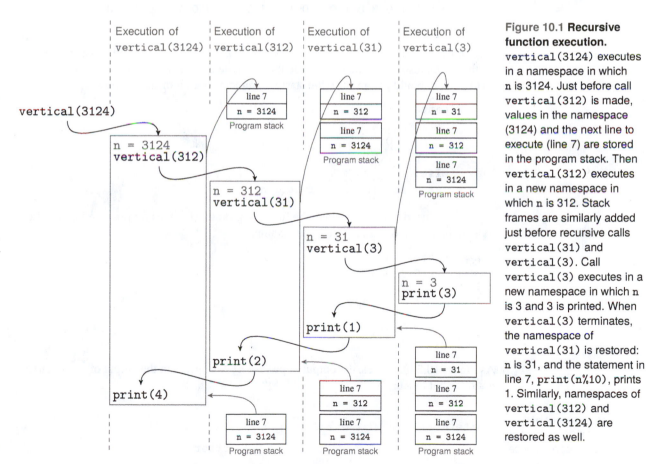

Figure 10.1 Recursive function execution. `vertical(3124)` executes in a namespace in which n is 3124. Just before call `vertical(312)` is made, values in the namespace (3124) and the next line to execute (line 7) are stored in the program stack. Then `vertical(312)` executes in a new namespace in which n is 312. Stack frames are similarly added just before recursive calls `vertical(31)` and `vertical(3)`. Call `vertical(3)` executes in a new namespace in which n is 3 and 3 is printed. When `vertical(3)` terminates, the namespace of `vertical(31)` is restored: n is 31, and the statement in line 7, `print(n%10)`, prints 1. Similarly, namespaces of `vertical(312)` and `vertical(3124)` are restored as well.

10.2 Examples of Recursion

In the previous section, we introduced recursion and how to solve problems using recursive thinking. The problems we used did not really showcase the power of recursion: Each problem could have been solved as easily using iteration. In this section, we consider problems that are far easier to solve with recursion.

Recursive Number Sequence Pattern

We start by implementing function `pattern()` that takes a nonnegative integer n and prints a number pattern:

```
>>> pattern(0)
0
>>> pattern(1)
0 1 0
>>> pattern(2)
0 1 0 2 0 1 0
>>> pattern(3)
0 1 0 2 0 1 0 3 0 1 0 2 0 1 0
>>> pattern(4)
0 1 0 2 0 1 0 3 0 1 0 2 0 1 0 4 0 1 0 2 0 1 0 3 0 1 0 2 0 1 0
```

How do we even know that this problem should be solved recursively? A priori, we do not, and we need to just try it and see whether it works. Let's first identify the base case. Based on the examples shown, we can decide that the base case is input 0 for which the function `pattern()` should just print 0. We start the implementation of the function:

```
def pattern(n):
    'prints the nth pattern'
    if n == 0:
        print(0)
    else:
        # remainder of function
```

We now need to describe what the function `pattern()` does for positive input n. Let's look at the output of `pattern(3)`, for example

```
>>> pattern(3)
0 1 0 2 0 1 0 3 0 1 0 2 0 1 0
```

and compare it to the output of `pattern(2)`

```
>>> pattern(2)
0 1 0 2 0 1 0
```

As Figure 10.2 illustrates, the output of `pattern(2)` appears in the output of `pattern(3)`, not once but twice:

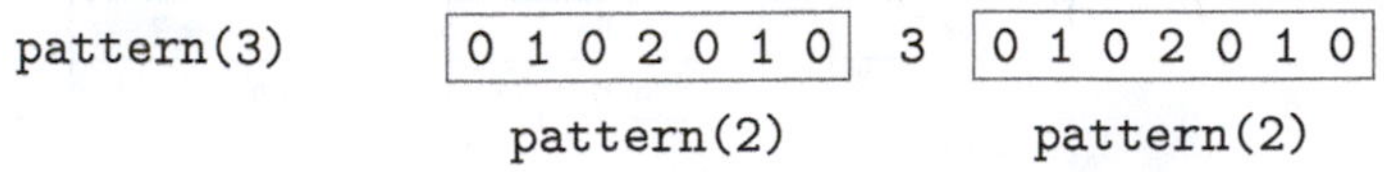

Figure 10.2 Output of `pattern(3)`. The output of `pattern(2)` appears twice.

pattern(3) | 0 1 0 2 0 1 0 | 3 | 0 1 0 2 0 1 0 |

                 pattern(2)   pattern(2)

It seems that the correct output of `pattern(3)` can be obtained by calling the function `pattern(2)`, then printing 3, and then calling `pattern(2)` again. In Figure 10.3, we illustrate the similar behavior for the outputs of `pattern(2)` and `pattern(1)`:

`pattern(2)` | 0 1 0 | 2 | 0 1 0 |
                    `pattern(1)`   `pattern(1)`

`pattern(1)` | 0 | 1 | 0 |
                    `pattern(0)`   `pattern(0)`

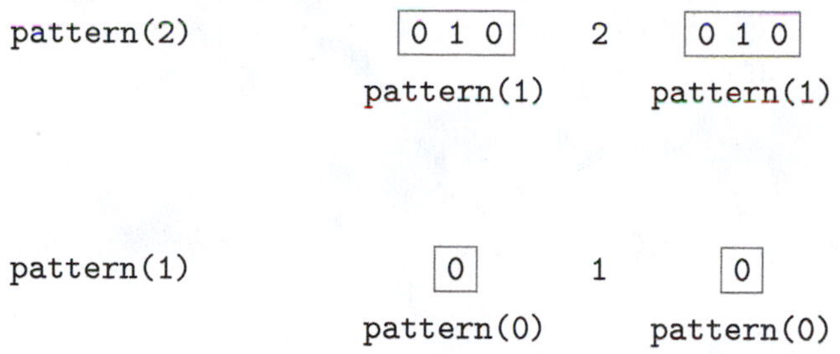

Figure 10.3 Outputs of `pattern(2)` **and** `pattern(1)`. The output of `pattern(2)` can be obtained from the output of `pattern(1)`. The output of `pattern(1)` can be obtained from the output of `pattern(0)`.

In general, the output for `pattern(n)` is obtained by executing `pattern(n-1)`, then printing the value of n, and then executing `pattern(n-1)` again:

```
        ... # base case of function
    else
        pattern(n-1)
        print(n)
        pattern(n-1)
```

Let's try the function as implemented so far:

```
>>> pattern(1)
0
1
0
```

Almost done. In order to get the output in one line, we need to remain in the same line after each print statement. So the final solution is:

Module: ch10.py

```
1  def pattern(n):
2      'prints the nth pattern'
3      if n == 0:              # base case
4          print(0, end=' ')
5      else:                   # recursive step: n > 0
6          pattern(n-1)            # print n-1st pattern
7          print(n, end=' ')       # print n
8          pattern(n-1)            # print n-1st pattern
```

Practice Problem 10.4

Implement recursive method `pattern2()` that takes a nonnegative integer as input and prints the pattern shown next. The patterns for inputs 0 and 1 are nothing and one star, respectively:

```
>>> pattern2(0)
>>> pattern2(1)
*
```

The patterns for inputs 2 and 3 are shown next.

```
>>> pattern2(2)
*
**
*
>>> pattern2(3)
*
**
*
***
*
**
*
```

Fractals

In our next example of recursion, we will also print a pattern, but this time it will be a graphical pattern drawn by a `Turtle` graphics object. For every nonnegative integer n, the printed pattern will be a curve called the *Koch curve* K_n. For example, Figure 10.4 shows Koch curve K_5.

Figure 10.4 Koch curve K_5. A fractal curve often resembles a snowflake.

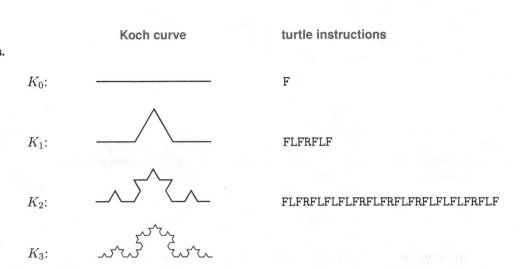

We will use recursion to draw Koch curves such as K_5. To develop the function that is used to draw this and other Koch curves, we look at the first few Koch curves. Koch curves K_0, K_1, K_2, and K_3 are shown on the left of Figure 10.5.

If you look carefully at the patterns, you might notice that each Koch curve K_i, for $i > 0$, contains within itself several copies of Koch curve K_{i-1}. For example, curve K_2 contains four copies of (smaller versions of) curve K_1.

Figure 10.5 Koch curves with drawing instructions. On the left, from top to bottom, are Koch curves K_0, K_1, K_2, and K_3. The drawing instructions for Koch curves K_0, K_1, and K_2 are shown as well. The instructions are encoded using letters F, L, and R corresponding to "move forward," "rotate left 60 degrees," and "rotate right 120 degrees."

	Koch curve	turtle instructions
K_0:	———————	F
K_1:		FLFRFLF
K_2:		FLFRFLFLFLFRFLFRFLFRFLFLFLFRFLF
K_3:		

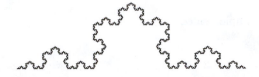

More precisely, to draw Koch curve K_2, a `Turtle` object should follow these instructions:

1. Draw Koch curve K_1.
2. Rotate left 60 degrees.
3. Draw Koch curve K_1.
4. Rotate right 120 degrees.
5. Draw Koch curve K_1.
6. Rotate left 60 degrees.
7. Draw Koch curve K_1.

Note that these instructions are described recursively. This suggests that what we need to do is develop a recursive function `koch(n)` that takes as input a nonnegative integer n and returns instructions that a `Turtle` object can use to draw Koch curve K_n. The instructions can be encoded as a string of letters F, L, and R corresponding to instructions "move forward," "rotate left 60 degrees," and "rotate right 120 degrees," respectively. For example, instructions for drawing Koch curves K_0, K_1, and K_2 are shown on the right of Figure 10.5. The function `koch()` should have this behavior:

```
>>> koch(0)
'F'
>>> koch(1)
'FLFRFLF'
>>> koch(2)
'FLFRFLFLFLFRFLFRFLFRFLFLFLFRFLF'
```

Now let's use the insight we developed about drawing curve K_2 in terms of drawing K_1 to understand how the instructions to draw K_2 (computed by function call `koch(2)`) are obtained using instructions to draw K_1 (computed by function call `koch(1)`). As Figure 10.6 illustrates, the instructions for curve K_1 appear in the instructions of curve K_2 four times:

koch(2)   FLFRFLF   L   FLFRFLF   R   FLFRFLF   L   FLFRFLF
                  koch(1)   koch(1)   koch(1)   koch(1)

Figure 10.6 Output of Koch(2). Koch(1) can be used to construct the output of Koch(2).

Similarly, the instructions to draw K_1, output by `koch(1)`, contain the instructions to draw K_0, output by `koch(0)`, as shown in Figure 10.7:

koch(1)   F   L   F   R   F   L   F
               koch(0)   koch(0)   koch(0)   koch(0)

Figure 10.7 Output of Koch(1). Koch(0) can be used to construct the output of Koch(1).

Now we can implement function `koch()` recursively. The base case corresponds to input 0. In that case, the function should just return instruction `'F'`:

```
def koch(n):
    if n == 0:
        return 'F'
    # remainder of function
```

For input $n > 0$, we generalize the insight illustrated in Figures 10.6 and 10.7. The instructions output by koch(n) should be the concatenation:

```
koch(n-1) + 'L' + koch(n-1) + 'R' + koch(n-1) + 'L' + koch(n-1)
```

and the function koch() is then

```
def koch(n):
    if n == 0:
        return 'F'
    return koch(n-1) + 'L' + koch(n-1) + 'R' + koch(n-1) + 'L' + \
           koch(n-1)
```

If you test this function, you will see that it works. There is an efficiency issue with this implementation, however. In the last line, we call function koch() on the *same input* four times. Of course, each time the returned value (the instructions) is the same. Our implementation is very wasteful.

CAUTION

Avoid Repeating the Same Recursive Calls

Often, a recursive solution is most naturally described using several identical recursive calls. We just saw this with the recursive function koch(). Instead of repeatedly calling the same function on the same input, we can call it just once and reuse its output multiple times.

The better implementation of function koch() is then:

Module: ch10.py

```
1  def koch(n):
2      'returns turtle directions for drawing curve Koch(n)'
3
4      if n == 0:         # base case
5          return 'F'
6
7      tmp = koch(n-1) # recursive step: get directions for Koch(n-1)
8                      # use them to construct directions for Koch(n)
9
10     return tmp + 'L' + tmp + 'R' + tmp + 'L' + tmp
```

The last thing we have to do is develop a function that uses the instructions returned by function koch() and draws the corresponding Koch curve using a Turtle graphics object. Here it is:

Module: ch10.py

```
1  from turtle import Screen, Turtle
2  def drawKoch(n):
3      'draws nth Koch curve using instructions from function koch()'
4
5      s = Screen()              # create screen
6      t = Turtle()              # create turtle
7      directions = koch(n)      # obtain directions to draw Koch(n)
8
```

```
9       for move in directions: # follow the specified moves
10          if move == 'F':
11              t.forward(300/3**n) # move forward, length normalized
12          if move == 'L':
13              t.lt(60)            # rotate left 60 degrees
14          if move == 'R':
15              t.rt(120)           # rotate right 60 degrees
16      s.bye()
```

Line 11 requires some explanation. The value 300/3**n is the length of a forward turtle move. It depends on the value of n so that, no matter what the value of n is, the Koch curve has width 300 pixels and fits in the screen. Check this for n equal to 0 and 1.

DETOUR

Koch Curves and Other Fractals

The Koch curves K_n were first described in a 1904 paper by the Swedish mathematician Helge von Koch. He was particularly interested in the curve K_∞ that is obtained by pushing n to ∞.

The Koch curve is an example of a *fractal*. The term *fractal* was coined by French mathematician Benoît Mandelbrot in 1975 and refers to curves that:

- Appear "fractured" rather than smooth
- Are *self-similar* (i.e., they look the same at different levels of magnification)
- Are naturally described recursively

Physical fractals, developed through recursive physical processes, appear in nature as snowflakes and frost crystals on cold glass, lightning and clouds, shorelines and river systems, cauliflower and broccoli, trees and ferns, and blood and pulmonary vessels.

Implement function `snowflake()` that takes a nonnegative integer n as input and prints a snowflake pattern by combining three Koch curves K_n in this way: When the turtle is finished drawing the first and the second Koch curve, the turtle should rotate right 120 degrees and start drawing a new Koch curve. Shown here is the output of `snowflake(4)`.

Practice Problem 10.5

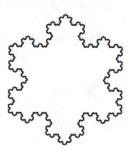

Virus Scanner

We now use recursion to develop a virus scanner, that is, a program that systematically looks at every file in the filesystem and prints the names of the files that contain a known *computer virus signature*. The signature is a specific string that is evidence of the presence of the virus in the file.

DETOUR

> #### Viruses and Virus Scanners
>
> A *computer virus* is a small program that, usually without the user's knowledge, is attached to or incorporated in a file hosted on the user's computer and does nefarious things to the host computer when executed. A computer virus may corrupt or delete data on a computer, for example.
>
> A virus is an executable program, stored in a file as a sequence of bytes just like any other program. If the computer virus is identified by a computer security expert and the sequence of bytes is known, all that needs to be done to check whether a file contains the virus is to check whether that sequence of bytes appears in the file. In fact, finding the *entire* sequence of bytes is not really necessary; searching for a carefully chosen fragment of this sequence is enough to identify the virus with high probability. This fragment is called the *signature* of the virus: It is a sequence of bytes that appears in the virus code but is unlikely to appear in an uninfected file.
>
> A *virus scanner* is a program that periodically and *systematically* scans every file in the computer filesystem and checks each for viruses. The scanner application will have a list of virus signatures that is updated regularly and automatically. Each file is checked for the presence of some signature in the list and flagged if it contains that signature.

We use a dictionary to store the various virus signatures. It maps virus names to virus signatures:

```
>>> signatures = {'Creeper':'ye8009g2h1azzx33',
                  'Code Red':'99dh1cz963bsscs3',
                  'Blaster':'fdp1102k1ks6hgbc'}
```

(While the names in this dictionary are names of real viruses, the signatures are completely fake.)

The virus scanner function takes, as input, the dictionary of virus signatures and the pathname (a string) of the top folder or file. It then visits every file contained in the top folder, its subfolders, subfolders of its subfolders, and so on. An example folder `'test'` is shown in Figure 10.8 together with all the files and folders that are contained in it, directly or indirectly. The virus scanner would visit every file shown in Figure 10.8 and could produce, for example, this output:

File: test.zip

```
>>> scan('test', signatures)
test/fileA.txt, found virus Creeper
test/folder1/fileB.txt, found virus Creeper
test/folder1/fileC.txt, found virus Code Red
test/folder1/folder11/fileD.txt, found virus Code Red
test/folder2/fileD.txt, found virus Blaster
test/folder2/fileE.txt, found virus Blaster
```

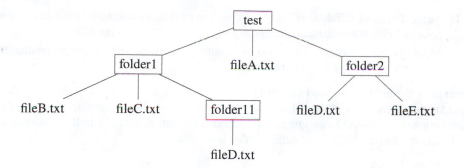

Figure 10.8 Filesystem fragment. Illustrated is folder `'test'` and all its descendant folders and files.

Because of the recursive structure of a filesystem (a *folder* contains files and other *folders*), we use recursion to develop the virus scanner function `scan()`. When the input pathname is the pathname of a file, the function should open, read, and search the file for virus signatures; this is the base case. When the input pathname is the pathname of a folder, `scan()` should recursively call itself on every file and subfolder of the input folder; this is the recursive step. The complete implementation is:

```python
import os
def scan(pathname, signatures):
    '''scans pathname or, if pathname is a folder, scans all files
       contained, directly or indirectly, in the folder pathname'''
    if os.path.isfile(pathname): # base case, scan pathname
        infile = open(pathname)
        content = infile.read()
        infile.close()

        for virus in signatures:
            # check whether virus signature appears in content
            if content.find(signatures[virus]) >= 0:
                print('{}, found virus {}'.format(pathname, virus))
        return

    # pathname is a folder so recursively scan every item in it
    for item in os.listdir(pathname):

        # create pathname for item relative
        # to current working directory
        # fullpath = pathname + '/' + item      # Mac only
        # fullpath = pathname + '\' + item      # Windows only
        fullpath = os.path.join(pathname, item) # any OS

        scan(fullpath, signatures)
```

Module: ch10.py

This program uses functions from the Standard Library module `os`. The module `os` contains functions that provide access to operating system resources such as the filesystem. The three `os` module functions we are using are:

a. `listdir()`. Takes, as input, an absolute or relative pathname (as a string) of a folder and returns the list of all files and subfolders contained in the input folder.

    b. `path.isfile()`. Takes, as input, an absolute or relative pathname (as a string) and returns True if the pathname refers to a regular file, `False` otherwise.

    c. `path.join()`. Takes as input two pathnames, joins them into a new pathname, inserting \ or / as needed, and returns it.

We explain further why we need the third function. The function `listdir()` *does not* return a list of *pathnames* but just a list of file and folder *names*. For example, when we start executing `scan('test')` (we ignore the second argument of `scan()` in this discussion), the function `listdir()` will get called in this way:

```
>>> os.listdir('test')
['fileA.txt', 'folder1', 'folder2']
```

If we were to make the recursive call `scan('folder1')`, then, when this function call starts executing, the function `listdir()` would get called on pathname `'folder1'`, with this result:

```
>>> os.listdir('folder1')
Traceback (most recent call last):
  File "<pyshell#387>", line 1, in <module>
    os.listdir('folder1')
OSError: [Errno 2] No such file or directory: 'folder1'
```

The problem is that the *current working directory* during the execution of `scan('test')` is the folder that contains the folder `test`; the folder `'folder1'` is not in there, thus the error.

    Instead of making the call `scan('folder1')`, we need to make the call on a pathname that is either absolute or relative with respect to the current working directory. The pathname of `'folder1'` can be be obtained by concatenating `'test'` and `'folder1'` as follows

```
'test' + '\' + 'folder1'
```

(on a Windows box) or, more generally, concatenating `pathname` and `item` as follows

```
path = pathname + '\' + item
```

This works on Windows machines but not on UNIX, Linux, or MAC OS X machines because pathnames use the forward slashes (/) in those operating systems. A better, portable solution is to use the `path.join()` function from module `os`. It will work for all operating systems and thus be system independent. For example, on a Mac:

```
>>> pathname = 'test'
>>> item = 'folder1'
>>> os.path.join(pathname, item)
'test/folder1'
```

Here is a similar example executed on a Windows box:

```
>>> pathname = 'C://Test/virus'
>>> item = 'folder1'
>>> os.path.join(pathname, item)
'C://Test/virus/folder1'
```

Linear recursion

The three problems we have considered in this section—printing the number sequence pattern, drawing the Koch curve, and scanning the filesystem for viruses—could all have been solved without recursion. Iterative solutions for these problems really do exist. The iterative solutions, however, require algorithms that are more complex than recursion and that are beyond the scope of an introductory computer science textbook.

The problems we considered in Section 10.1, on the other hand, have simple iterative solutions. Recursive functions `vertical()`, `reverse()`, `cheers()`, and `factorial()` from Section 10.1 could have as easily been developed using iteration. In fact, the recursive and iterative solutions are closely related. The two implementations of function `factorial()` from Practice Problem 10.3 and Practice Problem 5.4 can be used to illustrate this. While one implementation is recursive and the other is iterative, both functions use a similar process to compute $n!$: they both compute a sequence of intermediate results $i!$, for $i = 1, \ldots, n$, obtained by multiplying the previous intermediate result $(i-1)!$ with i. The recursive function can thus be viewed as a recursive implementation of this idea.

When the recursive step of a function is implemented using a single recursive call that computes the "previous" intermediate result and a "basic," nonrecursive (problem specific) operation that computes the "next" intermediate result, the function is said to use *linear recursion*. In function `vertical()`, for example, the recursive step consists of a single recursive call `vertical(n//10)` that prints all but the last digit of `n` and statement `print(n%10)` that prints the last digit.

Linear recursion is a particularly useful technique for implementing fundamental functions on lists. For example, a function that adds the numbers in a list of numbers can be implemented using linear recursion as follows:

Module: ch10.py

```
1  def recSum(lst):
2      'returns the sum of items in list lst'
3      if len(lst) == 0:
4          return 0
5      return recSum(lst[:-1]) + lst[-1]
```

Note that the recursive step consists of a single recursive call that sums all the numbers in the list but the last and a "basic" operation that adds the last number to this sum.

Using linear recursion, implement function `recNeg()` that takes a list of numbers as input and returns `True` if some number in the list is negative, and `False` otherwise.

```
>>> recNeg([3, 1, -1, 5])
True
>>> recNeg([3, 1, 0, 5])
False
```

Practice Problem 10.6

In the next example, we implement function `recIncr()` that takes a list of numbers as input and returns a copy of the list with every number in the list incremented by one:

```
>>> lst = [1, 4, 9, 16, 25]
>>> recIncr(lst)
[2, 5, 10, 17, 26]
```

We choose to implement the function using linear recursion instead of iteration:

Module: ch10.py

```
1  def recIncr(lst):
2      'returns list [lst[0]+1, lst[1]+1, ..., lst[n-1]+1]'
3      if len(lst) == 0:
4          return []
5      return recIncr(lst[:-1]) + [lst[-1]+1]
```

The recursive step consists of concatenating the list obtained by the recursive call and the list containing the last number in the list incremented by one.

The function `recIncr()` is an example of a function that takes a list and returns a copy of it in which the same operation was performed on every list item. Incrementing every number in the list by one is just one of the many operations one may wish to perform on items of a list. It would thus be useful to implement a more abstract function `recMap()` that takes, as input, the *operation* as well as the list and then applies the operation to every item in the list. What "operation" really means, of course, is a function. For example, if we wanted to use function `recMap()` to increment every number in a list of numbers, we would first have to define the function that we want to apply to every number:

```
>>> def f(i):
        return i + 1
```

Then we would use `recMap()` to apply function `f` to every number in the list:

```
>>> recMap(lst, f)
[2, 5, 10, 17, 26]
```

If, instead, we wanted to obtain a list containing the square roots of the numbers in list `lst`, we would apply the `math.sqrt` function instead:

```
>>> from math import sqrt
>>> recMap(lst, sqrt)
[1.0, 2.0, 3.0, 4.0, 5.0]
```

Note that the input argument of `recMap()` is `f`, not `f()`, or `sqrt`, not `sqrt()`. This is because we are simply passing a reference to the function object, not making a function call.

We can implement `recMap()` using linear recursion:

Module: ch10.py

```
1  def recMap(lst, f):
2      'returns list [f(lst[0]), f(lst[1]), ..., f(lst[n-1])]'
3      if len(lst) == 0:
4          return []
5      return recMap(lst[:-1], f) + [f(lst[-1])]
```

DETOUR

Higher-Order Functions

In function `recMap()`, the second input argument is a function. A function that takes another function as input or that returns a function is called a *higher-order function*. Treating a function like a value is a style of programming that is used extensively in the *functional programming* paradigm which we introduce in Section 12.3.

Python supports higher-order functions because the name of a function is treated no differently from the name of any other object, so it can be treated as a value. Not all languages support higher-order functions. A few other ones that do are LISP, Perl, Ruby, and JavaScript.

Using function `recMap()`, write a short statement that evaluates to a list containing the sums of the rows of a two-dimensional table of numbers called `table`.

Practice Problem
10.7

10.3 Run Time Analysis

The correctness of a program is of course our main concern. However, it is also important that the program is usable or even efficient. In this section, we continue the use of recursion to solve problems, but this time with an eye on efficiency. In our first example, we apply recursion to a problem that does not seem to need it and get a surprising gain in efficiency. In the second example, we take a problem that seems tailored for recursion and obtain an extremely inefficient recursive program.

The Exponent Function

We consider next the implementation of the exponent function a^n. As we have seen already, Python provides the exponentiation operator `**`:

```
>>> 2**4
16
```

But how is the operator `**` implemented? How would we implement it if it was not available? The straightforward approach is to just multiply the value of a n times. The accumulator pattern can be used to implement this idea:

```
1  def power(a, n):
2      'returns a to the nth power'
3      res = 1
4      for i in range(n):
5          res *= a
6      return res
```

Module: ch10.py

You should convince yourself that the function `power()` works correctly. But is this the best way to implement the function `power()`? Is there an implementation that would run faster? It is clear that the function `power()` will perform n multiplications to compute a^n. If n is 10,000, then 10,000 multiplications are done. Can we implement `power()` so significantly fewer multiplications are done, say about 20 instead of 10,000?

Let's see what the recursive approach will give us. We are going to develop a recursive function `rpower()` that takes inputs a and nonnegative integer n and returns a^n.

The natural base case is when the input n is 0. Then $a^n = 1$ and so 1 must be returned:

```
def rpower(a, n):
    'returns a to the nth power'
    if n == 0:                      # base case: n == 0
        return 1
    # remainder of function
```

Now let's handle the recursive step. To do this, we need to express a^n, for $n > 0$, recursively in terms of smaller powers of a (i.e., "closer" to the base case). That is actually not hard, and there are many ways to do it:

$$a^n = a^{n-1} \times a$$
$$a^n = a^{n-2} \times a^2$$
$$a^n = a^{n-3} \times a^3$$
$$\cdots$$
$$a^n = a^{n/2} \times a^{n/2}$$

The appealing thing about the last expression is that the two terms, $a^{n/2}$ and $a^{n/2}$, are the same; therefore, we can compute a^n by making only one recursive call to compute $a^{n/2}$. The only problem is that $n/2$ is not an integer when n is odd. So we consider two cases.

As we just discovered, when the value of n is even, we can compute rpower(a, n) using the result of rpower(a, n//2) as shown in Figure 10.9:

Figure 10.9 Computing a^n **recursively. When** n **is even,** $a^n = a^{n/2} \times a^{n/2}$.

$$\text{rpower(2, n)} \quad = \quad \underbrace{\boxed{2 \times 2 \times \ldots \times 2}}_{\text{power(2, n//2)}} \quad \times \quad \underbrace{\boxed{2 \times 2 \times \ldots \times 2}}_{\text{power(2, n//2)}}$$

When the value of n is odd, we still can use the result of recursive call rpower(a, n//2) to compute rpower(a, n), albeit with an additional factor a, as illustrated in Figure 10.10:

Figure 10.10 Computing a^n **recursively. When** n **is odd,** $a^n = a^{\lfloor n/2 \rfloor} \times a^{\lfloor n/2 \rfloor} \times a$.

$$\text{rpower(2, n)} \quad = \quad \underbrace{\boxed{2 \times 2 \times \ldots \times 2}}_{\text{power(2, n//2)}} \quad \times \quad \underbrace{\boxed{2 \times 2 \times \ldots \times 2}}_{\text{power(2, n//2)}} \quad \times \quad \boxed{2}$$

These insights lead us to the recursive implementation of rpower() shown next. Note that only one recursive call rpower(a, n//2) is made.

Module: ch10.py

```
1  def rpower(a, n):
2      'returns a to the nth power'
3      if n == 0:                  # base case: n == 0
4          return 1
5
6      tmp = rpower(a, n//2)    # recursive step: n > 0
7
8      if n % 2 == 0:
9          return tmp*tmp           # a**n = a**(n//2) * a**a(n//2)
10     else: # n % 2 == 1
11         return a*tmp*tmp         # a**n = a**(n//2) * a**a(n//2) * a
```

We now have two implementations of the exponentiation function, power() and rpower(). How can we tell which is more efficient?

Counting Operations

One way to compare the efficiency of two functions is to count the number of operations executed by each function on the same input. In the case of `power()` and `rpower()`, we limit ourselves to counting just the number of multiplications

Clearly, `power(2, 10000)` will need 10,000 multiplications. What about `rpower(2, 10000)`? To answer this question, we modify `rpower()` so it *counts* the number of multiplications performed. We do this by incrementing a `global` variable `counter`, defined outside the function, each time a multiplication is done:

Module: ch10.py

```
1  def rpower(a, n):
2      'returns a to the nth power'
3      global counter        # counts number of multiplications
4
5      if n==0:
6          return 1
7      # if n > 0:
8      tmp = rpower(a, n//2)
9
10     if n % 2 == 0:
11         counter += 1
12         return tmp*tmp         # 1 multiplication
13
14     else: # n % 2 == 1
15         counter += 2
16         return a*tmp*tmp       # 2 multiplications
```

Now we can do the counting:

```
>>> counter = 0
>>> rpower(2, 10000)
199506311688...792596709376
>>> counter
19
```

Thus, recursion led us to a way to do exponentiation that reduced the number of multiplications from 10,000 to 23.

Fibonacci Sequence

We introduced the Fibonacci sequence of integers in Chapter 5:

$$1, 1, 2, 3, 5, 8, 13, 21, 34, 55, 89, \dots$$

We also described a method to construct the Fibonacci sequence: A number in the sequence is the sum of the previous two numbers in the sequence (except for the first two 1s). This rule is recursive in nature. So, if we are to implement a function `rfib()` that takes a nonnegative integer n as input and returns the nth Fibonacci number, a recursive implementation seems natural. Let's do it.

Since the recursive rule applies to the numbers after the 0th and 1st Fibonacci number, it makes sense that the base case is when $n \leq 1$ (i.e., $n = 0$ or $n = 1$). In that case, `rfib()` should return 1:

```
def rfib(n):
    'returns nth Fibonacci number'
    if n < 2:                       # base case
        return 1
    # remainder of function
```

The recursive step applies to input $n > 1$. In that case, the nth Fibonacci number is the sum of the $n - 1$st and $n - 2$nd:

Module: ch10.py

```
1  def rfib(n):
2      'returns nth Fibonacci number'
3      if n < 2:                       # base case
4          return 1
5
6      return rfib(n-1) + rfib(n-2)   # recursive step
```

Let's check that function `rfib()` works:

```
>>> rfib(0)
1
>>> rfib(1)
1
>>> rfib(4)
5
>>> rfib(8)
34
```

The function seems correct. Let's try to compute a larger Fibonacci number:

```
>>> rfib(35)
14930352
```

Hmmm. It's correct, but it took a while to compute. (Try it.) If you try

```
>>> rfib(100)
...
```

you will be waiting for a very long time. (Remember that you can always stop the program execution by hitting Ctrl - c simultaneously.)

Is computing the 36th Fibonacci number really that time consuming? Recall that we already implemented a function in Chapter 5 that returns the nth Fibonacci number:

Module: ch10.py

```
1  def fib(n):
2      'returns nth Fibonacci number'
3      previous = 1    # 0th Fibonacci number
4      current = 1     # 1st Fibonacci number
5      i = 1           # index of current Fibonacci number
6
7      while i < n:    # while current is not nth Fibonacci number
8          previous, current = current, previous+current
9          i += 1
10
11     return current
```

Let's see how it does:

```
>>> fib(35)
14930352
>>> fib(100)
573147844013817084101
>>> fib(10000)
54438373113565...
```

Instantaneous in all cases. Let's investigate what is wrong with `rfib()`.

Experimental Analysis of Run Time

One way to precisely compare functions `fib()` and `rfib()`—or other functions for that matter—is to run them on the same input and compare their run times. As good (lazy) programmers, we like to automate this process, so we develop an application that can be used to analyze the run time of a function. We will make this application generic in the sense that it can be used on functions other than just `fib()` and `rfib()`.

Our application consists of several functions. The key one that measures the run time on one input is `timing()`: It is a higher-order function that takes as input (1) a function `func` and (2) an "input size" (as an integer), runs function `func` on an input of the given size, and returns the execution time.

Module: ch10.py

```python
1  import time
2  def timing(func, n):
3      'runs func on input returned by buildInput'
4      funcInput = buildInput(n)     # obtain input for func
5      start = time.time()           # take start time
6      func(funcInput)               # run func on funcInput
7      end = time.time()             # take end time
8      return end - start            # return execution time
```

Function `timing()` uses the `time()` function from the `time` module to obtain the current time before and after the execution of the function `func`; the difference between the two will be the execution time. (*Note:* The timing can be affected by other tasks the computer may be doing, but we avoid dealing with this issue.)

The function `buildInput()` takes an input size and returns an object that is an appropriate input for function `func()` and has the right input size. This function is dependent on the function `func()` we are analyzing. In the case of the Fibonacci functions `fib()` and `rfib()`, the input corresponding to input size n is just n:

Module: ch10.py

```python
1  def buildInput(n):
2      'returns input for Fibonacci functions'
3      return n
```

Comparing the run times of two functions on the same input does not tell us much about which function is better (i.e., faster). It is more useful to compare the run times of the two functions on *several* different inputs. In this way, we can attempt to understand the behavior of the two functions as the input size (i.e., the problem size) becomes larger. We develop, for that purpose, function `timingAnalysis` that runs an arbitrary function on a series of inputs of increasing size and report run times.

Module: ch10.py

```
1  def timingAnalysis(func, start, stop, inc, runs):
2      '''prints average run times of function func on inputs of
3         size start, start+inc, start+2*inc, ..., up to stop'''
4      for n in range(start, stop, inc):   # for every input size n
5          acc = 0.0                        # initialize accumulator
6
7          for i in range(runs):    # repeat runs times:
8              acc += timing(func, n)   # run func on input of size n
9                                       # and accumulates run times
10         # print average run times for input size n
11         formatStr = 'Run time of {}({}) is {:.7f} seconds.'
12         print(formatStr.format(func.__name__, n, acc/runs))
```

Function `timingAnalysis` takes, as input, function `func` and numbers `start`, `stop`, `inc`, and `runs`. It first runs `func` on several inputs of size `start` and prints the average run time. Then it repeats that for input sizes `start+inc`, `start+2*inc`, ... up to input size `stop`.

When we run `timinAnalysis()` on function `fib()` with input sizes 24, 26, 28, 30, 32, 34, we get:

```
>>> timingAnalysis(fib, 24, 35, 2, 10)
Run time of fib(24) is 0.0000173 seconds.
Run time of fib(26) is 0.0000119 seconds.
Run time of fib(28) is 0.0000127 seconds.
Run time of fib(30) is 0.0000136 seconds.
Run time of fib(32) is 0.0000144 seconds.
Run time of fib(34) is 0.0000151 seconds.
```

When we do the same on function `rfib()`, we get:

```
>>> timingAnalysis(rfib, 24, 35, 2, 10)
Run time of fibonacci(24) is 0.0797332 seconds.
Run time of fibonacci(26) is 0.2037848 seconds.
Run time of fibonacci(28) is 0.5337492 seconds.
Run time of fibonacci(30) is 1.4083670 seconds.
Run time of fibonacci(32) is 3.6589111 seconds.
Run time of fibonacci(34) is 9.5540136 seconds.
```

We graph the results of the two experiments in Figure 10.11.

Figure 10.11 Run time graph. Shown are the average run times, in seconds, of `fib()` and `rfib()` for inputs $n = 24$, 26, 28, 32, and 34.

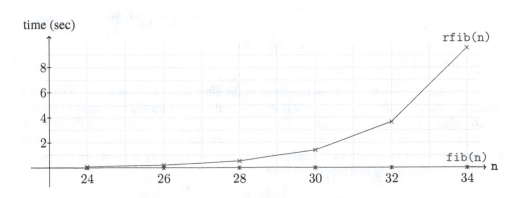

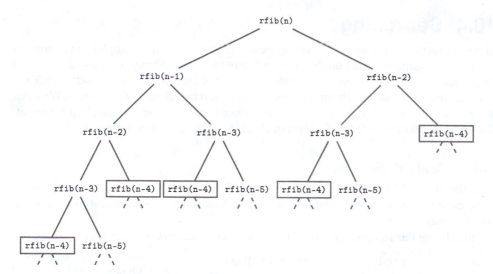

Figure 10.12 Tree of recursive calls. Computing `rfib(n)` requires making two recursive calls: `rfib(n-1)` and `rfib(b-2)`. Computing `rfib(n-1)` requires making recursive calls `rfib(n-2)` and `rfib(n-3)`; computing `rfib(n-2)` requires recursive calls `rfib(n-3)` and `rfib(n-4)`. The same recursive calls will be made multiple times. For example, `rfib(n-4)` will be recomputed five times.

The run times of `fib()` are negligible. However, the run times of `rfib()` are increasing rapidly as the input size increases. In fact, the run time more than doubles between successive input sizes. This means that the run time increases exponentially with respect to the input size. In order to understand the reason behind the poor performance of the recursive function `rfib()`, we illustrate its execution in Figure 10.12.

Figure 10.12 shows some of the recursive calls made when computing `rfib(n)`. To compute `rfib(n)`, recursive calls `rfib(n-1)` and `rfib(n-2)` must be made; to compute `rfib(n-1)` and `rfib(n-2)`, separate recursive calls `rfib(n-2)` and `rfib(n-3)`, and `rfib(n-2)` and `rfib(n-3)`, respectively, must be made. And so on.

The computation of `rfib()` includes two separate computations of `rfib(n-2)` and should therefore take more than twice as long as `rfib(n-2)`. This explains the exponential growth in run time. It also shows the problem with the recursive solution `rfib()`: It keeps making and executing the same function calls, over and over. The function call `rfib(n-4)`, for example, is made and executed five times, even though the result is always the same.

Using the run time analysis application developed in this section, analyze the run time of functions `power()` and `rpower()` as well as built-in operator `**`. You will do this by running `timingAnalysis()` on functions `power2()`, `rpower2()`, and `pow2()` defined next and using input sizes 20,000 through 80,000 with a step size of 20,000.

Practice Problem 10.8

```
def power2(n):
    return power(2,n)
def rpower2(n):
    return rpower(2,n)
def pow2(n):
    return 2**n
```

When done, argue which approach the built-in operator `**` likely uses.

10.4 Searching

In the last section, we learned that the way we design an algorithm and implement a program can have a significant effect on the program's run time and ultimately its usefulness with large data sets. In this section, we consider how reorganizing the input data set and adding structure to it can dramatically improve the run time, and usefulness, of a program. We focus on several fundamental search tasks and usually use sorting to give structure to the data set. We start with the fundamental problem of checking whether a value is contained in a list.

Linear Search

Both the `in` operator and the `index()` method of the `list` class search a list for a given item. Because we have been (and will be) using them *a lot*, it is important to understand how fast they execute.

Recall that the `in` operator is used to check whether an item is in the list or not:

```
>>> lst = random.sample(range(1,100), 17)
>>> lst
[28, 72, 2, 73, 89, 90, 99, 13, 24, 5, 57, 41, 16, 43, 45, 42, 11]
>>> 45 in lst
True
>>> 75 in lst
False
```

The `index()` method is similar: Instead of returning `True` or `False`, it returns the index of the first occurrence of the item (or raises an exception if the item is not in the list).

If the data in the list is not structured in some way, there is really only one way to implement `in` and `index()`: a systematic search through the items in the list, whether from index 0 and up, from index −1 and down, or something equivalent. This type of search is called *linear search*. Assuming the search is done from index 0 and up, linear search would look at 15 elements in the list to find 45 and *all of them* to find that 75 is not in the list.

A linear search may need to look at every item in the list. Its run time, in the worst case, is thus proportional to the size of the list. If the data set is not structured and the data items cannot be compared, linear search is really the only way search can be done on a list.

Binary Search

If the data in the list is comparable, we can improve the search run time by sorting the list first. To illustrate this, we use the same list `lst` as used in linear search, but now sorted:

```
>>> lst.sort()
>>> lst
[2, 5, 11, 13, 16, 24, 28, 41, 42, 43, 45, 57, 72, 73, 89, 90, 99]
```

Suppose we are searching for the value of `target` in list `lst`. Linear search compares `target` with the item at index 0 of `lst`, then with the item at index 1, 2, 3, and so on. Suppose, instead, we start the search by comparing `target` with the item at index i, for some arbitrary index i of `lst`. Well, there are three possible outcomes:

- We are lucky: `lst[i] == target` is true, or
- `target < lst[i]` is true, or
- `target > lst[i]` is true.

Let's do an example. Suppose the value of `target` is 45 and we compare it with the item at index 5 (i.e., 24). It is clear that the third outcome, `target > lst[i]`, applies in this case. Because list `lst` is sorted, this tells us that `target` cannot possibly be to the left of 24, that is, in sublist `lst[0:5]`. Therefore, we should continue our search for `target` to the right of 24 (i.e., in sublist `lst[6:17]`), as illustrated in Figure 10.13.

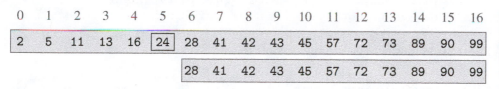

Figure 10.13 Binary search. By comparing 45, the value of `target`, with the item at index 5 of `lst`, we have reduced the search space to the sublist `lst[6:]`.

The main insight we just made is this: With just one comparison, between `target` and `list[5]`, we have reduced our search space from 17 list items to 11. (In linear search, a comparison reduces the search space by just 1.) Now we should ask ourselves whether a different comparison would reduce the search space even further.

In a sense, the outcome `target > lst[5]` was unlucky: `target` turns out to be in the larger of `lst[0:5]` (with 5 items) and `lst[6:17]` (with 11 items). To reduce the role of luck, we could ensure that both sublists are about the same size. We can achieve that by comparing `target` to 42—that is, the item in the middle of the list (also called the *median*).

The insights we just developed are the basis of a search technique called *binary search*. Given a list and a target, binary search returns the index of the target in the list, or −1 if the target is not in the list.

Binary search is easy to implement recursively. The base case is when the list `lst` is empty: `target` cannot possibly be in it, and we return −1. Otherwise, we compare `target` with the list median. Depending on the outcome of the comparison, we are either done or continue the search, recursively, on a sublist of `lst`.

We implement binary search as the recursive function `search()`. Because recursive calls will be made on sublists `lst[i:j]` of the original list `lst`, the function `search()` should take, as input, not just `lst` and `target` but also indices `i` and `j`:

Module: ch10.py

```
1  def search(lst, target, i, j):
2      '''attempts to find target in sorted sublist lst[i:j];
3         index of target is returned if found, -1 otherwise'''
4      if i == j:                          # base case: empty list
5          return -1                       # target cannot be in list
6
7      mid = (i+j)//2                      # index of median of l[i:j]
8
9      if lst[mid] == target:              # target is the median
10         return mid
11     if target < lst[mid]:               # search left of median
12         return search(lst, target, i, mid)
13     else:                               # search right of median
14         return search(lst, target, mid+1, j)
```

To start the search for `target` in `lst`, indices 0 and `len(lst)` should be given:

```
>>> target = 45
>>> search(lst, target, 0, len(lst))
10
```

Figure 10.14 Binary search. The search for 45 starts in list `1st[0:17]`. After 45 is compared to the list median (42), the search continues in sublist `1st[9:17]`. After 45 is compared to this list's median (72), the search continues in `1st[9:12]`. Since 45 is the median of `1st[9:12]`, the search ends.

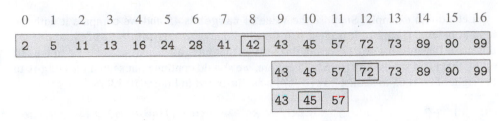

Figure 10.14 illustrates the execution of this search.

Linear versus Binary Search

To convince ourselves that binary search is, on average, much faster than linear search, we perform an experiment. Using the `timingAnalysis()` application we developed in the last section, we compare the performance of our function `search()` and the built-in list method `index()`. To do this, we develop functions `binary()` and `linear()` that pick a random item in the input list and call `search()` or invoke method `index()`, respectively, to find the item:

Module: ch10.py

```
1  def binary(1st):
2      'chooses item in list 1st at random and runs search() on it'
3      target=random.choice(1st)
4      return search(1st, target, 0, len(1st))
5
6  def linear(1st):
7      'choose item in list 1st at random and runs index() on it'
8      target=random.choice(1st)
9      return 1st.index(target)
```

The list `1st` of size `n` we will use is a random sample of `n` numbers in the range from 0 to $2n - 1$.

Module: ch10.py

```
1  def buildInput(n):
2      'returns a random sample of n numbers in range [0, 2n)'
3      1st = random.sample(range(2*n), n)
4      1st.sort()
5      return 1st
```

Here are the results:

```
>>> timingAnalysis(linear, 200000, 1000000, 200000, 20)
Run time of linear(200000) is 0.0046095
Run time of linear(400000) is 0.0091411
Run time of linear(600000) is 0.0145864
Run time of linear(800000) is 0.0184283
>>> timingAnalysis(binary, 200000, 1000000, 200000, 20)
Run time of binary(200000) is 0.0000681
Run time of binary(400000) is 0.0000762
Run time of binary(600000) is 0.0000943
Run time of binary(800000) is 0.0000933
```

It is clear that binary search is much faster and the run time of linear search grows proportionally with the list size. The interesting thing about the run time of binary search is that it does not seem to be increasing much. Why is that?

Whereas linear search may end up looking at every item in the list, binary search will look at far fewer list items. To see this, recall our insight that with every binary search comparison, the search space decreases by more than a half. Of course, when the search space becomes of size 1 or less, the search is over. The number of binary search comparisons in a list of size n is bounded by this value: the number of times we can halve n division before it becomes 1. In equation form, it is the value of x in

$$\frac{n}{2^x} = 1$$

The solution to this equation is $x = \log_2 n$, the logarithm base two of n. This function does indeed grow very slowly as n increases.

In the remainder of this section we look at several other fundamental search-like problems and analyze different approaches to solving them.

Uniqueness Testing

We consider this problem: Given a list, is every item in it unique? One natural way to solve this problem is to iterate over the list and for each list item check whether the item appears more than once in the list. Function dup1 implements this idea:

```
1  def dup1(lst):
2      'returns True if list lst has duplicates, False otherwise'
3      for item in lst:
4          if lst.count(item) > 1:
5              return True
6      return False
```

Module: ch10.py

The list method count(), just like the in operator and the index method, must perform a linear search through the list to count all occurrences of a target item. So, in duplicates1(), linear search is performed for every list item. Can we do better?

What if we sorted the list first? The benefit of doing this is that duplicate items will be next to each other in the sorted list. Therefore, to find out whether there are duplicates, all we need to do is compare every item with the item before it:

```
1  def dup2(lst):
2      'returns True if list lst has duplicates, False otherwise'
3      lst.sort()
4      for index in range(1, len(lst)):
5          if lst[index] == lst[index-1]:
6              return True
7      return False
```

Module: ch10.py

The advantage of this approach is that it does only one pass through the list. Of course, there is a cost to this approach: We have to sort the list first.

In Chapter 6, we saw that dictionaries and sets can be useful to check whether a list contains duplicates. Functions dup3() and dup4() use a dictionary or a set, respectively, to check whether the input list contains duplicates:

Module: ch10.py

```
1   def dup3(lst):
2       'returns True if list lst has duplicates, False otherwise'
3       s = set()
4       for item in lst:
5           if item in s:
6               return False
7           else:
8               s.add(item)
9       return True
10
11  def dup4(lst):
12      'returns True if list lst has duplicates, False otherwise'
13      return len(lst) != len(set(lst))
```

We leave the analysis of these four functions as an exercise.

Practice Problem 10.9

Using an experiment, analyze the run time of functions dup1(), dup2(), dup3(), and dup4(). You should test each function on 10 lists of size 2000, 4000, 6000, and 8000 obtained from:

```
import random
def buildInput(n):
    'returns a list of n random integers in range [0, n**2)'
    res = []
    for i in range(n):
        res.append(random.choice(range(n**2)))
    return res
```

Note that the list returned by this function is obtained by repeatedly choosing n numbers in the range from 0 to $n^2 - 1$ and may or may not contain duplicates. When done, comment on the results.

Selecting the *k*th Largest (Smallest) Item

Finding the largest (or smallest) item in an unsorted list is best done with a linear search. Finding the second, or third, largest (or smallest) kth smallest can be also done with a linear search, though not as simply. Finding the kth largest (or smallest) item for large k can easily be done by sorting the list first. (There are more efficient ways to do this, but they are beyond the scope of this text.) Here is a function that returns the kth smallest value in a list:

Module: ch10.py

```
1   def kthsmallest(lst, k):
2       'returns kth smallest item in list lst'
3       lst.sort()
4       return lst[k-1]
```

Computing the Most Frequently Occurring Item

The problem we consider next is searching for the most frequently occurring item in a list. We actually know how to do this, and more: In Chapter 6, we saw how dictionaries can be used to compute the frequency of *all* items in a sequence. However, if all we want is to find the most frequent item, using a dictionary is overkill and a waste of memory space.

We have seen that by sorting a list, all the duplicate items will be next to each other. If we iterate through the sorted list, we can count the length of each sequence of duplicates and keep track of the longest. Here is the implementation of this idea:

Module: ch10.py

```
1   def frequent(lst):
2       '''returns most frequently occurring item
3          in non-empty list lst'''
4       lst.sort()                    # first sort list
5
6       currentLen = 1               # length of current sequence
7       longestLen = 1               # length of longest sequence
8       mostFreq   = lst[0]          # item with longest sequence
9
10      for i in range(1, len(lst)):
11          # compare current item with previous
12          if lst[i] == lst[i-1]:   # if equal
13              # current sequence continues
14              currentLen+=1
15
16          else:                    # if not equal
17              # update longest sequence if necessary
18              if currentLen > longestLen:  # if sequence that ended
19                                           # is longest so far
20                  longestLen = currentLen  # store its length
21                  mostFreq   = lst[i-1]    # and the item
22              # new sequence starts
23              currentLen = 1
24
25      return mostFreq
```

Implement function `frequent2()` that uses a dictionary to compute the frequency of every item in the input list and returns the item that occurs the most frequently. Then perform an experiment and compare the run times of `frequent()` and `frequent2()` on a list obtained using the `buildInput()` function defined in Practice Problem 10.9.

Practice Problem
10.10

E-Book Case Study: Tower of Hanoi

In this case study, we consider the Tower of Hanoi problem, the classic example of a problem easily solved using recursion. We also use the opportunity to develop a visual application by developing new classes and using object-oriented programming techniques.

Chapter Summary

The focus of this chapter is recursion and the process of developing a recursive function that solves a problem. The chapter also introduces formal run time analysis of programs and applies it to various search problems.

Recursion is a fundamental problem-solving technique that can be applied to problems whose solution can be constructed from solutions of "easier" versions of the problem. Recursive functions are often far simpler to describe (i.e., implement) than nonrecursive solutions for the same problem because they leverage operating system resources, in particular the program stack.

In this chapter, we devolop recursive functions for a variety of problems, such as the visual display of fractals and the search for viruses in the files of a filesystem. The main goal of the exposition, however, is to make explicit how to do recursive thinking, a way to approach problems that leads to recursive solutions.

In some instances, recursive thinking offers insights that lead to solutions that are more efficient than the obvious or original solution. In other instances, it will lead to a solution that is far worse. We introduce run time analysis of programs as a way to quantify and compare the execution times of various programs. Run time analysis is not limited to recursive functions, of course, and we use it to analyze various search problems as well.

Solutions to Practice Problems

10.1 The function `reverse()` is obtained by modifying function `vertical()` (and renaming it, of course). Note that function `vertical()` prints the last digit after printing all but the last digit. Function `reverse()` should just do the opposite:

```
def reverse(n):
    'prints digits of n vertically starting with low-order digit'
    if n < 10:              # base case: one-digit number
        print(n)
    else:                   # n has at least 2 digits
        print(n%10)         # print last digit of n
        reverse(n//10)      # recursively print in reverse all but
                            # the last digit
```

10.2 In the base case, when $n = 0$, just `'Hurray!!!'` should be printed. When $n > 0$, we know that at least one `'Hip'` should be printed, which we do. That means that $n - 1$ strings `'Hip'` and then `'Hurray!!!'` remain to be printed. That is exactly what recursive call `cheers(n-1)` will achieve.

```
def cheers(n):
    'prints cheer'
    if n == 0:
        print('Hurray!!!')
    else: # n > 0
        print('Hip', end=' ')
        cheers(n-1)
```

10.3 By the definition of the factorial function $n!$, the base case of the recursion is $n = 0$ or $n = 1$. In those cases, the function `factorial()` should return 1. For $n > 1$, the recursive definition of $n!$ suggests that function `factorial()` should return `n * factorial(n-1)`:

```
def factorial(n):
    'returns n!'
    if n == 0:                  # base case
        return 1
    return factorial(n-1) * n # recursive step when n > 0
```

10.4 In the base case, when $n = 0$, nothing is printed. If $n > 0$, note that the output of `pattern2(n)` consists of the output of `pattern2(n-1)`, followed by a row of n stars, followed by the output of `pattern2(n-1)`:

```
def pattern2(n):
    'prints the nth pattern'
    if n > 0:
        pattern2(n-1)   # prints pattern2(n-1)
        print(n * '*')   # print n stars
        pattern2(n-1)   # prints pattern2(n-1)
```

10.5 As Figure 10.15 of `snowflake(4)` illustrates, a snowflake pattern consists of three patterns `koch(3)` drawn along the sides of an equilateral triangle.

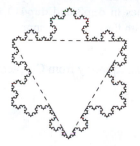

Figure 10.15 The pattern `snowflake(4)`.

To draw the pattern `snowflake(n)`, all we need to do is draw pattern `koch(n)`, turn right 120 degrees, draw `koch(n)` again, turn right 120 degrees, and draw `koch(n)` one last time.

```
def drawSnowflake(n):
    'draws nth snowflake curve using function koch() 3 times'
    s = Screen()
    t = Turtle()
    directions = koch(n)

    for i in range(3):
        for move in directions: # draw koch(n)
            if move == 'F':
                t.fd(300/3**n)
            if move == 'L':
                t.lt(60)
            if move == 'R':
                t.rt(120)
        t.rt(120)                   # turn right 120 degrees
    s.bye()
```

10.6 If the list is empty, the returned value should be `False`; otherwise, `True` should be returned if and only if `lst[:-1]` contains a negative number or `lst[-1]` is negative:

```
def recNeg(lst):
    '''returns True if some number in list lst is negative,
       False otherwise'''
    if len(lst) == 0:
        return False
    return recNeg(lst[:-1]) or lst[-1] < 0
```

10.7 The buil-in function `sum()` should be applied to every item (row) of `table`:

```
>>> table = [[1,2,3], [4,5,6]]
>>> recMap(table, sum)
[6, 15]
```

10.8 After running the tests, you will note that the run times of `power2()` are significantly worse than the run times of `pow2()` and `rpow2()` which are very, very close. It seems that the built-in operator `**` uses an approach that is equivalent to our recursive solution.

10.9 Even though `dup2()` has the additional sorting step, you will note that `dup1()` is much slower. This means that the multiple linear searches approach of `dup1()` is very inefficient. The dictionary and set approaches in `dup3` and `dup4()` did best, with the set approach winning overall. The one issue with these last two approaches is that they both use an extra container, so they take up more memory space.

10.10 You can use the function `frequency` from Chapter 6 to implement `freqent2()`.

Exercises

10.11 Using Figure 10.1 as a model, draw all the steps that occur during the execution of `countdown(3)`, including the state of the program stack at the beginning and end of every recursive call.

10.12 Swap statements in lines 6 and 7 of function `countdown()` to create function `countdown2()`. Explain how it differs from `countdown()`.

10.13 Using Figure 10.1 as a model, draw all the steps that occur during the execution of `countdown2(3)`, where `countdown2()` is the function from Exercise 10.12.

10.14 Modify the function `countdown()` so it exhibits this behavior:

```
>>> countdown3(5)
5
4
3
    BOOOM!!!
    Scared you...
2
1
Blastoff!!!
```

10.15 Using Figure 10.1 as a model, draw all the steps that occur during the execution of `pattern(2)`, including the state of the program stack at the beginning and end of every recursive call.

10.16 The recursive formula for computing the number of ways of choosing k items out of a set of n items, denoted $C(n, k)$, is:

$$C(n, k) = \begin{cases} 1 & \text{if } k = 0 \\ 0 & \text{if } n < k \\ C(n-1, k-1) + C(n-1, k) & \text{otherwise} \end{cases}$$

The first case says there is one way to choose no item; the second says that there is no way to choose more items than available in the set. The last case separates the counting of sets of k items containing the last set item and the counting of sets of k items *not* containing the last set item. Write a recursive function `combinations()` that computes $C(n, k)$ using this recursive formula.

```
>>> combinations(2, 1)
0
>>> combinations(1, 2)
2
>>> combinations(2, 5)
10
```

10.17 Just as we did for the function `rpower()`, modify function `rfib()` so that it counts the number of recursive calls made. Then use this function to count the number of calls made for $n = 10, 20, 30$.

Problems

10.18 Write a recursive method `silly()` that takes one nonnegative integer n as input and then prints n question marks, followed by n exclamation points. Your program should use no loops.

```
>>> silly(0)
>>> silly(1)
* !
>>> silly(10)
* * * * * * * * * * ! ! ! ! ! ! ! ! ! !
```

10.19 Write a recursive method `numOnes()` that takes a nonnegative integer n as input and returns the number of 1s in the binary representation of n. Use the fact that this is equal to the number of 1s in the representation of $n//2$ (integer division), plus 1 if n is odd.

```
>>> numOnes(0)
0
>>> numOnes(1)
1
>>> numOnes(14)
3
```

10.20 In Chapter 5 we developed Euclid's Greatest Common Divisor (GCD) algorithm using iteration. Euclid's algorithm is naturally described recursively:

$$gcd(a, b) = \begin{cases} a & \text{if } b = 0 \\ gcd(b, a\%b) & \text{otherwise} \end{cases}$$

Using this recursive definition, implement recursive function `rgcd()` that takes two non-negative numbers a and b, with $a > b$, and returns the GCD of a and b:

```
>>> rgcd(3,0)
3
>>> rgcd(18,12)
6
```

10.21 Write a method `rem()` that takes as input a list containing, possibly, duplicate values and returns a copy of the list in which one copy of every duplicate value was removed.

```
>>> rem([4])
[]
>>> rem([4, 4])
[4]
>>> rem([4, 1, 3, 2])
[]
>>> rem([2, 4, 2, 4, 4])
[2, 4, 4]
```

10.22 You're visiting your hometown and are planning to stay at a friend's house. It just happens that all your friends live on the same street. In order to be efficient, you would like to stay at the house of a friend who is in a central location in the following sense: the same number of friends, within 1, live in either direction. If two friends' houses satisfy this criterion, choose the friend with the smaller street address.

Write function `address()` that takes a list of street numbers and returns the street number you should stay at.

```
>>> address([2, 1, 8, 5, 9])
5
>>> address([2, 1, 8, 5])
2
>>> address([1, 1, 1, 2, 3, 3, 4, 4, 4, 5])
3
```

10.23 Develop a recursive function `tough()` that takes two nonnegative integer arguments and outputs a pattern as shown below. *Hint:* The first argument represents the indentation of the pattern, whereas the second argument—always a power of 2—indicates the number of "*"s in the longest line of "*"s in the pattern.

```
>>> f(0, 0)
>>> f(0, 1)
 *
>>> f(0, 2)
 *
**
 *
```

```
>>> f(0, 4)
 *
 **
  *
****
  *
 **
  *
```

10.24 Write a recursive method `base()` that takes a nonnegative integer n and a positive integer $1 < b < 10$ and *prints* the base-b representation of integer n.

```
>>> base(0, 2)
0
>>> base(1, 2)
1
>>> base(10, 2)
1010
>>> base(10, 3)
1 0 1
```

10.25 Implement function `permutations()` that takes a list `lst` as input and returns a list of all permutations of `lst` (so the returned value is a list of lists). Do this recursively as follows: If the input list `lst` is of size 1 or 0, just return a list *containing* list `lst`. Otherwise, make a recursive call on the sublist `lst[1:]` to obtain the list of all permutations of all items of `lst` except `lst[0]`. Then, for each such permutation (i.e., list) `perm`, generate permutations of `lst` by inserting `lst[0]` into all possible positions of `perm`.

```
>>> permutations([1, 2])
[[1, 2], [2, 1]]
>>> permutations([1, 2, 3])
[[1, 2, 3], [2, 1, 3], [2, 3, 1], [1, 3, 2], [3, 1, 2], [3, 2, 1]]
>>> permutations([1, 2, 3, 4])
[[1, 2, 3, 4], [2, 1, 3, 4], [2, 3, 1, 4], [2, 3, 4, 1],
 [1, 3, 2, 4], [3, 1, 2, 4], [3, 2, 1, 4], [3, 2, 4, 1],
 [1, 3, 4, 2], [3, 1, 4, 2], [3, 4, 1, 2], [3, 4, 2, 1],
 [1, 2, 4, 3], [2, 1, 4, 3], [2, 4, 1, 3], [2, 4, 3, 1],
 [1, 4, 2, 3], [4, 1, 2, 3], [4, 2, 1, 3], [4, 2, 3, 1],
 [1, 4, 3, 2], [4, 1, 3, 2], [4, 3, 1, 2], [4, 3, 2, 1]]
```

10.26 Implement function `anagrams()` that computes anagrams of a given word. An anagram of word A is a word B that can be formed by rearranging the letters of A. For example, the word pot is an anagram of the word top. Your function will take as input the name of a file of words and as well as a word, and print all the words in the file that are anagrams of the input word. In the next examples, use file `words.txt` as your file of words.

```
>>> anagrams('words.txt', 'trace')
crate
cater
react
```

File: words.txt

10.27 Write a function `pairs1()` that takes as inputs a list of integers and an integer target value and returns `True` if there are two numbers in the list that add up to the target and `False` otherwise. Your implementation should use the nested loop pattern and check all pairs of numbers in the list.

```
>>> pairs1([4, 1, 9, 3, 5], 13)
True
>>> pairs1([4, 1, 9, 3, 5], 11)
False
```

When done, reimplement the function so that it sorts the list first and then *efficiently* searches for the pair. Analyze the run time of both implementations using the `timingAnalysis()` app. (Function `buildInput()` should generate a tuple containing the list and the target.)

10.28 In this problem, you will develop a function that crawls through "linked" files. Every file visited by the crawler will contain zero or more links, one per line, to other files and nothing else. A link to a file is just the name of the file. For example, the content of file `file0.txt` is:

```
file1.txt
file2.txt
```

The first line represents the link o file `file1.txt` and the second is a link to `file2.txt`.

Implement recursive method `crawl()` that takes as input a file name (as a string), prints a message saying the file is being visited, opens the file, reads each link, and recursively continues the crawl on each link. The below example uses a set of files packaged in archive `files.zip`.

File: files.zip

```
>>> crawl('file0.txt')
Visiting  file0.txt
Visiting  file1.txt
Visiting  file3.txt
Visiting  file4.txt
Visiting  file8.txt
Visiting  file9.txt
Visiting  file2.txt
Visiting  file5.txt
Visiting  file6.txt
Visiting  file7.txt
```

10.29 Pascal's triangle is an infinite two-dimensional pattern of numbers whose first five lines are illustrated in Figure 10.16. The first line, line 0, contains just 1. All other lines start and end with a 1 too. The other numbers in those lines are obtained using this rule: The number at position i is the sum of the numbers in position $i - 1$ and i in the previous line.

Figure 10.16 Pascal's triangle. Only the first five lines of Pascal's triangle are shown.

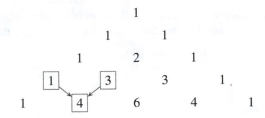

Implement recursive function `pascalLine()` that takes a nonnegative integer n as input and returns a list containing the sequence of numbers appearing in the nth line of Pascal's triangle.

```
>>> pascalLine(0)
[1]
>>> pascalLine(2)
[1, 2, 1]
>>> pascalLine(3)
[1, 3, 3, 1]
>>> pascalLine(4)
[1, 4, 6, 4, 1]
```

10.30 Implement recursive function `traverse()` that takes as input a pathname of a folder (as a string) and an integer d and prints on the screen the pathname of every file and subfolder contained in the folder, directly or indirectly. The file and subfolder pathnames should be output with an indentation that is proportional to their depth with respect to the topmost folder. The next example illustrates the execution of `traverse()` on folder `'test'` shown in Figure 10.8.

```
>>> traverse('test', 0)
test/fileA.txt
test/folder1
  test/folder1/fileB.txt
  test/folder1/fileC.txt
  test/folder1/folder11
    test/folder1/folder11/fileD.txt
test/folder2
  test/folder2/fileD.txt
  test/folder2/fileE.txt
```

File: test.zip

10.31 Implement function `search()` that takes as input the name of a file and the pathname of a folder and searches for the file in the folder and any folder contained in it, directly or indirectly. The function should return the pathname of the file, if found; otherwise, `None` should be returned. The below example illustrates the execution of `search('file.txt', 'test')` from the parent folder of folder `'test'` shown in Figure 10.8.

```
>>> search('fileE.txt', 'test')
  test/folder2/fileE.txt
```

File: test.zip

10.32 The Lévy curves are fractal graphical patterns that can be defined recursively. Like the Koch curves, for every nonnegative integer $n > 0$, the Lévy curve L_n can be defined in terms of Lévy curve L_{n-1}; Lévy curve L_0 is just a straight line. Figure 10.17 shows the Lévy curve L_8.

(a) Find more information about the Lévy curve online and use it to implement recursive function `levy()` that takes a nonnegative integer n and returns turtle instructions encoded with letters L, R and, F, where L means "rotate left 45 degrees," R means "rotate right 90 degrees," and F means "go forward."

```
>>> levy(0)
'F'
```

Figure 10.17 Lévy curve
L_8.

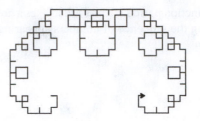

```
>>> levy(1)
'LFRFL'
>>> levy(2)
'LLFRFLRLFRFLL'
```

(b) Implement function `drawLevy()`) so that it takes nonnegative integer n as input and draws the Lévy curve L_n using instructions obtained from function `levy()`.

10.33 In the simple coin game you are given an initial number of coins and then, in every iteration of the game, you are required to get rid of a certain number of coins using one of the following rules. If n is the number of coins you have then:

- If n is divisible by 10, then you may give back 9 coins.
- If n is even, then you may give back exactly $n/2 - 1$ coins.
- If n is divisible by 3, then you may give back 7 coins.
- If n is divisible by 4, then you may give back 6 coins.

If none of the rules can be applied, you lose. The goal of the game is to end up with exactly 8 coins.

Note that more than one rule may be applied for some values of n. If n is 20, for example, rule 1 could be applied to end up with 11 coins. Since no rule can be applied to 11 coins, you would lose the game. Alternatively, rule 4 could be applied to end up with 14 coins, and then rule 2 could be applied to end up with 8 coins and win the game.

Implement a function `coins()` that takes as input the initial number of coins and returns `True` if there is some way to play the game and end up with 8 coins. The function should return `False` only if there is no way to win.

```
>>> coins(7)
False
>>> coins(8)
True
>>> coins(20)
True
>>> coins(66)
False
>>> coins(99)
True
```

10.34 Using linear recursion, implement function `recDup()` that takes a list as input and returns a copy of it in which every list item has been duplicated.

```
>>> recDup(['ant', 'bat', 'cat', 'dog'])
['ant', 'ant', 'bat', 'bat', 'cat', 'cat', 'dog', 'dog']
```

10.35 Using linear recursion, implement function `recReverse()` that takes a list as input and returns a reversed copy of the list.

```
>>> lst = [1, 3, 5, 7, 9]
>>> recReverse(lst)
[9, 7, 5, 3, 1]
```

10.36 Using linear recursion, implement function `recSplit()` that takes, as input, a list `lst` and a nonnegative integer `i` no greater than the size of `lst`. The function should split the list into two parts so that the second part contains exactly the last `i` items of the list. The function should return a list containing the two parts.

```
>>> recSplit([1, 2, 3, 4, 5, 6, 7], 3)
[[1, 2, 3, 4], [5, 6, 7]]
```

10.37 Implement a function that draws patterns of squares like this:

(a) To get started, first implement function `square()` that takes as input a `Turtle` object and three integers x, y, and s and makes the `Turtle` object trace a square of side length s centered at coordinates (x, y).

```
>>> from turtle import Screen, Turtle
>>> s = Screen()
>>> t = Turtle()
>>> t.pensize(2)
>>> square(t, 0, 0, 200)    # draws the square
```

(b) Now implement recursive function `squares()` that takes the same inputs as function `square` plus an integer n and draws a pattern of squares. When $n = 0$, nothing is drawn. When $n = 1$, the same square drawn by `square(t, 0, 0, 200)` is drawn. When $n = 2$ the pattern is:

Each of the four small squares is centered at an endpoint of the large square and has length $1/2.2$ of the original square. When $n = 3$, the pattern is:

The Web and Search

11.1 The World Wide Web   372

11.2 Python WWW API   379

11.3 String Pattern Matching   387

E-Book Case Study: Web Crawler   391

Chapter Summary   392

Solutions to Practice Problems   392

Exercises   394

Problems   395

IN THIS CHAPTER, we introduce the World Wide Web (the WWW or simply the web). The web is one of the most important developments in computer science. It has become the platform of choice for sharing information and communicating. Consequently the web is a rich source for cutting-edge application development.

We start this chapter by describing the three core WWW technologies: Uniform Resource Locators (URLs), the HyperText Transfer Protocol (HTTP), and the HyperText Markup Language (HTML). We focus especially on HTML, the language of web pages. We then go over the Standard Library modules that enable developers to write programs that access, download, and process documents on the web. We focus, in particular, on mastering tools such as HTML parsers and regular expressions that help us process web pages and analyze the content of text documents.

The skills taught in this chapter and the next are useful for mining data files such as web pages and developing applications such as search engines, recommender systems, and a multitude of other Big Data apps.

11.1 The World Wide Web

The World Wide Web (WWW or, simply, the web) is a distributed system of documents linked through hyperlinks and hosted on web servers across the Internet. In this section, we explain how the web works and describe the technologies that it relies on. We make use of these technologies in the web-based applications we develop in this chapter.

Web Servers and Web Clients

As mentioned earlier, the Internet is a global network that connects computers around the world. It allows programs running on two computers to send messages to each other. Typically, the communication occurs because one of the programs is requesting a resource (a file, say) from the other. The *program* that is the provider of the resource is referred to as a *server*. (The *computer* hosting the server program is often referred to as a *server* too.) The program requesting the resource is referred to as a *client*.

The WWW contains a vast collection of web pages, documents, multimedia, and other resources. These resources are stored on computers connected to the Internet that run a server program called a *web server*. Web pages, in particular, are a critical resource on the web as they contain *hyperlinks* to resources on the web.

A program that requests a resource from a web server is called a *web client*. The web server receives the request and sends the requested resource (if if exists) back to the client.

Your favorite browser (whether it is Chrome, Firefox, Internet Explorer, or Safari) is a web client. A browser has capabilities in addition to being able to request and receive web resources. It also processes the resource and displays it, whether the resource is a web page, text document, image, video, or other multimedia. Most important, a web browser displays the hyperlinks contained in a web page and allows the user to navigate between web pages by just clicking on the hyperlinks.

DETOUR

Brief History of the Web

The WWW was invented by English computer scientist Tim Berners-Lee while he worked at the European Organization for Nuclear Research (CERN). His goal was to create a platform that particle physicists around the world could use to share electronic documents. The first-ever web site was put online on August 6, 1991, and had the URL

```
http://info.cern.ch/hypertext/WWW/TheProject.html
```

The web quickly got accepted as a collaboration tool among scientists. However, it was not until the development of the Mosaic web browser (at the National Center for Supercomputing Applications at the University of Illinois at Urbana-Champaign) and its successor, Netscape, that its use among the general public exploded. The web has grown a lot since then. In late 2010, Google recorded a total of about 18 billion unique web pages hosted by servers in 239 countries.

The WWW Consortium (W3C), founded and headed by Berners-Lee, is the international organization that is in charge of developing and defining the WWW standards. Its membership includes information technology companies, nonprofit organizations, universities, governmental entities, and individuals from across the world.

"Plumbing" of the WWW

In order to write application programs that use resources on the web, we need to know more about the technologies that the web relies on. Before we go over them, let's understand what component of the web they implement.

In order to request a resource on the web, there must be a way to identify it. In other words, every resource on the web must have a unique name. Furthermore, there must be a way to locate the resource (i.e., find out which computer on the Internet hosts the resource). Therefore, the web must have a *naming* and *locator* scheme that allows a web client to identify and locate resources.

Once a resource is located, there needs to be a way to request the resource. Sending a message like "Hey dude, get me that mp3!" is just not going to fly. The client and server programs must communicate using an agreed-upon *protocol* that specifies precisely how the web client and the web server are supposed to format the request message and the reply message, respectively.

Web pages are a critical resource on the web. They contain formatted information and data and also hyperlinks that enable web surfing. In order to specify the format of a web page and incorporate hyperlinks into it, there needs to be a *language* that supports formatting instructions and hyperlink definitions.

These three components—the naming scheme, the protocol, and the web publishing language—were all developed by Berners-Lee and are the technologies that really define the WWW.

Naming Scheme: Uniform Resource Locator

In order to identify and access a resource on the web, each resource must have a unique identifier. The identifier is called the *Uniform Resource Locator* (URL). The URL not only uniquely identifies a resource but also specifies how to access it, just as a person's address can be used to find the person. For example, the mission statement of the W3C is hosted on the consortium's web site, and its URL is the string

```
http://www.w3.org/Consortium/mission.html
```

This string uniquely identifies the web resource that is the W3C mission document. It also specifies the way to access it, as illustrated in Figure 11.1.

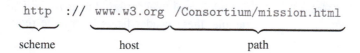

Figure 11.1 Anatomy of a URL. A URL specifies the scheme, the host, and the pathname of the resource.

The *scheme* specifies how to access the resource. In Figure 11.1, the scheme is the HTTP protocol that we will discuss shortly. The `host` (`www.w3c.org`) specifies the name of the server hosting the document, which is unique to each server. The *path* is the relative pathname (see the definition in Section 4.3) of the document relative to a special directory at the server called the *web server root directory*. In Figure 11.1, the path is (`/Consortium/mission.html`).

Note that the HTTP protocol is just one of many schemes that a URL may specify. Other schemes include the HTTPS protocol, which is the secure (i.e., encrypted) version of HTTP, and the FTP protocol, which is the standard protocol for transferring files over the Internet:

```
https://webmail.cdm.depaul.edu/
ftp://ftp.server.net/
```

Other examples include the `mailto` and `file` schemes, as in

```
mailto:lperkovic@cs.depaul.edu
file:///Users/lperkovic/
```

The `mailto` scheme opens an email client, such as Microsoft Outlook, to write an email (to me in the example). The `file` scheme is used to access folders or files in the local file system (such as my home directory /Users/lperkovic/).

Protocol: HyperText Transfer Protocol

A web server is a computer program that serves web resources it hosts upon request. A web client is a computer program that makes such a request (e.g., your browser). The client makes the request by first opening a network connection to the server (not unlike opening a file for reading and/or writing) and then sending a *request message* to the server through the network connection (equivalent to writing to a file). If the requested content is hosted at the server, the client will eventually receive—from the server and through the network connection—a *response message* that contains the requested content (equivalent to reading from a file).

Once the network connection is established, the communication schedule between the client and the server as well as the precise format of the request and response messages is specified by the *HyperText Transfer Protocol (HTTP)*.

Suppose, for example, that you use your web browser to download the W3C mission statement with URL:

```
http://www.w3.org/Consortium/mission.html
```

The request message your web browser will send to the host `www.w3.org` will start with this line:

```
GET /Consortium/mission.html HTTP/1.1
```

The first line of the request message is referred to as the *request line*. The request line must start with one of the *HTTP methods*. The method GET is one of the HTTP methods and is the usual way that a resource is requested. Following it is the path embedded in the resource's URL; this path specifies the identity *and* location of the requested resource relative to the web server's root directory. The version of the HTTP protocol used ends the request line.

The request message may contain additional lines, referred to as *request header fields*, following the request line. For example, these header fields follow the request line just shown:

```
Host: www.w3.org
User-Agent: Mozilla/5.0 (Windows; U; Windows NT 6.1; en-US; ...
Accept: text/html,application/xhtml+xml,application/xml;...
Accept-Language: en-us,en;q=0.5

...
```

The request header fields give the client a way to provide more information about the request to the server, including the character encoding and the languages (such as English) that the browser accepts, caching information, and so on.

When the web server receives this request, it uses the path that appears in the request line to find the requested document. If successful, it creates a reply message that contains the requested resource.

The first few lines of the reply message are something like:

```
HTTP/1.1 200 OK
Date: Mon, 28 Feb 2011 18:44:55 GMT
Server: Apache/2
Last-Modified: Fri, 25 Feb 2011 04:22:57 GMT
...
```

The first line of this message, called the *response line*, indicates that the request was successful; if it were not, an error message would appear. The remaining lines, called the *response header fields*, provide additional information to the client, such as the exact time when the server serviced the request, the time when the requested resource was last modified, the "brand" of the server program, the character encoding of the requested resource, and others.

Following the header fields is the requested resource, which in our example is an HTML document (describing the mission of the W3 Consortium). If the client receiving this response is a web browser, it will compute the layout of the document using the HTML codes and display the formatted, interactive document in the browser.

HyperText Markup Language

The W3C mission document `mission.html` downloaded when pointing the browser to the URL

```
http://www.w3.org/Consortium/mission.html
```

looks like a typical web page *when viewed in the browser*. It has headings, paragraphs, lists, links, pictures, all nicely arranged to make the "content" readable. However, if you look at the *actual content* of the text file `mission.html`, you will see this:

```
<!DOCTYPE html PUBLIC "-//W3C//DTD XHTML 1.0 Strict//EN" ...
<html xmlns="http://www.w3.org/1999/xhtml" xml:lang="en" ...
...
<script type="text/javascript" src="/2008/site/js/main" ...
</div></body></html>
```

(Only the beginning and the end of the file are shown.)

DETOUR

Viewing the Web Page Source File

You may view the actual content of the file that is displayed in your browser by clicking, for example, on menu [View] and then item [Page Source] in Firefox or on menu [Page] and then item [View Source] in Internet Explorer.

The file `mission.html` is the *source file* for the displayed web page. A web page source file is written using a publishing language called the *HyperText Markup Language* (HTML). This language is used to define the headings, lists, images, and hyperlinks of a web page and incorporate video and other multimedia into it.

HTML Elements

An HTML source file is composed of HTML *elements*. Each element defines one component (such as a heading, a list or list item, an image, or a link) of the associated web page. In order to see how elements are defined in an HTML source file, we consider the web page shown in Figure 11.2. It is a basic web page summarizing the W3C mission.

Figure 11.2 Web page w3c.html. A web page is composed of different types of HTML elements. Elements h1 and h2 specify the largest and second largest heading, p is the paragraph element, br is the line break element, ul is the list element, li is the list item element, and a is the anchor element, which is used to specify a hyperlink.

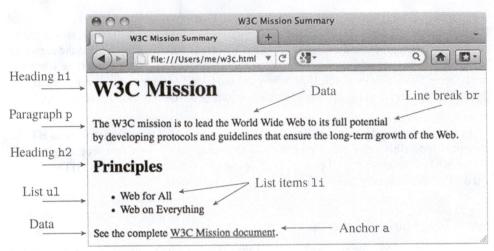

Indicated in the figure are web page components (headings of different size, a paragraph, a list, etc.) that correspond to the different elements of the document; what we actually see are the elements *after* they have been interpreted by the browser. The actual element definitions are in the web page source file:

File: w3c.html

```
1    <html>
2    <head><title>W3C Mission Summary</title></head>
3    <body>
4    <h1>W3C Mission</h1>
5    <p>
6    The W3C mission is to lead the World Wide Web to its full
7    potential<br>by developing protocols and guidelines that
8    ensure the long-term growth of the Web.
9    </p>
10   <h2>Principles</h2>
11   <ul>
12   <li>Web for All</li>
13   <li>Web on Everything</li>
14   </ul>
15   See the complete
16   <a href="http://www.w3.org/Consortium/mission.html">
17   W3C Mission document
18   </a>.
19   </body>
20   </html>
```

Consider the HTML element corresponding to heading "W3C Mission":

<h1>W3C Mission</h1>

This is a large heading element named h1. It is described using the *start tag* <h1> and the *end tag* `</h1>`. The text contained in between will be represented as a large heading by the browser. Note that the start and end tags contain the element name and are always delimited with < and > brackets; the end tag has a backslash as well.

In general, an HTML element consists of three components:

1. A pair of tags: the start tag and the end tag
2. Optional attributes within the start tag
3. Other elements or data between the start and end tag

In HTML source file `w3c.html`, there is an example of an element (`title`) contained inside another element (`head`):

```
<head><title>W3C Mission Summary</title></head>
```

Any element that appears between the start and end tag of another element is said to be contained in it. This containment relation gives rise to a treelike hierarchical structure between the elements of an HTML document.

Tree Structure of an HTML Document

The elements in an HTML document form a tree hierarchy similar to the tree hierarchy of a filesystem (see Chapter 4). The root element of every HTML document must be element `html`. Element `html` contains two elements (each optional but usually present). The first is element `head`, which contains document metadata information, such as a `title` element (which typically contains text data that is shown on top of the browser window when viewing the document). The second element is body, which contains all the elements and data that will be displayed within the browser window.

Figure 11.3 shows all the elements in file `w3c.html`. The figure makes explicit what element is contained in another and the resulting tree structure of the document. This tree structure and the HTML elements together determine the layout of the web page.

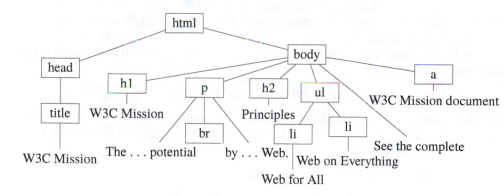

Figure 11.3 Structure of `w3c.html`. The elements of an HTML document form a hierarchical tree structure that specifies how the content is organized; the elements and the hierarchical structure are used by the browser to produce the web page layout.

Anchor HTML Element and Absolute Links

The HTML anchor element (a) is used to create hyperlinked text. In source file `w3c.html`, we create hyperlinked text in this way:

```
<a href="http://www.w3.org/Consortium/mission.html">
 W3C Mission document
</a>
```

This is an example of an HTML element with an *attribute*. As we said at the beginning of this section, the start tag of an element may contain one or more attributes. Each attribute is assigned a *value* in the start tag. The anchor element a requires attribute `href` to be present in the start tag; the *value* of the `href` attribute should be the URL of the linked resource. In our example, that is

```
http://www.w3.org/Consortium/mission.html
```

This URL identifies the web page containing the mission statement of the W3C and hosted on the server `www.w3.org`. The linked resource can be anything that can be identified with a URL: an HTML page, an image, a sound file, a movie, and so on.

The text contained in the anchor element (e.g., the text `W3C Mission document`) is the text displayed in the browser, in whatever format the browser uses to display hyperlinks. In Figure 11.2, the hyperlinked text is shown underlined. When the hyperlinked text is clicked, the linked resource is downloaded and displayed in the browser.

In our example, the URL specified in the hyperlink is an *absolute URL*, which means that it explicitly specifies all the components of a URL: the scheme, the host, and the complete path of the linked resource. In cases when the linked resource is accessible using the same scheme *and* is stored on the same host as the HTML document containing the link, a shortened version of the URL can be used, as we discuss next.

Relative Links

Suppose that you look at the source file of the web page with URL

```
http://www.w3.org/Consortium/mission.html
```

and find the anchor element

```
<a href="/Consortium/facts.html">Facts About W3C</a>
```

Note that the value of attribute `href` is not a complete URL; it is missing the scheme and host specification, and only has the path `/Consortium/facts.html`. What is the complete URL of the `facts.html` document?

The URL `/Consortium/facts.html` is a *relative URL*. Because it is contained in the document with URL

```
http://www.w3.org/Consortium/mission.html
```

the URL `/Consortium/facts.html` is relative to it, and the missing scheme and host-name are just `http` and `www.w3.org`. In other words, the complete URL of web page `/Consortium/facts.html` is:

```
http://www.w3.org/Consortium/facts.html
```

Here is another example. Suppose that the document with URL

```
http://www.w3.org/Consortium/mission.html
```

contains anchor

```
<a href="facts.html">Facts About W3C</a>
```

What is the complete URL of `facts.html`? Again, relative URL `facts.html` is relative to the URL of the document containing it, which is:

```
http://www.w3.org/Consortium/mission.html
```

In other words, `facts.html` is contained in directory `Consortium` on host `www.w3.org`. Therefore, its complete URL is

```
http://www.w3.org/Consortium/facts.html
```

DETOUR

> ### Learning More about HTML
>
> Web development and HTML is not a focus of this textbook. If you want to learn more about HTML, there are excellent free resources on the web, in particular the HTML tutorial at
>
> > `http://www.w3schools.com/html/default.asp`
>
> This tutorial also includes an interactive HTML editor that allows you to write HTML code and view the result.

11.2 Python WWW API

In the previous two sections, we went over basic WWW concepts and covered the three key technologies that make up the "plumbing" of the web. We have gained a basic understanding of how the web works and the structure of an HTML source file. Now we can use the web in our Python application programs. In this section we introduce a few of the Standard Library modules that allow Python developers to access and process resources on the web.

Module `urllib.request`

We typically use browsers to access web pages on the web. A browser is just one type of web client, however; any program can act as a web client and access and download resources on the web. In Python, the Standard Library module `urllib.request` gives developers this capability. The module contains functions and classes that allow Python programs to open and read resources on the web in a way similar to how files are opened and read.

The function `urlopen()` in module `urlib.request` is similar to the built-in function `open()` that is used to open (local) files. There are three differences however:

1. `urlopen()` takes as input a URL rather than a local file pathname.
2. It results in an HTTP request being sent to the web server hosting the content.
3. It returns a complete HTTP response.

In the next example, we use function `urlopen()` to request and receive an HTML document hosted at a server on the web:

```
>>> from urllib.request import urlopen
>>> response = urlopen('http://www.w3c.org/Consortium/facts.html')
>>> type(response)
<class 'http.client.HTTPResponse'>
```

The object returned by function `urlopen()` is of type `HTTPResponse`, which is a type defined in Standard Library module `http.client`. Objects of this type encapsulate the HTTP response from the server. As we saw earlier, the HTTP response includes the requested resource but also additional information. For example, the `HTTPResponse` method `geturl()`

returns the URL of the requested resource:

```
>>> response.geturl()
'http://www.w3.org/Consortium/facts.html'
```

To obtain all the HTTP response header fields, you can use method `getheaders()`:

```
>>> for field in response.getheaders():
        print(field)

('Date', 'Sat, 16 Jul 2011 03:40:17 GMT')
('Server', 'Apache/2')
('Last-Modified', 'Fri, 06 May 2011 01:59:40 GMT')
...
('Content-Type', 'text/html; charset=utf-8')
```

(Some header fields are omitted.)

The `HTTPResponse` object returned by `urlopen` contains the requested resource. The `HTTPResponse` class is said to be a *filelike* class because it supports methods `read()`, `readline()`, and `readlines()`, the same methods supported by the types of objects returned by the file-opening function `open()`. All these methods retrieve the content of the requested resource. For example, let's use the method `read()`:

```
>>> html = response.read()
>>> type(html)
<class 'bytes'>
```

The method `read()` will return the content of the resource. If the file is an HTML document, for example, then its content is returned. Note, however, that method `read()` returns an object of type `bytes`. This is because resources opened by `urlopen()` could very well be audio or video files (i.e., binary files). The default behavior for `urlopen()` is to assume that the resource is a binary file and, when this file is read, a sequence of bytes is returned.

If the resource happens to be an HTML file (i.e., a text file), it makes sense to decode the sequence of bytes into the Unicode characters they represent. We use the `decode()` method of the `bytes` class (and covered in Section 6.3) to achieve this:

```
>>> html = html.decode()
>>> html
'<!DOCTYPE html PUBLIC "-//W3C//DTD XHTML 1.0 Strict//EN"
"http://www.w3.org/TR/xhtml1/DTD/xhtml1-strict.dtd">\n
...
    </div></body></html>\n'
```

(Many lines are omitted.) Decoding an HTML document into a Unicode string makes sense because an HTML document is a text file. Once decoded into a string, we can use string operators and methods to process the document. For example, we can now find out the number of times string `'Web'` appears in (the source file of) web page

```
http://www.w3c.org/Consortium/facts.html
```

Here it is:

```
>>> html.count('Web')
26
```

With all we have learned so far, we can write a function that takes a URL of a web page as input and returns the content of the web page source file as a string:

Module: ch11.py

```
1  from urllib.request import urlopen
2  def getSource(url):
3      'returns the content of resource specified by url as a string'
4      response = urlopen(url)
5      html = response.read()
6      return html.decode()
```

Let's test it on Google web page:

```
>>> getSource('http://www.google.com')
'<!doctype html><html><head><meta http-equiv="content-type"
content="text/html; charset=ISO-8859-1"><meta name="description"
content="Search the world&#39;s information, including webpages,
...
```

Write method `news()` that takes a URL of a news web site and a list of news topics (i.e., strings) and computes the number of occurrences of each topic in the news.

```
>>> news('http://bbc.co.uk',['economy','climate','education'])
economy appears 3 times.
climate appears 3 times.
education appears 1 times.
```

Practice Problem 11.1

Module `html.parser`

Module `urllib.request` provides tools to request and download resources such as web pages from the web. If the downloaded resource is an HTML file, we can read it into a string and process it using string operators and methods. That may be sufficient to answer some questions about the web page content, but what about, for example, picking up all the URLs associated with anchor tags in the web page?

If you take a moment and think about it, it would be quite messy to use string operators and methods to find all the anchor tag URLs in an HTML file. Yet it is clear what needs to be done: Go through the file and pick up the value of the `href` attribute in every anchor start tag. To do this, however, we need a way to recognize the different elements of the HTML file (the title, headings, links, images, text data, etc.), in particular the anchor element start tags. The process of analyzing a document in order to break it into components and obtain its structure is called *parsing*.

The Python Standard Library module `html.parser` provides a class, `HTMLParser`, that parses HTML files. When it is *fed* an HTML file, it will process it from beginning to end, find all the start tags, end tags, text data, and other components of the source file, and "process" each one of them.

To illustrate the usage of a `HTMLParser` object and describe what "process" means, we use the HTML file `w3c.html` from Section 11.1.

Recall that file `w3c.html` starts with:

```
<html>
 <head><title>W3C Mission Summary</title></head>
 <body>
  <h1>W3C Mission</h1>
...
```

The `HMLPParser` class supports method `feed()` that takes, as input, the content of an HTML source file, in string form. Therefore, to parse file `w3c.html`, we first need to read it into a string and then feed it to the parser:

```
>>> infile = open('w3c.html')
>>> content = infile.read()
>>> infile.close()
>>> from html.parser import HTMLParser
>>> parser = HTMLParser()
>>> parser.feed(content)
```

When the last line is executed (i.e., when string `content` is fed to `parser`), this happens behind the scenes: The parser divides the string `content` into *tokens* that correspond to HTML start tags, end tags, text data, and other HTML components, and then *handles* the tokens in the order in which they appear in the source file. What this means is that for each token, an appropriate *handler* method is invoked. The handlers are methods of class `HTMLParser`. Some of them are listed in Table 11.1.

Table 11.1 Some HTMLParser handlers. These methods do nothing when invoked; they need to be overridden to produce the desired behavior.

Token	Handler	Explanation
`<tag attrs>`	`handle_starttag(tag, attrs)`	Start tag handler
`</tag>`	`handle_endtag(tag)`	End tag handler
`data`	`handle_data(data)`	Arbitrary text data handler

When the parser encounters a start tag token, handler method `handle_starttag()` is invoked; if the parser encounters a text data token, handler method `handle_data()` is invoked. Method `handle_starttag()` takes, as input, the start tag element name and a list containing the tag's attributes (or `None` if the tag contains no attributes). Each attribute is represented by a `tuple` storing the name and value of the attribute. Method `handle_data()` takes just the text token as input. Figure 11.4 illustrates the parsing of file `w3c.html`.

Figure 11.4 Parsing HTML file `w3c.html`. Tokens are handled in the order they appear. The first token, start tag `<html>`, is handled by `handle_starttag()`. The next token is the string between tags `<http>` and `<head>` consisting of a new line character and a blank space; considered text data, it is handled by `handle_data()`.

Token		Handler
`<http>`	→	`handle_starttag('http')`
`' '`	→	`handle_data('\n ')`
`<head>`	→	`handle_starttag('head')`
`' '`	→	`handle_data('')`
`<title>`	→	`handle_starttag('title')`
`'W3C Mission Summary'`	→	`handle_data('W3CMission Summary')`
`</title>`	→	`handle_endtag('title')`

What do the `HTMLParser` class handler methods (like `handle_starttag()`) really do? Well, nothing. The handler methods of class `HTMLParser` are implemented to do nothing when called. That is why nothing interesting happened when we executed:

```
>>> parser.feed(content)
```

The `HTMLParser` class handler methods are really meant to be overridden by user-defined handlers that implement the behavior desired by the programmer. In other words, class `HTMLParser` is not supposed to be used directly but rather as a super class from which the developer derives a parser that exhibits the parsing behavior desired by the programmer.

Overriding the `HTMLParser` Handlers

Let's develop a parser that prints the URL value of the `href` attribute contained in every anchor start tag of the fed HTML file. To achieve this behavior, the `HTMLParser` handler that needs to be overridden is method `handle_starttag()`. Recall that this method handles every start tag token. Instead of doing nothing, we want it now to check whether the input tag is an anchor tag and, if so, find the `href` attribute in the list of attributes and print its value. Here is the implementation of our `LinkParser` class:

Module: ch11.py

```
1  from html.parser import HTMLParser
2  class LinkParser(HTMLParser):
3      '''HTML doc parser that prints values of
4         href attributes in anchor start tags'''
5
6      def handle_starttag(self, tag, attrs):
7          'print value of href attribute if any'
8
9          if tag == 'a':                          # if anchor tag
10
11             # search for href attribute and print its value
12             for attr in attrs:
13                 if attr[0] == 'href':
14                     print(attr[1])
```

Note how, in lines 12 to 14, we search through the list of attributes to find the attribute `href`. Let's test our parser on this HTML file:

File: links.html

```
1   <html>
2   <body>
3   <h4>Absolute HTTP link</h4>
4   <a href="http://www.google.com">Absolute link to Google</a>
5   <h4>Relative HTTP link</h4>
6   <a href="w3c.html">Relative link to w3c.html.</a>
7   <h4>mailto scheme</h4>
8   <a href="mailto:me@example.net">Click here to email me.</a>
9   </body>
10  </html>
```

There are three anchor tags in the HTML file `links.html`: the first contains URL that is a hyperlink to Google, the second contains a URL that is a link to local file `w3c.html`, and the third contains a URL that actually starts the mail client. In the next code, we feed the file to our parser and obtain the three URLs:

```
>>> infile = open('links.html')
>>> content = infile.read()
>>> infile.close()
>>> linkparser = LinkParser()
>>> linkparser.feed(content)
http://www.google.com
test.html
mailto:me@example.net
```

Practice Problem 11.2

Develop class `MyHTMLParser` as a subclass of `HTMLParser` that, when fed an HTML file, prints the names of the start and end tags in the order that they appear in the document, and with an indentation that is proportional to the element's depth in the tree structure of the document. Ignore HTML elements that do not require an end tag, such as p and br .

File: w3c.html

```
>>> infile = open('w3c.html')
>>> content = infile.read()
>>> infile.close()
>>> myparser = MyHTMLParser()
>>> myparser.feed(content)
html start
    head start
        title start
        title end
    head end
    body start
        h1 start
        h1 end
        h2 start
        h2 end
        ul start
            li start
...
        a end
    body end
html end
```

Module `urllib.parse`

The parser `LinkParser` we just developed prints the URL value of *every* anchor `href` attribute. For example, when we run the following code on the W3C mission web page

```
>>> rsrce = urlopen('http://www.w3.org/Consortium/mission.html')
>>> content = rsrce.read().decode()
>>> linkparser = LinkParser()
>>> linkparser.feed(content)
```

we get an output that includes relative HTTP URLs like

```
/Consortium/contact.html
```

absolute HTTP URLs such as

```
http://twitter.com/W3C
```

and also non-HTTP URLs like

```
mailto:site-comments@w3.org
```

(We omit many lines of output.)

What if we are only interested in collecting the URLs that correspond to HTTP hyperlinks (i.e., URLs whose scheme is the HTTP protocol)? Note that we cannot just say "collect those URLs that start with string `http`" because then we would miss the relative URLs, such as `/Consortium/contact.html`. What we need is a way to construct an absolute URL from a relative URL (like `/Consortium/contact.html`) and the URL of the web page containing it (`http://www.w3.org/Consortium/mission.html`).

The Python Standard Library module `urllib.parse` provides a few methods that operate on URLs, including one that does exactly what we want, method `urljoin()`. Here is an example usage:

```
>>> from urllib.parse import urljoin
>>> url = 'http://www.w3.org/Consortium/mission.html'
>>> relative = '/Consortium/contact.html'
>>> urljoin(url, relative)
'http://www.w3.org/Consortium/contact.html'
```

Parser That Collects HTTP Hyperlinks

We now develop another version of the `LinkParser` class that we call `Collector`. It collects only HTTP URLs and, instead of printing them out, it puts them into a list. The URLs in the list will be in their absolute, rather than relative, format. Finally, the class `Collector` should also support method `getLinks()` that returns this list.

Here is a sample usage we expect from a `Collector` parser:

```
>>> url = 'http://www.w3.org/Consortium/mission.html'
>>> resource = urlopen(url)
>>> content = resource.read().decode()
>>> collector = Collector(url)
>>> collector.feed(content)
>>> for link in collector.getLinks():
        print(link)

http://www.w3.org/
http://www.w3.org/standards/
...
http://www.w3.org/Consortium/Legal/ipr-notice
```

(Again, many lines of output, all absolute URLs, are omitted.)

To implement `Collector`, we again need to override `handle_starttag()`. Instead of simply printing the value of the `href` attribute contained in the start tag, if any, the handler must process the attribute value so that that only absolute HTTP URLs are collected.

Therefore, the handler needs to do this with every `href` value it handles:

1. Transform the `href` value to an absolute URL.
2. Append it to a list if it is an HTTP URL.

To do the first step, the URL of the fed HTML file must be available to the handler. Therefore, an instance variable of the `Collector` parser object must store the URL. This URL must somehow be passed to the `Collector` object; we choose to pass the URL as an input argument of the `Collector` constructor.

For the second step, we need to have a `list` instance variable to store all the URLs. The list should be initialized in the constructor. Here is the complete implementation:

Module: ch11.py

```
1   from urllib.parse import urljoin
2   from html.parser import HTMLParser
3   class Collector(HTMLParser):
4       'collects hyperlink URLs into a list'
5
6       def __init__(self, url):
7           'initializes parser, the url, and a list'
8           HTMLParser.__init__(self)
9           self.url = url
10          self.links = []
11
12      def handle_starttag(self, tag, attrs):
13          'collect hyperlink URLs in their absolute format'
14          if tag == 'a':
15              for attr in attrs:
16                  if attr[0] == 'href':
17                      # construct absolute URL
18                      absolute = urljoin(self.url, attr[1])
19                      if absolute[:4] == 'http': # collect HTTP URLs
20                          self.links.append(absolute)
21
22      def getLinks(self):
23          'returns hyperlinks URLs in their absolute format'
24          return self.links
```

Practice Problem 11.3

Augment class `Collector` so that it also collects all the text data into a string that can be retrieved using method `getData()`.

```
>>> url = 'http://www.w3.org/Consortium/mission.html'
>>> resource = urlopen(url)
>>> content = resource.read().decode()
>>> collector = LinksCollector(url)
>>> collector.feed(content)
>>> collector.getData()
'\nW3C Mission\n  ...'
```

(Only the first few characters are shown.)

11.3 String Pattern Matching

Suppose we would like to develop an application that analyzes the content of a web page, or any other text file, and looks for all email addresses in the page. The string method `find()` can find only *specific* email addresses; it is not the right tool for finding all the substrings that "look like email addresses" or fit the pattern of an email address.

In order to mine the text content of a web page or other text document, we need tools that help us define text patterns and then search for strings in the text that match these text patterns. In this section, we introduce *regular expressions*, which are used to describe string patterns. We also introduce Python tools that find strings in a text that match a given string pattern.

Regular Expressions

How do we recognize email addresses in a text document? We usually do not find this very difficult. We understand that an email address follows a string pattern:

> An email address consists of a user ID—that is, a sequence of "allowed" characters— followed by the @ symbol followed by a hostname—that is, a dot-separated sequence of allowed characters.

While this informal description of the string pattern of an email address may work for us, it is not nearly precise enough to use in a program.

Computer scientists have developed a more formal way to describe a string pattern: a *regular expression*. A regular expression is a string that consists of characters and *regular expression operators*. We will now learn a few of these operators and how they enable us to precisely define the desired string pattern.

The simplest regular expression is one that doesn't use any regular expression operators. For example, the regular expression `best` matches only one string, the string `'best'`:

Regular Expression	Matching String(s)
best	best

The operator `.` (the dot) has the role of a wildcard character: It matches any (Unicode) character except the new line character (`'\n'`). Therefore `'be.t'` matches `best`, but also `'belt'`, `'beet'`, `'be3t'`, and `'be!t'`, among others:

Regular Expression	Matching String(s)
be.t	best, belt, beet, bezt, be3t, be!t, be t, ...

Note that regular expression `be.t` does not match string `'bet'` because operator `'.'` must match some character.

Regular expression operators `*`, `+`, and `?` match a particular number of repetitions of the previous character (or regular expression). For example, the operator `*` in regular expression `be*t` matches *0 or more* repetitions of the previous character (e). It therefore matches `bt` and also `bet`, `beet`, and so on:

Regular Expressions	Matching String(s)
be*t	bt, bet, beet, beeet, beeeet, ...
be+t	bet, beet, beeet, beeeet, ...
bee?t	bet, beet

The last example also illustrates that operator `+` matches *1 or more* repetitions, whereas `?` matches *0 or 1* repetition of the previous character (or regular expression).

The operator [] matches any one character listed within the square brackets: For example, regular expression [abc] matches strings a, b, and c and no other string. The operator -, when used within the operator [], specifies a range of characters. This range is specified by the Unicode character ordering. So regular expression [l-o] matches strings l, m, n, and o:

Regular Expressions	Matching String(s)
be[ls]t	belt, best
be[l-o]t	belt, bemt, bent, beot
be[a-cx-z]t	beat, bebt, bect, bext, beyt, bezt

In order to match a set of characters *not* in the range or not in a specified set, the caret character ^ is used. For example, [^0-9] matches any character that is not a digit:

Regular Expressions	Matching String(s)
be[^0-9]t	belt, best, be#t, . . . (but not be4t).
be[^xyz]t	belt, be5t, . . . (but not bext, beyt, and bezt).
be[^a-zA-Z]t	be!t, be5t, be t, . . . (but not beat).

The operator | is an "or" operator: If A and B are two regular expressions, then regular expression A|B matches any string that is matched by A or by B. For example, regular expression hello|Hello matches strings 'hello' and 'Hello':

Regular Expressions	Matching String(s)
hello|Hello	hello, Hello.
a+|b+	a, b, aa, bb, aaa, bbb, aaaa, bbbb, . . .
ab+|ba+	ab, abb, abbb, . . . , and ba, baa, baaa, . . .

The description of operators we just described is summarized in Table 11.2.

DETOUR

Additional Regular Expression Operators

Python supports many more regular expression operators; we have only scratched the surface in this section. To learn more about them, read the extensive documentation available online at:

    http://docs.python.org/py3k/howto/regex.html
and
    http://docs.python.org/py3k/library/re.html

Practice Problem 11.4

Each of the listed cases gives a regular expression and a set of strings. Select those strings that are matched by the regular expression.

Regular Expression	Strings
(a) [Hh]ello	ello, Hello, hello
(b) re-?sign	re-sign, resign, re-?sign
(c) [a-z]*	aaa, Hello, F16, IBM, best
(d) [^a-z]*	aaa, Hello, F16, IBM, best
(e) <.*>	<h1>, 2 < 3, <<>>>>, ><

Operator	Interpretation
.	Matches any character except a new line character.
*	Matches 0 or more repetitions of the regular expression immediately preceding it. So in regular expression ab*, operator * matches 0 or more repetitions of b, not ab.
+	Matches 1 or more repetitions of the regular expression immediately preceding it.
?	Matches 0 or 1 repetitions of the regular expression immediately preceding it.
[]	Matches any character in the set of characters listed within the square brackets; a range of characters can be specified using the first and last character in the range and putting '-' in between.
^	If S is a set or range of characters, then [^S] matches any character *not* in S.
|	If A and B are regular expressions, A|B matches any string that is matched by A or B.

Table 11.2 Some regular expression operator. Operators ., *, +, and ? apply to the regular expression preceding the operator. Operator \| is applied to the regular expression to the left and right of the operator.

Because operators *, ., and [have special meaning inside regular expressions, they cannot be used to match characters '*', '.', or '['. In order to match characters with special meaning, the escape sequence \ must be used. So, for example, regular expression *\[would match string '*['. In addition to serving as an escape sequence identifier, the backslash \ may also signal a *regular expression special sequence*. Regular expression special sequences represent predefined sets of characters that are commonly used together. Table 11.3 lists some of the regular expression special sequences.

Special Sequence	Set of Characters
\d	Matches any decimal digit; equivalent to [0-9]
\D	Matches any nondigit character; equivalent to [^0-9]
\s	Matches any whitespace character including the blank space, the tab \t, the new line \n, and the carriage return \r
\S	Matches any non-whitespace character
\w	Matches any alphanumeric character; this is equivalent to [a-zA-Z0-9_]
\W	Matches any nonalphanumeric character; this is equivalent to [^a-zA-Z0-9_]

Table 11.3 Some special regular expression sequences. Note that the listed escape sequences are to be used in regular expressions only; they should not be used in an arbitrary string.

For each of the listed informal pattern descriptions or sets of strings, define a regular expression that fits the pattern description or matches all the strings in the set and no other.

(a) aac, abc, acc

(b) abc, xyz

(c) a, ab, abb, abbb, abbbb, ...

(d) Nonempty strings consisting of lowercase letters in the alphabet (a, b, c, . . . , z)

(e) Strings containing substring oe

(f) String representing and HTML start or end tag

Practice Problem 11.5

Python Standard Library Module `re`

The module `re` in the Standard Library is Python's tool for regular expression processing. One of the methods defined in the module is method `findall()` that takes two inputs, a regular expression and a string, and returns a list of all substrings of the input string that the regular expression matches. Here are some examples:

```
>>> from re import findall
>>> findall('best', 'beetbtbelt?bet, best')
['best']
>>> findall('be.t', 'beetbtbelt?bet, best')
['beet', 'belt', 'best']
>>> findall('be?t', 'beetbtbelt?bet, best')
['bt', 'bet']
>>> findall('be*t', 'beetbtbelt?bet, best')
['beet', 'bt', 'bet']
>>> findall('be+t', 'beetbtbelt?bet, best')
['beet', 'bet']
```

If the regular expression matches two substrings such that one is contained in the other, the function `findall()` will match the longer substring only. For example, in

```
>>> findall('e+', 'beeeetbet bt')
['eeee', 'e']
```

the returned list does not contain substrings `'ee'` and `'eee'`. If the regular expression matches two overlapping substrings, the function `findall()` returns the left one. The function `findall()` in fact scans the input string from left to right and collects matches into a list in the order found. You can verify this when running:

```
>>> findall('[^bt]+', 'beetbtbelt?bet, best')
['ee', 'el', '?', 'e', ', ', 'es']
```

Here is another example:

```
>>> findall('[bt]+', 'beetbtbelt?bet, best')
['b', 'tbtb', 't', 'b', 't', 'b', 't']
```

CAUTION

Empty Strings Are Everywhere

Compare the last example with this one:

```
>>> findall('[bt]*', 'beetbtbelt?bet, best')
['b', '', '', 'tbtb', '', '', 't', '', 'b', '', 't', '', '',
 'b', '', '', 't', '']
```

Because regular expression `[bt]*` matches the empty string `''`, the function `findall()` looks for empty substrings in the input string `'beetbtbelt?bet, best'` that are not contained in a larger matching substring. It finds many empty strings, one before every character that is not b or t. That includes the empty substring between the first b and the first e, the empty substring between the first and second e, and so on.

Develop function `frequency()` that takes a string as input, computes the frequency of every word in the string, and returns a dictionary that maps words in the string to their frequency. You should use a regular expression to obtain the list of all words in the string.

Practice Problem
11.6

```
>>> content = 'The pure and simple truth is rarely pure and never\
        simple.'
>>> frequency(content)
{'and': 2, 'pure': 2, 'simple': 2, 'is': 1, 'never': 1,
 'truth': 1, 'The': 1, 'rarely': 1}
```

Another useful function defined in module `re` is `search()`. It also takes a regular expression and a string; it returns the first substring that is matched by the regular expression. You can think of it as a more powerful version of string method `find()`. Here is an example:

```
>>> from re import search
>>> match = search('e+', 'beetbtbelt?bet')
>>> type(match)
<class '_sre.SRE_Match'>
```

Method `search` returns a reference to an object of type `SRE_Match`, informally referred to as a *match object*. The type supports, for example, methods to find the start and end index of the match in the input string:

```
>>> match.start()
1
>>> match.end()
3
```

The matched substring of `'beetbtbelt?bet'` starts at index 1 and ends before index 3. Match objects also have an attribute variable called `string` that stores the searched string:

```
>>> match.string
'beetbtbelt?bet, best'
```

To find the matched substring, we need to get the slice of `match.string` from index `match.start()` to index `match.end()`:

```
>>> match.string[match.start():match.end()]
'ee'
```

E-Book Case Study: Web Crawler

In this case study, we apply recursion and what we have learned in this chapter to develop a basic *web crawler*, that is, a program that systematically visits web pages by following hyperlinks. A web crawler works by following a hyperlink and downloading the associated web page, parsing its content, collecting content data, and then recursively repeating this for every hyperlink contained in the web page. The recursive algorithm used by the crawler is an example of of depth-first search, a fundamental search algorithm.

Chapter Summary

In this chapter, we introduced the development of computer applications that search and collect data from documents near and far. We focused in particular on accessing, searching, and collecting data hosted on the World Wide Web.

The web is certainly one of the most important applications running on the Internet today. In the last 20 years, the web has revolutionized the way we work, shop, socialize, and get entertainment. It enables communication and the sharing of information on an unprecedented scale and has become an enormous repository of data. This data, in turn, provides an opportunity for the development of new computer applications that collect and process the data and produce valuable information. This chapter introduces the web technologies, the Python Standard Library web APIs, and the algorithms that can be used to to develop such applications,

We introduced the key web technologies: URLs, HTTP, and HTML. We also introduced the Python Standard Library APIs for accessing resources on the web (module `urllib.request`) and for processing web pages (module `html.parser`). We have seen how to use both APIs to download a web page HTML source file and parse it to obtain the web page content.

In order to process the content of a web page or any other text document, it is helpful to have tools that recognize string patterns in texts. This chapter introduces such tools: regular expressions and the Standard Library module `re`.

Solutions to Practice Problems

11.1 Once the HTML document is downloaded and decoded into a string, string methods can be used:

```python
def news(url, topics):
    '''counts in resource with URL url the frequency
       of each topic in list topics'''
    # download and decode resource to obtain all lowercase content
    response = urlopen(url)
    html = response.read()
    content = html.decode().lower()

    for topic in topics: # find frequency of topic in content
        n = content.count(topic)
        print('{} appears {} times.'.format(topic, n))
```

11.2 The methods `handle_starttag()` and `handle_endtag()` need to be overridden. Each should print the name of the element corresponding to the tag, appropriately indented.

The indentation is an integer value that is incremented with every start tag token and decremented with every end tag token. (We ignore elements `p` and `br`.) The indentation value should be stored as an instance variable of the parser object and initialized in the constructor.

Module: ch11.py

```python
1  from html.parser import HTMLParser
2  class MyHTMLParser(HTMLParser):
3      'HTML doc parser that prints tags indented by depth'
4
```

```
5       def __init__(self):
6           'initializes the parser and the initial indentation'
7           HTMLParser.__init__(self)
8           self.indent = 0              # initial indentation value
9
10      def handle_starttag(self, tag, attrs):
11          '''prints start tag with an indentation proportional
12             to the depth of the tag's element in the document'''
13          if tag not in {'br', 'p'}:
14              print('{}{} start'.format(self.indent*' ', tag))
15              self.indent += 4
16
17      def handle_endtag(self, tag):
18          '''prints end tag with an indentation proportional
19             to the depth of the tag's element in the document'''
20          if tag not in {'br', 'p'}:
21              self.indent -= 4
22              print('{}{} end'.format(self.indent*' ', tag))
```

11.3 You should initialize an empty string instance variable `self.text` in the `Collector` constructor. The handler `handle_data()` will then handle the text data token by concatenating it with `self.text`. The code is shown next.

Module: ch11.py

```
1       def handle_data(self, data):
2           'collects and concatenates text data'
3           self.text += data
4
5       def getData(self):
6           'returns the concatenation of all text data'
7           return self.text
```

11.4 The solutions are:
 (a) `Hello`, `hello`
 (b) `'re-sign'`, `'resign'`
 (c) `aaa`, `best`
 (d) `F16`, `IBM`
 (e) `<h1>`, `<<>>>>`

11.5 The solutions are:
 (a) `a[abc]c`
 (b) `abc|xyz`
 (c) `a[b]*`
 (d) `[a-z]+`
 (e) `[a-zA-Z]*oe[a-zA-Z]*`
 (f) `<[^>]*>`

11.6 We already considered this problem in Chapter 6. The solution here uses a regular expression to match words and is cleaner than the original solution.

```
def frequency(content):
    '''returns dictionary containing frequencies
       of words in string content'''
    pattern = '[a-zA-Z]+'
    words = findall(pattern, content)
    dictionary = {}
    for w in words:
        if w in dictionary:
            dictionary[w] +=1
        else:
            dictionary[w] = 1
    return dictionary
```

Exercises

11.7 In each of the next cases, select those strings that are matched by the given regular expression.

Regular Expression	Strings
(a) `[ab]`	ab, a, b, the empty string
(b) `a.b.`	ab, acb, acbc, acbd
(c) `a?b?`	ab, a, b, the empty string
(d) `a*b+a*`	aa, b, aabaa, aaaab, ba
(e) `[^\d]+`	abc, 123, ?.?, 3M

11.8 For each informal pattern description or set of strings below, define a regular expression that fits the pattern description or matches all the strings in the set and no other.

(a) Strings containing an apostrophe (')

(b) Any sequence of three lowercase letters in the alphabet

(c) The string representation of a positive integer

(d) The string representation of a nonnegative integer

(e) The string representation of a negative integer

(f) The string representation of an integer (whether positive or not)

(g) The string representation of a floating-point value using the decimal point notation

11.9 For each informal description listed next, write a regular expression that will match all the strings in file `frankenstein.txt` that match the description. Also find out the answer using the `findall()` function of the module `re`.

File: frankenstein.txt

(a) String 'Frankenstein'

(b) Numbers appearing in the text

(c) Words that end with substring 'ible'

(d) Words that start with an uppercase and end with 'y'

(e) List of strings of the form 'horror of <lowercase string> <lowercase string>'

(f) Expressions consisting of a word followed by the word 'death'

(g) Sentences containing the word 'laboratory'

11.10 Write a regular expression that matches the attribute `href` and its value (found in an HTML start tag) in an HTML source file.

11.11 Write a regular expression that matches strings that represent a price in U.S. dollars. Your expression should match strings such as `'$13.29'` and `'$1,099.29'`, for example. Your expression does not have to match prices beyond $9,999.99.

11.12 Write a regular expression that matches a string that represents a date given in the format DD/MM/YYY (where DD is a 2-digit day in the month, MM is a 2-digit representation of a month, and YYYY is a 4-digit year).

11.13 Write a regular expression that matches an email address. This is not easy so your goal should be to create an expression that matches email addresses as closely as you can.

11.14 Write a regular expression that matches an absolute URL that uses the HTTP protocol. Again, this is tricky, and you should strive for the "best" expression you can.

Problems

11.15 In this book, we have seen three ways to remove punctuation from a string: using string method `replace()` and string method `translate()` in Chapter 4, and using regular expressions in this chapter. Compare the running time of each using the experimental running time analysis framework from Section 10.3.

11.16 HTML supports ordered and unordered lists. An ordered list is defined using element `ol` and each item of the list is defined using element `li`. An unordered list is defined using element `ul` and each item of the list is defined using element `li` as well. For example, the unordered list in file `w3c.html` is described using HTML code:

```
<ul>
 <li>Web for All</li>
 <li>Web on Everything</li>
</ul>
```

File: w3c.html

Develop class `ListCollector` as a subclass of `HTMLParser` that, when fed an HTML file, creates a Python list for every ordered or unordered list in the HTML document. Each item of a Python list should be the text data that appears in one item of the corresponding HTML list. You may assume that every item of every list in the HTML document contains only text data (i.e. no other HTML element). The class `ListCollector` should support method `getLists()` that takes no input arguments but returns a list containing all the created Python lists.

```
>>> infile = open('lists.html')
>>> content = infile.read()
>>> infile.close()
>>> myparser = ListCollector()
>>> myparser.feed(content)
>>> myparser.getLists()
[['An item', 'Another', 'And another one'],
 ['Item one', 'Item two', 'Item three', 'Item four']]
```

File: lists.html

11.17 You would like to produce a unique scary dictionary but have a hard time remembering the thousands of words that should go into a dictionary. Your brilliant idea is to implement function `scary()` that reads in an electronic version of a scary book, say *Frankenstein* by Mary Wollstonecraft Shelley, picks up all the words in it using a regular expression, writes them in alphabetical order in a new file called `dictionary.txt`, and prints them as well. Your function should take the filename (e.g., `frankenstein.txt`) as input. The first few lines in `dictionary.txt` should be:

File: frankenstein.txt

```
a
abandon
abandoned
abbey
abhor
abhorred
abhorrence
abhorrent
...
```

11.18 Implement function `getContent()` that takes as input a URL (as a string) and prints only the text data content of the associated web page (i.e., no tags). Avoid printing blank lines that follow a blank line and strip the whitespace in every line printed.

```
>>> getContent('http://www.nytimes.com/')
The New York Times - Breaking News, World News &amp; Multimedia
Subscribe to The Times

Log In
Register Now

Home Page
...
```

11.19 Write function `emails()` that takes a document (as a string) as input and returns the set of email addresses (i.e., strings) appearing in it. You should use a regular expression to find the email addresses in the document.

```
>>> from urllib.request import urlopen
>>> url = 'http://www.cdm.depaul.edu'
>>> content = urlopen(url).read().decode()
>>> emails(content)
{'advising@cdm.depaul.edu', 'wwwfeedback@cdm.depaul.edu',
 'admission@cdm.depaul.edu', 'webmaster@cdm.depaul.edu'}
```

11.20 Develop an application that implements the web search algorithm we developed in Section 1.4. Your application should take as input a list of web page addresses and a list of target prices of the same size; it should print those web page addresses that correspond to products whose price is less than the target price. Use your solution to Problem 11.11 to find the price in an HTML source file.

11.21 Another useful function in the module `urllib.request` module is the function `urlretrieve()`. It takes as input a URL and a filename (both as strings) and copies the content of the resource identified by the URL into a file named `filename`. Use this function to develop a program that copies all the web pages from a web site, starting from the main web page, to a local folder on your computer.

Databases and Data Processing

12.1 Databases and SQL 400

12.2 Database Programming in Python 410

12.3 Functional Language Approach 415

12.4 Parallel Computing 423

E-Book Case Study: Data Interchange 431

Chapter Summary 432

Solutions to Practice Problems 432

Exercises 435

Problems 436

IN THIS CHAPTER, we introduce several approaches to handle the vast amounts of data that are created, stored, accessed, and processed in today's computing applications.

We start by introducing relational databases and the language used to access them, SQL. Unlike many of the programs we have developed so far in this book, real-world application programs usually make heavy use of databases to store and access data. This is because databases store data in a way that enables easy and efficient access to the data. For this reason, it is important to develop an early appreciation of the benefits of databases and how to make effective use of them.

The amount of data generated by web crawlers, scientific experiments, or the stock markets is so vast that no single computer can process it effectively. Instead, a joint effort by multiple compute nodes—whether computers, processors, or cores—is necessary. We introduce an approach to develop parallel programs that make effective use of the multiple cores of a modern microprocessor. We then use this to develop the MapReduce framework, an approach for processing data developed by Google that can scale from a few cores on a personal computer to hundreds of thousands of cores in a server farm.

12.1 Databases and SQL

Data that is processed by a program exists only while the program executes. In order for data to persist beyond the execution of the program—so it can be processed later by some other program, for example—the data must be stored in a file.

So far in this book, we have been using standard text files to store data persistently. The advantage of text files is that they are general purpose and easy to work with. Their disadvantage is that they have no structure; they have, in particular, no structure that permits data to be *efficiently* accessed and processed.

In this section, we introduce a special type of file, called a *database file* or simply a *database*, that stores data in a structured way. The structure makes the data in a database file amenable to efficient processing, including efficient insertion, update, deletion, and, especially, access. A database is a far more appropriate data storage approach than a general text file in many applications, and it is important to know how to work with databases.

Database Tables

In the Chapter 11 case study, we develop a web crawler—a program that visits web page after web page by following hyperlinks. The crawler scans the content of each visited web page and outputs information about it, including all the hyperlink URLs contained in the web page and the frequency of every word in the page. If we ran the crawler on the set of linked web pages shown in Figure 12.1, with each page containing names of some world cities with indicated frequencies, the hyperlink URLs would be output in this format:

```
URL              Link
one.html         two.html
one.html         three.html
two.html         four.html
...
```

Figure 12.1 Five linked web pages. Each page contains a few occurrences of some of the world's major cities. Page `one.html`, for example, contains three occurrences of `'Beijing'`, five of `'Paris'`, and five of `'Chicago'`. It also contains hyperlinks to web pages `two.html` and `three.html`.

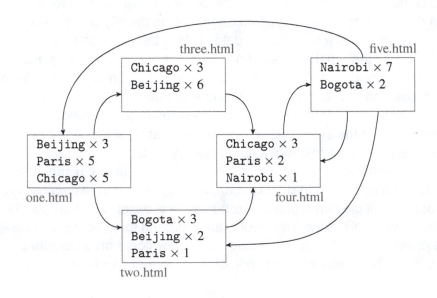

The first two lines, for example, indicate that page `one.html` contains links to pages `two.html` and `three.html`.

The crawler would output the frequency of every word in every web page in this format:

```
URL              Word           Freq
one.html         Beijing          3
one.html         Paris            5
one.html         Chicago          5
two.html         Bogota           3
...
```

So page `one.html` contains three occurrences of `'Beijing'`, five of `'Paris'`, and five of `'Chicago'`.

Suppose we are interested in analyzing the data set collected by the crawler. We might, for example, be interested in making queries such as:

1. In which web pages does word X appear in?
2. What is the ranking of web pages containing word X, based on the number of occurrences of word X in the page?
3. How many pages contain word X?
4. What pages have a hyperlink to page Y?
5. What is the total number of occurrences of the word 'Paris' across all web pages?
6. How many outgoing links does each visited page have?
7. How many incoming links does each visited page have?
8. What pages have a link to a page containing word X?
9. What page containing word X has the most incoming links?

Answering each of these questions on the data set produced by the crawler would be quite cumbersome. The text file format of the data set would require the file to be read into a string, and then ad hoc string operations would have to be used to retrieve the relevant data. For example, to answer question **1**, we would have to find all the lines in the file containing word X, split each line into words (i.e., strings separated by blanks), collect the first word in every line, and then eliminate duplicate URLs.

An alternative approach would be to save the information gathered by the crawler into a *database file* rather than a general-purpose text file. A database file stores data in a *structured* way that enables efficient access and processing of the data.

Structured means that data in a database file is stored in one or more *tables*. Each table is identified by a name, such as `Customers` or `Products`, and consists of columns and rows. Each *column* has a name and contains data of a specific type: string, integer, real (float), and so on. Each *row* of the table contains data corresponding to one *database record*.

In our example, the information obtained by the crawler on the web pages shown in Figure 12.1 could be stored in two database tables shown in Figure 12.2. The first table, called `Hyperlinks`, has columns named `Url` and `Link`. Each row (record) in that table has a string X in column `Page` and a string Y in column `Link` and refers to a hyperlink with URL Y in web page X. The second table, called `Keywords`, has columns named `Url`, `Word`, and `Freq`. Each record consists of strings X and Y in columns `Url` and `Word`, respectively, and integer Z in column `Freq`, and corresponds to word Y appearing in web page with URL X with frequency Z.

With data stored in database tables, we can make data queries using a special database programming language.

Url	Link
one.html	two.html
one.html	three.html
two.html	four.html
three.html	four.html
four.html	five.html
five.html	one.html
five.html	two.html
five.html	four.html

(a) Table Hyperlinks

Url	Word	Freq
one.html	Beijing	3
one.html	Paris	5
one.html	Chicago	5
two.html	Bogota	3
two.html	Beijing	2
two.html	Paris	1
three.html	Chicago	3
three.html	Beijing	6
four.html	Chicago	3
four.html	Paris	2
four.html	Nairobi	5
five.html	Nairobi	7
five.html	Bogota	2

(b) Table Keywords

Structured Query Language

Database files are not read from or written to by an application program using the usual file input/output interface. They typically are also not accessed directly. Instead, the application program usually sends commands to a special type of server program called a *database engine* or a *database management system* that manages the database; that program will access the database file on the application's behalf.

The commands accepted by database engines are statements written in a query language, the most popular of which is called *Structured Query Language*, typically referred to as *SQL*. Next we introduce a small subset of SQL that we can use to write programs that can make use of databases, when databases are the right choice for data storage.

Statement SELECT

The SQL statement SELECT is used to make queries into a database. In its simplest form, this statement is used to retrieve a column of a database table. For example, to retrieve column Link from table Hyperlinks, you would use:

```
SELECT Link FROM Hyperlinks
```

The result of executing this statement is stored in a *result table* (also called a *result set*), illustrated in Figure 12.3(a).

We use uppercase characters to highlight the SQL statement keywords; SQL statements are not case-sensitive so we could use lowercase characters. In general, the SQL statement SELECT retrieves a subset of columns from the table and has this format:

```
SELECT Column(s) FROM TableName
```

For example, to select the content of columns Url and Word from table Keywords, you would use:

```
SELECT Url, Word FROM Keywords
```

The result table that is obtained is shown in Figure 12.3(b). In order to retrieve *all* the columns of table Keywords, the wildcard symbol ∗ may be used:

```
SELECT * FROM Hyperlinks
```

Url	Word
one.html	Beijing
one.html	Paris
one.html	Chicago
two.html	Bogota
two.html	Beijing
two.html	Paris
three.html	Chicago
three.html	Beijing
four.html	Chicago
four.html	Paris
four.html	Nairobi
five.html	Nairobi
five.html	Bogota

Link
two.html
three.html
four.html
four.html
five.html
one.html
two.html
four.html

Link
two.html
three.html
four.html
five.html
one.html

```
SELECT Link
FROM Hyperlinks
```

(a)

```
SELECT Url, Word
FROM Keywords
```

(b)

```
SELECT DISTINCT Link
FROM Hyperlinks
```

(c)

Figure 12.3 Result tables for three queries. Each table is the result of the query appearing below it. Table (a) contains all the Link values in table Hyperlinks. Table (b) contains all the Url and Word values in table Keywords. Table (c) contains the *distinct* values in Link values in table Hyperlinks.

The result table obtained is the original table Hyperlinks shown in Figure 12.2(a). When we made the query

```
SELECT Link FROM Hyperlinks
```

the result set we obtained included multiple copies of the same link. If we wanted to retrieve only the distinct links in column Link, we could use the SQL DISTINCT keyword

```
SELECT DISTINCT Link FROM Hyperlinks
```

and we would obtain the result table shown in Figure 12.3(c).

DETOUR

Getting Your Hands Dirty with SQL

In the next section, we introduce the sqlite3 Python Standard Library module. It provides an application programming interface (API) that enables Python programs to access database files and execute SQL commands on them.

If you cannot wait and want to try running the SQL queries we just described, you can use the SQLite command-line shell. It is a stand-alone program that allows you to interactively execute SQL statements against a database file. You will, however, first need to download the precompiled shell binary from:

```
www.sqlite.org/download.html
```

Save the binary executable in a directory that contains the database file you want to work with. We illustrate next the usage of the SQLite command-line shell on database file links.db (whose two tables are shown in Figure 12.2), so we save the executable in the folder containing that file.

To run the SQLite command-line shell, you first need to open the command-line shell of your system. Then, switch the directory to the directory containing the `sqlite3` executable and run the code shown to access the database file `links.db`:

```
> ./sqlite3 links.db
SQLite version 3.7.7.1
Enter ".help" for instructions
Enter SQL statements terminated with a ";"
sqlite>
```

(This code works on Unix/Linux/Mac OS X systems; on MS Windows, you should use the command `sqlite3.exe links.db`.)

At the `sqlite>` prompt, you can now execute SQL statements against the database file `links.db`. The only additional requirement is that your SQL statement must be followed by a semicolon (`;`). For example:

```
sqlite> SELECT Url, Word FROM Keywords;
one.html|Beijing
one.html|Paris
one.html|Chicago
two.html|Bogota
two.html|Beijing
...
five.html|Nairobi
five.html|Bogota
sqlite>
```

(A few lines of output have been omitted.) You can use the SQLite command-line shell to execute every SQL statement described in this section.

Clause WHERE

In order to answer a question such as *"In which pages does word X appear in?"* we need to make a database query that selects only some records in a table (i.e., those that satisfy a certain condition). The SQL WHERE clause can be added to the SELECT statement to conditionally select records. For example, to select the URLs of web pages containing 'Paris', you would use

```
SELECT Url FROM Keywords
WHERE Word = 'Paris'
```

The result set returned is illustrated in Figure 12.4(a). Note that string values in SQL also use quotes as delimiters, just as in Python. In general, the format of the SELECT statement with the WHERE clause is:

```
SELECT column(s) FROM table
WHERE column operator value
```

The condition `column operator value` restricts the rows to which the SELECT statement is applied to only those that satisfy the condition. Operators that may appear in the condition are shown in Table 12.1. Conditions can be enclosed in parentheses, and logical operators AND and OR can be used to combine two or more conditions. *Note:* The format

Url
one.html
two.html
four.html

```
SELECT Url FROM Keywords
WHERE Word = 'Paris'
```

(a)

Url	Freq
one.html	5
four.html	2
two.html	1

```
SELECT Url, Freq FROM Keywords
WHERE Word = 'Paris'
ORDER BY Freq DESC
```

(b)

Figure 12.4 Result tables for two queries. Table (a) shows the URLs of pages containing the word 'Paris' in table Keywords. Table (b) shows the ranking of web pages containing the word 'Paris', based on the frequency of the word, in descending order.

of the WHERE clause is slightly different when the BETWEEN operator is used; it is

```
WHERE column BETWEEN value1 AND value2
```

Suppose we would like the result set in Figure 12.4(a) to be ordered by the frequency of the word 'Paris' in the web page. In other words, suppose the question is *"What is the ranking of web pages containing word X, based on the number of occurrences of string X in the page?"* To order the records in the result set by a specific column value, the SQL keyword ORDER BY can be used:

```
SELECT Url,Freq FROM Keywords
WHERE Word='Paris'
ORDER BY Freq DESC
```

This statement returns the result set shown in Figure 12.4(b). The keyword ORDER BY is followed by a column name; the records selected will be ordered based on values in that column. The default is an increasing ordering; in the statement, we used keyword DESC (which stands for "descending") to obtain an ordering that puts the page with most occurrences of 'Paris' first.

Operator	Explanation	Usage
=	Equal	column = value
<>	Not equal	column <> value
>	Greater than	column > value
<	Less than	column < value
>=	Greater than or equal	column >= value
<=	Less than or equal	column <= value
BETWEEN	Within an inclusive range	column BETWEEN value1 and value2

Table 12.1 SQL conditional operators. Conditions can be enclosed in parentheses, and logical operators AND and OR can be used to combine two or more conditions.

Write an SQL query that returns:

(a) The URL of every page that has a link to web page four.html
(b) The URL of every page that has an incoming link from page four.html
(c) The URL and word for every word that appears exactly three times in the web page associated with the URL
(d) The URL, word, and frequency for every word that appears between three and five times, inclusive, in the web page associated with the URL

Practice Problem 12.1

Built-In SQL Functions

To answer queries such as *"How many pages contain the word Paris?"* we need a way to count the number of records obtained through a query. SQL has built-in functions for this purpose. The SQL function COUNT(), when applied to a result table, returns the number of rows in it:

```
SELECT COUNT(*) FROM Keywords
WHERE Word = 'Paris'
```

The result table obtained, shown in Figure 12.5(a), contains just one column and one record. Note that the column no longer corresponds to a column of the table on which we made the query.

To answer *"What is the total number of occurrences of the word Paris across all web pages?"* we need to add up the values in column Freq of every row of table Keywords containing 'Paris' in the Word column. The SQL function SUM() can be used for this as shown next:

```
SELECT SUM(Freq) FROM Keywords
WHERE Word = 'Paris'
```

The result table is illustrated in Figure 12.5(b).

Figure 12.5 Result tables for three queries. Table (a) contains the number of pages in which the word 'Paris' appears. Table (b) is the total number of occurrences of the word 'Paris' across all web pages in the database. Table (c) contains the number of outgoing hyperlinks for each web page.

Url	
one.html	2
two.html	1
three.html	1
four.html	1
five.html	3

3

```
SELECT COUNT(*)
FROM Keywords
WHERE Word = 'Paris'
```

(a)

8

```
SELECT SUM(Freq)
FROM Keywords
WHERE Word = 'Paris'
```

(b)

```
SELECT Url, COUNT(*)
FROM Hyperlinks
GROUP BY Url
```

(c)

Clause GROUP BY

Suppose you now want to know *"How many outgoing links does each web page have?"* To answer this question, you need to add up the number of links for each distinct Url value. The SQL clause GROUP BY groups the records of a table that have the same value in the specified column. The next query will group the rows of table Hyperlinks by Url value and then count the number of rows in each group:

```
SELECT COUNT(*) FROM Hyperlinks
GROUP BY Url
```

We modify this query slightly to also include the Web page URL:

```
SELECT Url, COUNT(*) FROM Hyperlinks
GROUP BY Url
```

The result of this query is shown in Figure 12.5(c).

For each question, write an SQL query that answers it:

  (a) How many words, including duplicates, does page `two.html` contain?

  (b) How many distinct words does page `two.html` contain?

  (c) How many words, including duplicates, does each web page have?

  (d) How many incoming links does each web page have?

The result tables for questions (c) and (d) should include the URLs of the web pages.

Practice Problem
12.2

Making SQL Queries Involving Multiple Tables

Suppose we want to know *"What web pages have a link to a page containing the word 'Bogota'?"* This question requires a lookup of both tables Keywords and Hyperlinks. We would need to look up Keywords to find out the set S of URLs of pages containing the word 'Bogota', and then look up Keywords to find the URLs of pages with links to pages in S.

The SELECT statement can be used on multiple tables. To understand the behavior of SELECT when used on multiple tables, we develop a few examples. First, the query

```
SELECT * FROM Hyperlinks, Keywords
```

returns a table containing 104 records, each a combination of a record in Hyperlinks and a record in Keywords. This table, shown in Figure 12.6 and referred to as a *cross join*, has five named columns corresponding to the two columns of table Hyperlinks and three columns of table Keywords.

It is, of course, possible to conditionally select some records in the cross join. For example, the next query selects the 16 records (2 of which are shown in Figure 12.6) out of the 104 in the cross join that contain 'Bogota' in column Word of table Keywords:

```
SELECT * FROM Hyperlinks, Keywords
WHERE Keywords.Word = 'Bogota'
```

Do pay attention to the syntax of this last SQL query. In a query that refers to columns in multiple tables, you must add the table name and a dot before a column name. This is to avoid confusion if columns in different tables have the same name. To refer to column Word of table Keywords, we must use the notation `Keywords.Word`.

Hyperlinks		Keywords		
Url	**Link**	**Url**	**Word**	**Freq**
one.html	two.html	one.html	Beijing	3
one.html	two.html	one.html	Paris	5
one.html	two.html	one.html	Chicago	5
one.html	two.html	two.html	Bogota	3
...	...	...	...	...
five.html	four.html	four.html	Nairobi	5
five.html	four.html	five.html	Nairobi	7
five.html	four.html	five.html	Bogota	2

SELECT * FROM Hyperlinks, Keywords

Figure 12.6 Joining database tables.

The table consists of every combination of a row from table Hyperlinks and a row from table Keywords. Since there are 8 rows in table Hyperlinks and 13 in table Keywords, the cross join will have $8 \times 13 = 104$ rows. Only the first 3 and the last 3 rows are shown.

Here is another example. The next query picks up only those records in the cross join whose Hyperlink.Url and Keyword.Url values match:

```
SELECT * FROM Hyperlinks, Keywords
WHERE Hyperlinks.Url = Keywords.Url
```

The result of this query is shown in Figure 12.7.

Figure 12.7 Joining database tables. The table consists of those rows of the table in Figure 12.6 that have Hyperlinks.Link = Keywords.Url.

Hyperlinks		Keywords		
Url	**Link**	**Url**	**Word**	**Freq**
one.html	two.html	two.html	Bogota	3
one.html	two.html	two.html	Beijing	2
one.html	two.html	two.html	Paris	1
one.html	three.html	three.html	Chicago	3
...	...	...	...	...
five.html	four.html	four.html	Paris	2
five.html	four.html	four.html	Nairobi	5

```
SELECT * FROM Hyperlinks, Keywords
WHERE Hyperlinks.Url = Keywords.Url
```

Conceptually, the table in Figure 12.7 consists of records that associate a hyperlink (from Hyperlinks.Url to Hyperlinks.Link) to a word appearing in the web page pointed to by the hyperlink (i.e., the web page with URL Hyperlinks.Link).

Now, our original question was *"What web pages have a link to a page containing 'Bogota'?"* To answer this question, we need to select records in the cross join whose Keyword.Word value is 'Bogota' *and* whose Keyword.Url value is equal to the value of Hyperlinks.Link. Figure 12.8 shows these records.

Figure 12.8 Joining database tables. This table consists of those rows of the table in Figure 12.7 that have Keyword.Word = 'Bogota'.

Hyperlinks		Keywords		
Url	**Link**	**Url**	**Word**	**Freq**
one.html	two.html	two.html	Bogota	3
four.html	five.html	five.html	Bogota	2
five.html	two.html	two.html	Bogota	3

```
SELECT * FROM Hyperlinks, Keywords
WHERE Keywords.Word = 'Bogota' AND Hyperlinks.Link = Keywords.Url
```

To pick up all the URLs of web pages with a link to a page containing 'Bogota', we thus need to make the query shown and illustrated in Figure 12.9.

ure 12.9 Joining ase tables. This ble is just the perlinks.Url shown in

Hyperlinks
Url
one.html
four.html
five.html

```
SELECT Hyperlinks.Url FROM Hyperlinks, Keywords
WHERE Keywords.Word = 'Bogota' AND Hyperlinks.Link = Keywords.Url
```

Statement CREATE TABLE

Of course, before we can make queries to a database, we need to create the tables and insert records into it. When a database file is created, it will be empty and contain no table. The SQL statement CREATE TABLE is used to create a table and has this format:

```
CREATE TABLE TableName
(
   Column1 dataType,
   Column2 dataType,
   ...
)
```

We spread the statement across multiple lines and indent the column definitions for visual appeal, nothing else. We could have also written the whole statement in one line.

For example, to define the table Keywords, we would do:

```
CREATE TABLE Keywords
(
   Url text,
   Word text,
   Freq int
)
```

The CREATE TABLE statement explicitly specifies the name and data type of each column of the table. Columns Url and Word are of type text, which corresponds to the Python str data type. Column Freq stores integer data. Table 12.2 lists a few SQL data types and the corresponding Python data types.

SQL Type	Python Type	Explanation
INTEGER	int	Holds integer values
REAL	float	Holds floating-point values
TEXT	str	Holds string values, delimited with quotes
BLOB	bytes	Holds sequence of bytes

Table 12.2 **A few SQL data types.** Unlike Python integers, the SQL integers are limited in size (to the range from -2^{31} to $2^{31} - 1$).

Statements INSERT and UPDATE

The SQL statement INSERT is used to insert a new record (i.e., row) into a database table. To insert a complete row, with a value for every column of the database, this format is used:

```
INSERT INTO TableName VALUES (value1, value2, ...)
```

For example, to insert the first row of table Keywords, you would do

```
INSERT INTO Keywords VALUES ('one.html', 'Beijing', 3)
```

The SQL statement UPDATE is used to modify the data in a table. Its general format is

```
UPDATE TableName SET column1 = value1
WHERE column2 = value2
```

If we wanted to update the frequency count of 'Bogota' in page two.html, we would update the table Keywords in this way:

```
UPDATE Keywords SET Freq = 4
WHERE Url = 'two.html' AND Word = 'Bogota'
```

DETOUR

More on SQL

SQL is specifically designed to access and process data stored in a *relational database*, that is, a collection of data items stored in tables that can be accessed and processed in various ways. The term *relational* refers to to the mathematical concept of *relation*, which is a set of pairs of items or, more generally, tuples of items. A table can thus be viewed as a mathematical relation.

In this text, we have been writing SQL statements in an ad hoc fashion. The advantage of viewing tables through the prism of mathematics is that that the power of abstraction and mathematics can be brought to bear to understand what can be computed using SQL and how. *Relational algebra* is a branch of mathematics that has been developed for precisely this purpose.

There are good online resources if you would like to learn more about SQL, including

        www.w3schools.com/sql/default.asp

12.2 Database Programming in Python

With a bit of SQL under our belt, we can now write applications that store data in databases and/or make database queries. In this section, we show how to store the data grabbed by a web crawler into a database and then mine the database in the context of a simple search engine application. We start by introducing the database API we will use to access the database files.

Database Engines and SQLite

The Python Standard Library includes a database API module `sqlite3` that provides Python developers a simple, built-in API for accessing database files. Unlike typical database APIs, the `sqlite3` module is not an interface to a separate database engine program. It is an interface to a library of functions called SQLite that accesses the database files directly.

DETOUR

SQLite versus Other Database Management Systems

Application programs do not typically read from and write to database files directly. Instead, they send SQL commands to a *database engine* or, more formally, a relational database management system (RDBMS). An RDBMS manages the database and accesses the database files on the application's behalf.

The first RDBMS was developed at the Massachusetts Institute of Technology in the early 1970s. Significant RDBMSs in use today include commercial ones by IBM, Oracle, Sybase, and Microsoft as well as open source ones such as Ingres, Postgres, and MySQL. All these engines run as independent programs outside of Python. In order to access them, you must use an API (i.e., a Python module) that provides classes and functions that allow Python applications to send SQL statements to the engine.

SQLite, however, is a library of functions that implements an SQL database engine that executes in the context of the application rather than independent from it. SQLite is extremely lightweight and commonly used by many applications, including the Firefox and Opera browsers, Skype, Apple iOS and Google's Android operating system, to store data locally. For this reason, SQLite is said to be the most widely used database engine.

Creating a Database with `sqlite3`

We now demonstrate the usage of the `sqlite3` database API by going over the steps necessary to store word frequencies and hyperlink URLs scanned from a web page into a database. First, we need to create a connection to the database file, which is somewhat equivalent to opening a text file:

```
>>> import sqlite3
>>> con = sqlite3.connect('web.db')
```

The function `connect()` is a function in module `sqlite3` that takes as input the name of a database file (in the current working directory) and returns an object of type `Connection`, a type defined in the module `sqlite3`. The `Connection` object is associated with the database file. In the statement, if database file `web.db` exists in the current working directory, the `Connection` object `con` will represent it; otherwise, a new database file `web.db` is created.

Once we have a `Connection` object associated with the database, we need to create a cursor object, which is responsible for executing SQL statements. The method `cursor()` of the `Connection` class returns an object of type `Cursor`:

```
>>> cur = con.cursor()
```

A `Cursor` object is the workhorse of database processing. It supports a method that takes an SQL statement, as a string, and executes it: method `execute()`. For example, to create the database table `Keywords`, you would just pass the SQL statement, as a string, to the `execute()` method:

```
>>> cur.execute("""CREATE TABLE Keywords (Url text,
                                          Word text,
                                          Freq int)""")
```

Now that we've created table `Keywords`, we can insert records into it. The SQL `INSERT INTO` statement is simply passed as an input to the `execute()` function:

```
>>> cur.execute("""INSERT INTO Keywords
                   VALUES ('one.html', 'Beijing', 3)""")
```

In this example, the values inserted into the database (`'one.html'`, `'Beijing'` and 3) are "hardcoded" in the SQL statement string expression. That is not typical, as usually SQL statements executed within a program use values that come from Python variables. In order to construct SQL statements that use Python variable values, we use a technique similar to string formatting called *parameter substitution*.

Suppose, for example, that we would like to insert a new record into the database, one containing values:

```
>>> url, word, freq = 'one.html', 'Paris', 5
```

We construct the SQL statement string expression as usual, but we put a ? symbol as a placeholder wherever a Python variable value should be. This will be the first argument to the execute() method. The second argument is a tuple containing the three variables:

```
>>> cur.execute("""INSERT INTO Keywords
                   VALUES (?, ?, ?)""", (url, word, freq))
```

The value of each tuple variable is mapped to a placeholder as shown in Figure 12.10.

Figure 12.10 Parameter substitution. Placeholder ? is placed in the SQL string expression where the variable value should go.

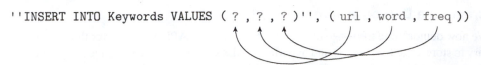

We can also assemble all the values into a tuple object beforehand:

```
>>> record = ('one.html','Chicago', 5)
>>> cur.execute("INSERT INTO Keywords VALUES (?, ?, ?)", record)
```

CAUTION

Security Issue: SQL Injection

It is possible to construct SQL statement string expressions using format strings and the string format() method. That is, however, insecure, as it is vulnerable to a security attack called an *SQL injection attack*. You should definitely not use format strings to construct SQL expressions.

Committing to Database Changes and Closing the Database

Changes to a database file—including table creation or deletion or row insertions and updates—are not actually written to the database file immediately. They are only recorded temporarily, in memory. In order to ensure that the changes are written, you must commit to the changes by having the Connection object invoke the commit() method:

```
>>> con.commit()
```

When you are done working with a database file, you need to close it just as you would close a text file. The Connection object invokes the close() method to close the database file:

```
>>> con.close()
```

**Practice Problem
12.3**

Implement function webData() that takes as input:

1. The name of a database file
2. The URL of a web page
3. A list of all hyperlink URLs in the web page
4. A dictionary mapping each word in the web page to its frequency in the web page

The database file should contain tables named `Keywords` and `Hyperlinks` defined as illustrated in Figures 12.2(a) and (b). Your function should insert a row into table `Hyperlinks` for every link in the list, and a row into table `Keywords` for every (word, frequency) pair in the dictionary. You should also commit and close the database file when done.

Querying a Database Using `sqlite3`

We now show how to make SQL queries from within a Python program. We make queries against database file `links.db`, which contains the tables `Hyperlinks` and `Keywords` shown in Figure 12.2.

```
>>> import sqlite3
>>> con = sqlite3.connect('links.db')
>>> cur = con.cursor()
```

File: links.db

To execute an SQL SELECT statement, we just need to pass the statement, as a string, to the cursor's `execute()` method:

```
>>> cur.execute('SELECT * FROM Keywords')
```

The SELECT statement should return a result table. So where is it?

The table is stored in the `Cursor` object `cur` itself. If you want it, you need to fetch it, which you can do in several ways. To obtain the selected records as a list of tuples, you can use the `fetchall()` method (of the `Cursor` class):

```
>>> cur.fetchall()
[('one.html', 'Beijing', 3), ('one.html', 'Paris', 5),
('one.html', 'Chicago', 5), ('two.html', 'Bogota', 3)
...
('five.html', 'Bogota', 2)]
```

The other option is to treat the `Cursor` object `cur` as an iterator and iterate over it directly:

```
>>> cur.execute('SELECT * FROM Keywords')
<sqlite3.Cursor object at 0x15f93b0>
>>> for record in cur:
        print(record)

('one.html', 'Beijing', 3)
('one.html', 'Paris', 5)
...
('five.html', 'Bogota', 2)
```

The second approach has the advantage of being memory efficient because no large list is stored in memory.

What if a query uses a value stored in a Python variable? Suppose we would like to learn what web pages contain the value of `word`, where `word` is defined as:

```
>>> word = 'Paris'
```

Once again, we can use parameter substitution:

```
>>> cur.execute('SELECT Url FROM Keywords WHERE Word = ?', (word,))
<sqlite3.Cursor object at 0x15f9b30>
```

The value of `word` is placed into the SQL query at the placeholder position. Let's check that the query does find all the web pages containing the word 'Paris':

```
>>> cur.fetchall()
[('one.html',), ('two.html',), ('four.html',)]
```

Let's try an example that uses values of two Python variables. Suppose we want to know the URLs of web pages containing more than n occurrences of `word`, where:

```
>>> word, n = 'Beijing', 2
```

We again use parameter substitution, as illustrated in Figure 12.11:

```
>>> cur.execute("""SELECT * FROM Keywords
                   WHERE Word = ? AND Freq > ?""", (word, n))
<sqlite3.Cursor object at 0x15f9b30>
```

Figure 12.11 Two parameter SQL substitution. The first variable is matched to the first placeholder, and the second variable to the second placeholder.

`'SELECT * FROM Keywords WHERE Word = ? AND Freq > ? ', ( word , n ))`

CAUTION

Two `Cursor` Pitfalls

If, after executing the `cur.execute()` statement, you run

```
>>> cur.fetchall()
[('one.html', 'Beijing', 3), ('three.html', 'Beijing', 6)]
```

you will get the expected result table. If, however, you run `cur.fetchall()` again:

```
>>> cur.fetchall()
[]
```

you get nothing. The point is this: The `fetchall()` method will empty the `Cursor` object buffer. This is also true if you fetch the records in the result table by iterating over the `Cursor` object.

Another problem occurs if you execute an SQL query without fetching the result of the previous query:

```
>>> cur.execute("""SELECT Url FROM Keywords
                   WHERE Word = 'Paris'""")
<sqlite3.Cursor object at 0x15f9b30>
>>> cur.execute("""SELECT Url FROM Keywords
                   WHERE Word = 'Beijing'""")
<sqlite3.Cursor object at 0x15f9b30>
>>> cur.fetchall()
[('one.html',), ('two.html',), ('three.html',)]
```

The `fetchall()` call returns the result of the second query only. The result of the first is lost!

A *search engine* is a server application that takes a keyword from a user and returns the URLs of web pages containing the keyword, ranked according to some criterion. In this practice problem, you are asked to develop a simple search engine that ranks web pages based on its frequency.

Write a search engine application based on the results of a web crawl that stored word frequencies in a database table Keywords just like the one in Figure 12.2(b). The search engine will take a keyword from the user and simply return the web pages containing the keyword, ranked by the frequency of the keyword, in decreasing order.

```
>>> freqSearch('links.db')
Enter keyword: Paris
URL             FREQ
one.html           5
four.html          2
two.html           1
Enter keyword:
```

12.3 Functional Language Approach

In this section we showcase MapReduce, a framework for data processing developed by Google. Its key feature is that it is *scalable*, which means that it is able to process very large data sets. It is robust enough to process large data sets using multiple compute nodes, whether the compute nodes are cores on one microprocessor or computers in a *cloud computing* platform. In fact, we show in the next section how to extend the framework we develop here to utilize all the cores of your computer's microprocessor.

In order to keep our MapReduce implementation as simple as possible, we introduce a new Python construct, *list comprehension*. Both list comprehension and the MapReduce framework have their origins in the functional programming language paradigm, which we describe briefly.

List Comprehension

When you open a text file and use method `readlines()` to read the file, you will obtain a list of lines. Each line in the list ends with the new line character \n. Suppose, for example, that list `lines` was obtained that way:

```
>>> lines
['First Line\n','Second\n','\n', 'and Fourth.\n']
```

In a typical application, character \n gets in the way of processing the lines, and we need to remove it. One way to do this would be to use a `for` loop and the familiar accumulator pattern:

```
>>> newlines = []
>>> for i in range(len(lines)):
        newlines.append(lines[i][:-1])
```

In each iteration `i` of the `for` loop, the last character of line `i` (the new line character \n) is removed and the modified line is added to accumulator list `newlines`:

```
>>> newlines
['First Line', 'Second', '', 'and Fourth.']
```

There is another way to accomplish the same task in Python:

```
>>> newlines = [line[:-1] for line in lines]
>>> newlines
['First Line', 'Second', '', 'and Fourth.']
```

The Python statement `[line[:-1] for line in lines]` constructs a new list from list `lines` and is Python's *list comprehension* construct. Here is how it works. Every item `line` in list `lines` is used in order from left to right to generate an item in the new list by applying `line[:-1]` to `line`. The order in which the items appear in the new list corresponds to the order in which the corresponding items appear in the original list `lines` (see Figure 12.12).

Figure 12.12 List comprehension. List comprehension constructs a new list from an existing list. The same function is applied to every item of the existing list to construct items of the new.

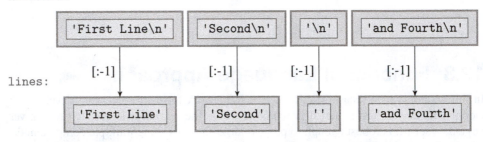

More generally, a list comprehension statement has this syntax:

```
[<expression> for <item> in <sequence/iterator>]
```

This statement evaluates into a list whose items are obtained by applying `<expression>`, a Python expression typically involving variable `<item>`, to each item of iterable container `<sequence/iterator>`. An even more general version may also include an optional conditional expression:

```
[<expression> for <item> in <sequence/iterator> if <condition>]
```

In this case, the list obtained has elements that are obtained by applying `expression` to each item of `sequence/iterator` for which `condition` is true.

Let's try a few examples. In the next modification of the last example, the new list will not contain blank strings that correspond to blank lines in the original file:

```
>>> [line[:-1] for line in lines if line != '\n']
['First Line', 'Second', 'and Fourth.']
```

In the next example, we construct a list of even numbers up to 20:

```
>>> [i for i in range(0, 20, 2)]
[0, 2, 4, 6, 8, 10, 12, 14, 16, 18]
```

In the last example, we compute the lengths of the strings in a list:

```
>>> [len(word) for word in ['hawk', 'hen', 'hog', 'hyena']]
[4, 3, 3, 5]
```

Let the list of strings `words` be defined as:

```
>>> words = ['hawk', 'hen', 'hog', 'hyena']
```

Write list comprehension statements that use `words` as the original list to construct lists:

(a) `['Hawk', 'Hen', 'Hog', 'Hyena']`

(b) `[('hawk', 4), ('hen', 3), ('hog', 3), ('hyena', 5)]`

(c) `[[('h', 'hawk'), ('a', 'hawk'), ('w', 'hawk'), ('k', 'hawk')],`
`    [('h', 'hen'), ('e', 'hen'), ('n', 'hen')], [('h', 'hog'),`
`    ('o', 'hog'), ('g', 'hog')], [('h', 'hyena'), ('y', 'hyena'),`
`    ('e', 'hyena'), ('n', 'hyena'), ('a', 'hyena')]]`

The list in (c) requires some explanation. For every string *s* of the original list a new *list* of tuples is created, such that each tuple maps a character of the string *s* to the string *s* itself.

Functional Programming

List comprehension is a programming construct borrowed from functional programming languages. With origins in the SETL and NPL programming languages, list comprehension became more widely known when incorporated in the functional programming language Haskell and, especially, Python.

The functional language paradigm differs from the imperative, declarative, and object-oriented paradigms in that it does not have "statements," only expressions. A functional language program is an expression that consists of a function call that passes data and possible other functions as arguments. Examples of functional programming languages include Lisp, Scheme, Clojure, ML, Erlang, Scala, F#, and Haskell.

Python is not a functional language, but it borrows a few functional language constructs that help create cleaner, shorter Python programs.

DETOUR

MapReduce Problem-Solving Framework

We consider, one last time, the problem of computing the frequency of every word in a string. We have used this example to motivate the dictionary container class and also to develop a very simple search engine. We use this problem now to motivate a new approach, called MapReduce, developed by Google for solving data processing problems.

Suppose we would like to compute the frequency of every word in the list

```
>>> words = ['two', 'three', 'one', 'three', 'three',
             'five', 'one', 'five']
```

The MapReduce approach for doing this takes three steps.

In the first step, we create a tuple `(word, 1)` for every `word` in the list `words`. The pair `(word, 1)` is referred to as a *(key, value)* pair, and the value of 1 for every key word captures the count of that particular instance of a word. Note that there is a `(word, 1)` pair for every occurrence of `word` in the original list `words`.

Figure 12.13 MapReduce for word frequency. List comprehension is used to map each word in list `words` to a list `[(word,1)]`. Those new lists are stored in list `intermediate1`. Then all `[(word,1)]` lists of `intermediate1` containing the same word are pulled together to create tuple `(word, [1,1,...,1])`. In the last step, the 1s in every such tuple are added up into variable `count`, and tuple `(word, count)` is added to list `frequency`.

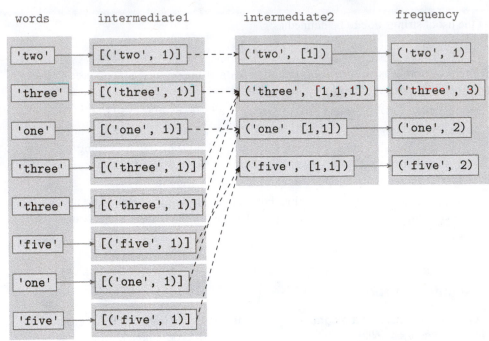

Each (key,value) pair is stored in its own list, and all these single-element lists are contained in the list `intermediate1`, as shown in Figure 12.13.

The intermediate step of MapReduce pulls together all (`word`, `1`) pairs with the same word key and create a new (key, value) pair (`word`, `[1,1,...,1]`) where `[1,1,...,1]` is a list of all the values 1 pulled together. Note that there is a 1 in `[1,1,...,1]` for every occurrence of `word` in the original list `words`. We refer to the list of (`key`, `value`) pairs obtained in this intermediate step as `intermediate2` (see Figure 12.13).

In the final step, a new pair (`word`, `count`) is constructed by adding up all the 1s in every (`word`, `[1,1,...,1]`) of `intermediate2`, as shown in Figure 12.13. We call this final list of (key, value) pairs `result`.

Let's see now how to do these steps in Python. The first step consists of constructing a new list from list `words` by applying function `occurrence()` to every word in list `words`:

Module: ch12.py

```
1   def occurrence(word):
2           'returns list containing tuple (word, 1)'
3           return [(word, 1)]
```

Using list comprehension, we can express the first step of MapReduce succinctly:

```
>>> intermediate1 = [occurrence(word) for word in words]
>>> intermediate1
[[('two', 1)], [('three', 1)], [('one', 1)], [('three', 1)],
 [('three', 1)], [('five', 1)], [('one', 1)], [('five', 1)]]
```

This step is referred to as the *Map* step of MapReduce, and function `occurrence()` is said to be the *map* function of the word frequency problem.

Map Step Returns a *List* of Tuples

The function `occurrence()` returns a list containing just one tuple. You may wonder why it does not return just the tuple itself.

The reason is that our goal is not just to solve the word frequency problem. Our goal is to develop a general framework that can be used to solve a range of problems. For problems other than the word frequency problem, the Map step may return more than one tuple. We will see an example of this later in this section. So we insist that the map function returns a list of tuples.

The intermediate step of MapReduce, called the *Partition* step, pulls together all pairs

```
(key, value1), (key, value2), ... (key, valuek)
```

contained in (sublists of) `intermediate1` with the *same* key. For each unique key, a new `(key, values)` pair is constructed where values is the list `[value1, value2, ..., valuek]`. This step is encapsulated in function `partition()`:

Module: ch12.py

```python
def partition(intermediate1):
    '''intermediate1 is a list containing [(key, value)] lists;
       returns iterable container with a (key, values) tuple for
       every unique key in intermediate1; values is a list that
       contains all values in intermediate1 associated with key
    '''
    dct = {}              # dictionary of (key, value) pairs

    # for every (key, value) pair in every list of intermediate1
    for lst in intermediate1:
        for key, value in lst:

            if key in dct: # if key already in dictionary dct, add
                dct[key].append(value) # value to list dct[key]
            else:          # if key not in dictionary dct, add
                dct[key] = [value]     # (key, [value]) to dct

    return dct.items()  # return container of (key, values) tuples
```

Function `partition()` takes list `intermediate1` and constructs list `intermediate2`:

```
>>> intermediate2 = partition(intermediate1)
>>> intermediate2
dict_items([('one', [1, 1]), ('five', [1, 1]), ('two', [1]),
            ('three', [1, 1, 1])])
```

Finally, the last step consists of constructing a new `(key, count)` pair from each `(key, values)` pair of `intermediate2` by just accumulating the values in `values`:

Module: ch12.py

```python
def occurrenceCount(keyVal):
    return (keyVal[0], sum(keyVal[1]))
```

Again, list comprehension provides a succinct way to perform this step:

```
>>> [occurrenceCount(x) for x in intermediate2]
[('six', 1), ('one', 2), ('five', 2), ('two', 1), ('three', 3)]
```

This is referred to as the *Reduce* step of MapReduce. The function `occurrenceCount()` is referred to as the *reduce* function for the word frequency problem.

MapReduce, in the Abstract

The MapReduce approach we used to compute word frequencies in the previous section may seem like an awkward and strange way to compute word frequencies. It can be viewed, as a more complicated version of the dictionary-based approach we have seen in Chapter 6. There are, however, benefits to the MapReduce approach. The first benefit is that the approach is general enough to apply to a range of problems. The second benefit is that it is amenable to an implementation that uses not one but many compute nodes, whether it is several cores on a central processing unit (CPU) or thousands in a cloud computing system.

We go into the second benefit in more depth in the next section. What we would like to do now is abstract the MapReduce steps so the framework can be used in a range of different problems, by simply defining the problem specific map and reduce functions. In short, we would like to develop a class `SeqMapReduce` that can be used to compute word frequencies as easily as this:

```
>>> words = ['two', 'three', 'one', 'three', 'three',
             'five', 'one', 'five']
>>> smr = SeqMapReduce(occurrence, occurrenceCount)
>>> smr.process(words)
[('one', 2), ('five', 2), ('two', 1), ('three', 3)]
```

We can then use the `SeqMapReduce` object `smr` to compute the frequencies of other things. For example, numbers:

```
>>> numbers = [2,3,4,3,2,3,5,4,3,5,1]
>>> smr.process(numbers)
[(1, 1), (2, 2), (3, 4), (4, 2), (5, 2)]
```

Furthermore, by specifying other, problem-specific, map and reduce functions, we can solve other problems.

These specifications suggest that the class `SeqMapReduce` should have a constructor that takes the map and reduce functions as input. The method `process` should take an iterable sequence containing data and perform the Map, Partition, and Reduce steps:

Module: ch12.py

```
1   class SeqMapReduce(object):
2       'a sequential MapReduce implementation'
3       def __init__(self, mapper, reducer):
4           'functions mapper and reducer are problem specific'
5           self.mapper = mapper
6           self.reducer = reducer
7       def process(self, data):
8           'runs MapReduce on data with mapper and reducer functions'
9           intermediate1 = [self.mapper(x) for x in data]   # Map
10          intermediate2 = partition(intermediate1)
11          return [self.reducer(x) for x in intermediate2] # Reduce
```

Input to MapReduce Should Be Immutable

Suppose we would like to compute frequencies of sublists in list `lists`:

```
>>> lists = [[2,3], [1,2], [2,3]]
```

It would seem that the same approach we used to count strings and numbers would work:

```
>>> smr = SeqMapReduce(occurrence, occurrenceCount)
>>> smr.process(lists)
Traceback (most recent call last):
...
TypeError: unhashable type: 'list'
```

So ... what happened? The problem is that lists cannot be used as keys of the dictionary `dct` inside the implementation of function `partition()`. Our approach can work only with hashable, immutable data types. By changing the lists to tuples, we are back in business:

```
>>> lists = [(2,3), (1,2), (2,3)]
>>> m.process(lists)
[((1, 2), 1), ((2, 3), 2)]
```

Inverted Index

We now apply the MapReduce framework to solve the *inverted index* problem (also referred to as the *reverse index* problem). There are many versions of this problem. The one we consider is this: Given a bunch of text files, we are interested in finding out which words appear in which file. A solution to the problem could be represented as a mapping that maps each word to the list of files containing it. This mapping is called an *inverted index*.

For example, suppose we want to construct the inverted index for text files `a.txt`, `b.txt`, and `c.txt` shown in Figure 12.14.

```
a.txt              b.txt              c.txt
Paris, Miami       Tokyo              Cairo, Cairo
Tokyo, Miami       Tokyo, Quito       Paris
```

Figure 12.14 Three text files. An inverted index maps each word to the list of files containing the word.

An inverted index would map, say, `'Paris'` to list `['a.txt', 'c.txt']` and `'Quito'` to `['b.txt']`. The inverted index should thus be:

```
[('Paris', ['c.txt', 'a.txt']), ('Miami', ['a.txt']),
('Cairo', ['c.txt']), ('Quito', ['b.txt']),
('Tokyo', ['a.txt', 'b.txt'])]
```

To use MapReduce to obtain the inverted index, we must define the map and reduce functions that will take the list of file names

```
['a.txt', 'b.txt', 'c.txt']
```

and produce the inverted index. Figure 12.15 illustrates how these functions should work.

Figure 12.15 MapReduce for the inverted index problem. The Map step creates a tuple (word, file) for every word in a file. The Partition step collects all the (word, file) tuples with the same word. The output of the Partition step is the desired inverted index that maps words to the files they are contained in. The Reduce step does not make any changes to the output of the Partition step.

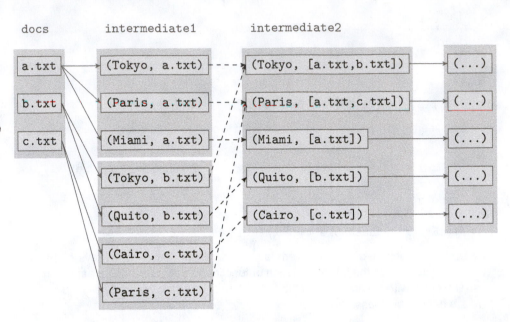

In the Map phase, the map function creates a list for every file. This list contains a tuple (word, file) for every word word in the file. Function getWordsFromFile() implements the map function:

Module: ch12.py

```
1  from string import punctuation
2  def getWordsFromFile(file):
3      '''returns list of items [(word, file)]
4         for every word in file'''
5      infile = open(file)
6      content = infile.read()
7      infile.close()
8
9      # remove punctuation (covered in Section 4.1)
10     transTable = str.maketrans(punctuation, ' '*len(punctuation))
11     content = content.translate(transTable)
12
13     # construct set of items [(word, file)] with no duplicates
14     res = set()
15     for word in content.split():
16         res.add((word, file))
17     return res
```

Note that this map function returns a set, not a list. That is not a problem because the only requirement is that the returned container is iterable. The reason we use a set is to ensure there are no duplicate entries [(word, file)], as they are not necessary and will only slow down the Partition and Reduce steps.

After the Map step, the partition function will pull together all tuples (word, file) with the same value of word and merge them into one tuple (word, files), where files is the list of all files containing word. In other words, the partition function constructs the inverted index.

This means that the Reduce step does not need to do anything. The reduce function just copies items to the result list, the inverted index.

```
1  def getWordIndex(keyVal):
2      return keyVal
```

Module: ch12.py

To compute the inverted index, you only need to do:

```
>>> files = ['a.txt', 'b.txt', 'c.txt']
>>> print(SeqMapReduce(getWordsFromFile, getWordIndex).
               process(files))
[('Paris', ['c.txt', 'a.txt']), ('Miami', ['a.txt']),
 ('Cairo', ['c.txt']), ('Quito', ['c.txt', 'b.txt']),
 ('Tokyo', ['a.txt', 'b.txt'])]
```

File: a.txt, b.txt, c.txt

Develop a MapReduce-based solution constructing an inverted "character index" of a list of words. The index should map every character appearing in at least one of the words to a list of words containing the character. Your work consists of designing the mapper function getChars() and reducer function getCharIndex().

Practice Problem 12.6

```
>>> mp = SeqMapReduce(getChars, getCharIndex)
>>> mp.process(['ant', 'bee', 'cat', 'dog', 'eel'])
[('a', ['ant', 'cat']), ('c', ['cat']), ('b', ['bee']),
 ('e', ['eel', 'bee']), ('d', ['dog']), ('g', ['dog']),
 ('l', ['eel']), ('o', ['dog']), ('n', ['ant']),
 ('t', ['ant', 'cat'])]
```

12.4 Parallel Computing

Today's computing often requires the processing of a tremendous amount of data. A search engine continuously extracts information out of billions of web pages. Particle physics experiments run at the Large Hadron Collider near Geneva, Switzerland, generate petabytes of data per year that must be processed to answer basic questions about the universe. Companies like Amazon, eBay, and Facebook keep track of millions of transactions daily and use them in their data mining applications.

No computer is powerful enough to tackle the type of problems we have just described by itself. Today, large data sets are processed in parallel using many, many processors. In this section, we introduce parallel programming and a Python API that enables us to take advantage of the multiple cores available on most current computers. While the practical details of parallel computing on a distributed system is beyond the scope of this text, the general principles we introduce in this chapter apply to such computing as well.

Parallel Computing

For several decades and until the mid-2000s, microprocessors on most personal computers had a single core (i.e., processing unit). That meant that only one program could execute at a time on such machines. Starting in the mid-2000s, major microprocessor manufacturers such as Intel and AMD started selling microprocessors with multiple processing units, typically referred to as *cores*. Almost all personal computers sold today and many wireless devices have microprocessors with two or more cores. The programs we have developed so far have not made use of more than one core. To take advantage of them, we need to use one of the Python parallel programming APIs.

DETOUR

> ### Moore's Law
>
> Intel cofounder Gordon Moore predicted in 1965 that the number of transistors on a microprocessor chip would double about every two years. Amazingly, his prediction has held up so far. Thanks to the exponential increase in transistor density, the processing power of microprocessors, measured in the number of instructions per second, has seen tremendous growth over the last several decades.
>
> Increasing transistor density can improve the processing power in two ways. One way is to use the fact that if transistors are closer together, then the instructions can execute quicker. We can thus reduce the time between the execution of instructions (i.e., increase the processor *clock rate*). Until the mid-2000s, that was exactly what microprocessor manufacturers were doing.
>
> The problem with increasing the clock rate is that it also increases power consumption, which in turn creates problems such as overheating. The other way to increase processing power is to reorganize the denser transistors into multiple cores that can execute instructions in parallel. This approach also ends up increasing the number of instructions that can be executed per second. Recently, processor manufacturers have begun using this second approach, producing processors with two, four, eight, and even more cores. This fundamental change in the architecture of microprocessors is an opportunity but also a challenge. Writing programs that use multiple cores is more complex than single-core programming.

Class `Pool` of Module `multiprocessing`

If your computer has a microprocessor with multiple cores, you can split the execution of *some* Python programs into several tasks, which can be run in parallel by different cores. One way to do this in Python is by using the Standard Library module `multiprocessing`.

If you do not know the number of cores on your computer, you can use the function `cpu_count()` defined in module `multiprocessing` to find out:

```
>>> from multiprocessing import cpu_count
>>> cpu_count()
8
```

Your computer may have fewer cores, or more! With eight cores, you could, theoretically, execute programs eight times faster. To achieve that speed, you would have to split the problem you are solving into eight pieces of equal size and then let each core handle a piece in parallel. Unfortunately, not all problems can be broken into equal-size pieces. But there are problems, especially data processing problems, that can be, and they are motivating this discussion.

We use the class `Pool` in module `multiprocessing` to split a problem and execute its pieces in parallel. A `Pool` object represents a pool of one or more *processes*, each of which is capable of executing code independently on an available processor core.

What Is a Process?

A process is typically defined as a "program in execution." But what does that really mean? When a program executes on a computer, it executes in an "environment" that keeps track of all the program instructions, variables, program stack, the state of the CPU, and so on. This "environment" is created by the underlying operating system to support the execution of the program. This "environment" is what we refer to as a process.

Modern computers are multiprocessing, which means that they can run multiple programs or, more precisely, multiple processes *concurrently*. The term *concurrently* does not really mean "at the same time." On a single-core microprocessor computer architecture, only one process can really be executing at a given point. What concurrently means in that case is that at any given point in time, there are multiple processes (programs in execution), one of which is actually using the CPU and making progress; the other processes are interrupted, waiting for the CPU to be allocated to them by the operating system. In a multicore computer architecture, the situation is different: Several processes can truly run at the same time, on different cores.

We illustrate the usage of the class `Pool` in a simple example:

Module: parallel.py

```python
from multiprocessing import Pool

pool = Pool(2)                  # create pool of 2 processes

animals = ['hawk', 'hen', 'hog', 'hyena']
res = pool.map(len, animals)    # apply len() to every animals item

print(res)                      # print the list of string lengths
```

This program uses a pool of two processes to compute the lengths of strings in list `animals`. When you execute this program in your system's command shell (not the Python interactive shell), you get:

```
> python parallel.py
[4, 3, 3, 5]
```

So, in program `parallel.py`, the `map()` method applies function `len()` to every item of list `animals` and then returns a new list from the values obtained. Expression

```python
pool.map(len, animals)
```

and the list comprehension expression

```python
[len(x) for x in animals]
```

really do the same thing and evaluate to the same value. The only difference is how they do it.

In the `Pool`-based approach, unlike the list comprehension approach, two processes are used to apply the function `len()` to each item of list `animals`. If the host computer has at least two cores, the processor can execute the two processes at the same time (i.e., in parallel).

To demonstrate that the two processes execute at the same time, we modify the program `parallel.py` to explicitly show that different processes handle different items of list `animal`. To differentiate between processes, we use the convenient fact that every process has a unique integer ID. The ID of process can be obtained using the `getpid()` function of the os Standard Library module:

Module: parallel2.py

```
1  from multiprocessing import Pool
2  from os import getpid
3
4  def length(word):
5      'returns length of string word'
6
7      # print the id of the process executing the function
8      print('Process {} handling {}'.format(getpid(), word))
9      return len(word)
10
11 # main program
12 pool = Pool(2)
13 res = pool.map(length, ['hawk', 'hen', 'hog', 'hyena'])
14 print(res)
```

The function `length()` takes a string and returns its length, just like `len()`; it also prints the ID of the process executing the function. When we run the previous program at the command line (not in the Python interactive shell), we get something like:

```
> python parallel2.py
Process 36715 handling hawk
Process 36716 handling hen
Process 36716 handling hyena
Process 36715 handling hog
[4, 3, 3, 5]
```

Thus, the process with ID 36715 handled strings `'hawk'` and `'hog'`, while the process with ID 36716 handled strings `'hen'` and `'hyena'`. On a computer with multiple cores, the processes can execute completely in parallel.

CAUTION

Why Don't We Run Parallel Programs in the Interactive Shell?

For technical reasons that go beyond the scope of this book, it is not possible, on some operating system platforms, to run programs using `Pool` in the interactive shell. For this reason, we run all programs that use a pool of processes in the command-line shell of the host operating system.

To change the pool size in `parallel2.py`, you only need to change the input argument of the `Pool` constructor. When a pool is constructed with the default `Pool()` constructor (i.e., when the pool size is not specified), Python will decide on its own how many processes to assign. It will not assign more processes than there are cores on the host system.

Practice Problem 12.7

Write program notParallel.py that is a list comprehension version of parallel2.py. Run it to check how many processes it uses. Then run parallel2.py several times, with a pool size of 1, 3, and then 4. Also run it with the default Pool() constructor.

Parallel Speedup

To illustrate the benefit of parallel computing, we consider a computationally intensive problem from number theory. We would like to compare the distribution of prime numbers in several arbitrary ranges of integers. More precisely, we want to count the number of prime numbers in several equal-size ranges of 100,000 large integers.

Suppose one of the ranges is from 12,345,678 up to but not including 12,445,678. To find the prime numbers in this range, we can simply iterate through the numbers in the range and check each whether it is prime. Function countPrimes() implements this idea using list comprehension:

Module: primeDensity.py

```python
from os import getpid

def countPrimes(start):
    'returns the number of primes in range [start, start+rng)'

    rng = 100000
    formatStr = 'process {} processing range [{}, {})'
    print(formatStr.format(getpid(), start, start+rng))

    # sum up numbers i in range [start, start_rng) that are prime
    return sum([1 for i in range(start,start+rng) if prime(i)])
```

The function prime() takes a positive integer and returns True if it is prime, False otherwise. It is the solution to Problem 5.36. We use the next program to compute the execution time of function countPrimes():

Module: primeDensity.py

```python
from multiprocessing import Pool
from time import time

if __name__ == '__main__':

    p = Pool()
    # starts is a list of left boundaries of integer ranges
    starts = [12345678, 23456789, 34567890, 45678901,
              56789012, 67890123, 78901234, 89012345]

    t1 = time()                        # start time
    print(p.map(countPrimes, starts))  # run countPrimes()
    t2 = time()                        # end time

    p.close()
    print('Time taken: {} seconds.'.format(t2-t1))
```

If we modify the line `p = Pool()` to `p = Pool(1)`, and thus have a pool with only one process, we get this output:

```
> python map.py
process 4176 processing range [12345678, 12445678]
process 4176 processing range [23456789, 23556789]
process 4176 processing range [34567890, 34667890]
process 4176 processing range [45678901, 45778901]
process 4176 processing range [56789012, 56889012]
process 4176 processing range [67890123, 67990123]
process 4176 processing range [78901234, 79001234]
process 4176 processing range [89012345, 89112345]
[6185, 5900, 5700, 5697, 5551, 5572, 5462, 5469]
Time taken: 47.84 seconds.
```

In other words, a single process handled all eight integer ranges and took 47.84 seconds. (The run time will likely be different on your machine.) If we use a pool of two processes, we get a dramatic improvement in running time: 24.60 seconds. So by using two processes running on two cores instead of just one process, we decreased the running time by almost one-half.

A better way to compare sequential and parallel running times is the *speedup*, that is, the ratio between the sequential and the parallel running times. In this particular case, we have a speedup of

$$\frac{47.84}{24.6} \approx 1.94.$$

What this means is that with two processes (running on two separate cores), we solved the problem 1.94 times faster, or almost twice as fast. Note that this is, essentially, the best we can hope for: Two processes executing in parallel can be at most twice as fast as one process.

With four processes, we get further improvement in running time: 16.78 seconds, which corresponds to a speedup of $47.84/16.78 \approx 2.85$. Note that the best possible speedup with four processes running on four separate cores is 4. With eight processes, we get some further improvement in running time: 14.29 seconds, which corresponds to a speedup of $47.84/14.29 \approx 3.35$. The best possible is, of course, 8.

MapReduce, in Parallel

With a parallel version of list comprehension in our hands, we can modify our first, sequential MapReduce implementation to one that can run the Map and Reduce steps in parallel. The only modification to the constructor is the addition of an optional input argument: the desired number of processes.

Module: ch12.py

```
1   from multiprocessing import Pool
2   class MapReduce(object):
3       'a parallel implementation of MapReduce'
4
5       def __init__(self, mapper, reducer, numProcs=None):
6           'initialize map and reduce functions, and process pool'
7           self.mapper = mapper
8           self.reducer = reducer
9           self.pool = Pool(numProcs)
```

The method `process()` is modified so that it uses the `Pool` method `map()` instead of list comprehension in the Map and Reduce steps.

Module: ch12.py

```
1    def process(self, data):
2        'runs MapReduce on sequence data'
3
4        intermediate1 = self.pool.map(self.mapper, data)  # Map
5        intermediate2 = partition(intermediate1)
6        return self.pool.map(self.reducer, intermediate2) # Reduce
```

Parallel versus Sequential MapReduce

We use the parallel implementation of MapReduce to solve the name cross-checking problem. Suppose that tens of thousands of previously classified documents have just been posted on the web and that the documents mention various people. You are interested in finding which documents mention a particular person, and you want to do that for every person named in one or more documents. Conveniently, people's names are capitalized, which helps you narrow down the words that can be proper names.

The precise problem we are then going to solve is this: Given a list of URLs (of the documents), we want to obtain a list of pairs (`proper`, `urlList`) in which `proper` is a capitalized word in any document and `urlList` is a list of URLs of documents containing `proper`. In order to use MapReduce, we need to define the map and reduce functions.

The map function takes a URL and should produce a list of (key, value) pairs. In this particular problem, there should be a (key, value) pair for every capitalized word in the document that the URL identifies, with the word being the key and the URL being the value. So the map function is then:

Module: ch12.py

```
1    from urllib.request import urlopen
2    from re import findall
3
4    def getProperFromURL(url):
5        '''returns list of items [(word, url)] for every word
6           in the content of web page associated with url'''
7
8        content = urlopen(url).read().decode()
9        pattern = '[A-Z][A-Za-z\'\-]*'        # RE for capitalized words
10       propers = set(findall(pattern, content)) # removes duplicates
11
12       res = []                   # for every capitalized word
13       for word in propers:       # create pair (word, url)
14           res.append((word, url))
15       return res
```

A regular expression, defined in line 8, is used to find capitalized words in line 9. (To review regular expressions, see Section 11.3.) Duplicate words are removed by converting the list returned by `re` function `findall()` to a set; we do that because duplicates are not needed and to speed up the Partition and Reduce steps that follow.

The Partition step of MapReduce takes the output of the Map step and pulls together all the (key, value) pairs with the same key. In this particular problem, the result of the Partition step is a list of pairs (`word, urls`) for every capitalized word; `urls` refers to the list of URLs of documents containing `word`. Since these are exactly the pairs we need, no further processing is required in the Reduce step:

Module: ch12.py

```
1  def getWordIndex(keyVal):
2      'returns input value'
3      return keyVal
```

How do our sequential and parallel implementations compare? In the next code, we develop a test program that compares the running times of the sequential implementation and a parallel implementation with four processes. (The tests were run on a machine with eight cores.) Instead of classified documents we use, as our test bed, eight novels by Charles Dickens, publicly made available by the Project Gutenberg:

Module: ch12.py

```
1   from time import time
2
3   if __name__ == '__main__':
4
5       urls = [                    # URLs of eight Charles Dickens novels
6             'http://www.gutenberg.org/cache/epub/2701/pg2701.txt',
7             'http://www.gutenberg.org/cache/epub/1400/pg1400.txt',
8             'http://www.gutenberg.org/cache/epub/46/pg46.txt',
9             'http://www.gutenberg.org/cache/epub/730/pg730.txt',
10            'http://www.gutenberg.org/cache/epub/766/pg766.txt',
11            'http://www.gutenberg.org/cache/epub/1023/pg1023.txt',
12            'http://www.gutenberg.org/cache/epub/580/pg580.txt',
13            'http://www.gutenberg.org/cache/epub/786/pg786.txt']
14
15       t1 = time()    # sequential start time
16       SeqMapReduce(getProperFromURL, getWordIndex).process(urls)
17       t2 = time()    # sequential stop time, parallel start time
18       MapReduce(getProperFromURL, getWordIndex, 4).process(urls)
19       t3 = time()    # parallel stop time
20
21       print('Sequential: {:5.2f} seconds.'.format(t2-t1))
22       print('Parallel:   {:5.2f} seconds.'.format(t3-t2))
```

Let's run this test:

```
> python ch12.py
Sequential: 19.89 seconds.
Parallel:   14.81 seconds.
```

So, with four cores, we decreased the running time by 5.08 seconds, which corresponds to a speedup of

$$\frac{19.89}{14.81} \approx 1.34.$$

The best possible speedup with four cores is 4. In the previous example, we are using four cores to get a speedup of 1.34, which is not close to the theoretically best speedup of 4.

DETOUR

Why Cannot We Get a Better Speedup?

One reason we cannot get a better speedup is that there is always overhead when running a program in parallel. The operating system has extra work to do when managing multiple processes running on separate cores. Another reason is that while our parallel MapReduce implementation executes the Map and Reduce steps in parallel, the Partition step is still sequential. On problems that produce very large intermediate lists to be processed in the Partition step, the Partition step will take the same long time as on the sequential implementation. This effectively reduces the benefit of parallel Map and Reduce steps.

It is possible do the Partition step in parallel, but to do so you would need access to an appropriately configured distributed file system of the kind Google uses. In fact, this distributed file system is the real contribution made by Google in developing the MapReduce framework. To learn more about it, you can read the original Google paper that describes the framework:

```
http://labs.google.com/papers/mapreduce.html
```

In Practice Problem 12.8, you will develop a program that has a more time-intensive Map step and a less intensive Partition step; you should see a more impressive speedup.

Practice Problem 12.8

You are given a list of positive integers, and you need to compute a mapping that maps a prime number to those integers in the list that the prime number divides. For example, if the list is [24,15,35,60], then the mapping is

```
[(2, [24, 60]), (3, [15, 60]), (5, [15, 35]), (7, [35])]
```

(Prime number 2 divides 24 and 60, prime number 3 divides 15 and 60, etc.)

You are told that your application will get very large lists of integers as input. Therefore, you must use the MapReduce framework to solve this problem. In order to do so, you will need to develop a map and a reduce function for this particular problem. If named `mapper()` and `reducer()`, you would use them in this way to get the mapping described:

```
>>> SeqMapReduce(mapper, reducer).process([24,15,35,60])
```

After implementing the map and reduce functions, compare the running times of your sequential and parallel MapReduce implementations, and compute the speedup, by developing a test program that uses a random sample of 64 integers between 10,000,000 and 20,000,000. You may use the `sample()` function defined in the module `random()`.

E-Book Case Study: Data Interchange

In the Chapter 11 case study, we have developed a simple web crawler that collects information about web pages it visits. This information can in turn be used to build a search engine. By saving the crawl data into a file, we can make that data available to other programs. In this case study, we look at *data interchange* or how to format and save data so it is accessible, easily and efficiently, to any program that requires it.

Chapter Summary

This chapter focuses on modern approaches to processing data. Behind almost every modern "real" computer application, there is a database. Database files are often more suitable than general-purpose files for storing data. This is why it is important to get an early exposure to databases, understand their benefits, and know how to use them.

This chapter introduces a small subset of SQL, the language used to access a type of database files. We also introduce the Python Standard Library module `sqlite3`, which is an API for working with such files. We demonstrate the usage of SQL and the `sqlite3` module in the context of storing the results of a web crawl in a database file and then making search engine-type queries.

Scalability is an important issue with regard to data processing. The amount of data generated and processed by many current computer applications is huge. Not all programs can scale and handle large amounts of data, however. We are thus particularly interested in programming approaches that can scale (i.e., that can be run in parallel on multiple processors or cores). We introduce in this chapter several scalable programming techniques that have their roots in functional languages. We introduce first list comprehensions, a Python construct that enables, using a succinct description, the execution of a function on every item of a list. We then introduce the function `map()`, defined in the Standard Library module `multiprocessing`, that essentially enables the execution of list comprehensions in parallel using the available cores of a microprocessor. We then build on this to describe and develop a basic version of Google's MapReduce framework. Google and other companies use this framework to process really big data sets.

While our programs are implemented to run on a single computer, the concepts and techniques introduced in this chapter apply to distributed computing in general and especially to modern cloud computing systems.

Solutions to Practice Problems

12.1 The SQL queries are:

(a) SELECT DISTINCT Url FROM Hyperlinks WHERE Link = 'four.html'

(b) SELECT DISTINCT Link FROM Hyperlinks WHERE Url = 'four.html'

(c) SELECT Url, Word from Keywords WHERE Freq = 3

(d) SELECT * from Keywords WHERE Freq BETWEEN 3 AND 5

12.2 The SQL queries are:

(a) SELECT SUM(Freq) From Keywords WHERE Url = 'two.html'

(b) SELECT Count(*) From Keywords WHERE Url = 'two.html'

(c) SELECT Url, SUM(Freq) FROM Keywords GROUP BY Url

(d) SELECT Link, COUNT(*) FROM Hyperlinks GROUP BY Link

12.3 Make sure you use parameter substitution correctly, and do not forget to commit and close:

```
import sqlite3
def webData(db, url, links, freq):
    '''db is the name of a database file containing tables
        Hyperlinks and Keywords;
```

```
    url is the URL of a web page;
    links is a list of hyperlink URLs in the web page;
    freq is a dictionary that maps each word in the web page
    to its frequency;

    webData inserts row (url, word, freq[word]) into Keywords
    for every keyword in freq, and record (url, link) into
    Hyperlinks, for every link in links
    '''
    con = sqlite3.connect(db)
    cur = con.cursor()
    for word in freq:
        record = (url, word, freq[word])
        cur.execute("INSERT INTO Keywords VALUES (?,?,?)", record)
    for link in links:
        record = (url, link)
        cur.execute("INSERT INTO Keywords VALUES (?,?)", record)
    con.commit()
    con.close()
```

12.4 The search engine is a simple server program that iterates indefinitely and serves a user search request in every iteration:

```
def freqSearch(webdb):
    '''webdb is a database file containing table Keywords;

    freqSearch is a simple search engine that takes a keyword
    from the user and prints URLs of web pages containing it
    in decreasing order of frequency of the word'''
    con = sqlite3.connect(webdb)
    cur = con.cursor()

    while True:    # serve forever
        keyword = input("Enter keyword: ")
        # select web pages containing keyword in
        # decreasing order of keyword frequency
        cur.execute("""SELECT Url, Freq
                    FROM Keywords
                    WHERE Word = ?
                    ORDER BY Freq DESC""", (keyword,))
        print('{:15}{:4}'.format('URL', 'FREQ'))
        for url, freq in cur:
            print('{:15}{:4}'.format(url, freq))
```

12.5 The list comprehension constructs are:

(a) `[word.capitalize() for word in words]`: Every word is capitalized.

(b) `[(word, len(word)) for word in words]`: A tuple is created for every word.

(c) `[[(c,word) for c in word] for word in words]`: Every word is used to create a list; the list is constructed from every character of the word, which can be done using list comprehension too.

12.6 The map function should map a word (string) to a list of tuples (`c, word`) for every character c of word.

```
def getChars(word):
    '''word is a string; the function returns a list of tuples
       (c, word) for every character c of word'''
    return [(c, word) for c in word]
```

The input to the reduce function is a tuple (`c, lst`) where `lst` contains words containing c; the reduce function should simply eliminate duplicates from `lst`:

```
def getCharIndex(keyVal):
    '''keyVal is a 2-tuple (c, lst) where lst is a list
       of words (strings)

       function returns (c, lst') where lst' is lst with
       duplicates removed'''
    return (keyVal[0], list(set(keyVal[1])))
```

12.7 The program is:

Module: notParallel.py

```
1  from os import getpid
2
3  def length(word):
4      'returns length of string word'
5      print('Process {} handling {}'.format(getpid(), word))
6      return len(word)
7
8  animals = ['hawk', 'hen', 'hog', 'hyena']
9  print([length(x) for x in animals])
```

It will, of course, use only one process when executed.

12.8 The map function, which we name `divisors()`, takes number and returns a list of pairs (`i, number`) for every prime i dividing number:

```
from math import sqrt
def divisors(number):
    '''returns list of (i, number) tuples for
       every prime i dividing number'''
    res = []             # accumulator of factors of number
    n = number
    i = 2
    while n > 1:
        if n%i == 0:  # if i is a factor of n
            # collect i and repeatedly divide n by i
            # while i is a factor of n
            res.append((i, number))
            while n%i == 0:
                n //= i
        i += 1           # go to next i
    return res
```

The Partition step will pull together all pairs (i, number) that have the same key i. The list it constructs is actually the desired final list, so the Reduce step should only copy the (key, value) pairs:

```
def identity(keyVal):
    return keyVal
```

Here is a test program:

```
from random import sample
from time import time
if __name__ == '__main__':
    # create list of 64 large random integers
    numbers = sample(range(10000000, 20000000), 64)
    t1 = time()
    SeqMapReduce(divisors, identity).process(numbers)
    t2 = time()
    MapReduce(divisors, identity).process(numbers)
    t3 = time()
    print('Sequential: {:5.2f} seconds.'.format(t2-t1))
    print('Parallel:   {:5.2f} seconds.'.format(t3-t2))
```

When you run this test on a computer with a multicore microprocessor, you should see the parallel MapReduce implementation run faster. Here is the result for a sample run using four cores:

```
Sequential: 26.77 seconds.
Parallel:   11.18 seconds.
```

The speedup is 2.39.

Exercises

12.9 Write SQL queries on tables Hyperlinks and Keywords from Figure 12.2 that return these results:

(a) The distinct words appearing in web page with URL four.html

(b) URLs of web pages containing either 'Chicago' or 'Paris'

(c) The total number of occurrences of every distinct word, across all web pages

(d) URLs of web pages that have an incoming link from a page containing 'Nairobi'

12.10 Write SQL queries on table WeatherData in Figure 12.16 that return:

(a) All the records for the city of London

(b) All the summer records

(c) The city, country, and season for which the average temperature is less than 20°

(d) The city, country, and season for which the average temperature is greater than 20° and the total rainfall is less than 10 mm

(e) The maximum total rainfall

(f) The city, season, and rainfall amounts for all records in descending order of rainfall

(g) The total yearly rainfall for Cairo, Egypt

(h) The city name, country, and total yearly rainfall for every distinct city

Figure 12.16 A world weather database fragment. Shown are the 24-hour average temperature (in degrees Celsius) and total rainfall amount (in millimeters) for Winter (1), Spring (2), Summer (3), and Fall (4) for several world cities.

City	Country	Season	Temperature	Rainfall
Mumbai	India	1	24.8	5.9
Mumbai	India	2	28.4	16.2
Mumbai	India	3	27.9	1549.4
Mumbai	India	4	27.6	346.0
London	United Kingdom	1	4.2	207.7
London	United Kingdom	2	8.3	169.6
London	United Kingdom	3	15.7	157.0
London	United Kingdom	4	10.4	218.5
Cairo	Egypt	1	13.6	16.5
Cairo	Egypt	2	20.7	6.5
Cairo	Egypt	3	27.7	0.1
Cairo	Egypt	4	22.2	4.5

12.11 Using module `sqlite3`, create a database file `weather.db` and table `WeatherData` in it. Define the column names and types to match those in the table in Figure 12.16; then enter all the rows shown into the table.

12.12 Using `sqlite3` and within the interactive shell, open the database file `weather.db` you created in Problem 12.11 and execute the queries from Problem 12.10 by running appropriate Python statements.

12.13 Let list `lst` be defined as

```
>>> lst = [23, 12, 3, 17, 21, 14, 6, 4, 9, 20, 19]
```

Write list comprehension expression based on list `lst` that produce these lists:
- (a) `[3, 6, 4, 9]` (the single-digit numbers in list `lst`)
- (b) `[12, 14, 6, 4, 20]` (the even numbers in list `lst`)
- (c) `[12, 3, 21, 14, 6, 4, 9, 20]` (the numbers divisible by 2 or 3 in list `lst`)
- (d) `[4, 9]` (the squares in list `lst`)
- (e) `[6, 7, 3, 2, 10]` (the halves of the even numbers in list `lst`)

12.14 Run program `primeDensity.py` with one, two, three, and four cores, or up to as many cores as you have on your computer, and record the running times. Then write a sequential version of the `primeDensity.py` program (using list comprehension, say) and record its running time. Compute the speedup for each execution of `primeDensity.py` with two or more cores.

12.15 Fine-tune the run time analysis of program `ch12.py` by recording the execution time of each step—Map, Partition, and Reduce—of MapReduce. (You will have to modify the class MapReduce to do this.) Which steps have better speedup than others?

Problems

12.16 Write function `ranking()` that takes as input the name of a database file containing a table named `Hyperlinks` of the same format as the table in Figure 12.2(a). The function should add to the database a new table that contains the number of *incoming* hyperlinks for every URL listed in the Link column of Hyperlinks. Name the new table and its columns Ranks, Url, and Rank, respectively. When executed against database file links.db, the wildcard query on the Rank table should produce this output:

```
>>> cur.execute('SELECT * FROM Ranks')
<sqlite3.Cursor object at 0x15d2560>
>>> for record in cur:
        print(record)

('five.html', 1)
('four.html', 3)
('one.html', 1)
('three.html', 1)
('two.html', 2)
```

File: links.db

12.17 Develop an application that takes the name of a text file as input, computes the frequency of every word in the file, and stores the resulting (word, frequency) pairs in a new table named Wordcounts of a new database file. The table should have columns Word and Freq for storing the (word, frequency) pairs.

12.18 Develop an application that displays, using Turtle graphics, the n most frequently occurring words in a text file. Assume that the word frequencies of the file have already been computed and stored in a database file such as the one created in Problem 12.17. Your application takes as input the name of this database file and the number n. It should then display the n most frequent words at random positions of a turtle screen. Try using different font sizes for the words: a very large font for the most frequently occurring word, a smaller font for the next two words, an even smaller font for the next four words, and so on.

12.19 In Practice Problem 12.4, we developed a simple search engine that ranks web pages based on word frequency. There are several reasons why that is a poor way to rank web pages, including the fact that it can be easily manipulated.

Modern search engines such as Google's use hyperlink information (among other things) to rank web pages. For example, if a web page has few incoming links, it probably does not contain useful information. If, however, a web page has many incoming hyperlinks, then it likely contains useful information and should be ranked high.

Using the links.db database file obtained by crawling through the pages in Figure 12.1, and also the Rank table computed in Problem 12.16, redevelop the search engine from Practice Problem 12.4 so that it ranks web pages by number of incoming links.

```
>>> search2('links.db')
Enter keyword: Paris
URL             RANK
four.html          3
two.html           2
one.html           1
Enter keyword:
```

File: links.db

12.20 The UNIX text search utility grep takes a text file and a regular expression and returns a list of lines in the text that contain a string that matches the pattern. Develop a parallel version of grep that takes from the user the name of a text file and the regular expression and then uses a pool of processes to search the lines of the file.

12.21 We used the program `primeDensity.py` to compare the densities of prime numbers in several large ranges of very large integers. In this problem, you will compare the densities of *twin primes*. Twin primes are pairs of primes whose difference is 2. The first few twin primes are 3 and 5, 5 and 7, 11 and 13, 17 and 19, and 29 and 32. Write an application that uses all the cores on your computer to compare the number of twin primes across the same ranges of integers we used in `primeDensity.py`.

12.22 Problem 10.26 asks you to develop function `anagram()` that uses a dictionary (i.e., a list of words) to compute all the anagrams of a given string. Develop `panagram()`, a parallel version of this function, that takes a list of words and computes a list of anagrams for each word.

12.23 At the end of this book there is an index, which maps words to page numbers of pages containing the words. A line index is similar: It maps words to line numbers of text lines in which they appear. Develop, using the MapReduce framework, an application that takes as input the name of a text file and creates a line index. Your application should output the index to a file so words appear in alphabetical order, one word per line; the line numbers, for each word, should follow the word and be output in increasing order.

12.24 Redo Problem 12.16 using MapReduce to compute the number of incoming links for every web page.

12.25 A *web-link graph* is a description of the hyperlink structure of a set of linked web pages. One way to represent the web-link graph is with a list of (url, linksList) pairs with each pair corresponding to a web page; url refers to the URL of the page, and linksList is a list of URLs of hyperlinks contained in the page. Note that this information is easily collected by a web crawler.

The *reverse web-link graph* is another representation of the hyperlink structure of the set of web pages. It can be represented as a list of (url, incomingList) pairs with url referring to the URL of a web page and incomingList referring to a list of URLs of *incoming* hyperlinks. So the reverse web-link graph makes explicit incoming links rather than outgoing links. It is very useful for efficiently computing the Google PageRank of web pages.

Develop a function that takes a web-link graph, represented as described, and returns the reverse web-link graph.

12.26 A web server usually creates a log for every HTTP request it handles and appends the log string to a log file. Keeping a log file is useful for a variety of reasons. One particular reason is that it can be used to learn what resources—identified by URLs—managed by the server have been accessed and how often—referred to as the URL access frequency. In this problem, you will develop a program that computes the URL access frequency from a given log file.

Web server log entries are written in a well-known, standard format known as the *Common Log Format*. This is a standard format used by the Apache httpd web server as well as other servers. A standard format makes it possible to develop log analysis programs that mine the access log file. A log file entry produced in a common log format looks like this:

```
127.0.0.1 - - [16/Mar/2010:11:52:54 -0600] "GET /index.html HTTP/1.0" 200 1929
```

This log contains a lot of information. The key information, for our purposes, is the requested resource, `index.html`. Write a program that computes the access frequency for each resource appearing in the log file and writes the information into a database table with columns for the resource URL and the access frequency. Writing the access frequency into a database makes the URL access frequency amenable to queries and analysis.

12.27 Write an application that computes a concordance of a set of novels using MapReduce. A *concordance* is a mapping that maps each word in a set of words to a list of sentences from the novels that contain the word. The input for the application is the set of names of text files containing the novels and the set of words to be mapped. You should output the concordance to a file.

Index

!= operator
    number not equal, 19, 36
    overloading, 258
    set not equal, 179, 180
    string not equal, 23
** exponentiation operator, 17, 36
* operator
    list repetition, 28
    number multiplication, 16, 36
    overloading, 258
    in regular expression, 387, 389
    string repetition, 24, 25
+= increment operator, 135
+ operator
    list concatenation, 28
    number addition, 16, 36
    overloading, 258
    in regular expression, 387, 389
    string concatenation, 24, 25
- operator
    negation unary operator, 36
    overloading, 258
    set difference, 179, 180
    subtraction binary operator, 16, 36
.. parent folder, 109
. regular expression operator, 387, 389
// quotient operator, 17, 36
/ operator
    number division, 16, 36
    overloading, 258
<= operator
    number less than or equal, 19, 36
    overloading, 258
    SQL less than or equal, 405
    subset of, 179, 180
<> SQL not equal operator, 405
< operator
    number less than, 18, 36
    overloading, 258
    proper subset of, 179, 180
    SQL less than, 405
    string less than, 23
== operator
    number equal, 19, 36
    overloading, 258, 261, 262
    set equal, 179, 180
    string equal, 23
    versus = assignment operator, 22
= SQL equal operator, 405
= assignment statement, 12, 20–22, 74–78
    and mutability, 76–77
    multiple assignment, 78
    simultaneous assignment, 78
    swapping, 77–78
    versus == equal operator, 22
>= operator
    number greater than or equal, 19, 36
    overloading, 258
    SQL greater than or equal, 405
    superset of, 179, 180
> operator
    number greater than, 18, 36
    overloading, 258
    proper superset of, 179, 180
    SQL greater than, 405
    string greater than, 23
>>> prompt, 9, 16
? regular expression operator, 387, 389
[] operator
    dictionary indexing, 169
    list indexing, 27, 28
    list slicing, 95
    in regular expression, 387, 389
    string indexing, 25–27
    string slicing, 94–95
    tuple indexing, 30
    two-dimensional list indexing, 141

% remainder operator, 17, 36
& set intersection operator, 179, 180
^ operator
    in regular expression, 388, 389
    set symmetric difference, 179, 180
| operator
    in regular expression, 388, 389
    set union, 179, 180

abs() built-in function, 17, 36
absolute pathname, 108
abstraction, 3, 10
accumulator
    for integer sum, 135
    for integer product, 136
    for list concatenation, 136
    loop pattern, *see* iteration pattern
    for string concatenation, 136
acronym() function, 136
__add__() method, 257
add() set method, 180
algebraic
    expression, 16–18
    operators, 16, 17, 36
algorithm, 3, 11
    running time, *see* run time analysis
alignment in formatted output, 103
American Standard Code for Information
    Interchange (ASCII), 182–183
anchor, *see* HTML
and Boolean operator, 19, 20
Animal class, 247, 268
append() list method, 32
Application Programming Interface
    (API), 7
approxE() function, 146
approxPi() function, 188
Ariane rocket accident, 220
ARPANET, 6
assignment, *see* = assignment statement
attribute
    class, *see* class
    of HTML element, *see* HTML
    instance, *see* instance
    module, *see* module
automation, 3
average.py program, 69

background widget option, 293, 296
backslash in file path, 109

base case, *see* recursion
before0() function, 150
Berners-Lee, Tim, 372, 373
BETWEEN SQL operator, 405
binary operator, 20
binary search, 354
bind() widget method, 306–311
binding, *see* event
Bird class, 267, 268
bool Boolean type, *see* Boolean
George Boole, 20
Boolean
    algebra, 20
    expression, 18–20
    mutability, 75
    operators, 19
    type, 18
    values, 18
borderwidth widget option, 293, 296
break statement, 149–150
browser, *see* web
bubblesort() function, 139
buffer overflow attack, 210
bug, *see* computer bug
builtins module, 226
bus, 5
Button tkinter class, 299–302
    command option, 300
    event handler, 300
bytes built-in type, 186, 380

camelCase, 22
canonical string representation, 260–262
Canvas tkinter class, 308–313
capitalize() string method, 96, 98
Card class, 250–251
ceil() math module function, 42
central processing unit (CPU), 4, 425
character encoding, 181–186
    ASCII, 182–183
    of files, 186
    Unicode, 183–186
    UTF encodings, 185–186
cheers() recursive function, 334
choice() random module function, 189
chr() built-in function, 183
cities() function, 148
cities2() function, 148
class, 34, 40
    attribute, 230–231

attribute inheritance, 244–245

attribute search, 268–269

code reuse, 264

constructor, 37

constructor and `repr()` contract, 260–264

default constructor, 249–250

defining new class, 240–275

defining new container, 251–256

documentation, 246

extending a method, 270

inheritance, 264–272

inheritance patterns, 270–271

method implementation, 231

namespace, 230–231, 241–242

overloaded constructor, 248–250

overloaded operator, 256–264

overriding a method, 267–270

subclass, 265, 266

superclass, 266

`class` statement, 243, 245, 267

`clear()` set method, 180

`ClickIt` class, 314

`clickit.py` module, 300, 301, 313

client, *see* web

clock rate, 424

`close()`

Connection method, 412

file method, 110, 112

code point (Unicode), 183

code reuse

with classes, 264

with functions, 204

`Collector` class, 385

column formatted output, 102

column `grid()` method option, 298

`columnspan grid()` method option, 298

command `Button` widget option, 300

command line, 53

comment, 72

`commit()` Connection method, 412

comparison operators, 36

for numbers, 18–19

for sets, 180

for strings, 23

compiler, 7

`complete()` function, 173

computational thinking, 9–13

computer applications, 2

computer bug, 7

computer science, 2–4, 13

computer system, 3–7

computer virus, *see* virus

concatenation, *see* + operator

concurrent, 425

condition

in multiway `if` statement, 128–131

in one-way `if` statement, 59, 128

in two-way `if` statement, 62, 128

in `while` loop statement, 143

mutually exclusive, 130

`connect()` sqlite3 function, 411

`Connection` sqlite3 class, 411

method `close()`, 412

method `commit()`, 412

method `cursor()`, 411

constructor, *see* class

container class, *see* class

`continue` statement, 150–151

core (CPU), 424

`cos()` math module function, 42

`count()` list method, 32

`count()` string method, 96, 98

`COUNT()` SQL function, 406

`countdown()` recursive function, 330–332

counter loop pattern, *see* iteration pattern

counting operations, 349

`cpu_count()` multiprocessing function, 424

`CREATE TABLE` SQL statement, 409

`create_line()` widget method, 309, 310

`create_rectangle()` widget method, 310

`create_oval()` widget method, 310

cross join, *see* SQL

`crosscheck.py` module, 429–430

current working directory, 108

cursor, 111

`Cursor` sqlite3 class, 411

as an iterator, 413

method `execute()`, 411

method `fetchall()`, 413, 414

`cursor()` Connection method, 411

data type, 11–12

database, 400–415

column, 401

engine, 402, 410

file, 400, 401

management system, 402

programming, 410

record, 401

row, 401

SQLite, 410

SQLite command-line shell, 403

sqlite3 module, 410–415

structured data storage, 401

table, 401

Day class, 316

day.py module, 303, 304, 315

debugger, 7

decimal precision in formatted output, 103

decision structure, *see* if statement

Deck class, 252–254

decode() bytes method, 186, 380

def function definition statement, 68

default constructor, *see* class

default exception handler, *see* exception

delete() widget method, 310

for Entry, 303

for Text, 305

delimiter for method split(), 96

DESC SQL clause, 405

developer, 2–4

dict dictionary type, *see* dictionary

dictionary, 166–176

for counting, 173–176

dict() constructor, 168

key-value pair, 167

methods, 170–172

multiway condition substitute, 173

mutability, 168

operators, 169–170

user-defined indexes, 166–167

view object, 172

dictionary order (strings), 24, 185

directory, 108

DISTINCT SQL clause, 403

divisors() function, 136

docstring, 72

documentation, 72, 246

double quotes, *see* string

Draw class, 318

draw.py module, 309, 310, 317

drawKoch() function, 340

dynamic.py module, 71

e math module Euler constant *e*, 42

editor, 52, 54

elif statement, *see* if statement

else clause, *see* if statement

emoticon() function, 204

EmptyQueueError exception class, 274

encapsulation

with classes, 275

with functions, 205

with user-defined exceptions, 272, 274

end argument, *see* print()

Entry tkinter class, 302–304

deleting entry, 303

reading entry, 303

epoch, 106

__eq__() method, 261, 263

__len__() method, 263

error, *see* exception

escape sequence, 93

\", 92

\', 92

\n, 93, 112

interpreted by print(), 93

in regular expressions, 389

eval() built-in function, 56

event, 301

binding to event handler, 306–311

handler, 300, 301, 306

loop, 301

pattern, 306–311

type, 306

Event tkinter class, 306–308

attributes, 306

except statement, *see* exception

exception, 116–119, 215

catching a type of, 218

catching and handling, 216–223

default handler, 215, 218, 221

defining new, 272–275

exceptional control flow, 215–223

handler, 217, 218, 222

multiple handlers, 219

object, 118

raising, 215

raising in a program, 273

try/except statements, 217–218

type, 118

Exception class, 274

execute() Cursor method, 411

execution control structure, 12–13
    decision, 57–62, 128–131
    iteration, 62–67, 131–151
`expand pack()` method option, 296
experimental run time analysis, 351–353
expression
    algebraic, *see* algebraic
    Boolean, *see* Boolean
    evaluation, 17
Extender class, 270

`factorial()`
    iterative function, 136, 345
    recursive function, 334, 345
False value, 18
`feed()` HTMLParser method, 382
`fetchall()` Cursor method, 413, 414
`fibonacci()` function, 146
Fibonacci numbers, 145, 349
field width in formatted output, 103
file, 107–116
    appending to, 110
    binary, 107, 110, 380
    character encoding, 186
    closing, 115
    cursor, 111
    database, 400
    flushing output, 116
    mode, 110
    opening, 109–111
    reading, 110–115
    reading and writing, 110
    reading patterns, 112–115
    storage, 5
    text, 107, 110
    writing, 110, 115–116
filesystem, 107–109
    absolute pathname, 108
    current working directory, 108
    directory, 108
    folder, 108
    pathname, 108
    recursive structure, 342
    relative pathname, 108
    root directory, 108
    tree structure, 108
`fill pack()` method option, 296
`find()` string method, 95, 98
`findall()` re function, 390
First-In First Out (FIFO), 254

`float` type, *see* floating point
floating point
    `float()` constructor, 38
    mutability, 75
    type, 16
    values, 16, 35
`floor()` math module function, 42
flowchart, 52
    one-way `if` statement, 58, 59
    three-way `if` statement, 129
    two-way `if` statement, 61
    `while` loop statement, 143
flushing output, 116
folder, 108
`font` widget option, 293
`for` loop statement, 62–65, 131
    iteration patterns, 131–143
    loop variable, 64
`foreground` widget option, 293, 296
`format()` string method, 100–105
format string, 100
    for time, 106
formatted output, 98–105
forward slash in file path, 109
fractal, 338–342
    Koch curve, 338
    snowflake, 341
`Fraction fractions` class, 42
    difference between `float` and, 43
`fractions` Standard Library module, 42–43
`Frame tkinter` class, 311–313
`frequency()` function, 175
`frequent()` function, 359
`from` module import keyword, 229
function
    built-in math, 17
    call, 31
    code reuse, 204
    encapsulation, 205
    higher-order, 346
    input arguments, 68–69
    local variable, 205–207
    modifying global variable inside, 214
    modularity, 205
    recursive, *see* recursion
    user-defined, 67–74
functional language, 346, 417
    list comprehension, 415–417

geometry (of GUI), *see* widget
get() dictionary method, 171
get() widget method
    for Entry, 303
    for Text, 305
getheaders() HTTPResponse method, 380
getpid() os function, 426
getSource() function, 381
geturl() HTTPResponse method, 380
getWordsFromFile() function, 422
global keyword, 214
global scope, 211–215
global variable, 211
    storing state in, 310
gmtime() time function, 106
Google, 417
graphical user interface (GUI)
    development, 292–318
    history, 302
    object-oriented approach, 313–318
graphics interchange format (GIF), 294
grid() widget method, 297–299
GROUP BY SQL clause, 406
growthrates() function, 105

handle_data() HTMLParser method, 382
handle_endtag() HTMLParser method, 382
handler
    exception, *see* exception
    GUI event, *see* event
    HTML document parser, 382
handle_starttag() HTMLParser method, 382
hard drive, 5
hardware, 4
height widget option, 293, 294
hello() function, 70, 73
hello.py module, 52
hello2() function, 147
help() built-in function, 40
higher-order function, 346
HTML, 375–379
    a anchor element, 377
    absolute hyperlink, 378
    body element, 377
    document parsing, 381–384
    document tree structure, 377

    element, 376–377
    element attribute, 377, 378
    head element, 377
    heading element, 376
    href attribute, 378
    html element, 377
    hyperlink, 372, 377, 385
    relative hyperlink, 378
    resources, 379
    tag, 376
    title element, 377
HTMLParser html.parser class, 381
html.parser Standard Library module, 381–384
HTTP, 374–375
    hyperlink, *see* HTML
http.client Standard Library module, 379
HTTPResponse http.client class, 379
hyperlink, *see* HTML
HyperText Markup Language, *see* HTML
HyperText Transfer Protocol, *see* HTTP

IDLE, 8
    editor, 52
    running program, 52
if statement
    elif statement, 128
    else clause, 60, 128
    multiway, 128–131
    one-way, 57–60, 128
    ordering of conditions, 130–131
    two-way, 60–62, 128
ignore0() function, 151
image widget option, 293, 294
immutable, 29, 75
    parameter passing, 79–80
import statement, *see* module, 54
ImportError exception, 225
in operator
    for dictionaries, 169
    for lists, 28
    for sets, 179, 180
    for strings, 24, 25
incr2D() function, 142
incrementing, *see* += increment operator
indentation, 60
indented block
    in class definition, 243, 245

in `for` loop statement, 65
in function definition, 68
in multiway `if` statement, 128
in one-way `if` statement, 59, 128
in two-way `if` statement, 62, 128
in `while` loop statement, 143
index, 25
in two-dimensional list, 141
`IndexError` exception, 117, 118
indexing operator, *see* `[]` operator
infinite loop pattern, *see* iteration pattern
inheritance, 264–272
extending a method, 270
by objects, 244–245
overriding a method, 270
patterns, 270–271
subclass, 266
superclass, 266
`Inheritor` class, 270
`__init__()` method, 249–250, 255
`input()` built-in function, 55
`input.py` module, 55
`insert()` list method, 32
`insert()` widget method
for `Entry`, 303
for `Text`, 305
INSERT INTO SQL statement, 409
instance
attribute, 244
variable, 243–244
`int` integer type, *see* integer
integer
`int()` constructor, 37, 38
mutability, 75
type, 16
values, 16, 35
integrated development environment (IDE), 7, 8, 52, 54
interactive shell, 8
restarting, 52
`interest()` function, 144
Internet, 6
interpreter, 7, 17
inverted index, 421–423
`IOError` exception, 119
`items()` dictionary method, 171, 172
iteration
through indexes of a list, 132–134
through integers in a range, 66–67, 132

through a list, 64, 131
through a string, 63, 131
iteration pattern
accumulator loop, 134–137
counter loop, 132–134
infinite loop, 147
iteration loop, 131–132
loop and a half, 147–149
nested loop, 137–139, 141–143
sequence loop, 145–146
iteration structure
for loop, *see* `for` loop statement
while loop, *see* `while` loop statement

`jump()` function, 204

key-value pair
dictionary, 167
MapReduce, 417
`KeyboardInterrupt` exception, 118
`KeyError` exception, 168
`keyLogger.py` module, 307
`keys()` dictionary method, 170, 171
keyword (reserved), 23
`koch()` recursive function, 339
Koch curve, 338–342
`kthsmallest()` function, 358

`Label` tkinter class, 292–298
for images, 294–297
for text, 292–293
language
HTML, 373
SQL, 402
left-to-right, 36
left-to-right evaluation, 16
`len()` built-in function
for dictionaries, 169
for lists, 28
for sets, 179
for strings, 25
overloading, 258, 263
lexicographic order, 185
library, 7
line ending in text file, 112
linear recursion, 345–347
linear search, 354
`LinkParser` class, 383
Linux, 6

list, 27–33
  comprehension, 415–417
  concatenation, *see* + operator
  indexing, *see* [] operator
  length, *see* `len()` built-in function
  `list()` constructor, 38
  methods, 31–33
  mutability, 29, 75, 76
  operators, 27–29
  repetition, *see* * operator
  slicing, *see* [] operator
  two-dimensional, 140–143
  type, 27
  value, 27
`listdir()` os module function, 343
local scope, 211–212
local variable, 205–207
`localtime()` time function, 106
`log()` math module function, 42
loop and a half pattern, *see* iteration pattern
`lower()` string method, 98

Mac OS X, 5
`__main__` module, 226
main memory, 4
`mainloop()` widget method, 292
`maketrans()` string method, 97
`map()` Pool method, 425
map MapReduce function, 420
MapReduce class, 428
MapReduce, 417–423, 428–431
  inverted index, 421–423
  name cross-checking, 429
  sequential versus parallel, 430
  word frequency, 417–420
master (widget), *see* widget
match object (regular expression), 391
math Standard Library module, 41–42
`max()` built-in function, 18, 28
method, 32, 33
  call, 40
  extending, 270
  as a function in a namespace, 231
  inheriting, 270
  overriding, 267–270
Microsoft Windows, 5
`min()` built-in function, 18, 28
mode, *see* file mode
model, 3, 10

modularity
  through classes, 276
  through functions, 205
module, 41, 54, 223–230
  attribute, 223–224
  current working directory, 108
  importing, 41, 223–230
  importing all attributes, 229
  importing module name, 228
  importing some attributes, 228
  `__main__` module, 226
  `__name__` variable, 226–228
  namespace, 224–230
  search path, 224, 227
  top-level, 226–228
  user-defined, 54
Moore's Law, 424
`move()` widget method, 310
multiple assignment, 78
`multiprocessing` Standard Library module, 424–431
  class Pool, 424–431
  function `cpu_count()`, 424
multiway, *see* if statement
mutable, 29, 75
  parameter passing, 80–81
mutually exclusive conditions, 130
MyList class, 265

`__name__` variable, 226–228
NameError exception, 117, 118
namespace, 207
  class, 241–242
  function call, 206–207
  global, 211–215
  local, 212
  module, 224–230
  object, 242
  and the program stack, 207–211
negative index, 26, 27
`nested()` function, 138
nested loop pattern, *see* iteration pattern
nested statements, 65–66
`nested2()` function, 139
network, 5, 6
not Boolean operator, 19, 20
`numChars()` function, 112
`numLines()` function, 114
`numWords()` function, 113

object, 33
    class attributes inheritance, 244–245
    instance variable, 243–244
    namespace, 242
    type, 33
    value, 33, 35
object-oriented programming (OOP), 40, 240–276
    GUI development, 313–318
    Python, 34
occurrences
    most frequently occurring item, 359
    number of, 173–176
    using MapReduce, 417–420
one-way, *see* `if` statement
`oneWay.py` module, 58
`oneWay2.py` module, 59
`open()` built-in function, 186
`open()` function
    built-in, 109–111
open source, 6
operating system, 5–6
operator, 33
    Boolean, *see* Boolean
    algebraic, *see* algebraic
    as class method, 257–258
    dictionary, *see* dictionary
    as a function in a namespace, 258
    list, *see* list
    overloaded, *see* class
    precedence, *see* precedence rule
    regular expression, 387–391
    set, *see* set
    string, *see* string
`or` Boolean operator, 19, 20
`ord()` built-in function, 182
ORDER BY SQL clause, 405
os Standard Library module, 343
    `getpid()` function, 426
    `listdir()` function, 343
    `path.isfile()` function, 343
    `path.join()` function, 343
`OverflowError` exception, 35, 118
overloaded, *see* class
overriding a method, 267–269

`pack()` widget method, 293, 295–297
packing widgets, *see* widget
padx, pady widget options, 293, 296

`parallel.py` module, 425
parallel computing, 423–431
    versus concurrent, 425
    speedup, 427
`parallel2.py` module, 426
parameter passing, 78–81
    immutable parameter, 79–80
    mutable parameter, 80–81
    passing functions, 346
parameter substitution (SQL), 411
parent folder, 109
parser, 116
    HTML document, *see* HTML
`partition()` MapReduce function, 419
pass statement, 119, 151
`path` sys module variable, 227
`pathsys` module variable, 224
`path.isfile()` os module function, 343
`path.join()` os module function, 343
pathname, 108
    absolute, 108
    relative, 108
`pattern()` recursive function, 336
`peace.py` module, 294
`phone.py` module, 297
`PhotoImage` tkinter class, 294
`pi math` module constant π, 42
placeholder
    in format string, 100
    in SQL query, 412
`plotter.py` module, 311
Point class, 240–246, 248–250
    constructor and `repr()` contract, 260–262
    implementation, 242–243
    methods, 240
    overloaded operators, 256
    string representation, 258–260
Pool multiprocessing class, 424–431
    method `map()`, 425
`pop()` method
    dictionary, 170, 171
    list, 32
precedence rule, 16, 18, 36–37
`primeDensity.py` module, 427
`print()` built-in function, 52, 54, 98–100
    end argument, 99
    sep argument, 98

versus `return` statement, 70
`print2D()` function, 141
process, 424
    ID, 426
program, 2, 3, 52
    editing, 52
    executing, 52, 53
program stack, 207–211
    buffer overflow attack, 210
    stack frame, 209
programming, 7
    language, 7
Project Gutenberg, 430
prompt
    `input()` function, 55
    Python shell, *see* >>> prompt
protocol, 373
    HTTP, *see* HTTP
pseudocode, 11
pseudorandom number generator, 186
Python
    background, 8
    Standard Library, *see* Standard Library modules

Queue class, 254–256, 272, 275
    empty queue exception, 274
    overloaded operators, 257, 262–264
    as subclass of `list`, 271
Queue2 class, 271
quotes, *see* string

`raise()` built-in function, 273
raising exception, *see* exception
`random` Standard Library module, 186–190
random access memory (RAM), *see* main memory
randomness, 188
`randrange()` random module function, 187
`range()` built-in function, 66–67
    in counter loop pattern, 132
`re` Standard Library module, 390–391
`read()` file method, 110, 111
`read()` HTTPResponse method, 380
`readline()` file method, 110, 111
`readlines()` file method, 110, 114
real numbers, 35
`recNeg()` function, 345

`recSum()` function, 345
recursion, 330–357
    base case, 331
    filesystem traversal, 342–344
    fractal, 338–342
    function, 330
    linear, 345–347
    and the program stack, 334–335
    recursive call, 330
    recursive step, 332
    recursive thinking, 330, 332–334
    repeated recursive calls, 340
    stopping condition, 331
    virus scanning, 342–344
reduce MapReduce function, 420
regular expression, 387–391
    escape sequences, 389
    operators, 387–391
    resources, 388
relational
    algebra, 410
    database, 410
relative pathname, 108
`relief` widget option, 293, 296
`remove()` method
    for lists, 32
    for sets, 180
`replace()` string method, 96, 98
Replacer class, 270
`__repr__()` method, 264
`repr()` built-in function, 259
    contract with constructor, 260–264
    overloading, 258, 259, 263
reserved keywords, 23
result table, *see* SQL
`return` statement, 68–71
    versus `print()` built-in function, 70
`reverse()` list method, 32
`reverse()` recursive function, 334
reverse index, *see* inverted index
`rfib()` recursive function, 349
    run time analysis, 352
`rlookup()` function, 169
root directory, 108
row `grid()` method option, 298
rowspan `grid()` method option, 298
`rpower()` recursive function, 347
run time analysis, 347–353
    experimental, 351–353

linear versus binary search, 356

`safe_open()` function, 220
`sample()` random module function, 189
scalability, 415
`scan()` recursive function, 343
scientific notation, 35
scope, 211
`search()` recursive function, 355
`search()` re function, 391
search of a list, 354–359
    binary, 354
    duplicates, 357
    linear, 354
    linear versus binary, 356
search path, *see* module
SELECT SQL statement, 402–404
selecting kth smallest, 358
`sep` argument, *see* `print()`
SeqMapReduce class, 420
sequence loop pattern, *see* iteration pattern
server, *see* web
set, 177–181
    comparison, 179
    constructor, 178
    for duplicate removal, 178
    empty set, 178
    methods, 180–181
    operators, 179–180
setup (of Python IDE), 8
shell, *see* interactive shell
`shuffle()` random module function, 189
`side pack()` method option, 295
simultaneous assignment, 78
`sin()` math module function, 42
single quotes, *see* string
slicing, *see* `[]` operator
`smileyPeace.py` module, 295
snowflake fractal, 341
software, 4
software library, 7
`sort()` list method, 32
`sorted()` function, 134
speedup (parallel), 427, 430
`spelling.py` module, 63
`split()` string method, 96, 98
SQL, 402–410
    conditional operators, 405

`COUNT()` function, 406
CREATE TABLE statement, 409
cross join, 407
DESC clause, 405
DISTINCT clause, 403
GROUP BY clause, 406
INSERT INTO statement, 409
ORDER BY clause, 405
parameter substitution, 411
querying multiple tables, 407
resources, 410
result table, 402
SELECT statement, 402–404
SQL injection, 412
SUM() function, 406
UPDATE statement, 409
WHERE clause, 404–406
SQLite, 410
    command-line shell, 403
`sqlite3` Standard Library module, 410–415
    class Connection, 411
    class Cursor, 411
    function `connect()`, 411
`sqrt()` math module function, 41, 42
stack
    frame, *see* program stack
Standard Library modules, 41
    `fractions`, *see* `fractions`
    `html.parser`, *see* `html.parser`
    `http.client`, *see* `http.client`
    `math`, *see* `math`
    `multiprocessing`, *see* `multiprocessing`
    `os`, *see* `os`
    `random`, *see* `random`
    `re`, *see* `re`
    `sqlite3`, *see* `sqlite3`
    `sys`, *see* `sys`
    `time`, *see* `time`
    `tkinter`, *see* `tkinter`
    `turtle`, *see* `turtle`
    `urllib.parse`, *see* `urllib.parse`
    `urllib.request`, *see* `urllib.request`
`str()` string constructor
    informal string representation, 260
    overloading, 258
`str` string type, *see* string
`strftime()` time function, 106
string, 23–27, 92–98
    comparison, 24, 184

concatenation, *see* + operator
encoding, *see* character encoding
formatting, 100–105
methods, 95–98
methods return copy, 96
mutability, 29, 75
operators, 23–27
pattern matching, 387–391
quotes, 23, 92
repetition, *see* * operator
representation, 92–93
representation of object, 98, 259–262
slicing, *see* [] operator
`str()` constructor, *see* `str()` constructor
triple quotes, 93
type, 23
value, 23
`strip()` string method, 98
structured data storage, *see* database
Structured Query Language, *see* SQL
subclass, 265, 266
substring, 25
`sum()` built-in function, 28
SUM() SQL function, 406
superclass, 266
swapping, 77–78
syntax error, 116
sys Standard Library module, 224, 227

table, *see* database
TCP/IP, 6
`temperature()` function, 129
Text tkinter class, 305–308
text widget option, 293
text entry box
multiline, *see* Text tkinter class
single-line, *see* Entry tkinter class
`time()` time function, 105
time format directive, 106
`time` Standard Library module, 105–107
`timing()` function, 351
`timingAnalysis()` function, 352
Tk tkinter class, 292
tkinter Standard Library module, 292
coordinate system, 312
resources, 299
widgets, *see* widget

top-level module, 226–228
`translate()` string method, 97, 98
tree
filesystem, 108
of recursive calls, 353
root, 377
structure of HTML document, 377
triple quotes, 93
True value, 18
truth table, 20
try statement, *see* exception
tuple, 29–31
as dictionary keys, 176–177
methods, 33
mutability, 29, 176
one-element tuple, 30
Turtle graphics, 338
two-dimensional list, 140–143
two-way, *see* if statement
`twoWay.py` module, 61
type, 11–12, 33
in formatted output, 104
`type()` built-in function, 34
type conversion
explicit, 39
implicit, 17, 38
TypeError exception, 117, 118

unary operator, 20
Unicode, 183–186
`uniform()` random module function, 188
Uniform Resource Locator, *see* URL
uniqueness testing, 357
UNIX, 5
`update()` dictionary method, 170, 171
UPDATE SQL statement, 409
`upper()` string method, 96, 98
URL, 373–374
absolute, 378
host, 373
pathname, 373
relative, 378
scheme, 373
`urljoin()` urllib.parse function, 385
`urllib.request` Standard Library module, 379–381
`urllib.parse` Standard Library module, 384–385

`urlopen() urllib.request` function, 379

user-defined
function, 67–74
module, 54

user-defined indexes, *see* dictionary

UTC time, 106

UTF encodings, 185–186

`ValueError` exception, 118

Van Rossum, Guido, 8

variable, 20–21
evaluation of, 21
global, 211
instance, 243–244
local, 205–207
naming convention, 22
naming in Python 3, 22
naming rules, 22–23
type, 34
unassigned, 21

`vertical()` recursive function, 332

view object, 172

virus, 342
scanner, 342–344
signature, 342

web, 372
browser, 372, 375, 376
client, 372
page source file, 375
server, 372
server root directory, 373

WHERE SQL clause, 404–406

`while` loop statement, 143–144
iteration patterns, 145–149

widget, 292
`Button` tkinter class, 299–302
`Canvas` tkinter class, 308–313
constructor options, 292–298
coordinate system, 312
`Entry` tkinter class, 302–304
`Frame` tkinter class, 311–313
`Label` tkinter class, 292–298
for images, 294–297
for text, 292–293
`mainloop()` widget method, 292
master, 293, 311
mixing `pack()` and `grid()`, 298
placement, 293
placement with `Frame`, 311–313
placement with `grid()`, 297–299
placement with `pack()`, 295–297
`Text` tkinter class, 305–308
Tk, 292

`width` widget option, 293, 294

`wordcount()` function, 175

World Wide Web, *see* WWW

`write()` file method, 110, 115

WWW, 6, 372–379
history, 372
HTML, *see* HTML
HTTP, *see* HTTP
locator scheme, 373
naming scheme, 373
Python web API, 379–387
technologies, 373
URL, *see* URL

`ZeroDivisionError` exception, 117, 118